HISTORICAL ATLAS OF
JERUSALEM

HISTORICAL ATLAS OF
JERUSALEM

MEIR BEN-DOV

CONTINUUM
New York • London

2002

HISTORICAL ATLAS OF JERUSALEM

First English-language edition published in 2002 by

The Continuum Publishing Group Inc
370 Lexington Avenue, New York, NY 10017

The Continuum Publishing Group Ltd
The Tower Building, 11 York Road, London SE1 7NX

Translated from the original Hebrew by David Louvish

Designed and produced by Carta, Jerusalem
Managing Editor: Barbara Ball

Library of Congress Cataloging-in-Publication Data

Ben-Dov, M.
   Historical atlas of Jerusalem.
    p. cm.
   "First English-language edition published in 2002 by The Continuum
Publishing Group Inc."
   Translated from the original Hebrew by David Louvish.
   Copyright 2000, 2002, Carta, The Israel Map and Publishing Company,
Ltd.
   ISBN 0-8264-1379-X
   1. Jerusalem–Historical geography–Maps.   2. Jerusalem–Maps. I.
Title: Atlas of Jerusalem. II. Karta (Firm). III. Title.
   G2239.J4S1 B4 2002
   911'.5694'42–dc21

                                  2001018266

Printed in Israel

TABLE OF CONTENTS

JERUSALEM

FR. BARGIL PIXNER, O.S.B.

THE CITY OF JERUSALEM was the cradle of Jesus' life and activities in the days preceding his Crucifixion. Together with his disciples, he made a pilgrimage to Jerusalem; there he found lodgings in a small village to the east of Jerusalem whence he would pass along the slopes of the Mount of Olives, enter the city and visit the Temple Mount and Temple. On one such visit he foretold the destruction of the Temple and even grieved for it. In Jerusalem Jesus arranged with his disciples where to celebrate the Passover—the place of the Last Supper. Here too, he was surrendered to the Roman consul Pontius Pilate, and brought to trial before him: this was the Praetorium, from where Jesus was taken to the site of the Crucifixion carrying his own heavy wooden cross. This was the revered Via Dolorosa which today is walked by myriads of emotionally stirred pilgrims.

From the Cross Jesus was taken to a burial cave donated for this purpose by Joseph of Arimathea. When his followers came to his tomb, they discovered that Jesus' body had disappeared even though the opening had been locked and sealed with wax. Two youths from Emmaus related that Jesus had appeared before them, risen from the dead. Traditional lore tells that he sheltered in a cave in Gethsemane where he preached to chosen disciples the tenets of his faith and then ascended in a storm to heaven. The site of Ascension is believed to be the ridge of the Mount of Olives which overlooks Jerusalem.

There is no doubt that Jerusalem was the central stage for events of the last days of Jesus' life on earth; after his Crucifixion many sites became foci of veneration and destinations of pilgrimages by his followers.

In the first centuries CE under Roman rule, Christianity was hounded and its believers persecuted. Only in the fourth century, at the time of Constantine the Great, did Christianity gain recognition and was proclaimed the preferred religion in the Eastern Roman Empire.

The emperor's mother, Helena, visited Jerusalem and began to search for sites associated with Jesus' last days. She identified the place of the Crucifixion, burial and Resurrection and had a church built over it—the Church of the Holy Sepulcher. She also identified the Mount of Olives as the place of the Ascension. During her day many churches and monasteries were built in and around Jerusalem to commemorate Jesus' life, and also that of Mary, Jesus' mother; one is her burial place close to Gethsemane in the Kidron Valley.

During the reign of the emperor Justinian, in the sixth century, the city witnessed a building boom so grandiose that it is reminiscent of that of Herod. One other important church built at that time was in honor of Mary, the Theotokus, called by the inhabitants of Jerusalem at that time *Nea*, "the new." But hard times fell upon Jerusalem again. At the beginning of the seventh century, the city was conquered by the Persians. A mere fourteen years later the Byzantine emperor, Heraclius, reconquered it, and once again the sound of builders' hammers were heard in Jerusalem. Stormy times followed. Ten years later Jerusalem and the rest of the country found itself in the hands of Islam's second caliph, Omar. This was a major turning point in the history of Jerusalem, although Christianity and its institutions survived.

From Islamic rule until the Crusader conquest and the restoration of Christian rule, a period of some one hundred years, Jerusalem experienced many ups and downs. There were harsh Muslim rulers such as the Egyptian Fatimid Al-Hakim Bi-Amr Allah who destroyed the Church of the Holy Sepulcher and pillaged the holy tomb.

This and other misfortunes were instrumental in inspiring the Crusades, during whose reign the city once again enjoyed Christian restoration and building.

But, not for long; again Muslims returned to rule, first the Mamluks and then the Ottomans. The Ottoman sultan, Suleiman the Magnificent, forged links with Francis I, king of France, and Christians were accorded many privileges in the city and in the country. Thus even under Muslim rule, Christianity flourished. Francis I endowed the Franciscan order with the title to all the holy sites making them the custodians of the Holy Land, *Custodia de Terra Sancta*. However, little by little, other orders took up residence and they too restored many Christian holy places. Yet another burst of Christian building activity occurred in the nineteenth century.

The twentieth century too was of great impact—British Mandatory rule followed the conquest of Palestine by British forces in 1917, and scarcely thirty years later there followed the United Nations' decision in 1947 to establish within Palestine two homelands, one Jewish and one Arab with international status proposed for Jerusalem.

This century also witnessed the visit to Jerusalem of two popes, Paul VI in 1964, and John Paul II in 2000. These visits were indeed milestones in the history of the city and the faith, and an inspiration to Christians within the Holy Land and the world.

Jerusalem's importance for Christians preceded the coming of Jesus; the biblical city of King David and his son King Solomon, who built the First

Temple, and even earlier, Melchizedek the priest, whose seat was in Jerusalem, are all revered by Christians.

One can safely say that Jerusalem is unique in the history of the world, and in the annals of faith it is a story which has a beginning but not an end. Day by day new finds are being made and new ideas are raised and interpretations offered on every conceivable subject. Not always is there agreement, but the multiplicity of views makes Jerusalem that much richer.

This book appears at the beginning of the third millennium and covers the story of the city from five thousand years ago till the beginning of the millennium. It addresses events and ideas from its inception (a time of two thousand years before King David) until the present time. Richly illustrated, it furnishes the geographical and historical context in which to view Jerusalem from imperial Egyptian rule onward, through biblical days, the Middle Ages and to modern times, by documenting valuable archaeological and historical evidence which brings places and events to life before the very eyes of the reader.

It is praiseworthy that the author has presented conflicting views on specific issues, for instance, the identification of the location of the Praetorium, the scene of Jesus' judgment before Pontius Pilate, and the route taken from the Praetorium to the Crucifixion site. Or take the theory of the disappearance of the tombstones of the Crusader kings from the Church of the Holy Sepulcher, the reasons for granting custody to the various Christian groups by Suleiman the Magnificent, and more. Particularly riveting and innovative is the theory on circumstances surrounding the building of the walls of Jerusalem by the Ottoman sultan.

The author specifically relates to the visits of the popes, Paul VI and John Paul II, as well as the significance of Jerusalem as a universally revered holy city. He proposes solutions for the awesome controversies inherent in a city holy to so many, such as the prophets of Israel might have proposed. These solutions seem to be utopian, but often vision leads to activity. After all, the visionary of Zionism, Theodor Herzl, when predicting the establishment of the state of Israel, used the phrase *"if you wish it, it is not a dream."*

I believe this book contributes to understanding the history of Jerusalem and the Holy Land as a whole, and the religious issues which have inspired man throughout history.

*For my sons,
Eran, Guy and Yuval,
Who love Jerusalem, the city of their birth*

INTRODUCTION

J ERUSALEM'S DESTINY was ordained nearly five thousand years ago when a small number of families decided to settle on the lowest of the Jerusalem hills. They chose this hill because of the abundant water flowing beneath it—the Gihon Spring—and the nearby fertile valleys and beautiful ridges for planting vineyards, which ensured sustenance. In time, the hill would become known as the City of David.

After a short time the entire country fell under Egyptian rule, and eventually became known as the Province of Canaan, named for one of the area's important ethnic groups. Under the Egyptians, a number of cities emerged in Canaan which gained ascendancy; these were established along international trade routes and at crossroads, and many of their citizens earned a livelihood by providing services for passing caravans. One of these cities was Jerusalem, lying on an important crossroad connecting the Via Maris to the King's Highway. During the next two thousand years Jerusalem's fate did not differ from that of other Canaanite

Archaeological excavations at the foot of the Temple Mount, aerial photograph.

cities: Gaza, Ashkelon, Joppa, Megiddo, Gezer, Aphek, Hazor and others. The turning point in Jerusalem's history came when it was conquered by King David, some three thousand years ago.

The big change came when King David decided to make Jerusalem the capital of his kingdom. There he established his royal court and Temple, thus uniting both the political and the religious branches of his authority. The Temple inspired Israel's spiritual leaders: the prophets, whose teachings became the foundation of the moral doctrines of the entire western world. King David came to symbolize the ideal ruler, and the prophecies that the future would bring good rulers referred to the descendants of David and the Messiah who would reign as king at the End of Days. As Christianity and Islam derived their moral doctrines and practices from Judaism, they too have always held Jerusalem to be a holy and important city. It should be stressed here that, apart from the period when it was the capital of the Crusader kingdom, only the Jews have ever made Jerusalem their political capital and most important holy city. The Muslim Umayyad caliphs failed in their attempt to make Jerusalem their political capital.

Despite its sanctity and the meaning of the word *shalom*—"peace"—which is part of its Hebrew name, *Yerushalayim*, the city has known many wars. No fighting force has passed through the Middle East without bringing suffering to the holy city. The city's destruction and subsequent rebuilding became one of its distinguishing characteristics. The strong feelings awakened by the city resulted in extensive construction within its walls, as well as terrible destruction when captured by members of a different faith. Important chapters of Jerusalem's history and architectural features were thus buried under the soil and covered with debris.

Interest in Jerusalem's history, its status, buildings and everyday life has never waned since the days of David; pilgrims, Crusaders and others visited the city, many of them recording their impressions in writing and, in more recent centuries, also in drawings. Despite the large range of descriptions of Jerusalem, surpassing that of any other of the world's ancient cities, a lack of sufficient information was felt, because of both the extensive destruction and the thirst for more knowledge. Systematic research into the city's history began in the nineteenth century, based on the study of historical sources and attempts to understand them in the light of the remains and buildings in the area. With the birth of modern archaeology, Jerusalem became a focus of activity; countless excavations were carried out in the city and its surroundings for over one hundred years, until 1967. The knowledge uncovered by the diggers' tools and the numerous surveys have provided a clearer picture of the city's past.

Nevertheless, the most important work has been carried out since the 1967 Six-Day War. Extensive development work in the Old City and its surroundings, coupled with the thirst for knowledge of a generation of Israeli scholars who knew the Old City solely from literature and observation from afar, aroused a wave of archaeological activity unknown anywhere else in the world.

Even now, before all the information has been reviewed and conclusions drawn, it can be safely said that we are already better informed about Jerusalem's past than we were before 1967. The story of Jerusalem through the ages now differs from that known and written before the Six-Day War. This justifies the presentation of this history of the city for scholars and other interested people.

Although this is not the first study of Jerusalem's history, and probably not even the last, it brings many innovations. For the first time, the city's history is presented not in separate installments, but as a chain, its links firmly connected to form a single entity. This chain of history also includes characters behind the events, each of whom contributed in his own way to molding the city's character.

In the nineteenth century, Jerusalem broke out of its narrow confines and the construction of new neighborhoods began. This new chapter in the city's history began toward the end of the Ottoman period and continued under the British Mandate. In 1948 the State of Israel was established and Jerusalem was proclaimed its capital; after 2,000 years, Jerusalem was once again the political capital of the Jewish people. This was followed by the events of 1967 when, in the wake of the Six-Day War, the Old City also came under Jewish rule, opening a new chapter in the city's recorded history. In presenting Jerusalem's history it is important to consider the significance of events, as has been done here.

This study is accompanied by hundreds of specially prepared drawings and photographs. An abundance of maps illustrate the chapters of Jerusalem's history. Many maps and drawings are presented three-dimensionally, in order to help the reader understand the often complex problems and situations.

The bibliography at the end of the book shows that this study is based on the work of many of the best Jerusalem scholars through the ages. Many have devoted much thought to the study of Jerusalem, and I have tried to make my own small contribution. The nature of an overall study does not permit the development of ideas, only their presentation for the reader's consideration.

A study of this kind cannot be carried out without teamwork, and this is the place to acknowledge the assistance of many colleagues. First and foremost is Martha Ritmeyer, a Dutch-born artist who had worked with me for many years. Beginning as a young student illustrator at the excavations near the Temple Mount, she became one of the best archaeological illustrators in Israel. Her work is characterized by its clean lines and understanding of the construction and the buildings. Martha was also skilled at sketching portraits, with singular success. Most of the drawings in this study are her work. A few drawings were done by other artists who have worked with me at various times, including Yitzhak Rachlin, Claudia Himmelman, Hans Pugels and Eran Ben-Dov. I am indebted to all of them. The presentation of the sketches, the measurements and everything connected with their interpretation are my work, and any error is solely my responsibility. Some of the photographs were taken by myself; others are the work of my friend Avinoam Glick, the former archaeological team photographer.

Thanks are also due to the many individuals without whom this book could not have been completed: David Louvish, who ably translated the text from the original Hebrew version and offered valuable comments; the staff at Carta and especially Barbara Ball who, with her usual diligence, was instrumental in designing and shaping the book and also translated the map texts. Tsahi Ben-Ami did yeoman's work in converting the numerous maps and illustrations to computer language—not an easy task. My thanks also to Pauline Shomer, with whom I embarked on the English translation; to Eli Kellerman, the art director at Carta, who oversaw production from beginning to end, and to all others who at various times were recruited to see this project to its speedy and successful conclusion.

Last but not least are the members of my immediate family: my wife, Zippi, and my sons Eran, Guy and Yuval, who have shown understanding and patience during the writing and preparation of this book. All deserve my warm appreciation and thanks.

I have found it appropriate to dedicate this study to my sons, all born in Jerusalem. I wish them the gift of a tranquil and good future for Jerusalem—the city sacred to so many, destined to serve as a beacon to all peoples and a focus for the message of peace in the spirit of the prophecy of Isaiah (2:2–4):

> *It shall come to pass in the latter days that the*
> *   mountain of the house of the LORD*
> *Shall be established as the highest of the mountains.*
> *And shall be raised above the hills;*
> *And all the nations shall flow to it, and many peoples*
> *   shall come, and say:*
> *"Come, let us go up to the mountain of the LORD,*
> *To the house of the God of Jacob;*
> *That he may teach us his ways*
> *And that we may walk in his paths."*
> *For out of Zion shall go forth the law,*
> *And the word of the LORD from Jerusalem.*
> *He shall judge between the nations,*
> *And shall beat their swords into plowshares,*
> *And their spears into pruning hooks:*
> *Nation shall not lift up sword against nation,*
> *Neither shall they learn war any more.*

Meir Ben-Dov
Jerusalem, 2001

Chapter 1:

BEFORE THE CITY EXISTED: FIRST STEPS

1. BETWEEN SEA AND DESERT: THE FERTILE CRESCENT

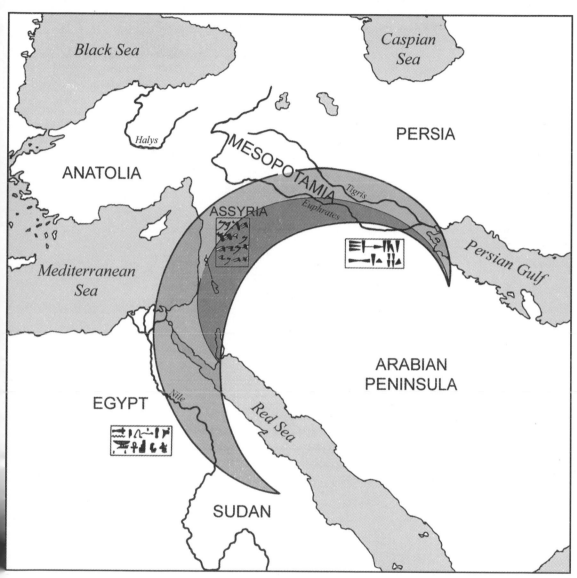

The Middle East—cradle of western civilization. The area between the Euphrates and the Tigris rivers in Mesopotamia, south and west of the Halys River in Anatolia and along the eastern Mediterranean coast—present-day Syria, Lebanon, Jordan and Israel—is known as the Fertile Crescent. It was here, and along the Nile in Egypt, that the first western civilizations arose.

WESTERN civilization was born in the Middle East, in two major centers: Egypt and Mesopotamia (today Iraq and southern Iran). The valleys and broad plains of Mesopotamia, between the Euphrates and Tigris rivers, offered ample sources of sustenance, and people learned to utilize and improve what was provided

(above) Wall painting from an Egyptian tomb (Medinet Habu): a caravan of Semitic merchants, probably Canaanites, going down to Egypt along the Fertile Crescent.

Engraving of a merchant ship on the wall of a burial cave in Beth She'arim. By the beginning of the 2nd millennium BCE, merchants and armies were plying the routes along the Mediterranean coast, between the ports of Egypt and those of Syria and the Holy Land.

by nature to meet their needs. To control and subjugate the forces of nature called for great effort; this is the plain meaning of the story of the expulsion from the Garden of Eden: "In the sweat of your face you shall eat bread" (Gen. 3:19). Eventually, surpluses were produced and sold, leading to the accumulation of riches; improvement in food production technologies led to savings in manpower and time. The wealth thus amassed and the free time created were the foundations of all human progress, without which no higher civilization could be created.

The domestication of the camel in the 12th century BCE opened up new possibilities for international trade.

As in Mesopotamia, so also in Egypt. The Nile Delta and the north, along the river up to Sudan, provided the same basic conditions and circumstances for another great civilization to develop and flourish. These two civilizations became the foundation of western civilization.

Between these two great powers lies an area some 800 km long and 100 km wide—the location of today's Syria and the Holy Land. This area does not enjoy the same conditions. It is very mountainous, stony and rocky, its soil is not fertile nor easy to cultivate, and it has neither the natural fertilization brought by river silt nor abundant, readily available water. A buffer zone, it was bordered on the north by the powers that arose in Mesopotamia and in the south by Egypt, on the west by the Mediterranean Sea and on the east by the great Arabian-Syrian Desert.

The accumulated abundance and riches, which needed protection, inspired the creation of forms of government and rule able to protect property and lives. The needs of government required the ability to record and write, and so it was in this region that the earliest forms of writing were invented: cuneiform in Mesopotamia and hieroglyphics in Egypt.

In the course of time, Mesopotamia and Egypt became aware of each other. Extensive ties gradually developed, based on the need for barter trade: there were important basic commodities in the fields of economy and religion that one did not have but the other did. Large caravans carrying goods began to travel between Egypt and Mesopotamia, utilizing donkeys as the main beasts of burden. The desert could not be crossed, for the camel had not yet been domesticated; neither had sea routes been opened up.

The two powers were not always at peace with one another: at times the rulers of one power coveted the property and land of the other, and war chariots plied the caravan routes. The needs of both peace and war required convenient routes to cross the buffer zone—the mountains of Syria and the Holy Land.

2. International Routes in the Fertile Crescent

Via Maris and the King's Highway

Two main routes served international travel in the Middle East. One later became known as the "Via Maris" ("way of the sea") because large sections of it, especially in the south, passed along the Mediterranean shore. It began east of the Nile Delta and crossed Sinai along the Mediterranean coast from west to east. Upon reaching the Holy Land, the Via Maris turned north, again along the coast, passing Gaza, Ashkelon, Ashdod and Jabneh, where it turned northeast toward Aphek in the Sharon and passed through Nahal Iron, entering the Jezreel Valley near Megiddo. The eastward turn, at the foot of the Samarian Hills, was necessary in order to bypass the perennial streams that obstructed travel in this area, such as the Yarkon and Alexander,

among others. From Megiddo the road continued north toward Hazor in the Galilee, then turned through the Golan Heights toward Damascus. Another branch of the route continued northward, through the city of Ijon, to Beirut, and from there northward to Aleppo and beyond, finally reaching the Upper Euphrates River.

The other route left Mesopotamia, descended to the southwest and crossed Syria, toward Damascus. From Damascus it ran south, crossing the Bashan and Gilead plains through the towns of Ramoth-gilead (Ramta), Gerasa, Rabbath-bene-ammon (Amman) and Kirmoab, all the way to Elath on the Red Sea. From Elath the route turned west, crossed the center of the Sinai Peninsula

Slate pallette engraved with depiction of the Egyptian King Narmer, Third Dynasty (3000 BCE), smiting a Canaanite prisoner.

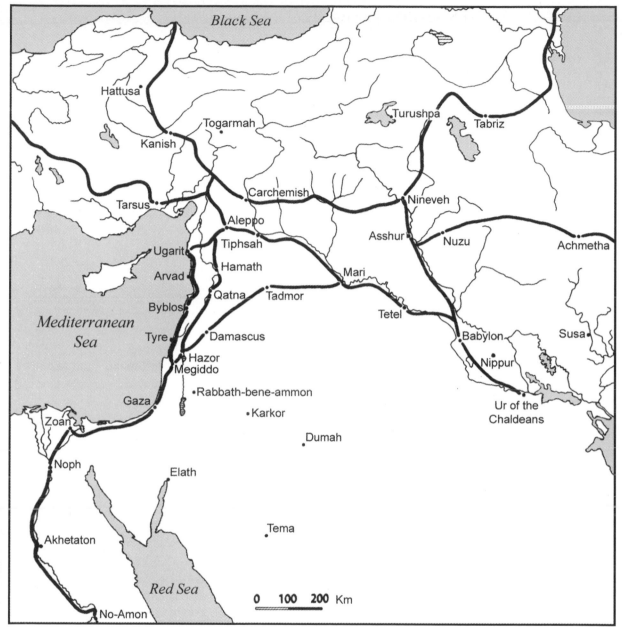

Map of the network of international routes throughout the ancient Middle East.

and reached the Delta. This route was known as the "King's Highway," because of the official status bestowed on it by royalty and the protection given those traversing it. Even in modern times it was known by its Arabic name Darb al-Sultan, the Sultan's Route, for the Ottoman sultan who gave it his protection. Another name is Darb al-Hajj (Pilgrims' Route), because one of its branches goes on to Mecca and Medina, serving the multitudes of Muslims who made the pilgrimage to the sacred cities in the Arabian Peninsula. The King's Highway was also an international trade route to Yemen and Ethiopia, operated by Arab traders who also plied trade routes to India and China.

3. JERUSALEM AND THE INTERNATIONAL ROUTES

Egyptian military campaign in Canaan; detail from Egyptian relief recording Egyptian military exploits.

THE international routes in the Holy Land were established outside the hilly region that runs the length of the country: the Via Maris along the Sharon Plain at the foot of the hills of Ephraim and Samaria, the King's Highway east of the Jordan Valley. Supplementing these two main routes was an extensive internal road network, part of which merged with the international routes. The routes of the country's roads were dictated by the central mountain range. A range of rocky hills rises from the Beersheba Valley in the south to the Jezreel Valley in the north: its southern section, from the Beersheba Valley to Jerusalem, is called the Judean Hills; its northern section, from Jerusalem to the approaches of the Jezreel Valley, is called the Hills of Ephraim. In the south (around Hebron and Halhul), the hills rise to a height of 1,000 meters above sea level (a.s.l.); while in the north (in the area of Shechem [Nablus], Mount Gerizim and Mount Ebal) it reaches 950 meters. West of these ranges lies the Mediterranean Sea and to the east the Jordan Valley (part of the Rift Valley). In this area the Rift Valley falls to 250–400 meters below sea level: the Dead Sea is the lowest point on earth.

These mountain ranges form the country's watershed. The clouds release their rain onto them, and from there the water flows westward in riverbeds to the Mediterranean Sea, and eastward toward the Jordan River. Since the riverbeds interfere with the movement of foot travelers, a central travel route took shape along the crest of the ridge, from south to north, that forms the watershed. This route was used by caravans throughout history. The main inhabited sites along this route today are Dahariyya, Hebron, Halhul, Bethlehem, Jerusalem, Ramallah, Nablus and Jenin.

A parallel south-north route traversed the Jordan Valley, from Jericho through Beth-shean to the Sea of Galilee—a convenient route for caravans, as the rivers cutting through it were passable. Furthermore, the dry climate prevented the growth of heavy vegetation, while springs in the riverbeds provided water for man and beast.

In sum, three main routes ran the length of the Holy Land: the western route—a section of the Via Maris coming up from Rafah, Gaza, Ashkelon, Ashdod, Jabneh, Gezer, Aphek, Iron, Megiddo and Hazor; the central route—along the mountain ridge (or along the watershed), coming up from the Beersheba Valley through Dahariyya, Hebron, Halhul, Bethlehem, Jerusalem, Ramallah, Bethel and Shechem to Jenin; and the eastern one—along the Jordan Valley, to the west of the river, from Jericho through Phasaelis, Hamath, Rehob, Beth-shean, Zemah and the Sea of Galilee to Hazor. Besides these three longitudinal routes west of the Jordan, a fourth ran east of the river—the King's Highway.

Travelers along these routes were often attacked and robbed; in view of the high taxes and service fees demanded from caravans, they preferred to split up among the various longitudinal routes. This created the need for connecting routes across the width of the country in the highlands of the Holy Land.

Such cross-routes—two main routes and a number of secondary ones—ran through various valleys and wadis which were convenient for regular travel. The main routes branched off the Via Maris, providing easy access to the King's Highway. One left Via Maris in the area of Gezer and climbed up to Jerusalem along an easy route—through Ma'aleh Beth-horon; it continued down from Jerusalem through Ma'aleh Adummim and Wadi Qelt to Jericho, and from there eastward to the King's Highway, or northward along the Jordan Valley to Beth-shean. The other cross-route left Via Maris in the area of the present-day city of Netanya toward Tulkarm and Shechem, along an easily negotiated riverbed. From Shechem the road des-

Via Maris and the King's Highway were joined by cross routes. One of the most important of these went up from the coastal plain, crossed the crest of the hill country near Jerusalem and descended from there to the Jordan Valley and eastward toward the King's Highway. Map and cross section.

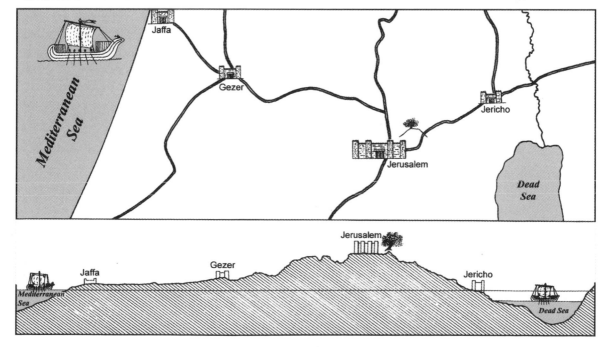

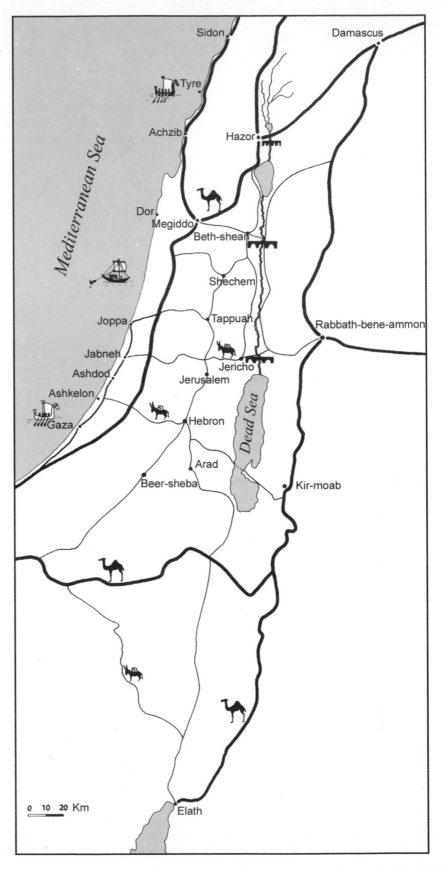

Network of international routes crossing Paslestine in the province of Canaan.

Mediterranean Sea

Sidon

Damascus

Tyre

Achzib

Hazor

Dor

Megiddo

Beth-shean

Shechem

Joppa

Tappuah

Rabbath-bene-ammon

Jabneh

Jericho

Ashdod

Jerusalem

Ashkelon

Dead Sea

Gaza

Hebron

Arad

Beer-sheba

Kir-moab

0 10 20 Km

Elath

cended to the Jordan Valley through Wadi Far'a (Nahal Tirzah), continuing eastward to the Jordan and beyond to the King's Highway, or northward to Beth-shean and the Sea of Galilee. Both routes crossed the Jordan on permanent bridges, two of which have been in use throughout history: one on the Jerusalem–Jericho–Amman road (today's "Allenby Bridge"), and the other, the Adam (Damiyya) Bridge, which crosses the Jordan at the end of the Shechem (Nablus)–Wadi Far'a road.

In addition to these, some travelers used partial cross-routes that approached the north-south watershed route from the west. One of these ascended from Beth Guvrin and joined the hill route in the area of Halhul, continuing to the north along the watershed to Jerusalem; from there it proceeded to the Ma'aleh Adummim–Wadi Qelt route, the traditional cross-route in this area. Similarly, in the northern section of the Jordan Valley a route climbed up to the ridge through Wadi al-Malih to Tayyasir and Tubas, continuing along the ridge and from there winding westward along the traditional cross-route through Tulkarm and Netanya to meet the Via Maris. Thus, since antiquity, a ramified network of longitudinal and latitudinal routes assigned Jerusalem and Shechem a key role among the cities of the Holy Land.

4. "THE MOUNTAINS ROUND ABOUT JERUSALEM"

THROUGHOUT history—in biblical times, during the time of the Second Temple, under Byzantine, Arab and Crusader rule, right up to the Ottoman period— Jerusalem consisted only of what is now known as the Old City, to the west of the watershed, which reaches its peak high in the Jerusalem hills, 800 meters or more a.s.l. Only toward the close of the Ottoman period, and more especially during the British Mandate, did the city's neighborhoods venture west of the watershed line. The watershed in the Jerusalem area lies along a north-south line, running from the slopes of Mount Scopus down to the Ge'ula quarter,

View from the south toward the Jerusalem hills, before the city was founded. The City of David ridge is lower and smaller in area than the neighboring hills.

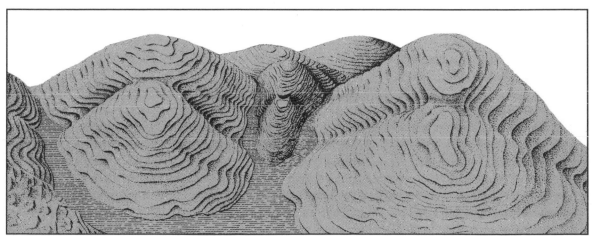

Mount Zion   City of David   Mount of Olives

"The mountains round about Jerusalem." Topographical map of the Jerusalem hills before the city was founded.

thence toward Rehavia, through Gonen (Katamon) to the old section of Talpiot and Ramat Rahel. Runoff from the watershed drains along streams coming down the Jerusalem hills, some flowing toward the Mediterranean and others toward the Dead Sea. The largest and most important of the westward streams are Nahal Sorek, whose source is in northern Jerusalem, and Nahal Refa'im, in the south of the city. The main channel carrying rainwater to the east is Nahal Kidron, which rises on the hill slopes in northern Jerusalem. In its upper reaches the Kidron flows for a few kilometers from north to south, turning west toward the Dead Sea at the spur of the hill on which the City of David was built.

Thus, the city of Jerusalem was built to the east of the watershed, alongside the Kidron Valley. Several other valleys or riverbeds inside Jerusalem have been concealed from view by extensive construction through the ages. The southernmost one is the Hinnom Valley, only about three kilometers long, which originates in the area of present-day Independence Park and the Mamilla Pool, running into the Kidron Valley south of the hill of David's City. It drops sharply, falling 200 meters along a stretch of only 3 kilometers, from 800 meters a.s.l. to its confluence with the Kidron Valley, at a level of 600 meters a.s.l. This sharp drop has created high, impressive cliffs on both sides of the valley. The southern cliff is still visible today, at the foot of the Abu Tor neighborhood, but the northern cliff—the southern slope of Mount Zion—has been buried for centuries under stones and debris. The valley is named for the Ben-Hinnom family, which owned the land; the fertile land was cultivated, particularly for viticulture. In ancient times one of the most fearsome cults in Jerusalem's history was practiced in the southern part of the gorge, in the shadow of the forbidding cliff: human beings, mainly children,

were sacrificed there in the a cult brought to Jerusalem from Tyre, which aroused wrathful prophecies of the prophets of Israel. The Hebrew word *gehinnom* (Greek *gehenna*), meaning simply "Valley of Hinnom," became an appellation for the place where the souls of the wicked would be tormented after death.

Another short valley, 2 kilometers long, runs from the north of the Valley of Hinnom, in today's Morasha (Musrara) quarter, draining into the Kidron. Before the existence of the city it flowed under today's Damascus Gate, then along present-day Hagai (the Valley) Street to the Western Wall Plaza, and from there under the southwest corner of the Temple Mount, joining the Kidron near the Siloam Pool. This so-called Central Valley—which has been inside the city for most of its existence—is so covered with stones and debris that it is difficult to identify, despite its depth: along its brief, 2-kilometer-long course it drops 150 meters (from 770 meters a.s.l. at source to 620 meters where it joins the Kidron). The rocky cliffs thus created on both sides of the valley were long buried under building debris and ruins. Excavations in the southwest section of the Western Wall Plaza, opposite Robinson's Arch and along the stairway leading up to the Jewish Quarter, have exposed sections of the cliffs along the western bank of the channel.

Another short tributary of the Kidron has its source in the area of the Hulda Gates in the Ophel. In just a few hundred meters it drops from an altitude of 730 meters a.s.l. to the level of the Kidron at 650 meters. It was still visible in 1970, but following the death of two youths while searching in the debris, the Jerusalem Municipality filled the channel with thousands of cubic meters of debris, almost completely concealing it.

The northernmost riverbed of Second Temple Jerusalem and its immediate surroundings is known as the Beth Zetha

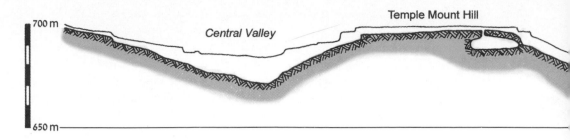

Topographical section of the Jerusalem hills.

Valley. It originates in the heart of the Sheikh Jarrah quarter, near the watershed, at a height of 780 meters a.s.l. It drops 100 meters along a one-kilometer stretch, to join the Kidron at 680 meters a.s.l.

These various valleys and riverbeds lie between several hills or ridges. In the course of time, up to the nineteenth century, the city was built on some of these hills; others were used as burial fields for the city's inhabitants. It was the lowest of these hills that was used for Jerusalem's earliest construction. Known today as the City of David, it is bordered on the east by the Kidron Valley and on the west by the Central Valley, which in that area are only 150 meters apart. Between the confluence of the two valleys is the southern spur of the hill; its northern border is a small topographical saddle—a few meters south of the present-day road to Jericho from the Dung Gate. The center of the hill rises 690 meters a.s.l.

In the past, another small hill rose to the north of this one, reaching 725 meters a.s.l. Described by Josephus Flavius, it is no longer visible owing to construction and quarrying. Intended by King Solomon for the construction of his administrative and religious center, this hill was known in antiquity as the Ophel Hill or the Millo. Its northern edge is now buried beneath Al-Aqsa Mosque. Farther to the north stands yet another hill, rising 745 meters a.s.l., on which the Temple was ultimately constructed; this later became known as the Temple Mount.

The northern boundary of the Temple Mount is marked by the course of the

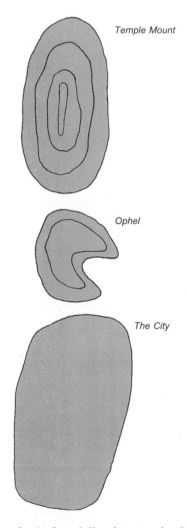

Jerusalem's three hills: the city, the Ophel and the Temple Mount.

12

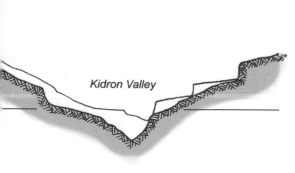

Kidron Valley

Beth Zetha Valley. The northern bank of this valley is very gentle, climbing gradually up to the watershed. The topography makes this slope very favorable for construction, and when settlement expanded in the Second Temple period it became a residential quarter. Today the area is a large stretch of empty ground between the Morasha and Sheikh Jarrah quarters, extending up to the eastern parts of the latter, along the street leading from Damascus Gate to the Tombs of the Kings.

Three peaks form a single hill or ridge to the west of the City of David: the present-day Jewish Quarter, at an altitude of 760 meters, the Armenian Quarter, at 775 meters, and Mount Zion, at 765 meters. In the Second Temple period the entire area was known, according to the historian Josephus Flavius, as the Upper City.

The entire hill is bordered on the west and south by the Hinnom Valley, and on the east, by the Central Valley; its northern border is the so-called Transversal Valley, marked today by David Street and the Street of the Chain, descending from Jaffa Gate to the Temple Mount. A further peak, to the north, rises to 780 meters. On its slopes is the hill of Golgotha (the supposed site of the Crucifixion), some 750 meters a.s.l.; this is the location of the Church of the Holy Sepulcher.

To the east of these hills, now the site of the Old City of Jerusalem, stand the Mount of Olives and Mount Scopus, rising to 830 meters a.s.l.; their slopes were the city's main burial grounds for many generations.

To the south, Government Hill overlooks the city, with an elevation of 800 meters a.s.l.; a magnificent Canaanite tomb was uncovered there. To the west, closer to the city (where the Scottish Church now stands) lies the Hinnom ridge, where impressive tombs of the First and Second Temple periods have been discovered.

5. WATER SOURCES IN JERUSALEM AND ENVIRONS

JERUSALEM sits athwart the watershed of the Holy Land. The sharp drop of the mountain slopes from their peak in Jerusalem toward the east greatly influences the amount of rainfall: west of Jerusalem, in the area of Abu Ghosh, Kiryat Anavim and Tzuba, annual rainfall averages from 600 to 680 mm; in Jerusalem itself, west of the watershed, in the Romema, Beit Hakerem and Katamon quarters, the average annual rainfall drops from 570 to 520 mm; within the Old City it is slightly less, 480 to 500 mm; while just one kilometer to the east, near the el-Azariya quarter, it drops to 380 mm. Except in years of severe drought, the quantity of rainfall within the city and to the east is suitable for the cultivation of crops not requiring irrigation, such as wheat and barley, olives and grapes.

The drop in rainfall also affects the springs in the Jerusalem area: to the west of the watershed there are numerous small springs, but the number of springs to its east falls practically to zero.

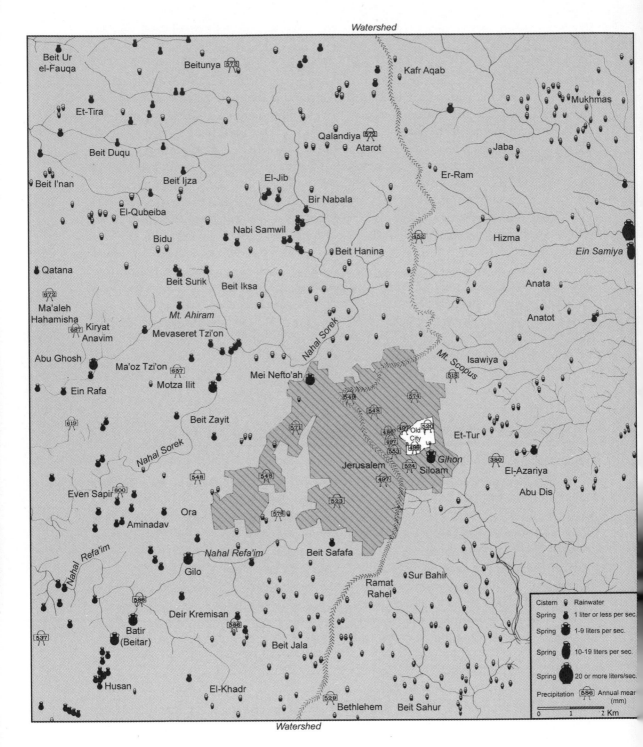

Map of precipitation and water sources in and around Jerusalem. East of the watershed, precipitation falls sharply, so that springs supply meager quantities of water. Most water supply in the east is based on the collection of rainwater (especially flood waters from the west), and storing it in cisterns.

Residents of the areas east of the town always relied for drinking water on artificial, plastered cisterns and pools, whose supply depended on the collection of rainwater. In the west of the city, too, the springs flow mainly along riverbeds, so that people living on the hilltops were forced to dig wells or to go down to the spring. The yield of the springs is usually low, only few of them supplying 80 to 90 cubic meters a day; the majority yield at most 3 to 5 cubic meters.

Two springs are exceptionally abundant: Mei Nefto'ah (the Waters of Nephtoah) and Gihon. The first gushes west of the watershed, in the now abandoned Arab village of Lifta, at the head of a small channel, flowing into Nahal Sorek on its southern bank; Mei Nefto'ah supplies 500 to 600 cubic meters a day. The other spring, located east of the watershed in the Kidron Valley below the City of David, is known by its biblical name Gihon, so called because its waters burst forth forcefully at intervals. It supplies over 1,000 cubic meters a day. In the past there was another spring, En-rogel, in the riverbed a few hundred meters south of the Gihon Spring. Despite its relatively small flow it used to contribute a reasonable quantity of water to Nahal Kidron. In biblical times En-rogel was considered sacred, and the kings of Judah were anointed there. The source of En-rogel's water may have been overflow from the Gihon percolating into the upper strata of the Kidron riverbed. In modern times this spring is known as a well, called in Arabic Bir Ayyub, that is, Job's Well. In recent years it has dried up, probably because of water drilling in the area.

6. Cultivated Land and Agriculture

In its early years, until its conquest by David, Jerusalem extended over an area of 12.5 to 15 acres (50,000–60,000 square meters). Assuming a population density as established by historical and archaeological research for such a city, we may assume that the population was probably around 3,000 souls, or 500 families. Some twenty percent of families (about 100) were occupied in providing services; the remaining 400 families subsisted on agriculture. The smallest agricultural holding that could support its owners at that time was about 25 acres, which means that the cultivated areas totaled around 10,000 acres.

The cultivated areas around Jerusalem were sufficient to meet the needs of the city's population. The main areas lay on the slopes of what is today Emek Refa'im (biblical Valley of Rephaim); in the vicinity of today's German and Greek colonies; in the upper reaches of the Kidron Valley, between the Temple Mount and the slopes of the Mount of Olives and Mount Scopus; in the areas north of the Temple Mount (the Morasha quarter) up to Me'a She'arim; and of course in the lower Kidron Valley, from the Siloam Pool and several kilometers to the southeast. The valley is relatively wide and suitable for cultivation. The limits of Jerusalem's agricultural hinterland lay some 3 or 4 kilometers from the city; beyond lay areas cultivated by neighboring towns or other settlements.

The main crops were wheat and barley for both man and beast, covering an area of 5,000 acres, or half the cultivated area. Based on the estimated average yield of Arab agriculture one hundred years ago, this area could produce a harvest of 1,200 tons of seed, calculated at 240 kilograms per acre. Half the crop would be barley for fodder, and the other half, wheat, for human consumption. This quantity—600

The economy of ancient Jerusalem was based mainly on agriculture. Most of its wheat and barley was grown in the Rephaim Valley and on the hilltops and slopes north of the city. Olive groves were planted on the western slopes of the Mount of Olives, and grapevines on the western hill. Dates, figs and pomegranates were grown in the Kidron Valley, from the Siloam Pool eastward. Cattle was reared in the basin of the Kidron Valley, close to the city; sheep, camels and horses were pastured in the semi-arid areas south of Jerusalem.

(opposite) Basic foods in antiquity were bread, oil and the produce of the vine—wine, honey and raisins; as long as these were available, a person's sustenance and livelihood were ensured. Their preparation involved arduous labor: felling trees, plowing and sowing wheat, pressing olives, harvesting and treading grapes.

Pressing olives for oil

Felling trees

Plowing

Treading grapes to produce wine

Vintage

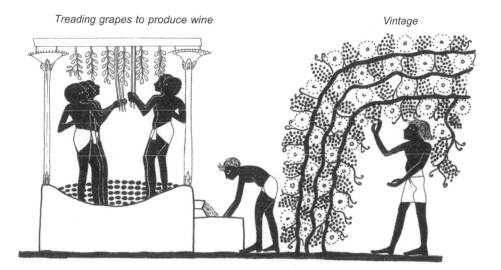

The seven basic foods native to the Holy Land; as they were all grown in and around Jerusalem, they did not have to be imported.

Wheat

Barley

Grapes

Figs

Pomegranates

Olives

Dates

tons—could feed the city's population for an entire year, even leaving a quantity to be sold or put aside for sowing in the following year. Accordingly, farmers would have been left with grain surpluses for barter trading. The other half of the cultivated area was used for growing olives, grapes, figs and dates: the Mount of Olives was so named for the olive groves planted on its slopes since antiquity. The New Testament story of Jesus' life mentions farmhouses on the slopes of the Mount of Olives, with wine vats, winepresses and oil presses, attesting to the mountain's agricultural past. Figs, grapes and especially dates were used to produce honey—the main sweetener used in ancient times, before the advent of cane sugar.

In addition to agricultural crops, live-stock was also kept. The desert's close proximity to the city made it possible to rear sheep and goats for their milk, meat and wool. The climate of the Judean Desert is ideal for grazing: during the winter, when it is cold in the hills, weeds are already sprouting in the desert, and there are ample cattle pastures. The abundant waters of the Gihon left a sufficient surplus for irrigation, providing vegetables and fruit to enrich the food supply. In the pastures, Jerusalem farmers also kept horses, camels, donkeys and cattle, for which the barley was an important feed component.

In sum, Jerusalem and its environs offered ideal natural conditions for a community subsisting on agriculture: precipitation, springs and arable land.

7. Foundation of the City

THE founder, planner and builder of a city—the head of a family or tribe—would select the location of a settlement according to four criteria:

1. Suitable land for agriculture;
2. water for man and beast;
3. accessibility;
4. security.

Since the establishment of cities in early history depended on agriculture, the proximity of fields and areas suitable for cultivation, with yields sufficient to feed the inhabitants, was of paramount importance. In antiquity, fields not requiring extensive preparation for cultivation, such as terracing, were preferred. As tools were simple and plow blades made of soft metal (bronze at best), land without large quantities of rock and stones was favored. Such natural fields were available in the wide riverbeds surrounding the area that was to become Jerusalem.

Our description of the water sources in the Jerusalem hills shows that the most suitable location for establishing a settle-

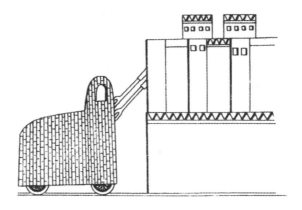

A city built on level ground was readily attacked, as the enemy could easily bring up siege engines to breach the walls (top). On the other hand, fortifications built on a steep incline hindered the enemy's use of heavy siege equipment.

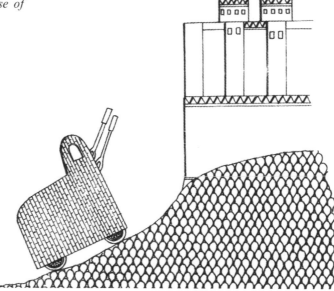

ment was close by the Gihon Spring, because of the abundant water available from there and from En-rogel.

Ancient planners sought to set up settlements at crossroads, preferably of international routes. This ensured sufficient jobs and livelihood in addition to agricultural work, such as provision of supplies and services for caravan travelers and their animals.

The natural crossroads in the Jerusalem hills lies a few kilometers north of the city. A traveler taking the cross-route from Gezer, ascending the Beth-horon–Gibeon route, reached the north-south mountain road near Beit Hanina, some 2 kilometers north of Mount Scopus; from there it was easy to go down to Wadi Qelt, thence to Jericho and onward to the longitudinal route along the Jordan Valley, or to the bridges crossing the Jordan River to the east bank and then to the King's Highway. However, it being difficult to find a location meeting all criteria, the planners compromised between what was desirable and what was actually possible. One location meeting most of the criteria was Megiddo: it lies at the outlet of the Nahal Iron road to the Jezreel Valley, at the crossroads between this road and the road from Beth-shean to the Mediterranean (Haifa and Acre); moreover, there is a small spring at the foot of the hill on which Megiddo was built.

Not so Jerusalem: the crossroads lay some distance from the Gihon, the sole source of flowing water; since water supply was of the utmost importance, the settlement was established on the hill of the City of David, 50 meters above the Gihon. A traveler climbing up into the highlands from the west was thus obliged to make a 2 or 3 kilometer detour in order to stock up on food and water in the city, and to receive travel services and sleeping facilities, before continuing eastward through Ma'aleh Adummim to Wadi Qelt and Jericho.

To a modern observer, the location of Jerusalem at this particular spot seems to violate the security criterion. Anyone standing on one of the hills of Jerusalem or on one of the surrounding hills and looking toward the Lower City will realize that it is lower than its surroundings on every side, as the Bible says: "… the mountains round about Jerusalem." However, this conclusion, based as it is on our conceptions of modern warfare, is basically wrong: from the time of the city's establishment until the Middle Ages, weapons had a very short range. Arrows fired from bows had a maximum range of some 50 meters. Hence the height of the hills surrounding the City of David was of no consequence: it enabled observers to look down into the city but not to fire into it. Another consideration dictating the planner's choice of location was also, most probably, that the available area on the hill should suit the size of the planned settlement. Moreover, the city walls, built as they were on the rocky slopes of the hill, were essentially a continuation of the natural barriers provided by the site. On the other hand, if the hill had been too large, i.e., larger than the fortified area of the city, the result would have been military inferiority: attacking armies would then have ample space to assemble outside the walls, severely hampering the city's defense. This was indeed the situation in the Middle Ages, when the southern wall of Jerusalem did not include Mount Zion in the fortified area.

According to archaeological data, the earliest construction of the city dates to around 3000 BCE, that is, five thousand years ago. As a compromise between all the criteria for the location of the settlement, early Jerusalem was eventually established on the hill of the City of David—the lowest of Jerusalem's hills, an elongated spur between the Kidron Valley on one side and the Central Valley on the other. In the north it extended as

Spring water

The location of an ancient city was based on four factors: arable land, fresh water for man and beast, proximity to crossroads and, of course, convenient topography for fortifications.

Agriculture

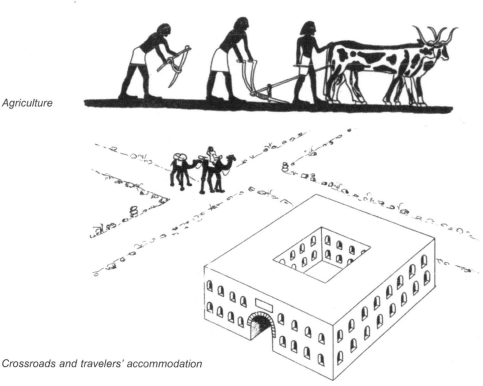

Crossroads and travelers' accommodation

Fortified natural hill

Ancient cities were fortified with three types of wall: (1) straight, thick wall; (2) casemate wall (utilizing the thickness of the wall for storage space); (3) offset-inset wall, not built in a straight line—the "insets" avoided the creation of blind spots for the defenders.

far as the Ophel Hill, which was at first uninhabited. Since the foundations were laid for the city's first houses until modern times, a period of five thousand years, Jerusalem has never ceased to exist—a rare continuity in the history of urban settlement throughout the world.

Recorded historical information about Jerusalem dates back only four thousand years, beginning about one thousand years after the city's establishment: Jerusalem is first clearly mentioned in the Egyptian Execration Texts (see below).

Excavations at the City of David, carried out by an expedition headed by Montague Parker in the early days of archaeological research, uncovered pottery utensils characteristic of the Early Bronze Age; these findings date the earliest settlement of the site to the end of the fourth millennium BCE and the beginning of the third millennium BCE—five thousand years ago. More recent excavations in the City of David, headed by Yigal Shiloh, have confirmed this date.

8. Names of the City Through the Ages

Jerusalem is first mentioned by name in documents discovered in Egypt. In the early Execration Texts (twentieth century BCE) and the later ones (eighteenth to sixteenth centuries BCE), a list of towns in the Holy Land includes a name usually transliterated as ꜣwš ꜣ mm. Since it was customary at the time of the Egyptian Middle Kingdom to transliterate both Western Semitic sounds r and l, which did not exist in Egyptian, by the same sign ꜣ, representing a glottal stop similar to the Hebrew aleph, this transliteration is generally read rushalimum. The doubling of the last letter (m) is found elsewhere in the Execration Texts, being associated with Semitic syntax. In the El-Amarna letters (fourteenth century BCE), the name "Jerusalem" appears in Accadian cuneiform script as Urusalim.

In the Bible, the name is almost always ירושלַ ם yrwšlm (read: Yerushalayim), and only rarely ירושלַים yrušlym (with the letter yod added after the lamed). In biblical texts in Aramaic the name of the city is written as ירושלֵם (read: Yerushlem). The spelling ירושָׁלַים is later, apparently influenced by the endings of other place names of the same noun pattern, such as Adorayim or Eglayim (also Karnayim). The Assyrian transliteration in Sennacherib's inscription, for example, is Urusilimu. Centuries later we have the Greek spelling in the Septuagint: Ιερουσαλημ. The ancient evidence thus points to the original Hebrew name of Jerusalem being ירושלֵם, read Yerushalem.

Many places in the Holy Land were named for their god or patron deity, prefixing the word beth (= house, i.e., temple, of ...) to the god's name, as in Beth Yerah—a town built around the temple of the moon god (Heb. yerah = moon); Beth-el—the temple (house) of El; Beth-lehem—a city whose central temple was dedicated to its patron, the god Lehem. Early scholars interpreted the name Yerushalem in this way: since the meaning of the word yeru in Sumerian is "settlement" or "city," Yerushalem is the city of the god Shalem. Other scholars, however, question the intrusion of Sumerian, suggesting that the solution should be sought on the basis of a Semitic language only. They derive the first part of the name from the Semitic/Hebrew verb yarah, meaning "to lay a cornerstone" (as in the verse, "who laid its cornerstone," Job 38:6). The name would thus refer to laying the cornerstone of a temple of the god Shalem. This god is a known member of the Western Semitic pantheon; he is known in the Accadian pantheon as Shalim and in the Assyrian pantheon as Shulmanu—the god of the setting sun and the nether world, as well as the god of health and perfection. Noteworthy in this connection is the title of Melchizedek, "king of S(h)alem" (Genesis 14:18); it is also interesting that the Book of Psalms identifies Salem with Jerusalem, or Zion: "His abode has been established in Salem, his dwelling place in Zion" (v. 76:2). Some of the princes and kings of the House of David had names derived from that of the god Shalem, such as Absalom (Heb. Avshalom), Solomon (Heb. Shelomo) and Shallum.

Jerusalem was also called "Zion," but the meaning of each occurrence of this name in the Bible is not sufficiently clear. At times "Mount Zion" refers to the Temple Mount, but it may also refer to the hill of the city south of the Temple Mount. In the biblical account of David's conquest of Jerusalem, the name "Zion" refers to the city's fortress or stronghold: "David took the stronghold of Zion, that is, the city of David" (2 Sam. 5:7). As to the origin of the name Zion, there is so

1. Egyptian hieroglyphics; 2. Accadian cuneiform script; 3. Paleo-Hebrew script (First Temple period); 4. Paleo-Hebrew script (Persian-Hellenistic period); 5. "Square" Hebrew script; 6. "Aelia Capitolina" (Latin); 7. "Hierosolima" (Greek, Byzantine period)

The first written reference to Jerusalem by name apparently occurs in the Egyptian Execration Texts, although the exact transliteration of the hieroglyphics is uncertain. The first certain occurrence of the name "Jerusalem" is in the El-Amarna letters (14th century BCE) in Accadian cuneiform script, and this name was used from then on. At different times in its history, Jerusalem received other names, including some that survived for centuries but eventually fell into disuse, such as Aelia Capitolina. The city also had various other designations, some actually used, such as the Arabic al-Quds, others specific to literature and poetry. More than any other city in the world, Jerusalem's name has been absorbed in many languages and in many different scripts. A number of examples are illustrated here.

far no universally accepted explanation. One suggestion is that it is derived from a Hebrew root meaning a dry place—perhaps an appropriate designation for a city overlooking the desert.

Another biblical appellation of Jerusalem is ethnic in nature and refers to its residents in a certain period: Jebus (Heb. *Yevus*)—". . . Jebus (that is, Jerusalem)" (Jg. 19:10); the meaning of the name is in fact explained in the Bible itself: "...the Jebusites who dwelt in Jerusalem" (Jg. 1:21). This name dated back to a time when certain Jebusite families,

probably of Hittite extraction, settled in the city and gained positions of power: the last king of the city before it was conquered by David was Araunah the Jebusite. The Jebusites left such a mark on the city that it was named for them. Another biblical city named for its inhabitants is the southern city referred to as "the city of Amalek" (1 Sam. 15:5).

Yet another biblical name associated with Jerusalem is "city of David," clearly deriving from King David's capture of the city and his choice of it as the capital of his kingdom: "Nevertheless David

Medieval Latin (Crusader period)

took the stronghold of Zion, that is, the city of David.... And David dwelt in the stronghold, and called it the city of David" (2 Sam. 5:7–9). It was traditional in the East and in particular in the Holy Land to rename a city for the conquering king who established his seat of power there. Thus, when Gibeah of Benjamin, for a time the seat of a Philistine governor, was conquered by King Saul, he built his capital there and renamed it Gibeah of Saul. Antiochus IV Epiphanes built a large fortified quarter in Jerusalem to protect the Hellenizers, with the Acra fortress at its center, and named it for himself: "Antiochia."

It is not certain which parts of the city were designated as "the City of David"— David's stronghold only, or the entire city. Neither do we know whether, when the city extended to the western hill as well (the "Upper City" of Second Temple times) in the late First Temple period, the new quarter was also part of the "City of David."

The El-Amarna letters (fourteenth century BCE) indicate that Jerusalem also gave its name to its environs, where there were several other towns subject to its authority. Thus, the phrase "land of Jerusalem" appears beside "city of Jerusalem." Conversely, much later, in the post-Exilic period, Jerusalem was sometimes referred to by the name of the entire province as "city of Judah."

Seal impressions on pottery handles, dated to the end of the Persian period and the beginning of the Hellenistic period, record the name of the city as *yršlm*. However, other seal impressions of the same type display the name *yhd* (= Yehud?). It is as yet unclear whether these inscriptions refer to the city by its two names (Jerusalem or City of Judah), or, conversely, to the entire province.

Although the Roman emperor Hadrian finally succeeded in suppressing the Bar Kokhba Revolt, the effort exacted a terrible price and the feeling of humiliation haunted him for a long time. Determined to eradicate Judaism and its religion entirely, he changed the name of

25

1. Modern Hebrew
2. Russian (19th century)
3. Hebrew (Ottoman period)
4. Paleo-Hebrew script on coin
5. "Ilya" (Arabic)
6. "Aelia Capitolina
   Commodiana" (Latin)

the country from Judea to "Palaestina," i.e., Philistia, the land of the Philistines. He also changed the name of the city of Jerusalem, from which Jews had been barred since its destruction by Hadrian's predecessor Titus, to Colonia (= the imperial colony of) Aelia Capitolina, after himself (his full name was Aelius Hadrianus) and the Capitol Hill in Rome, the site of the main temple of the Roman god Jupiter. At the same time, he initiated the construction of a temple to Jupiter on the site of the ruined Temple. The new name was prominently displayed in public inscriptions and coins, thus entering the long procession of different names given to Jerusalem. The name Aelia was retained during the reign of the pagan emperors who succeeded Hadrian, though some added their own names; thus, during the reign of Commodus it was known as Capitolina Commodiana. Perhaps it was only in the time of that emperor that the construction of public buildings gained momentum, thus justifying the addition of his name to that of the city.

In the fourth century CE, after the emperor Constantine the Great had recognized Christianity as the state religion, the leaders of the Christian community began to construct their institutions. They attached the utmost importance to Jerusalem, which had been the scene of Jesus' life and death. Around this time, therefore, "Jerusalem" reappeared as the city's name, alongside the abbreviated name "Aelia." It is puzzling that the early Christians, who had fought bitterly against paganism, apparently continued to use the pagan name "Aelia" of the city under Hadrian, who had also persecuted the Christians (perhaps out of hatred for the Jews, who were indeed persecuted by Constantine). Though we have no documentation for the use of the name Aelia at this time, the fact is that in the seventh century CE, when the Arabs conquered Jerusalem, they called the city *Ilya*, presumably adopting the previously existing name; some of them, however, believed that it was named for the prophet Elijah (*Ilyas* in Arabic). The first coins the Arabs minted in Jerusalem bore that name in Arabic script. Only later, when they had consolidated their rule,

(top row) "Zion" (Armenian)

(bottom, left to right) "Al-Quds" (Arabic); "Dar es-Salaam" ("House of Peace," Arabic); "Ilya" on coin (Arabic, Early Arab period)

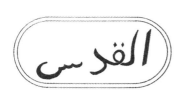 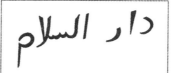

the Arab conquerors realized the need to stress the importance of the city for the Muslims through a suitable name, instead of the previous, heathen name. They therefore began to refer to the city as *Madinat Bayt al-Maqdis*—the city of the Temple; this was eventually shortened to *al-Maqdis*, later distorted colloquially to *al-Quds*—the Holy City. (Interestingly enough, the Arabs associated the name of the city with the Jewish Temple and not with Muhammad's legendary nocturnal flight to Jerusalem.)

The Crusaders revived the city's Hebrew name in a Latin form, Hierosolima. It is this name, or other derivatives of the original Hebrew *Yerushalayim*, that has persisted all over western and eastern Europe, though each nation has its own individual pronunciation.

Besides all these "official" names, Jerusalem has been given a great number of epithets representative of love and affection for the city—more than any other city in the world. Some of these "nicknames" have become popular and widely used, while others are merely literary expressions. One such popular name is "Ariel," the lion (Heb. *aryeh*) being the emblem of the tribe of Judah and eventually of the kingdom of Judah/Judea.

Chapter 2:
CANAANITE JERUSALEM
FROM *YQR'M* TO ARAUNAH 3000–1000 BCE

1. THE FIRST THOUSAND YEARS

Early Bronze Age pottery (3rd millennium BCE) discovered in the south of the biblical city, on the lower hill ("City of David").

AGRICULTURAL land for cultivation; proximity to the main crossroads; a hill suiting the size of the planned city, with rocky ridges on which to construct fortifications; and, above all, an abundant supply of fresh water, available from the Gihon Spring—all these factors prompted the head of some family or some tribal elder, the first (anonymous) "king" of Jerusalem, to make the best of the rather limited natural advantages and build his city on the lower hill. Archaeological finds date the foundation of the settlement some 5,000 years ago: tombs dated to that period—on the basis of the pottery they contained—have been found on the rocky cliffs to the south of the city, near the Valley of Kidron. This conclusion has been corroborated by the discovery of actual remains of contemporary construction, albeit meager, in more recent excavations on the eastern slope of the lower hill, the hill of the City of David. Neither the size of the city at that time nor its name are known; it was presumably given the name known to us from a thousand years later—*Yerushalem*, Jerusalem, for the temple established there in honor of the city's patron, the god Shalem.

At that early stage of its existence, Jerusalem was a fortress city on the country's travel routes. Evidence from Egypt shows that the Egyptians' military expeditions in this area and toward Mesopotamia took not only the main roads (the Via Maris and the King's Highway) but also the secondary routes. Archaeological finds in the Holy Land attest to the establishment of large and powerful cities not only along the main routes, but also in the secondary areas. Thus Arad was established in the Judean Desert, and later Beth Yerah on the shore of the Sea of Galilee. These towns clearly had trade ties with Egypt and were particularly large, each with an area of between 50 and 75 acres. Ancient towns were not always so large; some were little more than fortified posts whose importance lay in their location and role and not in the size of their area or population; such were Jerusalem and Beth-shean. Nevertheless, as long as the western part of the lower city of Jerusalem has not been excavated, its size in the Early Bronze Age cannot be estimated. The existence of a large town in the Early Bronze Age where there would later be a relatively small one is a phenomenon known from other mounds excavated in the Holy Land.

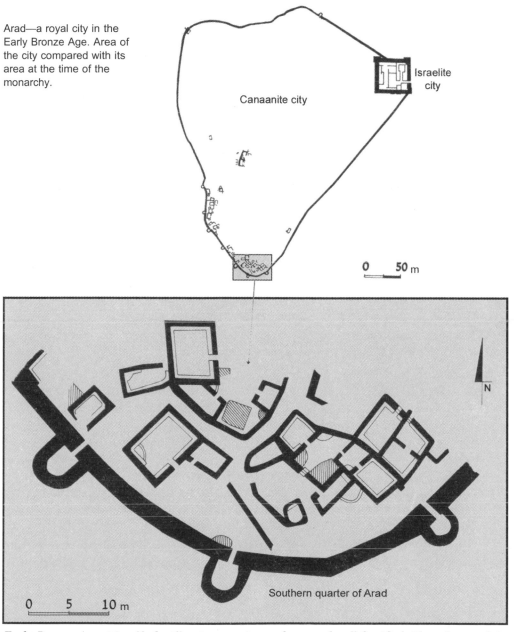

Arad—a royal city in the Early Bronze Age. Area of the city compared with its area at the time of the monarchy.

Canaanite city

Israelite city

0   50 m

0   5   10 m

Southern quarter of Arad

Early Bronze Age cities (3rd millennium BCE) were large and well fortified. Plan of part of the fortifications of the Canaanite city of Arad, northern Negev.

2. *YQRʿM* AND *ŠSʿN*, KINGS OF JERUSALEM

PERIOD OF THE EXECRATION TEXTS 20TH–18TH CENTURIES BCE

JERUSALEM is first mentioned by its present name in historical documents uncovered in Egypt, known as the Execration Texts. These are in three groups: the first dates from the twentieth to nineteenth centuries BCE, and the other two, from the nineteenth to eighteenth centuries BCE. Those in the first group were written in ink on pottery vessels, while the other two groups were inscribed on pottery figurines representing a prisoner with hands tied behind his back. At that time the mighty Egyptian empire ruled the Holy Land, Libya and Sudan. When an unexpected change of government occurred (such as the sudden demise of a king), the Egyptian priests held magical ceremonies in their temples, in which they invoked curses upon potential rebels by breaking and then

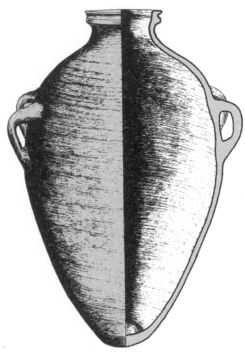

(above) Pottery jar from the Middle Bronze Age (20th–18th century BCE) from a dwelling of that period excavated in the lower city of Jerusalem ("City of David").

(right) One of the pottery figurines inscribed with the later Execration Texts, discovered in Egypt (now in the Brussels Museum). Inscribed on the figurine in hieratic script are the names of kings and cities suspected of disloyalty to the kings of Egypt. One of the cities mentioned is possibly Jerusalem.

burying figurines and jars inscribed with execrations against persons in Egypt and its empire who might take advantage of the situation and rebel. They believed that the actual writing of the execration would intimidate potential rebels. The execration texts are of historical importance because of the valuable information they convey about places, countries and towns, as well as the names of contemporary rulers. Jerusalem and its kings are listed in all three groups of texts, among towns and rulers liable to rebel against authority. While the rulers' names are undecipherable in the later groups, the name of the city is clear; in the first group (20th to 19th centuries BCE) the names of the city and of two or three rulers are legible: *Yqr'm* and *Šs'n*, both Semitic names. It may perhaps be inferred from the texts that Jerusalem had three population groups, or three clans, each headed by a different ruler.

In addition to this important historical information, archaeological excavations have confirmed the existence of the town at the time the execrations were written. Parts of a well-built wall have been uncovered on the eastern slope of the city, with abutting buildings containing pottery which could be dated to the Middle Bronze Age II, i.e., the twentieth and nineteenth centuries BCE. The remains indicate that this wall was so sturdy and strong that its foundations were still used for walls built in the First Temple period. The size and status of the city may be gauged from the existence of large quantities of contemporary pottery sherds a considerable distance away, on the slopes of the western hill near Robinson's Arch. These sherds were brought there and used as raw material to fill in stairs and level the ground. We cannot tell, however, whether the fill was taken from nearby or brought from the lower hill. Whatever the case, the Jerusalem of *Yqr'm* and *Šs'n* assumes physical dimensions.

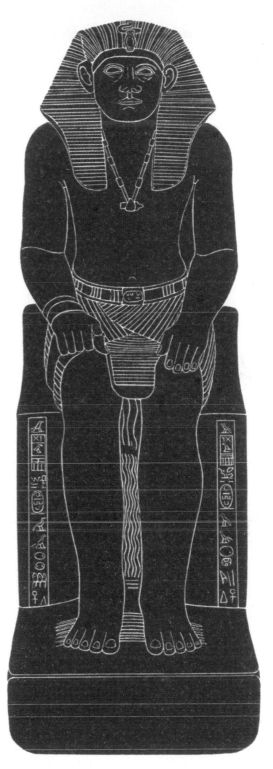

Royal statue of Pharaoh Sesostris III, one of the greatest Twelfth Dynasty kings of Egypt, who reigned in the 19th century BCE and conducted military campaigns into Canaan. The Execration Texts were probably written in his time.

3. Melchizedek, King of Shalem, Priest of God Most High

HISTORICAL and archaeological research sees the Holy Land of the eighteenth and seventeenth centuries BCE as the backdrop for the stories of the Patriarchs in the Book of Genesis. One impressive event of the time was the war that Abraham—then still called Abram— fought against four kings who came from the far north to fight against the cities of the plain of the Dead Sea. During the fighting they captured Lot, Abraham's nephew, with his family and property. After Abraham had defeated them and returned all their spoils to the owners, he was met by Melchizedek, King of Shalem (or Salem), who also held the title "Priest of God Most High."

The encounter took place in the Valley of Shaveh, later known as the Valley of the King. There Melchizedek blessed Abraham and in return received a tithe from the spoils, intended for the temple of God Most High in the town of Shalem. The city of Shalem was already identified with Jerusalem in biblical times; Melchizedek was the king of the city, who was also the high priest of the local temple. We should note, however, that some early authorities placed the god Shalem in the city of Shechem;

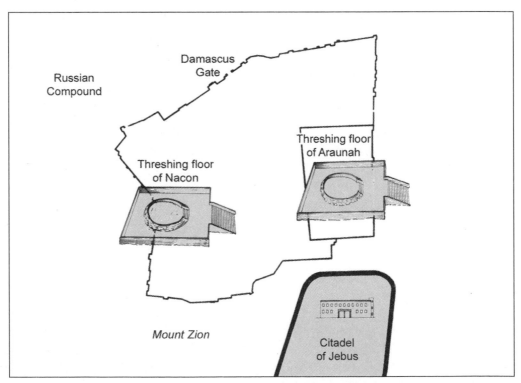

There were two cult places in Jerusalem, which subsequently became known as the "threshing floors" of Araunah and of Nacon. Located on high ground to the north and northwest of the city, they were probably used by two different populations living in the city on the eve of its conquest by David—Amorites (Nacon) and Jebusites (Araunah).

Jerusalem still maintains a tradition of two important sacred sites—the Temple Mount and the Holy Sepulcher.

perhaps there was a temple dedicated to Shalem in Shechem as well.

Since antiquity, the principle of the separation of powers has generally been applied, to prevent too much authority being concentrated in one person's hands. In particular, kingship and priesthood were two important positions that had to be separated. In ancient societies, the priesthood had many powers revolving around the temple and spiritual affairs: higher education, adjudication, even the administration of state funds, and more, were in the hands of the High Priest. The monarchy, on the other hand, was responsible for defense and relations with other cities and states, as well as internal administration. This separation of powers was intended for the benefit of the people. At times, however, a strong leader would concentrate all powers in his own hands. This was to occur in the second and first centuries BCE, when the Hasmoneans ruled as both kings and high priests (see below); but we have a far earlier case here—Melchizedek, King of Shalem, who was also high priest of his city-state.

This story demonstrates the importance of Jerusalem in the hill country, as a city with which the Semitic families then roaming the Holy Land maintained close ties. It was most probably the same city mentioned a hundred years before in the Execration Texts, remains of whose walls and fortifications, as well as some houses, have been uncovered in archaeological excavations.

4. THE PATRIARCH ABRAHAM AND THE SACRIFICE OF ISAAC—MOUNT MORIAH

ONE of the best known stories of Abraham describes his attempt to sacrifice Isaac. At the end of the episode, God promises Abraham that his descendants would become a great nation. The story contains several messages for mankind, which may be counted among the most important in human civilization. At the center of the narrative, Abraham is subjected to the most difficult test of all: God demands that he offer his only son, born in his old age, as a sacrifice, to prove his devotion and absolute trust in God. The testing of a person is a central element of the religious world of the Bible, and the story of the sacrifice of Isaac is one of the peaks of biblical narrative—a few words that convey so much and arouse such powerful emotions. Two further moral principles demonstrated by the story are perhaps even more significant than devotion to God. One is the prohibition of human sacrifice, which was common at the time, and its replacement, in fulfillment of God's will, by animal sacrifice. The second principle is of general, humanitarian significance: your son's life does not belong to you, and you may not sacrifice it. Although you, the father, gave him his life, once he has taken his first breath you cannot end that life. This is the principal message of "Do not raise your hand against the boy" (Genesis 22:12), a generally accepted humanitarian principle that is still engaging the attention of thinkers and philosophers.

The Bible describes this important episode as having taken place in "the land of Moriah," on a certain mountaintop. Jewish theology of that time considered identification of the site of utmost importance. Ultimately, in the time of David and Solomon, the peak in the land of Moriah was identified as the threshing floor of a Jebusite named

The biblical story of Abraham's attempt to sacrifice his son Isaac—known in Jewish tradition as the "Binding of Isaac"—has long attracted the attention of theologians and philosophers, on the one hand, and of artists, on the other. Jewish tradition identifies the site of the event, Mount Moriah, with the Temple Mount in Jerusalem, but the antiquity of this tradition is not known. The Samaritans, who follow the tradition of the northern Kingdom of Israel, identify Mount Moriah with Mount Gerizim, near Shechem (Nablus).

The sacrifice of Isaac.

Araunah in northern Jerusalem—the present site of the Temple Mount, also known as Mount Moriah. This was the subsequent site of the Temple; indeed, perhaps its identification as the place where Isaac was almost sacrificed was the reason for building the Temple there. (See also below, in our discussion of David and his establishment of Jerusalem as his capital.) Incidentally, the identification of the peak in the land of Moriah with the Temple Mount in Jerusalem was not always universally accepted. In the northern Kingdom of Israel, which seceded from Judah after King Solomon's death, Mount Moriah was identified with Mount Gerizim. The tradition that the binding of Isaac took place on Mount Gerizim, still upheld by the Samaritans, who in fact built their temple there, probably originated in the northern Kingdom of Israel.

5. *ABDI HEB/PA*, RULER OF JERUSALEM

THE EL-AMARNA PERIOD, 14TH CENTURY BCE

OUR historical information about Jerusalem in the fourteenth century BCE comes from an archive of letters discovered at El-Amarna in Egypt over one hundred years ago. In a mound near a village named El-Amarna, farmers digging for clay to improve the soil in their fields discovered a collection of letters, written in Accadian cuneiform script on baked clay tablets. Scholars and collectors purchased the finds, and subsequently regular archaeological excavations were conducted at the site. The excavators unearthed the ruins of the town of Akhetaton, capital city of the pharaoh Akhenaton (formerly Amenhotep IV), who placed the sun god Aton at the head of the Egyptian pantheon—a religious revolution that had significant political repercussions in Egypt, including the transfer of the capital to a new location, with the construction of a temple to the god Aton and a palace for the ruler Akhenaton. Among the ruins of the palace, some 400 tablets were found; some were letters sent to the pharaoh and his predecessor Amenhotep III, and others, copies of letters that he had written. The correspondence was in the Accadian language and script, at that time the *lingua franca* of the Middle East. Some of the archive consisted of correspondence between the major powers of the time: Egypt, Hatti, Babylon and Assyria. Most of the letters, however, were sent from cities of Syria and the Holy Land, which were then vassal-states of the Egyptian authorities, though they enjoyed a large degree of autonomy.

The letters reveal the atmosphere of the

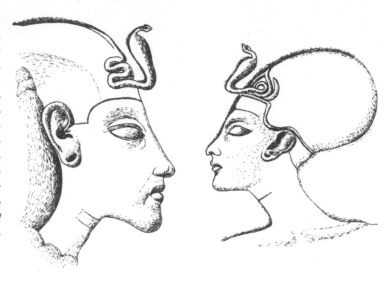

fourteenth century BCE, on the eve of the settlement of the Israelite tribes in the Holy Land: nomadic bands, some regarded as outlaws by the Egyptians and referred to as *Habiru*, were roaming the country and harassing the Egyptian authorities. The weakness of the supreme authority was also exploited by the rulers of the Canaanite towns, who tried to expand the areas under their control at the expense of their neighbors. All this is expressed in the El-Amarna letters, which convey repeated requests to the supreme power for arms to protect Egyptian interests in the large Egyptian province of Canaan. Although the Bible refers to the rulers of the Canaanite cities as "kings," they did not use this title in the letters to their overlord, the pharaoh; he alone possessed this exalted title. The rulers of the cities are referred to as "man of...," meaning the head of the town, some-

Late Bronze Age pottery from a Canaanite tomb in Jerusalem. No occupation strata of this period have been found in archaeological excavations in the tel of ancient Jerusalem. The only evidence of the period in Jerusalem has come from the chance discovery of tombs.

times also governing a number of neighboring villages and estates.

One distinguished writer from the Judean Hills was "*Abdi Heb/pa*, man of Jerusalem," "king" of Jerusalem in the fourteenth century BCE. He wrote six letters, all requesting arms and assistance to protect Egyptian interests against the Habiru marauders and other Canaanites, neighbors of the king of Jerusalem. *Abdi Heb/pa* of course declares his unreserved loyalty to Pharaoh. These letters reveal Jerusalem's status in the fourteenth century BCE as an important city of the hilly region, as well as the name of its king—the overlord of the city.

Despite the relatively large volume of historical information about this period of Jerusalem's history—the Late Bronze Age (LBA)—no remains of buildings dated to this period have been found in excavations as yet. Only thorough excavation in the heart of the City of David might help to uncover the secrets of *Abdi Heb/pa*'s city. Nevertheless, graves with abundant pottery dating to the LBA have been uncovered not far from the city: at Government House (Armon Hanatziv), in the Mahaneh Yehuda quarter and on the Mount of Olives. These rich finds attest to the presence in the city of a relatively prosperous population.

In sum, Late Bronze Age Jerusalem seems to have possessed some political importance in the hilly areas of Judah and Ephraim, controlling the routes along the length and breadth of the hilly regions.

6. THE CITY-STATE OF JERUSALEM

THE Egyptians established small city-states in Canaan—a system of "divide and rule" that permitted efficient control of the mountainous country of Canaan. Each city was surrounded by a number of villages and farms, together forming the territory of the city-state. The extent of these territories may be inferred from the El-Amarna letters (see above).

The complaints of *Abdi Heb/pa*, king of Jerusalem, about his neighbors reveal that Gezer—ruled by *Milhi-ilu*—was a city-state, west of Jerusalem, whose status equaled that of Jerusalem. This

Jerusalem in the El-Amarna period was a kind of city-state, ruling over a number of nearby villages and small towns, including Manahat, Mei Neftoah and perhaps also Bethlehem. The El-Amarna letters refer to a city named "Beit Ninip," identified by some scholars as Bethlehem. Among the city-states mentioned in the Shephelah are Gezer, Gath and Lachish.

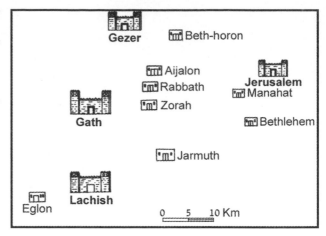

also applied to Gath and its ruler *Shuwardata* and the town of Lachish. The king of Jerusalem expresses anger at the rulers of these towns for trying to seize some of his land to their east, on the inland plain and the mountain; he complains in his letter and appeals to his overlord the Pharaoh. The territory of the city-state of Jerusalem may be estimated from the list of places mentioned in the El-Amarna letters: its area was about half that of the province of Yehud (Judah) under Persian rule (see below). It is an interesting point that, around one thousand years later, territories of a similar area were defined as administrative units.

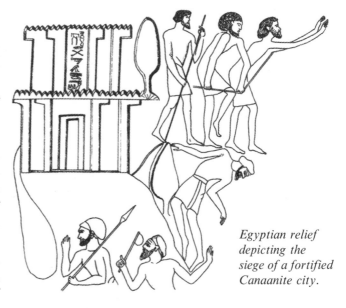

Egyptian relief depicting the siege of a fortified Canaanite city.

7. JERUSALEM ON THE EVE OF JOSHUA'S CONQUEST
THE KINGDOM OF ADONI-ZEDEK 13TH CENTURY BCE

IN the second half of the thirteenth century BCE, the Israelite tribes, led by Joshua, entered Canaan and began their conquests. Their first battles were successful. The battle for the city of Ai, for example, demonstrated considerable initiative, guile and tactical ability. The hilly land northwest of Jerusalem (in the area of today's Nabi Samwil) and farther west was the home of a special ethnic group, probably the Hivites of the Bible. They commanded a hilly region with four fortified towns, between which were small unwalled villages. The capital of the region was Gibeon, and the other three towns were Chephirah, Beeroth and Kiriath-jearim (the latter is now the site of the village of Abu Ghosh). This

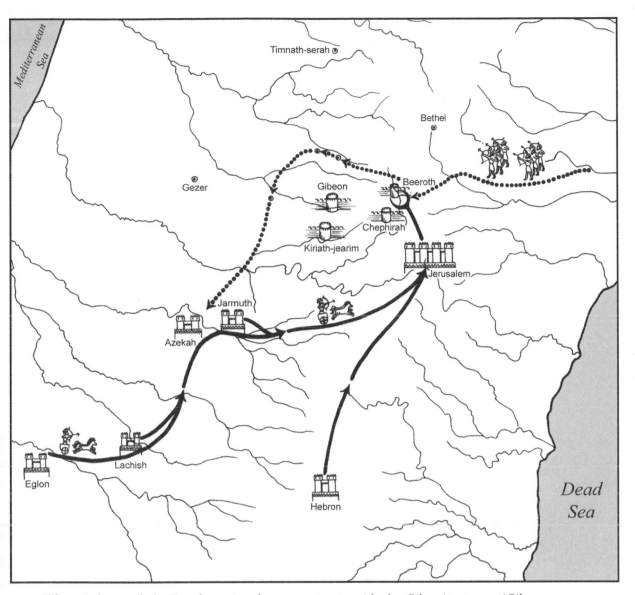

Labels on map: Mediterranean Sea, Timnath-serah, Bethel, Gezer, Gibeon, Beeroth, Chephirah, Kiriath-jearim, Jerusalem, Jarmuth, Azekah, Lachish, Eglon, Hebron, Dead Sea

When Joshua and the Israelites signed a peace treaty with the Gibeonite towns (Gibeon, Chephirah, Beeroth and Kiriath-jearim), King Adoni-zedek of Jerusalem declared war on the Gibeonites. With aid from the kings of Lachish, Hebron and other cities, he went to battle. The Gibeonites appealed for help to their new allies, Joshua and the Israelites. In a fierce battle, later known as the battle of Gibeon and the Valley of Aijalon, the Israelites were victorious and the Canaanite kings were slain after they had hidden in a cave in Makkedah.

population—known as the Gibeonites, after the name of their capital—concluded a treaty with the invading Israelite tribes that would spare their lives; they paid dearly, forfeiting the relative freedom they had had in Canaan. The neighboring kings disapproved of their action, fearing that it initiated a process that would eventually bring all of Canaan under the rule of the Israelite tribes, terminating the autonomy they had enjoyed as the rulers of the Canaanite city-states. The first ruler to become aware of this danger was Adoni-zedek, king of Jerusalem—the name recalls that of Melchizedek, King of Shalem, who had reigned a few hundred years earlier. Adoni-zedek therefore turned to his

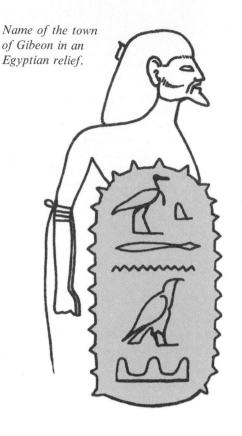

Name of the town of Gibeon in an Egyptian relief.

and a military coalition was formed. The Gibeonites accordingly appealed to their new allies, the Israelite tribes and their leader Joshua, and requested help. After bitter, exhausting battles against five cities, headed by Jerusalem, the Israelite tribes under Joshua won a resounding victory. The coalition forces were routed and their kings were killed in a cave in the town of Makkedah. Some of the cities were conquered, but not settled by the Israelites. We have no information about the fate of Jerusalem, the leader of the coalition. Was it conquered, destroyed or burnt, or did it remain intact, easy prey to other nomadic tribes seeking to settle in Canaan? These questions remain unanswered by both recorded history and archaeological findings. Later evidence, from the Book of Judges, indicates that, from the period of the judges until David's time, Jerusalem was considered a foreign enclave. At any rate, it was either not captured by the Israelite tribes or, if conquered, was eventually abandoned and occupied by another ethnic group, the Jebusite-Hittites, together with some Amorite families.

neighbors, the cities of the Shephelah and the hill country, and summoned them to fight the Gibeonites. Hebron, Eglon, Debir and Lachish responded to his call

8. JERUSALEM-JEBUS, HITTITE AND AMORITE CITY

THE KINGDOM OF ARAUNAH 12TH–11TH CENTURIES BCE

IN one of his prophecies, the prophet Ezekiel describes Jerusalem prior to its capture by David in the following terms: "Your origin and your birth are of the land of the Canaanites; your father was an Amorite, and your mother a Hittite" (Ezekiel 16:3). This is an apt description of the Jerusalem of that time: a city in the land of Canaan, with a mixed population of Amorites and Hittites. Not only Canaanites dwelt in the Egyptian province of Canaan, but also other peoples, referred to in the Bible as the "seven nations." One of them, the Amorites,

lived in the inland plain and in the hill country, including Jerusalem. There are various indications that another people, the Hittites, inhabited the hill country: Abraham purchased the cave of Machpelah in Hebron from a person named Ephron the Hittite. The Jebusites associated with Jerusalem were a Hittite family; it has been suggested that the biblical Uriah the Hittite, who served in David's court, was one of the original Jebusite inhabitants of Jerusalem. After the war against Jerusalem's king Adonizedek, the city passed into the hands of

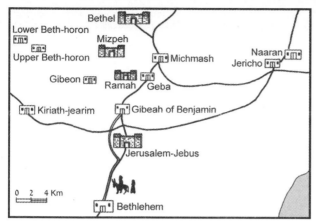

The Bible tells us that in the time of the Judges, just before the establishment of the monarchy, Jerusalem was inhabited by Jebusites. A Levite from the hill country of Ephraim was traveling home with his concubine from Bethlehem. Toward evening he found himself close to Jebus/Jerusalem, but chose not to spend the night there because it was not an Israelite city. He therefore turned off the highway and spent the night at Gibeah of Benjamin.

the Amorites and Hittites—that is, the Jebusites, who were its principal rulers until its occupation by David. The last king of the city, Araunah, was a Jebusite. The rulers of the city gave it their name, and it became known as the "town of the Jebusites" or briefly "Jebus."

Jerusalem-Jebus occupied the site of the Canaanite city from its foundation, that is, the lower ridge, above the Gihon Spring. Some authorities believe that its area was even smaller, based on the sections of walls uncovered halfway down the eastern slope, above the Middle Bronze Age walls. However, it is probably still too early to determine the dimensions of Jebus, because these walls may be part of the ruler's citadel, which is known to have stood in this area. There were two citadels in Jerusalem, one in the north, south of the Ophel (south of the present-day road from the Dung Gate to Jericho), built during Solomon's reign; and the other in the south of the city, where the Central Valley joins the Kidron Valley, close to the later site of the Siloam Pool. The northern citadel was the rulers' fortified palace, while the southern one protected one of Jerusalem's weak points: the southern ridge of the city, which is relatively low in comparison with the Kidron Valley. One of the citadels also came to be known as "Zion"—an as yet unexplained name, later applied to the Temple Mount

and later to Jerusalem's western hill, outside the present Zion Gate—but that is a much later story.

In those days, an independent city had one or more cult places. The city priests officiated at the cult place, the temple or "high place" (*bamah*), also acting in various administrative capacities. Of special importance were their roles of adjudication and education, which were carried out at the site of the temple. Because of the modest dimensions of Jerusalem/Jebus, its ancient cult places were outside the city and probably fortified in some way. In Shechem, too, there were cult places some distance outside the city, on Mount Ebal and Mount Gerizim.

One cult place in Jerusalem was on the northern hill—today's Temple Mount or what was then known as the "threshing floor" of Araunah. The other was on the hill near today's Jaffa Gate, the "threshing floor" of Nacon. The Hebrew word *goren*, "threshing floor," also denotes a circular place—most threshing floors in antiquity were of necessity circular—but the word was also commonly used for a cult place, which is presumably how it should be understood in Jerusalem. David purchased Araunah's "threshing floor," that is, the Jebusite cult place with its appurtenances, for the purposes of worship, because that had also been its previous use. As such an idea offended

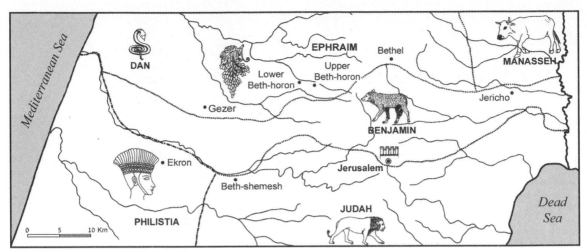

On the eve of David's conquest of Jerusalem, it was a small Jebusite town surrounded by territory already occupied by Israelite tribes. The town itself was in the territory of Benjamin, though part of its agricultural hinterland was in the territory of Judah. The Philistines would sometimes come up into the hill country from the west to collect protection money and taxes from the Israelite families that had settled there. It is not known what relations, if any, there were between the Philistines and Jebus/Jerusalem.

the late editor of the biblical narrative, he described the transaction, in which David purchased cattle and wood for cultic purposes, as applying to the agricultural equipment of a threshing floor (see 2 Samuel ch. 24).

Another cult place mentioned in a cultic context is the so-called "threshing floor of Nacon," where it was intended to bring the Ark of the Covenant, which had been captured by the Philistines, from Kiriath-jearim; because of the death of Uzzah on the way to the "threshing floor," the Bible names the site Perez-uzzah (meaning "the misfortune of Uzzah"; see 2 Samuel 6:1–23). A similarly named site (the "garden of Uzzah") is mentioned in the Bible as the burial place of two kings of Judah; it is apparently located in the area of today's Jaffa Gate (for tombs found there, see below). The transfer of the Ark of the Covenant to the threshing floor of Nacon having failed, it was taken into the City of David, after being kept for a few months in the home of one Obed-edom the Gittite (from the city of Gath). The idea

of building a temple at the threshing floor of Araunah, where the Ark would be kept permanently, arose only toward the end of David's reign; it was implemented only by his son Solomon.

The plain meaning of the biblical text is that the original intention was to accommodate the Ark on the western hill, at the threshing floor of Nacon. This plan apparently met with objections, because of the disasters that had befallen the Ark and its bearers on the way there. As a compromise, a cult place was established, with the Ark, elsewhere. However, allocation of an area for that purpose within the city would have adversely affected the quality of life within the small and presumably overcrowded area. Ultimately, the cult place was established at the threshing floor of Araunah, located outside the city to its north.

Perhaps Nacon's threshing floor was an Amorite cult place, while Araunah's threshing floor was that of the Jebusite majority; only further investigation may settle this question.

Chapter 3:

JERUSALEM IN THE FIRST TEMPLE PERIOD
THE HOUSE OF DAVID, FROM DAVID TO ZEDEKIAH
1000–586 BCE

1. FROM JEBUS TO THE CITY OF DAVID

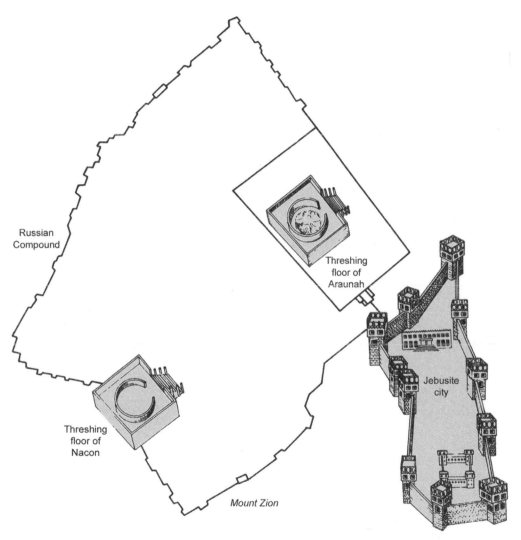

Jerusalem, the Jebusite city that David conquered and made his capital. There were two cult places outside the city, to the north and the northwest. After the city had become the capital of David's kingdom it became known as the "City of David."

THE revolutionary change in Jerusalem's history came with its conquest by David and his decision to make it his capital. Jerusalem would thus acquire a status held by no other city: the birthplace of western civilization and the sacred capital of the western world.

David was born in 1037 BCE in

Imaginary portrait of King David, from a wall painting in the church of the Monastery of the Cross, Jerusalem.

Bethlehem, 8 to 9 kilometers south of Jerusalem. In 1007 BCE, at the age of thirty, he was crowned king of the tribe of Judah and the affiliated ethnic units—the Simeonites, the Jerahmeel and Jeroham clans and their southern neighbors. David established his capital at Hebron, a status which it retained when he was anointed king of all Israel two years later. In 999 BCE David conquered Jerusalem-Jebus and it became part of his kingdom. Before that event, Jerusalem had become smaller in area, the city and the neighboring fields remaining a small enclave between the Israelite cities of Judah and Benjamin. Although some scholars believe that the battle for Jerusalem and its conquest was a major military campaign, there is no evidence of this: the Jebusite population was unharmed and did not leave. They seem to have submitted quite quickly, after a brief show of resistance. The Bible describes the episode as follows: "...who said to David, 'You will not come in here, but the blind and the lame will ward you off'" (2 Samuel 5:6). Yigael Yadin cited this verse as evidence that the Jebusites were of Hittite stock, since the Hittites, in defense of a besieged city, would parade their blind and lame on the walls in a magical rite, invoking similar afflictions upon the attackers if they captured the city. There is no further hint in the Bible of a battle, and indeed, if the Jebusites had to employ such magical means, they surely did not have a powerful army at their disposal. Another puzzling biblical allusion to the conquest is David's proclamation: "Whoever would smite the Jebusites, let him get up the water shaft (*zinnor*)" (2 Samuel 5:8). This obscure phrase has been interpreted for decades as describing some stratagem employed to enter the city. After archaeologists discovered the water-supply system known as Warren's Shaft, it was believed that the word *zinnor* referred to this concealed system, through which David's forces penetrated the city. In recent years, however, it has been shown that Warren's Shaft postdates David's reign, making this interpretation untenable (see below, "Water in Times of Siege").

After the conquest, David took up residence in the citadel, in the Palace of Araunah, the last Jebusite king. In that same year (999 BCE), he decided to transfer the capital of the combined kingdom from Hebron to Jebus-Jerusalem, which has since been called the City of David. It was indeed customary in the ancient Near East, including the Holy Land, to name a conquered city for the conqueror and to establish his capital there. Thus, when Saul captured Gibeah of Benjamin, the site of the citadel in which the Philistine army was garrisoned, he made it his capital, renaming it Gibeah of Saul (that is, "Hill of Saul"). Another example comes from the late years of the Second Temple period, when

Remains of fortifications from the Jebusite period found in archaeological excavations on the eastern slope of the lower hill.

Herod, after occupying the region southeast of Bethlehem, built an administrative center there and called it Herodis or Herodium.

There were several reasons for the decision to move from Hebron to Jerusalem, chief among which was the desire to unite the northern and southern Israelite tribes and establish a united kingdom, ruled by a single monarch. David chose the path of compromise, foregoing his prestige to placate the northern tribes: Jerusalem was a good choice as capital, because it lay within the territory of Benjamin, on the border of Judah. Another factor was Jerusalem's wonderful geographic location: a city situated at the kingdom's crossroads, but also protected because it was in the heart of the region and not at its edge. After Jerusalem had been taken it be-

came the king's private possession, and he now granted land to his large retinue of courtiers, princes, priests, army commanders and other members of the administrative staff. Most of the Jebusites were moved out of the city; a few remained and entered David's service, as did Uriah the Hittite.

For the first time in its history, Jerusalem became the chief city of the country. Previously a provincial town, on a par with the important Canaanite cities of Shechem, Ashkelon, Gaza, Gezer, Aphek and others, it was now the capital of the kingdom. It was to retain that status—capital of all of the Holy Land, from Dan to Beersheba—for many centuries; and it remained the capital when further conquests enlarged the country, annexing territories in the south, north and east.

2. From Capital City to Royal Temple and Seat

The Ark of the Covenant was carried in a Philistine ox-drawn wagon like that illustrated here.

THE priesthood fulfilled important functions in the administration of the state in antiquity—including adjudication, education, care of the state's treasury—and, of course, in the religious realm. The Levites were the executive branch of the priesthood, and the center of the priesthood developed around the temples. With the establishment of Jerusalem as the capital, it was natural that David would also make it the spiritual center and build the main temple there.

Two years after the conquest, in 997 BCE, David decided to bring the Ark of the Covenant up to Jerusalem. Having been captured by the Philistines and retrieved, it had been kept at Kiriath-jearim (today the village of Abu Ghosh). As already noted, David probably first established a cult site at the threshing floor of Nacon (2 Samuel 6:6; referred to in 1 Chronicles 13:9 as the threshing floor of Chidon), west of the city (in the area of today's Jaffa Gate). However, as the first attempt to bring the Ark to Jerusalem had disastrous results, a place was found for it in a tent in the City of David, after it had been left for three months in the home of Obed-edom the Gittite (outside the walls of the city, to the south).

Although David wished to establish a permanent temple for the Ark, he was too preoccupied with security and state affairs to be able to do so. Possibly, he also feared that the construction of a temple in Jerusalem might offend the northern tribes—before its capture, the Ark had been kept at Shiloh, in the

During their war with the Philistines, the Israelites took the Ark of the Covenant from its permanent home at Shiloh to battle at Eben-ezer. The Philistines captured it, but quickly returned it to Judah after a series of disasters befell their cities. At first the Ark was kept at Beth-shemesh, in the Shephelah; it was later moved to Kiriath-jearim, a Gibeonite town in the Jerusalem hills.

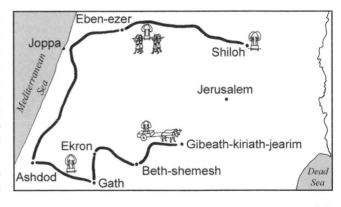

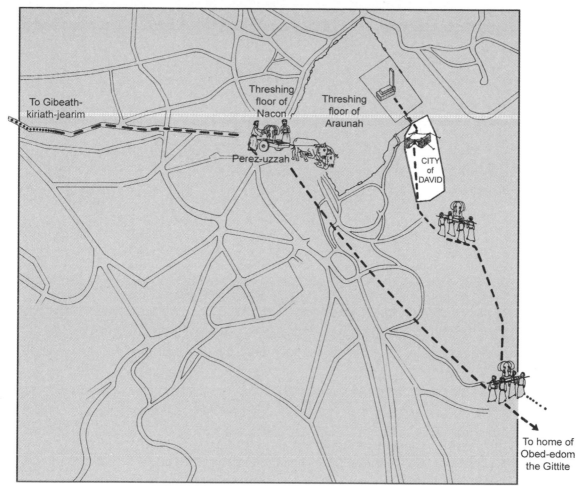

From Kiriath-jearim the Ark was taken to Jerusalem and kept at the threshing floor of Nacon near the city. After one of the company who had carried the Ark died mysteriously, it was moved to the home of one Obed-edom the Gittite (from the city of Gath), probably in the Kidron Valley near Ma'aleh Adummim. It was eventually moved to Jerusalem and placed in the City of David, close to the royal palace. After the Temple had been constructed at the threshing floor of Araunah, the Ark was placed in the Holy of Holies in the Temple.

territory of Ephraim, which was consequently considered a sacred site; hence the permanent transfer of the religious center to Jerusalem-Jebus might be seen by the northern tribes as too innovative. Perhaps this was the principal reason for placing the Ark in temporary quarters in Jerusalem. Moreover, possibly no construction site was available at the time, and only years later was David able to purchase the threshing floor of Araunah.

Twenty-four years after the Ark had been transferred to Jerusalem, in 973 BCE, David succeeded in purchasing the Jebusite cult place; a severe epidemic was ravaging the people, and David tried to contain it by building a permanent altar and a Temple. It was for this purpose that he bought the threshing floor of Araunah. Now, after many years, public opposition to establishing Jerusalem as the religious center had died down. Rebellions against David's rule had been put down; his conquests brought the country economic prosperity and stability and strengthened his status even among the northern tribes. All these factors helped to speed the planning and construction of the Temple.

The site's standing as a symbol of national identity would naturally be enhanced by association with one of the stories of the Patriarchs, who were venerated by all the tribes. The association of an event with a certain place involves the choice of a narrative that lacks a clearly identified geographical location. Such was the story of Abraham's sacrifice of Isaac; and indeed, the "land of Moriah" referred to in the story was identified with a hilltop outside the City of David to the north, possibly in keeping with ancient traditions. Such linkage of a narrative to a sacred site is a familiar element in the religious world of the Ancient East; in fact, many centuries later the story of Muhammad's ascent into heaven was also associated with the Temple Mount.

The choice of the threshing floor of Araunah as the site for the altar and the Temple determined the destiny of Jerusalem for generations, influencing its history for the next three thousand years.

3. SOLOMON BUILDS THE FIRST TEMPLE

SOLOMON, born in 986 BCE, was crowned at the age of sixteen, reigning for the first four years at his father David's side. The forty years of Solomon's rule were an era of peace and tranquility throughout his large kingdom.

It now appeared that David's idea of a third state between the two great powers was becoming a reality for the first time in the history of the Ancient East. The success of the idea depended on unity among the tribes, the stability of the

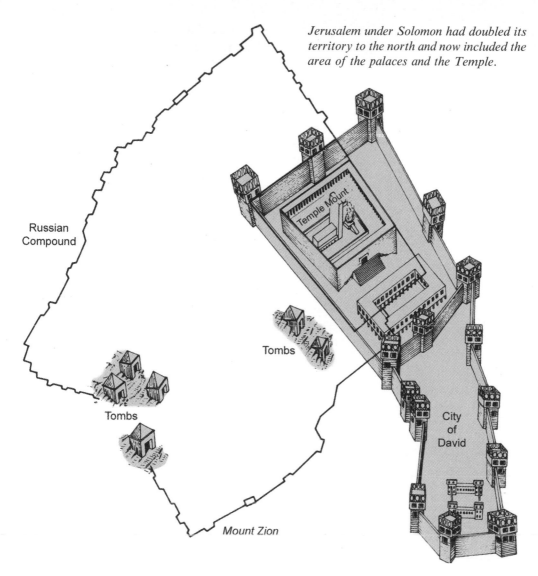

Jerusalem under Solomon had doubled its territory to the north and now included the area of the palaces and the Temple.

Russian
Compound

Temple Mount

Tombs

Tombs

City
of
David

Mount Zion

kingdom and its strength as a durable entity. Superficially, Solomon's kingdom seemed united and stable, and he was able to devote his efforts to accelerated development and extensive construction. Favorable economic conditions and international trade filled his coffers, providing large sums for construction projects—especially in Jerusalem. After he had built the Millo, where he estab-

(opposite) Solomon's foreign, economic and internal policies earned him a reputation as a wise king. This imaginary portrait of Solomon is based on a miniature of the Judgment of Solomon from a 13th century illuminated Hebrew manuscript.

lished his administrative center and its various components—the royal palace, the women's house, granaries, storerooms and stables—the construction of the Temple became the primary challenge. Most of Solomon's construction work began after David's death and after he had consolidated his rule. Jewish tradition questions why the Temple, the special symbol of Judaism, was built by Solomon and not by his father, the founder of the House of David. The Book of Chronicles gives an interesting explanation: David was not privileged to build the Temple, the embodiment of peace, because he was a man of war, whose hands had shed blood, in the spirit

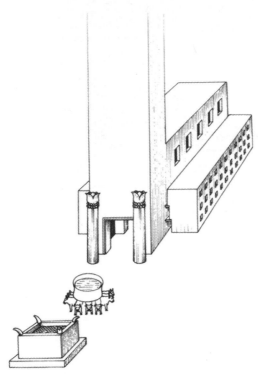

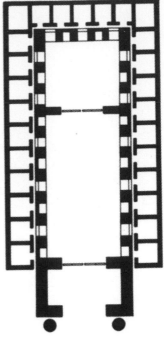

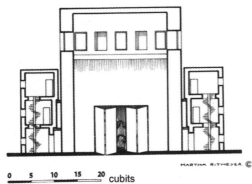

Reconstructed view from the east toward the façade of Solomon's Temple: flanking the entrance are the columns "Jachin" and "Boaz," and in front of them—the altar and the laver; (below) plan of the façade.

General plan of the Temple (above) and north-south section.

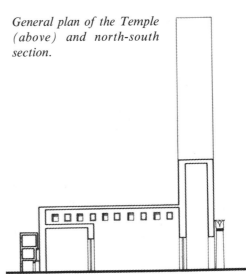

later expressed so aptly by the prophet Zechariah (4:6): "Not by might, nor by power, but by my Spirit, says the LORD of hosts."

While Araunah's threshing floor was a suitable site for the Temple, it lay outside the city, as did Jerusalem's other earlier cult place, the threshing floor of Nacon. However, unlike the latter, it was close enough to permit its inclusion in the city boundaries. In order to link the hill of the

threshing floor with the city, the northern topographical saddles were filled in: one north of the City of David outside the wall, the other, north of the Ophel hill. The three hills—the city, the Ophel and the Temple Mount—were henceforth one continuous unit; physically linked by terraces built into the hillside on the fill, known in Hebrew as *millo* (filling). The hill just north of the City of David and a few dozen meters higher was now desig-

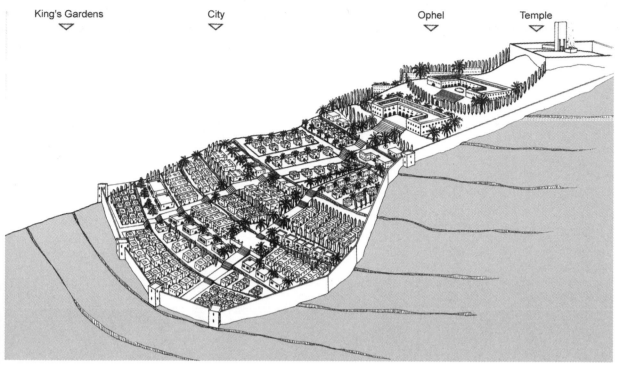

Jerusalem in the days of Solomon, reconstruction, looking westward. The city doubled in size, in a northward direction, and now included the area of the palaces and the Temple.

nated for the construction of the administrative center and was called the Ophel, meaning "acropolis." The third hill, higher still than the Ophel, was the threshing floor of Araunah, the intended site of the Temple. From then on it was called the Temple Mount or Mount Moriah; some Psalms and literary descriptions refer to it as Mount Zion.

At birth Solomon had been given the name "Jedidiah" ("friend of God"), apparently receiving the royal name Solomon only later. Perhaps he was given the name Solomon, *Shelomo* in Hebrew, in recognition of the construction of the Temple at the site where the god Shalem—the patron of Jerusalem—had formerly been worshiped; another theory explains the name as derived from the Hebrew *shalem*, "complete," because he completed the construction of the Temple planned by his father, a project which gave Jerusalem its position as "a king's sanctuary and a royal place."

With the completion of the Temple,

Jerusalem possessed a magnificent building, a spiritual and cultural beacon for life in the city. It left its mark on all the subsequent history of Jerusalem and determined its character and special status.

Two immense freestanding bronze columns were placed at the front entrance to the Temple, topped with capitals, a design familiar from the Ancient East. These columns were known as Jachin and Boaz, perhaps symbolizing the unification of the two cult places, the threshing floors of Araunah and Nacon, at one site. The name Boaz may derive from the name of the founder of the royal family, David's forefather; the other column, Jachin, may have been named for the threshing floor of Nacon (the two names have the same root in Hebrew). From the name of Jachin came the names of some kings of Judah, including Jeconiah-Jehoiachin, just as the names Solomon, Absalom and Shallum were derived from Shalem.

51

4. The City Expands Westward, to the Upper Hills

From Jehoshaphat to the Destruction of the First Temple

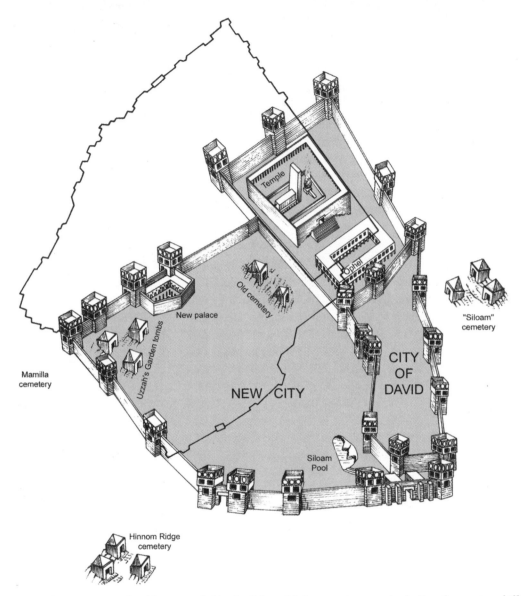

Jerusalem was considerably expanded in the 9th and 8th centuries BCE, including the western hills in the inhabited and fortified area. In the Second Temple period the western hills, which were higher than the older part of the city, were known as the Upper City.

UNDER Solomon, Jerusalem's population and area doubled for the first time in its history: from around 15 acres to approximately 35 acres, including the Ophel and the Temple Mount. The city's hills were settled in accordance with a logical social order: the lowest hill was inhabited by the common folk, the Ophel above it housed the administrative center and in the north rose the Temple Mount, from which the Temple towered above the royal palace and the rest of the city.

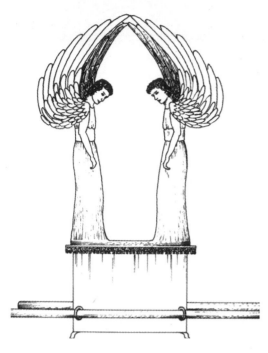

(left) Reconstruction of the Ark and the cherubim in the Holy of Holies of Solomon's Temple.

(below) Phoenician portrayal of a cherub. Phoenician art also influenced Israelite art.

We have already noted that the Temple Mount and the Ophel were new additions to the city boundaries. The Ophel hill, the first of these new areas, was from the outset part of the royal estate; for many generations thereafter, it was indeed used exclusively for public building.

From 999 BCE, the year of David's conquest of the city, until 586 BCE, when it was conquered by Nebuchadnezzar, Jerusalem was the capital of the kingdom: of the united kingdom under David and Solomon; and of the kingdom of Judah from Rehoboam's reign until the destruction of the Temple. For over 400 years, the kingdom was ruled by a single

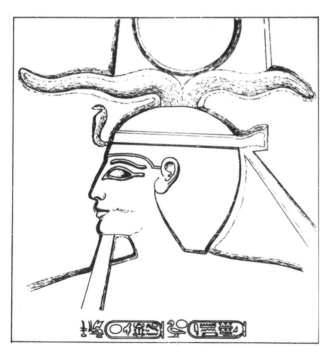

Portrait of the Egyptian Pharaoh Shishak, based on an Egyptian relief.

Excavations in the Jewish Quarter exposed a tower from the monarchic period in the northern city wall. The fortification remains were reused in the Second Temple period, alongside structures built by different techniques.

dynasty, with power being transferred from father to son—an almost unprecedented phenomenon in ancient history.

Several kings played a prominent role in Jerusalem's history. Rehoboam, through wasteful policies that destroyed the achievements of his father and grandfather, was most probably responsible for the division of the united kingdom. On the other hand, he may be credited with saving the city from conquest by the Egyptian Pharaoh Shishak by paying him tribute. Another king who stands out among the early kings of David's dynasty was Jehoshaphat, who introduced important religious-legal reforms (his name

establishing the religious significance of Jerusalem and its Temple. His achievements in foreign policy were also significant, but he failed in his attempt to restore the situation that had existed during David's reign and reestablish Judah as a strong buffer state between the great powers. Many other kings contributed to strengthening the capital: some built new walls, others reinforced old walls and added to them, endeavoring to cultivate Jerusalem as a splendid and impressive capital.

The principal activities of the kings of Judah are known to us from the biblical books of Kings and Chronicles; beyond these rather meager historical records, however, archaeological research has contributed important information about Jerusalem in the days of the First Temple.

For many generations, right up to the Six-Day War of 1967, most scholars believed that until its destruction by the Babylonians Jerusalem occupied the same area as under Solomon: the Lower City, the Ophel and the Temple Mount. A minority disputed this view, arguing that the city had also spread to the western hill, known in Second Temple times as the Upper City. This minority opinion was indeed corroborated by major discoveries in excavations in the Jewish Quarter of today's Old City, at Mount Zion and at the foot of the western wall of the Old City. The discovery of a northern line of fortification with towers revealed that residential quarters were already being built on the

in fact means "the Lord judged"). Much of his fame derives from his cordial relations with the northern kingdom (he married into the Omrid dynasty) and his extensive commercial and economic ties with the kings of Tyre and Sidon. During Jehoshaphat's reign, fortifications and water systems for time of siege were built, similar to those of the north—about which more details are given further on. Another great king of Judah, although a leper, was Uzziah; he, too, fortified Jerusalem—"Uzziah built towers in Jerusalem...and fortified them" (2 Chronicles 26:9)—and developed and expanded settlement in the Negeb. King Hezekiah is particularly known for his successful resistance to the Assyrian king Sennacherib, who besieged Jerusalem; he thus gave the kingdom and the city over one hundred additional years of independence. Hezekiah's grandson, Josiah, instituted major religious reforms, firmly

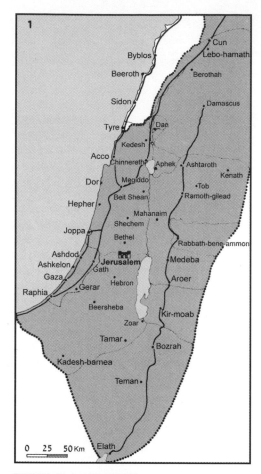

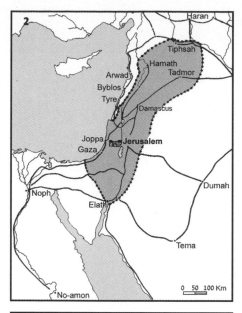

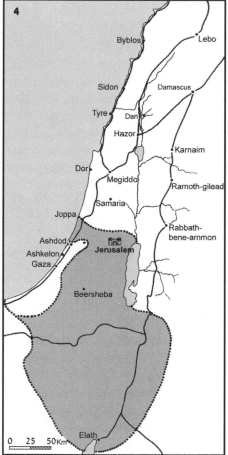

Jerusalem served as the capital of the united kingdom of Israel and as the capital of Judah after the division of the kingdom. (1) David's kingdom. (2) Solomon's kingdom. (3) Rehoboam's kingdom. (4) Uzziah's kingdom.

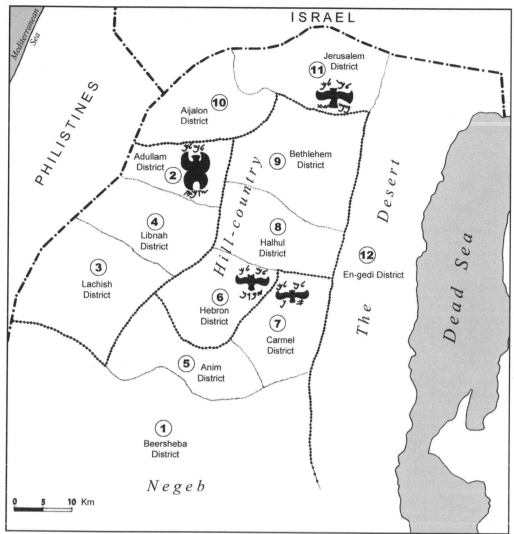

Excavations and surveys in the kingdom of Judah have unearthed thousands of pottery jar handles bearing the seal impression of a royal symbol and the word la-melekh, *meaning "(belonging) to the king," as well as the name of one of four cities: Hebron, Ziph, Socoh and* mmšt. *The first three are known cities in Judah, but the fourth is known neither from the Bible nor elsewhere. The suggestion that* mmšt *is a name for Jerusalem cannot be confirmed.*

Scholars differ in their interpretations of the seal impressions. Some believe that they represent royal land and vineyards owned by the king around the cities named. Other theories suggest that these cities had royal pottery workshops or royal winepresses. Alternatively, it has been proposed that these four cities represent the administrative division of Judah into four districts instead of the twelve traditional ones. On this approach, Jerusalem was referred to as mmšt *in its capacity as district capital, in contrast to its special status as capital of the kingdom.*

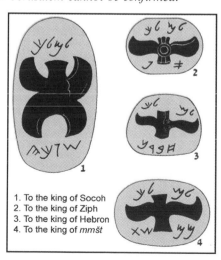

1. To the king of Socoh
2. To the king of Ziph
3. To the king of Hebron
4. To the king of *mmšt*

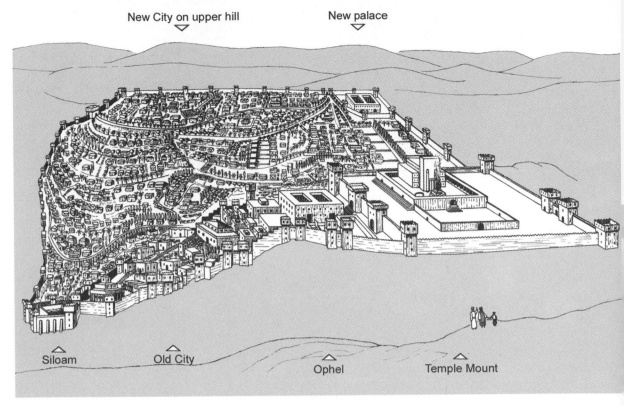

New City on upper hill   New palace

Siloam   Old City   Ophel   Temple Mount

Jerusalem, capital of the Kingdom of Judah: reconstruction, view from the Mount of Olives. To the right: the Temple Mount and the government seat on the Ophel. Top right: the new royal citadel on the peak of the western hill, today in the heart of the Jewish Quarter.

western hill in the time of the First Temple; these neighborhoods were subsequently fortified with sturdy walls. Thanks to such archaeological discoveries, it is now clear that at some time during the First Temple period the city expanded beyond the area that it had occupied under Solomon.

While the identity of the king in whose reign this expansion took place is as yet unknown, he is commonly identified as Hezekiah, who reigned toward the end of the eighth century BCE. This opinion is based on a story according to which refugees from the northern kingdom arrived in Judah after the Assyrian invasion and found a place to settle in Jerusalem; this presumably involved enlarging the city. Nevertheless, I believe that the findings reveal that the expansion took place and the new neighbor-

hoods were fortified before Hezekiah's reign, under either Jehoshaphat or—which is more likely—Uzziah. It seems probable that the Siloam Pool, which was inside the fortified area of the city together with the Siloam Channel, predate Hezekiah's Tunnel. If this is so (see next section), it supports our conclusion that the western hill was fortified before the close of the eighth century BCE. Incidentally, pottery finds in these particular excavations do not help to date the remains, since pottery from the end of the eighth century BCE is indistinguishable from that of the late ninth or early eighth centuries BCE. Corroboration for the fortification of the western hill in the Upper City during the First Temple period must be based on historical considerations, since precise archaeological evidence is lacking.

5. WATER IN TIME OF SIEGE

WARREN'S SHAFT, THE SILOAM CHANNEL, HEZEKIAH'S TUNNEL

ONE problem facing military planners in the ancient world was the supply of water during siege. As it was very costly to excavate wells and plaster them to prevent seepage, any water-supply system depended on spring water. Springs are generally found in valleys and deep places, while towns were built on the top of a hill or mountain, placing them some distance from the water source. In times of war, therefore, the enemy did not lack for water, whereas the besieged city was cut off from its source of water. Ancient engineers solved the problem by excavating well-designed water systems which permitted covert access to the water from inside the city, while the spring was sealed from the outside to deny the enemy access. Such systems have been discovered at Megiddo, Ibleam, Hazor, Gezer, Gibeon and Jerusalem—and probably also at Lachish and Beersheba. When they were first discovered, it was assumed that these were Canaanite work, but Yigael Yadin, in his studies of the water systems at Megiddo and Hazor, proved that they date to the era of Israelite rule, especially the Omrid dynasty. The water system at Gibeon was also most certainly constructed in the First Temple period and not the Late Bronze (Late Canaanite) Age. It may be assumed that the other systems, which are very similar, also date from that period. The most probable date for the water-supply system in Judah is the reign of Jehoshaphat, the ally of the Omrid kings.

The main idea of these water systems was to dig a tunnel and a shaft, from the center of the city to the water source; the spring was then sealed to prevent access

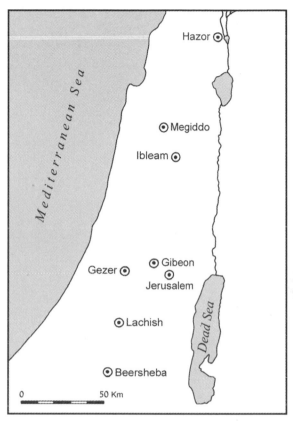

Cities in Judah and Israel equipped with water-supply systems for times of siege, all dating from the 9th to 8th centuries BCE.

from outside. Such a plan was feasible provided the spring supplied a relatively small quantity of water daily, say about 2 to 5 cubic meters—a quantity that is easily drawn off. This was the case for the springs supplying the water systems built in the Holy Land. At Hazor, the quarriers reached groundwater before getting to the spring; this solved the problem, since the groundwater level remains constant no matter how much is removed, obviating the need to dig a tunnel to the spring in the riverbed outside the city. This is probably the situation in the water system at Gezer, though further research is needed for verification.

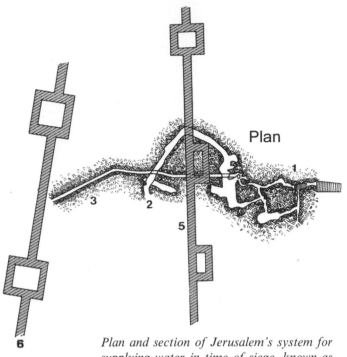

Plan

Plan and section of Jerusalem's system for supplying water in time of siege, known as Warren's Shaft. The system is located outside the wall of the Jebusite city but within the walled city of the Davidic dynasty (9th–8th centuries BCE).

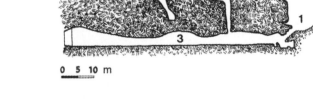

Section

0 5 10 m

(opposite, top to bottom):

(1) Plan and section of Hazor water system: rock-cut vertical shaft and diagonal tunnel. While work was in progress the workers reached the water table and so it was not necessary to dig any farther to reach the spring water flowing outside the city.

(2) Plan and section of Megiddo water system: vertical shaft and horizontal tunnel leading to spring outside the city.

(3) Plan and section of Gibeon water system: diagonal tunnel descending from the center of the city to the spring. Another tunnel beginning at the spring was never finished; it may have been intended to reach the nearby (unfinished) vertical shaft.

(4) Plan and section of second water system at Gibeon: unfinished vertical shaft near the diagonal tunnel. The vertical shaft is actually a wide cylindrical cistern with steps cut into the sides.

1. Gihon Spring

2. Shaft entrance from the city

3. Hezekiah's Tunnel

4. Vault from Second Temple period

5. Eastern city wall at time of monarchy

6. Jebusite city wall

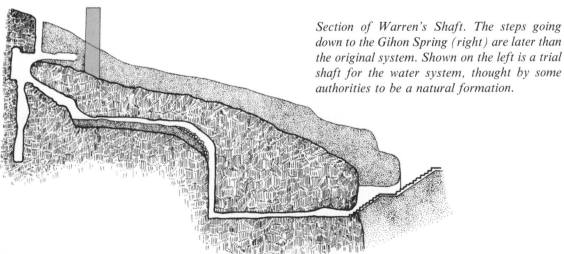

Section of Warren's Shaft. The steps going down to the Gihon Spring (right) are later than the original system. Shown on the left is a trial shaft for the water system, thought by some authorities to be a natural formation.

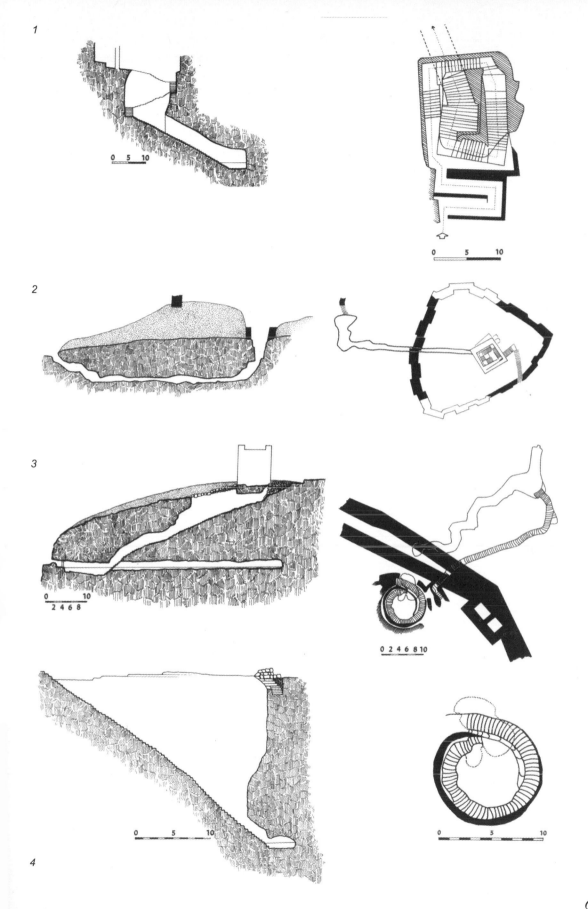

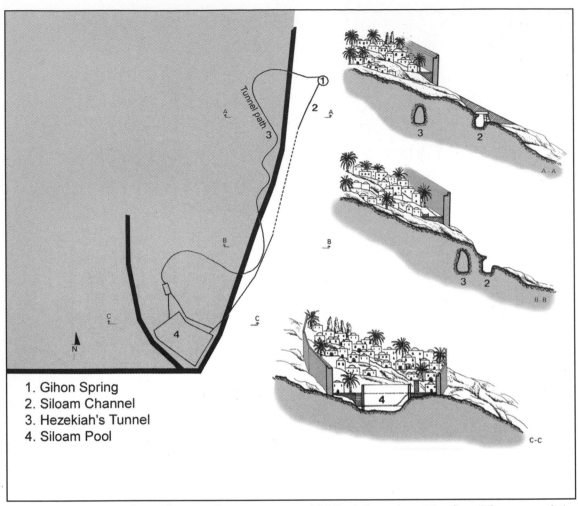

Stages in the sophisticated water system of biblical Jerusalem. The first Siloam tunnel (or channel) was partly hewn into the rock and partly built on the outer slope of the City of David. Although the built sections were covered over, enemies could expose the tunnel and cut off the flow of water. In consequence, a new tunnel was excavated through the rock for its entire length, under the hill of the city, in Hezekiah's time. Thanks to Hezekiah's tunnel, it was possible to seal off access to the Gihon Spring from the Kidron Valley and conceal it from the enemy.

In Jerusalem, the water system now known as Warren's Shaft had to solve a problem unknown elsewhere in the country: the Gihon Spring supplies hundreds of cubic meters of water per day, too much to be removed by pumping. The strong flow of water also makes it impossible to seal off the spring from the outside. The planners devised an original solution: they employed a vertical shaft—difficult to climb but easy to defend—through which it would be possible to descend to the water and return up to the city. (Incidentally, this is the factual basis for one explanation of the phrase "to reach the *zinnor*" [see above] in the story of David's conquest of Jerusalem.) It is now believed that Warren's Shaft is mostly natural and not man-made. It is nevertheless possible that, despite its natural elements, the system as a whole was planned and constructed by the Israelites, as was most certainly the case at the other water systems mentioned.

Jerusalem's water-supply system was

The text engraved on the tunnel wall, not far from its entrance into the Siloam Pool (the famous "Siloam Inscription"), expresses the exhilaration felt by the two teams of diggers, who had been working simultaneously from both directions, when they met.

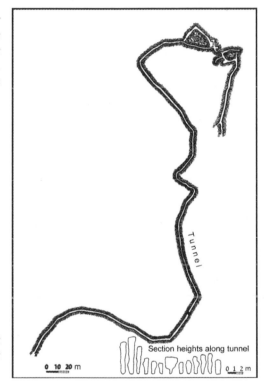

Plan and sections of Hezekiah's Tunnel at various points along its length. In its last part the tunnel is very high, reaching 5 meters.

Section heights along tunnel

0 10 20 m

0 1 2 m

later improved in various ways, specifically, by the construction of the Siloam Channel and Hezekiah's Tunnel. Once the city had been extended to the western hill (Mount Zion and today's Jewish and Armenian Quarters) and fortified by a wall, the lower stretch of the Central Valley could be utilized as a large water reservoir within the city walls—it was only necessary to channel the water there. To that end, water was directed from the Gihon Spring through a concealed channel—partly hewn in the rock and partly built and covered with stone slabs—to the pool in the lower part of the Central Valley. This channel and the pool are now known as the Siloam Channel and Siloam Pool. The original Hebrew name, *shiloah*, derives from a verb meaning "to send, transport," thus simply meaning that the channel was used to carry water from one place to another. It seems clear, incidentally, that the Siloam Tunnel was not intended solely for irrigation purposes, for if that were the case there would have been no need to conceal it. It therefore follows that it was intended for the city's needs, in fact predating Hezekiah's Tunnel. In any case, the system transferred water covertly from the Gihon to the Siloam Pool. Thus, it was now possible to seal off the Gihon and conceal it from sight, as water flowed from it continuously to the pool; when the latter filled up, the overflow was directed outside to irrigate the king's gardens, and a practical solution had thus been found to the problem of Jerusalem's water supply in time of siege.

There was one disadvantage: the enemy could discover the system, open the stone covers of the conduit and redirect the waters of the Gihon to the Kidron Valley. Moreover, they could also get into the pool through the Siloam Channel, and of course penetrate the city from there. Hezekiah's Tunnel was meant to prevent such an eventuality. The entire tunnel was hewn in the rock, with the laborers working in both directions simultaneously until they met halfway. The tunnel carried water from the spring to the pool, and once access to the spring had been sealed off, it was inaccessible from outside. The design and execution of Hezekiah's Tunnel are most impressive. Some contemporary scholars believe that the system was based on a natural tunnel or crevice, which the diggers had only to adapt or improve. However, there is no proof of this; indeed, had this been the case there would have been no need to build the Siloam Channel. Moreover, the famous inscription, with its graphic expression of the celebration and excitement when the two teams met, would have been superfluous if they had merely widened an existing tunnel. In any event, by building the tunnel, Hezekiah freed Jerusalem from dependence on wells during siege and enhanced its defensive abilities, undoubtedly an important factor in his confrontation with Sennacherib. The existence of a simpler water system, constructed before Hezekiah's time, shows that the Siloam Pool predated him. This is also proof that the fortification of the Upper City began before Hezekiah's reign. Hence the expansion of Jerusalem to the western hill and the fortification of the new section may well have taken place under Uzziah.

6. Palaces Outside the City

THE city's expansion toward the western hill—the Upper City—presumably created an embarrassing situation for the kings of Judah. Their palaces and administrative center in the Ophel, formerly towering above the homes of the citizenry, now lay between the Upper and Lower City. Clearly, the rulers would soon want to transfer the administrative center to the Upper City. This was indeed done in the Hasmonean and Herodian period. It appears, however, that some steps toward such a move were already taken during the First Temple period. In the north of today's Jewish Quarter, near the northern wall of the city in the First Temple period, part of a massive wall dating to that period, known today as the Broad Wall, was uncovered. This wall was part not of the city's fortifications, but of some independent, internal system of fortification; to my mind, it must have been part of a palace or citadel built by the kings of Judah on the crest of the western hill, near the northern city wall of that time and one of its gates. (Many centuries later, Herod's fortress was built not far from there—near his palace, in the area of today's Jaffa Gate.) The palace was perhaps enlarged by Josiah's son Shallum (Jehoahaz), arousing the prophet Jeremiah's wrathful condemna-

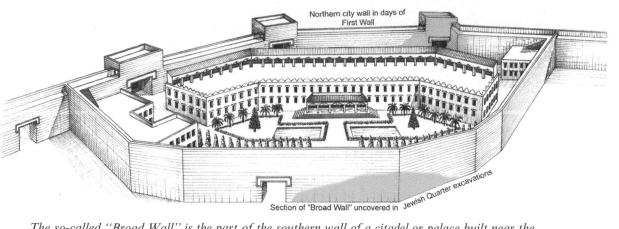

Northern city wall in days of
First Wall

Section of "Broad Wall" uncovered in Jewish Quarter excavations

The so-called "Broad Wall" is the part of the southern wall of a citadel or palace built near the northern wall of the city on the slope of the upper hill (today's Jewish Quarter). Shown here is a reconstruction, looking north.

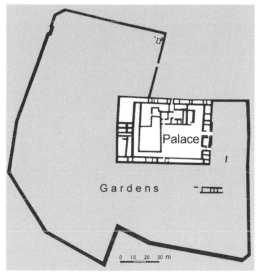

Palace

Gardens

0 10 20 30 m

Kibbutz Ramat Rahel today lies on the main road from Jerusalem to Bethlehem. Near the kibbutz were found the remains of a luxurious palace dating to the period of the kings of Judah. Plan of the fortified palace from the First Temple period at Ramat Rahel.

Window balustrade with a woman looking out of the window—a popular subject in biblical times, especially in ivory carvings.

tion of that king's oppressive rule and violation of his subjects' civil rights: "Woe to him who builds his house by unrighteousness, and his upper rooms by injustice" (Jeremiah 22:13).

The king's desire to build a large palace with adjacent gardens and abundant open space could not be fulfilled inside the crowded city of Jerusalem, for lack of space, so it was necessary to look for a site just outside the city. Such a palace was built in the Jerusalem area, on the main road from Jerusalem to Bethlehem, at the site now occupied by Kibbutz Ramat Rahel, 4 kilometers south of the city, where impressive remains and royal artifacts were uncovered. Though an exact date cannot be established, the remains can be attributed to the period between Jehoshaphat and the destruction

(left) Proto-Aeolic capital from the excavations at Ramat Rahel, one of the finest
examples of Israelite royal art. Similar capitals
have been found at the City of David, Samaria,
Megiddo and Hazor.

(below) Details of a window balustrade made
of soft limestone, from the palace at Ramat
Rahel.

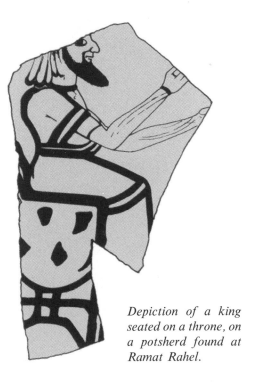

Depiction of a king
seated on a throne, on
a potsherd found at
Ramat Rahel.

(below) Reconstruction of the royal palace and
gardens at Ramat Rahel.

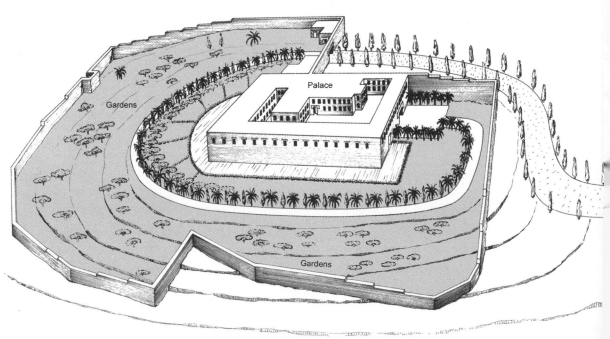

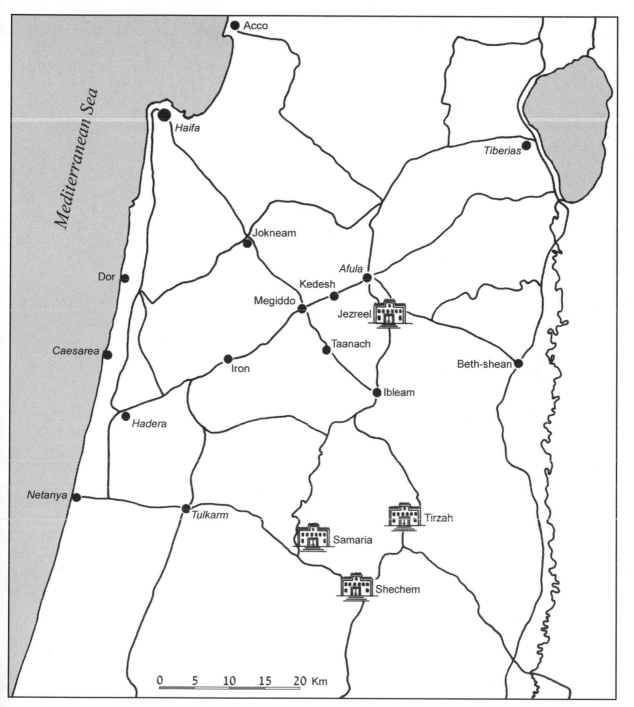

David transferred his capital from Hebron to Jerusalem, and from that time there was no other capital, even after the division of the kingdom. In the northern kingdom of Israel, however, the capital was transferred from Shechem to Tirzah and then to Samaria. There was also a winter palace at Jezreel, and there may have been an attempt to build a palace at Jericho during Ahab's reign.

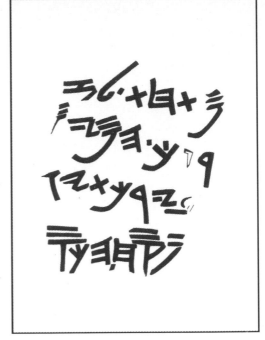

Excavations by the Temple Mount unearthed the gem (semi-precious stone) of a ring engraved with a griffin. This was a seal for use on documents of the period of the monarchy.

(right) Fragment of a monumental royal inscription in Paleo-Hebrew script, from excavations in the area of the palace on the Ophel, Jerusalem.

of the First Temple. The palace may have been built by the ruthless queen Athaliah; alternatively, it could have been built for Uzziah or any other king. Among the pottery finds in the fills of the palace floor were jars stamped with the word *lamelekh*, "(belonging) to the king," dating from Hezekiah's time. As the palace, whose floors were repaved many times, was still in use during the Persian period, precise archaeological dating of its con-struction is difficult. The palace, which was surrounded by walled gardens, was undoubtedly used by the last kings of Judah. Several hundred years later, with similar intentions, King Herod also built a palace and administrative center at Herodium, 15 kilometers from Jerusalem. And in more modern times, too, the French king Louis XIV built the palace of Versailles, 15 kilometers from crowded and noisy Paris, for similar reasons.

7. THE NECROPOLIS
TOMBS OF JERUSALEM'S KINGS AND ARISTOCRACY

As far back as the First Temple period, the Jews buried their dead outside the populated area of the city, that is, outside the city walls. First Temple period tombs discovered in Jerusalem thus help to identify the city limits and the direction of its expansion. As it turns out, the information thus obtained accords with the latest research on the city's walls. The most impressive of these burial grounds consists of a large number of monumental tombs quarried into the slopes now occupied by the village of Siloam (*Shiloah*), just outside today's Old City walls. One of these tombs has been dated, on the basis of an inscription on its façade, to some time between the eighth and seventh centuries BCE.

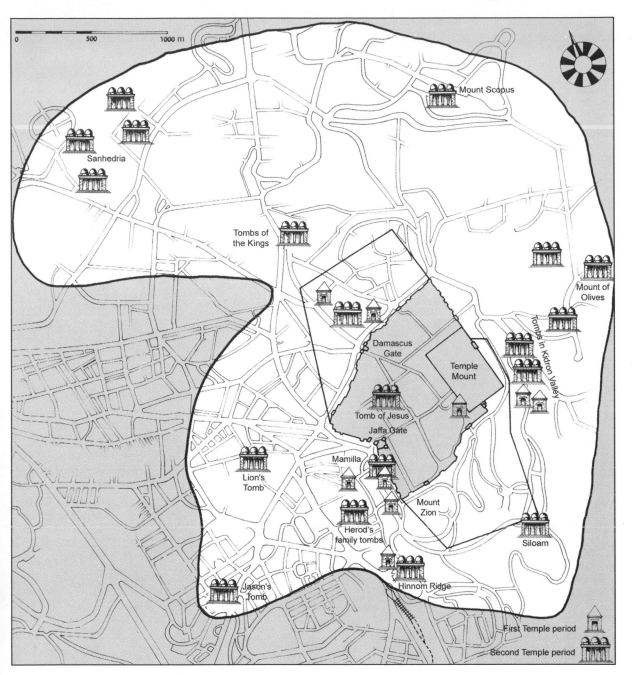

During the First Temple period, burial fields were located outside the city, on all sides. When the city expanded towards a burial field, burials there were probably discontinued, but the tombs themselves were preserved. Some of these burial grounds (but only those outside the city borders) continued to be used during the Second Temple period.

69

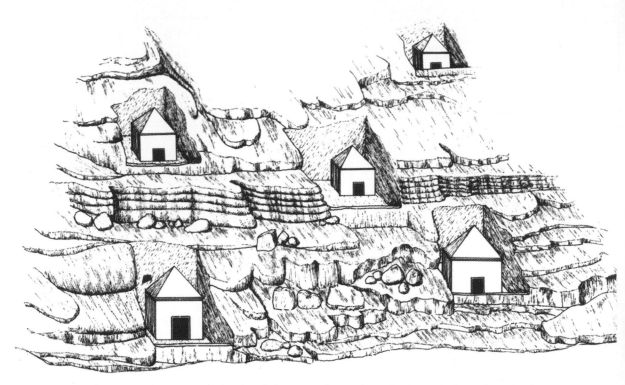

When Jerusalem consisted only of the City of David on the lower hill (10th and 9th centuries BCE), a monumental necropolis lay to the west of the administrative seat on the Ophel (today the slope near Robinson's Arch). Reconstruction of the necropolis.

Impressive remains of a First Temple period tomb were found in the necropolis of the village of Siloam. Today this is popularly known as the "Tomb of Pharaoh's Daughter." Reconstructed view of the tomb on the cliff.

In the grounds of St. Etiènne's Monastery, north of Damascus Gate, there is an impressive tomb from the First Temple period. The tomb consists of a large entrance hall surrounded by burial chambers, which contain benches for the bodies with rock-cut headrests. Once the flesh had dried, the bones were collected and kept in a repository under the bench. Sectional view of the tomb.

One of the tombs in Siloam village bore an impressive Hebrew inscription, now in the British Museum, London, identifying it as the tomb of a senior official of the royal court.

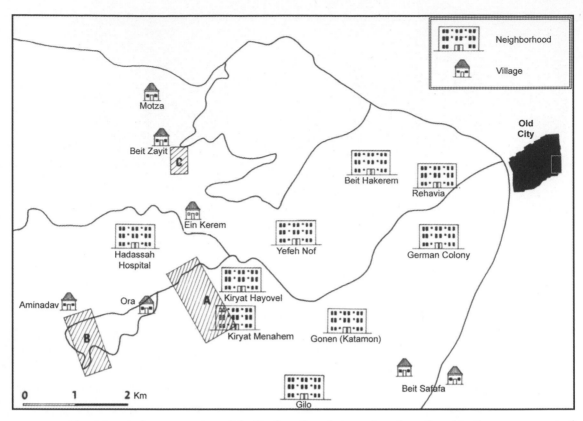

About twenty barrows or tumuli built of earth and stones have been found in three areas west of Jerusalem, close to Kiryat Menahem, Aminadav and Beit Zayit. They vary in size from 4 to 30 meters in diameter and from 1 to 2 meters in height. No similar structures have been found anywhere else in Israel. Trial excavations in some tumuli have dated them to the First Temple period. They may have had some ritual purpose, but as yet no plausible explanation has been proposed. Some scholars have associated them with the cult of "high places"; another suggestion is that they mark sites where incense was burnt to mourn a king's death. Most, but not all, of the tumuli are on hilltops.

Impressive tombs have been discovered to the west of the city as well, across the Hinnom Valley (near the present-day Scottish Church), at the foot of the Old City walls and on the western slopes of the western hill (some actually touching the Citadel at Jaffa Gate). In the north of the city, too, in the vicinity of Damascus Gate and to the north, magnificent tombs of the First Temple period have been found, dating from the ninth to eighth centuries BCE.

According to the Bible, there was a burial field within the city itself, where the kings of the House of David, including David himself, were interred. There were several royal cemeteries; when one was full, another site was used. One such cemetery has been unearthed near the southwest corner of the Temple Mount, opposite Robinson's Arch. So far the remains of seven spacious single tombs have been uncovered, none of them containing bones or offerings because the tombs were robbed as early as the Second Temple period. Near one tomb, though not inside, a heap of pottery votive vessels was found. Based on their form, these tombs were planned and excavated in the style of Phoenician tombs which have been discovered near Achziv, still containing bones and offer-

First Temple period cave tomb discovered on the western slope of the hill of the Upper City. The tomb contained, besides the bones of the deceased, pottery vessels for offerings, one of which bore the owner's name. The tomb is at the edge of the large necropolis extending toward the Citadel and the adjacent area.

ings, and dated to the ninth to seventh centuries BCE; the considerable resemblance between them and the Jerusalem tombs indicates that the latter should be dated to the same period. Perhaps this burial field was used by the kings of Judah before the city spread to the western hill; its tombs were left intact and abandoned only during the Second Temple period. A similar cemetery, also in use up to the Second Temple period, has been found in the area of Jaffa Gate and the Citadel; this may also be one of the burial grounds of the kings of Judah. It is surely no accident that this area has long been known as the Tower of David;

near the Citadel and the Tower of David there are tombs from the First Temple period, not inconceivably belonging to kings of the House of David. There is in fact a report by the historian Josephus Flavius that John Hyrcanus and Herod, who built a fortress at this site, opened the tombs of the House of David.

Other structures in west Jerusalem connected with death rituals are barrows or tumuli. Gabriel Barkay, pointing out that the number of tumuli on hilltops to the west of the city is identical to the number of kings of Judah, has associated them with certain religious rites mentioned in the Bible; these ceremonies

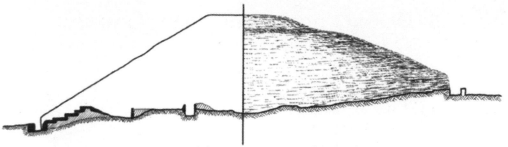

Section of the structure in tumulus no. 6.

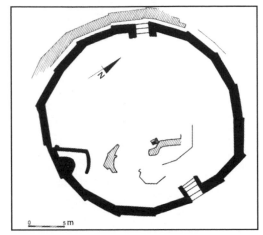

Plan of tumulus no. 6.

involved the burning of incense and apparently also the construction of a monument in the form of a large mound or tumulus. Excavations of some of these tumuli date them to the period of the kings of Judah. The tumuli, found in this form only in the hill country to the west of Jerusalem, have yet to be explained in a satisfactory manner.

Map of tumuli in the Kiryat Menahem area, west Jerusalem.

8. Destruction of the First Temple

Babylonian Rule, Nebuchadnezzar and Jerusalem 586 BCE

THE death of King Josiah at the battle of Megiddo marked the beginning of the decline of Judah and its capital Jerusalem. Josiah's heirs were inept rulers, who contributed to the decline, which culminated in the conquest of Judah by King Nebuchadnezzar of Babylon. Not content with merely occupying Jerusalem, Nebuchadnezzar destroyed the Temple, burned down much Jerusalem, demolished its fortifications and deported its people to foreign parts.

Once the situation had calmed down, the Babylonians granted the remaining people of Judah a certain degree of autonomy, under the administration of Jewish officials. The capital of the state, however, and the administrative center moved to Mizpeh, a small town to the

Portrait of Sennacherib, King of Assyria, who conquered Lachish after a difficult war and siege, but failed in his attempt to conquer heavily fortified Jerusalem.

Aramaic inscription found in Jerusalem (the exact location is unknown) stating that the bones of King Uzziah were removed from their resting place in the Second Temple period and transferred to another burial site. It is not known whether this was done because of construction in the area of the Citadel carried out by John Hyrcanus I or in Herod's time. (Both of them are reported to have tampered with the tombs of the House of David.) In either case, it appears that the burial ground in the "Garden of Uzzah" had to be moved.

75

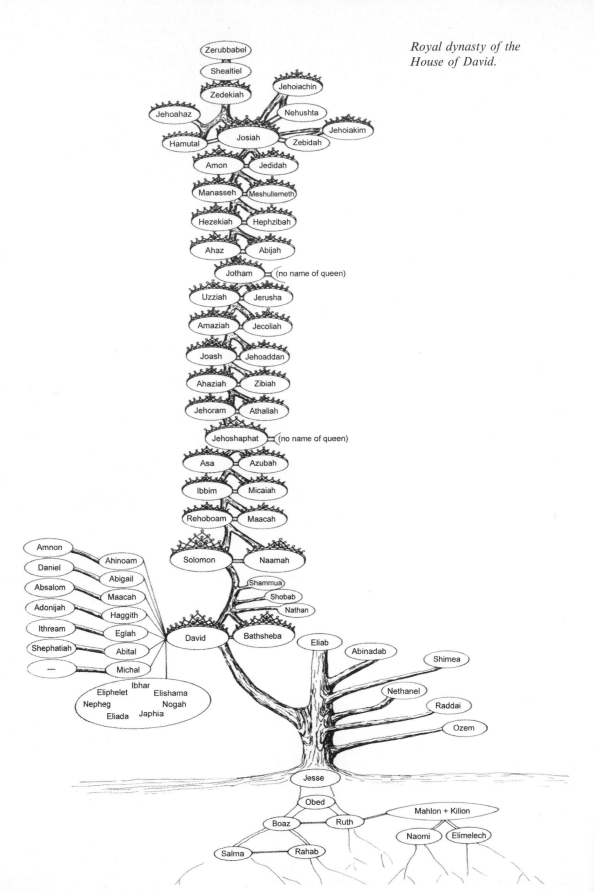

Royal dynasty of the House of David.

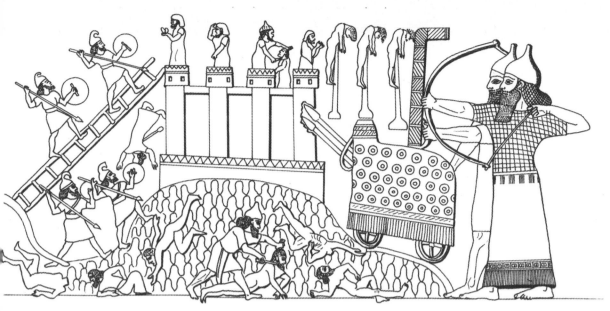

Depiction of an Assyrian siege, based on an Assyrian relief.

Seal impression: "(Belonging) to Jehoahaz, son of the king."

The excavations on the Ophel uncovered a large storehouse, destroyed when Jerusalem was conquered by the Babylonians (586 BCE). One of the rooms contained dozens of pottery vessels, including jars.

north of Jerusalem, near the former border between Judah and the northern kingdom. The people of Judah continued to dream of restoring their independence, and especially rebuilding Jerusalem and the Temple. However, further attempts to rebel against the Babylonians were quickly subdued and more Judahites were deported. Jerusalem and the Temple remained in ruins. The leaders and elite of Judah, exiled to Babylon, lamented their bitter fate: "By the waters of Babylon, there we sat down and wept, when we remembered Zion....If I forget you, O Jerusalem, let my right hand wither! Let my tongue cleave to the roof of my mouth, if I do not remember you" (Psalms 137:1–6). These verses accompanied the people of Israel throughout their exile: the memory of Jerusalem and its Temple would remain in the heart of every Jew, awaiting the Redemption.

9. JERUSALEM—CITY OF PROPHETS

"JERUSALEM and Athens," "Jerusalem and Rome"—such phrases attest to the contribution of these cities to western civilization. Athens and Rome made a major contribution to humanity in the spheres of architecture and construction, as well as intellectual life, philosophy and the sciences. Jerusalem's contribution belongs above all to the spiritual realm. This was due in no little measure to the prophets of Israel, some of whom came from Jerusalem, others from surrounding towns, but all were divinely inspired and acted in the shadow of the Temple. The

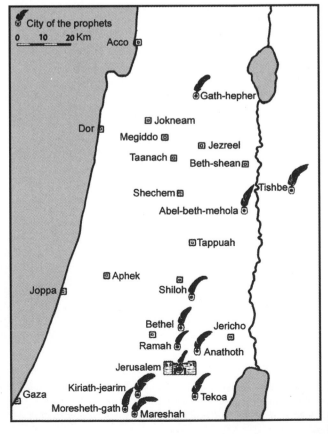

Cities of the prophets. Some of the prophets are explicitly reported to be natives of Jerusalem. Others were born in nearby towns and villages, and a few still farther away. According to traditions dating from the period of the Mishnah and the Talmud, every prophet whose place of birth is not specified in the Bible was born in Jerusalem. Their prophecies were inspired by the Holy City and its Temple.

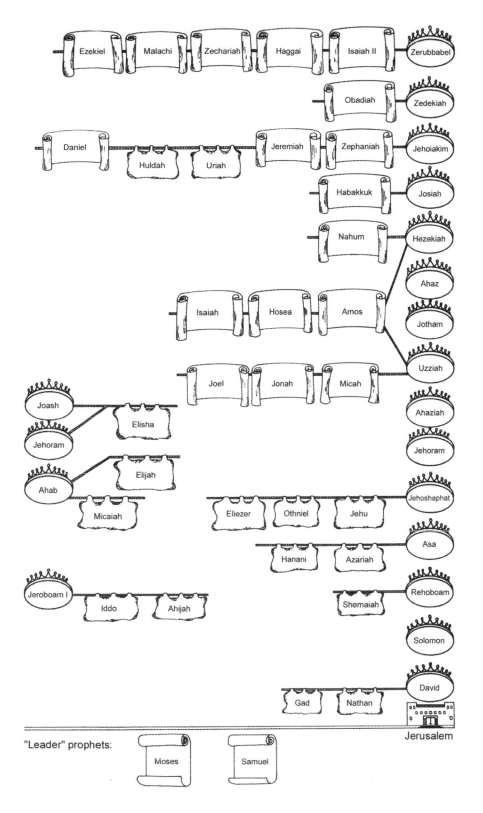

Ezekiel · Malachi · Zechariah · Haggai · Isaiah II · Zerubbabel

Obadiah · Zedekiah

Daniel · Huldah · Uriah · Jeremiah · Zephaniah · Jehoiakim

Habakkuk · Josiah

Nahum · Hezekiah

Ahaz

Isaiah · Hosea · Amos · Jotham

Uzziah

Joel · Jonah · Micah · Ahaziah

Joash · Jehoram

Elisha

Jehoram

Ahab · Elijah · Jehoshaphat

Micaiah · Eliezer · Othniel · Jehu

Asa

Hanani · Azariah

Jeroboam I · Iddo · Ahijah · Rehoboam

Shemaiah

Solomon

David

Gad · Nathan

Jerusalem

"Leader" prophets: Moses · Samuel

The prophecies of some of the prophets have been preserved in books of the Bible named for them (these are known as the classical, or literary, prophets); while other prophets are known today only from accounts given by other people. The prophets of both categories were spiritual giants who laid the moral foundations of western civilization.

79

prophets were outstanding thinkers who fearlessly reprimanded kings and their representatives. Aware of the kings' needless political entanglements and realizing that social injustice would destroy the nation, these spiritual giants publicly proclaimed their message, with no thought for the possible consequences to themselves. Even the Holy City and the Temple itself were not spared: "Therefore because of you Zion shall be plowed as a field," warned Micah (3:12). Daily, they warned that the city would be destroyed if the people failed to correct their ways or the kings their injustices. At the same time, the prophets tempered their rebukes and predictions of doom with messages of consolation and future redemption.

The prophecies heard in Jerusalem and recorded in the Bible are now the abiding heritage of all civilization. More than its buildings and riches, these prophets of doom and consolation have engraved Jerusalem in the hearts of western civilization.

Artist's impression of the prophet Jeremiah, standing on the Mount of Olives and prophesying the destruction of Jerusalem.

Chapter 4:

JERUSALEM IN THE SECOND TEMPLE PERIOD
UNDER PERSIA, GREECE AND ROME: FROM ZERUBBABEL TO JOHANAN BEN ZAKKAI, OR FROM CYRUS TO TITUS
538 BCE–70 CE

1. ZERUBBABEL BEN SHEALTIEL AND JOSHUA BEN JEHOZADAK

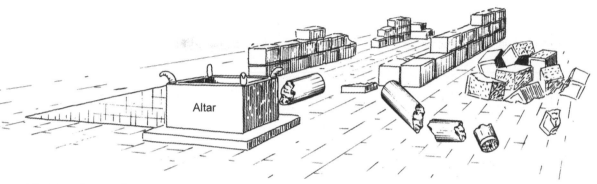

The Temple is still in ruins, but the altar has been restored and sacrifices are being offered.

SINCE the empires of the Ancient East began to wage wars of conquest, they faced the problem of how to maintain rule over conquered areas for a long period. In the early stages of history this goal was achieved through the exercise of violence, terror and fear, with little or no concern for human life. With passing time, the limited efficacy of such means became obvious. As the ancient civilized world came to resort less and less to violence and murder against both groups and individuals, such methods were no longer suitable. Moreover, violence, liquidation or depletion of entire populations was disadvantageous to the conquerors: as occupied lands lost their inhabitants, fertile agricultural land gave way to wasteland and desert.

The kings of Assyria and Babylon

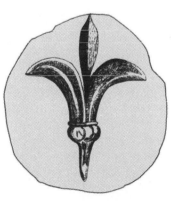

Coin of the province of Yehud (Judah), from the Persian period.

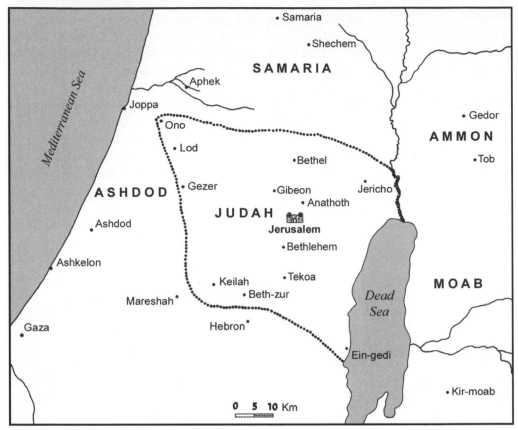

Borders of the province of Yehud (Judah), with its capital, Jerusalem. The province had no direct access to the sea.

treated the territories they conquered differently: their method was exile and deportation. The elites, such as priests, administrators, teachers and the most skilled farmers, were deported from their homes to foreign lands. People of similar status were brought from other conquered lands in their place; thus, the local ethnic leadership was replaced by a different, foreign ethnic element of similar standing. The goal was to separate the ordinary people from its leadership, through a system of "divide and rule." On a long-term basis, however, this method also proved inefficient: in time, local people and deportees banded together to oppose the conquering power.

When the Persians extended their conquests, they developed a new method of rule in their new possessions, and none better has yet been proposed until the present day. King Cyrus II, known in Jewish sources simply as Cyrus the Great, believed that administration of the territory and most of the authority involved should be entrusted to the defeated people. The local inhabitants were made responsible for their own day-to-day administration and permitted, in particular, to preserve their culture and religious beliefs; the only privileges denied to them were operation of an army and the conduct of foreign policy. Security (army) and foreign policies came under the sole authority of the conquering nation (in this instance, Persia), and were administered by satraps—officials representing the ruler—who were also responsible for tax collection for the royal treasury. The conquerors divided their territories into several small units, all more or less equally powerful. With

82

this method of "divide and rule," a large occupying army was unnecessary and the heavy financial burden of administering conquered territory was avoided, while the centrality of the supreme government was ensured. The description of the Persian Empire in the Book of Esther, as comprising one hundred and twenty-seven provinces, aptly expresses this doctrine.

After defeating the Babylonian Empire, Cyrus II headed a mighty empire, known in the Bible as the kingdom of Persia and Media. On accession to power he immediately applied these principles in the conquered territories; he called on the Judahite exiles in Babylon to return to their country and reestablish their capital, Jerusalem, and its cultural-religious center, the Temple. Thus, the movement of "the Return to Zion," known to historians as the Restoration, began to take shape. Sheshbazzar, a descendant of one of the exiles, was appointed to head the project. In 538 BCE, entrusted with the treasures that Nebuchadnezzar had pillaged from the Temple in Jerusalem, he led a large group to Judah. After no more than fifty years of exile, Jerusalem was returned once more to its owners. However, as Sheshbazzar was an old man, the leadership of the returnees passed to two younger men: Zerubbabel son of Shealtiel, grandson of the exiled King Jehoiachin, and a priest named Joshua son of Jehozadak, grandson of the last High Priest who had served in the Temple in Jerusalem. With the return to Jerusalem of the first exiles (518 BCE), work commenced on setting up the altar and planning the rebuilding of the Temple, as foretold by the prophets. However, the returnees' main aim—to rebuild the Temple and the city walls—was not achieved. The leaders of the neighboring autonomous territories, Tobiah the Ammonite, Sanballat the Horonite (Samaritan) and Geshem the Arab, alarmed lest the province of Judah become too strong, protested to the Persian king in an attempt to have the work halted. The reaction of the Persian

Tomb of Cyrus the Great, King of Persia, in Pasargadae.

authorities was even harsher, and Zerubbabel was sent back to Babylon. From that time on, the Persians took care not to appoint any descendant of the House of David as governor of Judah, and they now transferred the main authority in the administration of the autonomy to the High Priest. Consequently, the returnees were demoralized: the ruined, unprotected city of Jerusalem was only slightly rebuilt; the walls, which they had just began to construct, were destroyed by hostile neighbors and the city gates were burned. Depression and frustration reigned, causing a decline in the social and cultural spheres; education in Jerusalem and Judah dropped to its lowest level. Jerusalem was to recover only with the arrival of Ezra and Nehemiah.

2. EZRA AND NEHEMIAH

FOLLOWING its devastation, Jerusalem now entered an era of rejuvenation under the leadership of Ezra and Nehemiah. Ezra, a scribe and spiritual leader, came to Jerusalem first, followed some years later by Nehemiah, an outstanding administrator. Before going to the Holy Land Nehemiah had been cupbearer to the Persian king Artaxerxes—a senior official at the royal court and trusted servant of the king, responsible for running the royal household and personally supervising the king's meals. Deeply distressed by the disheartening news from Jerusalem, he appealed to the king to appoint him governor of the province of Yehud, as Judah was now called, as representative of the central power.

His request granted, Nehemiah arrived in Jerusalem in the year 445 BCE. His stay, planned to last only a short time, extended to twelve years. He went back to Persia for only a short time, and then returned to Jerusalem to continue the labor of restoration. He undertook the administration and organization of the work, for which he was well suited, while Ezra, a man of learning and culture, took up the burden of education and building a new society. They worked as a team, each the perfect complement of the other.

The two leaders set out to rebuild and restore the Temple. When they had

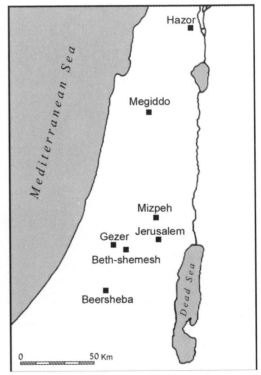

Biblical cities where archaeological excavations have uncovered fortifications and gates. One finding from these excavations is that cities of the size of Jerusalem and even slightly larger usually had only one gate, sometimes two—but never more (see opposite, above).

succeeded in this, Nehemiah turned to building the city walls and gates. Mobilizing the people of Judah *en masse*, he divided them into teams, some doing

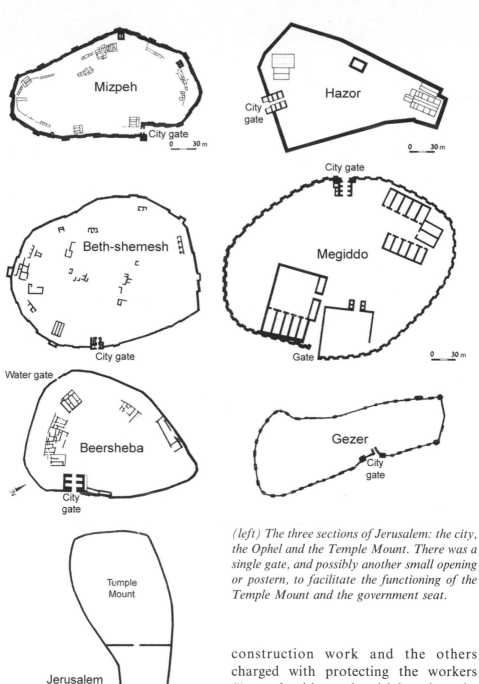

Mizpeh

Hazor

City gate

0 30 m

0 30 m

Beth-shemesh

City gate

City gate

Megiddo

0 30 m

Gate

Water gate

Beersheba

City gate

Gezer

City gate

Temple Mount

Jerusalem

Ophel

City gate

The City

(left) The three sections of Jerusalem: the city, the Ophel and the Temple Mount. There was a single gate, and possibly another small opening or postern, to facilitate the functioning of the Temple Mount and the government seat.

construction work and the others charged with protecting the workers ("...each with one hand labored on the work and with the other held his weapon"; Nehemiah 4:17). The work took fifty-two days, indicating that it consisted mostly of restoration, as entire sections of the walls of the First Temple period still stood to a considerable height, and only gaps had to be repaired, as did the tops of the walls. According to the Book of Nehemiah, the area surrounded by the walls was quite large, while the popula-

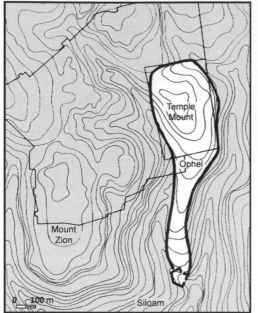

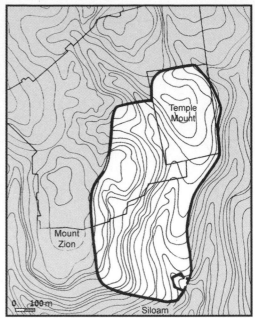

1. Avi-Yonah and Tsafrir: small city of small area, limited to the City of David.

2. Grafman: medium-sized city, occupying the City of David and half of the Upper City.

(above) Three proposals for the course of Nehemiah's wall.

(below) Three proposals for the location of the gates in Nehemiah's wall.

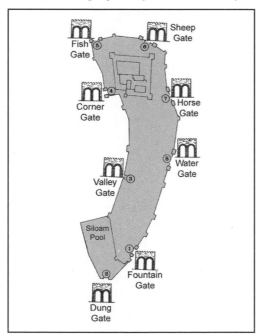

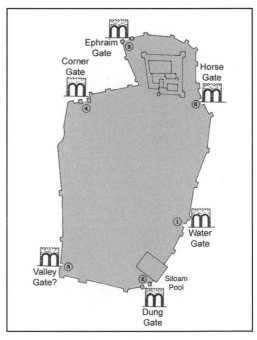

1. Large number of gates in a small city (eight gates—Avi-Yonah and Tsafrir). Improbable.

2. Six gates in a medium-sized city (Grafman). Plausible.

86

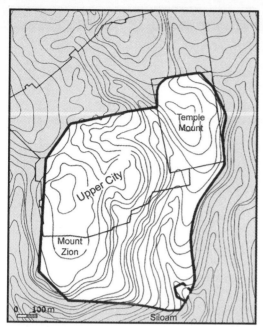

3. Ben-Dov: large city, similar to the biblical city destroyed by the Babylonians.

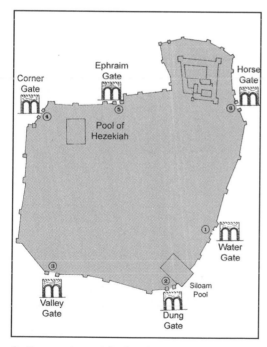

3. Large city, with the six gates necessary to function efficiently. In several periods in Jerusalem's history, when the city was the same size as under Nehemiah, there were 4 to 6 gates in the wall. (Ben-Dov)

tion was small—"The city was wide and large, but the people within it were few" (Nehemiah 7:4). The biblical description fits a city of approximately the dimensions of Jerusalem toward the end of the First Temple period, indicating that Nehemiah's main achievement to rebuild the walls had been destroyed by Nebuchadnezzar in 586 BCE.

Until the Six-Day War in 1967 scholars believed that Nehemiah's Jerusalem occupied the same area as the city of the First Temple period, that is, only the lower hill. Now that, as noted previously, archaeological research has shown that toward the end of the First Temple period the city already extended to the upper hill, this must also have been true for the large city restored by Nehemiah. The fact that the reconstructed wall had six gates supports this assertion, since a settlement the size of the City of David—as some scholars believe it was at the time of Nehemiah—would only have needed one gate. Too many gates would have weakened defense against an enemy attack. Other cities of the same size, and even larger, had only one gate, such as Megiddo, Tyre, Gezer, Ashdod, Dan, Mizpeh, Beersheba, Beth-shemesh and others. As in other biblical cities, when Jerusalem was confined to the lower hill, it had only one gate—the "Valley Gate" in the west. With the expansion of the city to include the Ophel and the Temple Mount, one or two additional gates may have been built, although this too would have been exceptional. In any case, it is not plausible that a small city would have six gates. In the Middle Ages, the walls built around Jerusalem by the Ottoman sultan Suleiman contained only six gates, two of which were actually small posterns—and Jerusalem was then of approximately the same size as in biblical times and in the days of Ezra and Nehemiah.

One of Nehemiah's projects in Jerusalem was the construction of the fortress

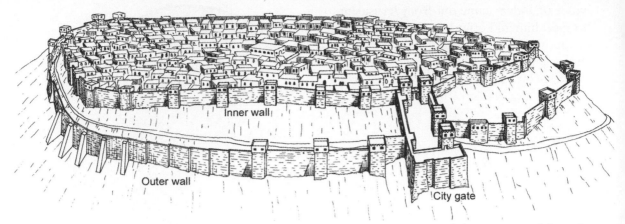

Lachish toward the end of the First Temple period. Reconstruction of the city, viewed from the south. Lachish, which was similar in size to biblical Jerusalem, had only one gate.

on a hill northwest of the Temple Mount, outside the sacred compound and outside the city. The fortress was built in order to increase security and to confront invasion from the topographically vulnerable north, as in the biblical description, "Out of the north evil shall break forth" (Jeremiah 1:14). This fortress was known in Hebrew as the *birah*. There may have been a fortress at the same site in the First Temple period, as indicated by the biblical term *sar ha-birah*, "the governor of the castle" (Nehemiah 7:2). The construction of the eastern gate, in the eastern wall of the Temple Mount, should also be dated to Nehemiah's time, or in any event to the Persian period; this gate was known as the "Priest's Gate" or the "Shushan Gate." The Mishnah explains the latter name by the fact that the palace (or castle) of Shushan (the Persian capital) was depicted on it—perhaps a token of gratitude and submission to Persian rule. Similarly, in a later period, Herod affixed a gold eagle (the emblem of Rome) to the gates of the Temple.

3. JERUSALEM UNDER GREEK RULE

THE PTOLEMIES AND THE SELEUCIDS

THE year 333 BCE saw major changes in the Middle East. The superpower ruling an immense Mediterranean empire was now Greece, whose center lay in the northeastern Mediterranean. The curtain had fallen on the hegemony of the eastern or southern states, Egypt, Assyria, Babylon and Persia. The greatest military commander of the ancient world, Alexander the Great, now stood at the head of the ruling power after his defeat of Darius, king of Persia. Fascinated by eastern civilization, its lifestyles and systems of government, Alexander instituted no significant administrative changes: the autonomous Persian provinces that had surrendered to him continued to be ruled in the same manner as before.

On his way to conquer Egypt, Alexander passed through the coastal region in the west of Judah, or, as we shall now call it, Judea. The High Priest, who wielded supreme authority in the province of Judea, came out from Jerusalem to meet him and offer him the submission of Jerusalem and Judea, thus bringing Judea under the sway of Greece without battle. The High Priest—Jewish sources identify him as Simeon the Just—presumably understood that this was not the time to rebel or to seek political independence; his proposal to the invading king was a necessary evil. Alexander, impressed by the demeanor and personality of the High Priest, welcomed the surrender and promised the Jews all the freedoms that they had enjoyed under Persian rule, even adding some privileges for the Jerusalem Temple, such as tax concessions and gifts to its treasury.

Macedonian rule of Judea did not last long: Alexander died young, and a bitter war of succession erupted among the Diadochi—his military commanders, who divided the immense young empire into a number of independent kingdoms. Syria and the Holy Land were divided between two kingdoms. The largest of the Hellenistic kingdoms, headed by Seleucus, included Iraq and Syria; the other,

Portrait of Antiochus IV Epiphanes.

ruled by Ptolemy, included Egypt and the Holy Land—the latter important to all the new kingdoms as a buffer zone between them. In the third century BCE the provinces of the Holy Land, including Judea and its capital Jerusalem, were ruled by kings of the Egyptian Ptolemaic

After the death of Alexander the Great, his empire was divided up among his generals. The Middle East was split between two kingdoms, one ruled by Ptolemy and the other by Seleucus. Palestine and Jerusalem were part of the Ptolemaic kingdom for a hundred years, but were then conquered by the Seleucid king Antiochus III.

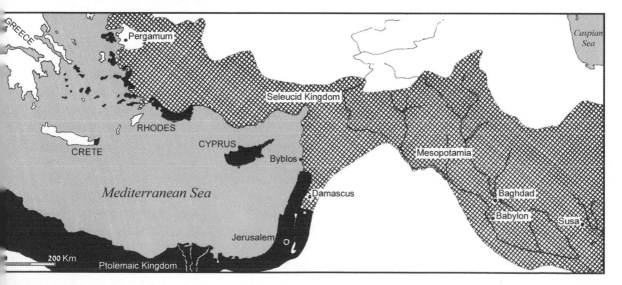

Greek inscription engraved on a stone, found in excavations at the foot of the Temple Mount, in a large building from the Second Temple period. It reports a monetary contribution toward the renovation of the paving, probably of the building, which was used as a community center.

dynasty. The Ptolemies adopted a very liberal attitude toward the province of Judea, its citizens and religion. Although the Jewish religion was incomprehensible to them, they continued to aid the religious center in Jerusalem.

The good relations with the ruling power and its sympathetic attitude held a hidden danger for Judaism and the Jews: the influence of Hellenistic culture. Hellenization became a threat to the continued existence of the Jewish culture and religion. In 198 BCE Antiochus III, one of the greatest Seleucid kings, conquered Judea and Jerusalem from the Ptolemies. Antiochus treated the Jews well: in order to earn their support he granted them many additional privileges and tax concessions, even contributing toward the purchase of cattle for sacrifice in the Temple. Under Antiochus III's rule Hellenization intensified, helped along by the liberal attitude of the rulers. His successors, Seleucus IV and Antiochus IV Epiphanes, behaved similarly; however, Antiochus Epiphanes later changed his attitude, and Jewish sources nicknamed him "Antiochus the Wicked."

Any confrontation between different cultures, particularly between conqueror and conquered, influences both sides. Absorption of values from a different culture is usually a very fruitful and beneficial process, but when those on the receiving end adopt mainly the external trappings of the other culture, with no consideration for its underlying values, they lose their identity and become assimilated. This was essentially the kind of Hellenization that took place in Judea. Most of the population, who willingly accepted the yoke of Greek culture, in fact only took on its outer forms, learning nothing of its basic values. Were it not for the political events that overtook the area—the rise of Rome and the resulting power struggle—Hellenization, which had now infiltrated the elite of Jerusalem society, might have caused the Jewish nation to assimilate completely, gradually disappearing from the stage of history.

4. Jerusalem Under the Hasmoneans

From Mattathias to Mattathias

In the third century BCE, three powers dominated the east: the Ptolemies in Egypt, the Seleucids in Syria, Iraq and Anatolia, and the Parthians in the region of the Upper Euphrates and Tigris rivers and in northern Persia. In the west, a mighty battle for hegemony in western Europe and North Africa was being fought by two powers: Rome and the Punic kingdom of Carthage.

The balance of power shifted at the end of the third century BCE and the beginning of the second century. In the east, the Seleucids prevailed over their opponents, while Rome increased its power in the west. Clearly, after defeating Carthage, Rome would direct its efforts to the east. Indeed, enticed by the attractions and rich treasures of the Middle East, Rome began expanding eastward toward Greece and Anatolia. Antiochus IV Epiphanes, fearing Rome's spread toward his territories, decided to forestall the danger. Despite his relative power in the east, Antiochus believed that resistance to his Hellenizing policies among any of the peoples under his rule might undermine the stability of his regime; he therefore embarked on a course of enforced Hellenization, resolved to impose cultural and national unity and thus to create a consolidated front against Rome.

On the advice of his Hellenized Jewish allies, Antiochus decided to deal severely with pockets of Jewish opposition to Hellenization. Since so many had willingly accepted Greek culture, he did not

Floor of a large storage pool for rainwater, discovered south of the Temple Mount. It probably served the Acra fortress.

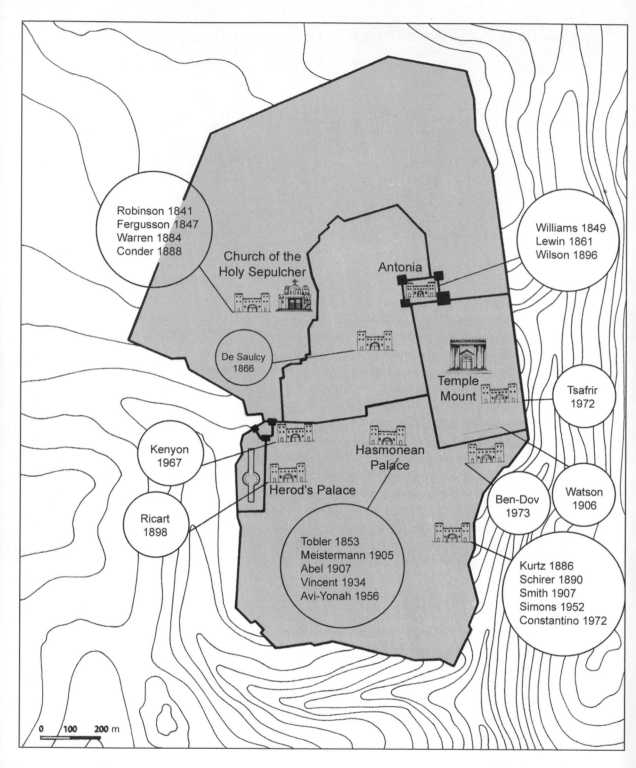

Different scholars' proposals for the location of the Acra and the Antiochia quarter.

Remains of the basement of a large building in the style of a barracks, uncovered near the southern wall of the Temple Mount; probably part of the foundations of the Acra fortress.

(right) The Acra, a fortified fortress built by Antiochus IV south of the Temple Mount.

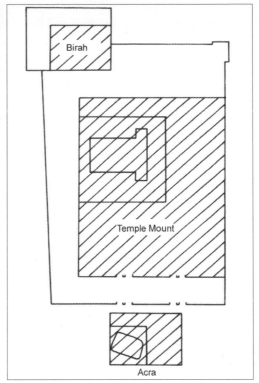

believe that a small minority could successfully withstand the pressure. This is the background to the measures known in Jewish history as the "edicts of the wicked Antiochus." The king's efforts to impose Hellenization met with determined opposition on the part of small groups of Jews. In the struggle to impose Greek culture and the cult of his personality, Antiochus desecrated the Temple in Jerusalem and converted it into a pagan shrine. After eight hundred years, Jerusalem, with the Temple—the religious-cultural symbol of the Jewish people since the days of David and Solomon—now faced the danger of losing its special position, anchored in the tenets of the Jewish faith. The edicts were intensified in 167 BCE, two years after the king had plundered the Temple treasures.

The edicts in fact strengthened the Jewish opposition to Hellenization, and the minority that still clung to a pure Jewish faith challenged the king and his edicts. While most of these elements lived outside Jerusalem, there were also groups in the city who preached active opposition and attacked Hellenized Jews as collaborators. In order to protect the latter, Antiochus built a fortified quarter on public land south of the Temple Mount, in the Ophel and in the upper part of the City of David (in the area of government center of biblical times). This quarter was named "Antiochia of Jerusalem" in honor of the king. Besides residential housing it contained a fortress, known as the "Acra," which overlooked the Temple Mount, making it possible to supervise those entering the Temple enclosure. In addition, a large pool was dug in Antiochia as a rainwater reservoir for times of emergency. Subsequently, during the rule of Simeon the Hasmonean—in the year 141 BCE—this quarter and its fortress were completely destroyed. Through a hundred years of Jerusalem research, scholars tried to determine the location of the Acra. Only in 1970 did Meir Ben-Dov identify its

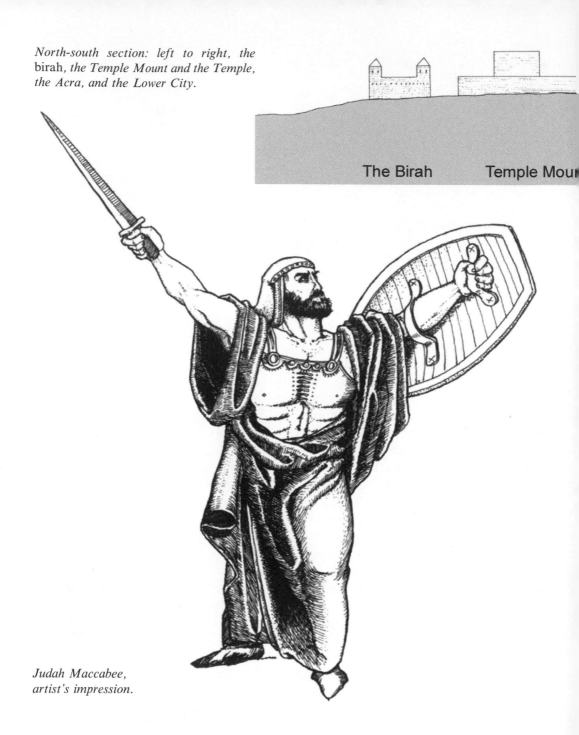

The Birah   Temple Mou[nt]

Judah Maccabee,
artist's impression.

remains in the archaeological excavations at the foot of the Temple Mount. This discovery verified the sparse information about the fortress in written sources. In addition to building the Acra fortress south of the Temple Mount, Antiochus strengthened the capital's fortifications to the north of the Temple, around the same time as he began to enforce his edicts.

These activities helped to strengthen the rule of the Greeks and the Hellenizers in Jerusalem.

The fall of Antiochus, his army and ideas was brought about by a priest named Mattathias, of a family known as the Hasmoneans, from the small village of Modi'in in the Lod plain, and his sons. In 164 BCE, his son Judah,

Acra	City of David

known as Maccabee, conquered all of Jerusalem, except for the Antiochia quarter and the Acra; he then purified the defiled Temple. These events have since been celebrated throughout the generations by the festival of Hanukkah. Three years later, in 161 BCE, the Greek commander Bacchides recaptured Jerusalem. The Jews retook the city from the Greeks only in 152 BCE—this time under the leadership of Jonathan, Mattathias' youngest son. After Jonathan was murdered in captivity, command passed to Simeon, the last survivor of Mattathias' five sons. Simeon, like his brother Jonathan a gifted statesman and soldier, seized the opportunity to declare the independence of the state of Judea, with Jerusalem as its capital. Alongside its main role as a holy city, the cultural-religious capital of the Jewish nation, the city once more became the political capital of the state of Judea, with the same borders as the Persian province of Yehud.

Simeon the Hasmonean had himself appointed as both High Priest and secular ruler, bearing the title of ethnarch (or *nasi* in Jewish tradition). His heirs, the kings of the Hasmonean dynasty, continued in his footsteps, expanding the borders of the new state and rebuilding their capital, Jerusalem. Among the most prominent of these royal builders were John Hyrcanus I, his son Alexander Yannai and the latter's widow Queen Salome. Toward the end of the second century BCE, John Hyrcanus I began to build a new fortress in the west of the

Pottery wine jar, with seal impressions on the handles indicating its provenance and its date: Rhodes, 2nd century BCE. Discovered among the remains of the Acra south of the Temple Mount. Hundreds of handles of Rhodian wine jars were discovered farther to the south, in the City of David but still within the Antiochia quarter.

95

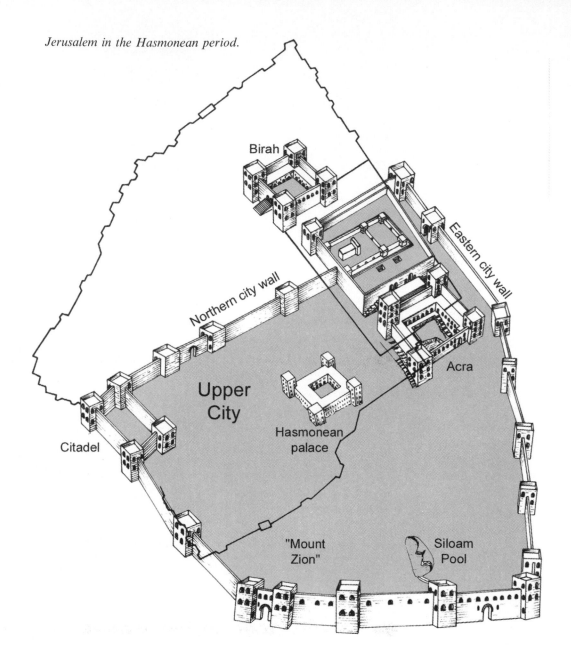

Jerusalem in the Hasmonean period.

city, and in the last decade of the first century BCE, a Hasmonean royal palace of the Hasmoneans was built on the crest of the western hill, in the Upper City. During the same period, a palace was also built outside the city. Like the kings of Judah, who had built themselves a palace at Ramat Rahel, the Hasmoneans sought to build themselves a country palace, far from the noise and bustle of the city. They chose Jericho, both because of its mild winter climate and because of its special agricultural produce, the perfumes and dates, which were the backbone of the new state's economy. The cultivation of perfume and medicinal plants, spices and dates in the Jordan Valley required the kings' close supervision.

While the damaged walls of Jerusalem had been repaired, agreements between the Hasmoneans and the Seleucid rulers sometimes made it necessary to demolish and later rebuild them. Excavations by

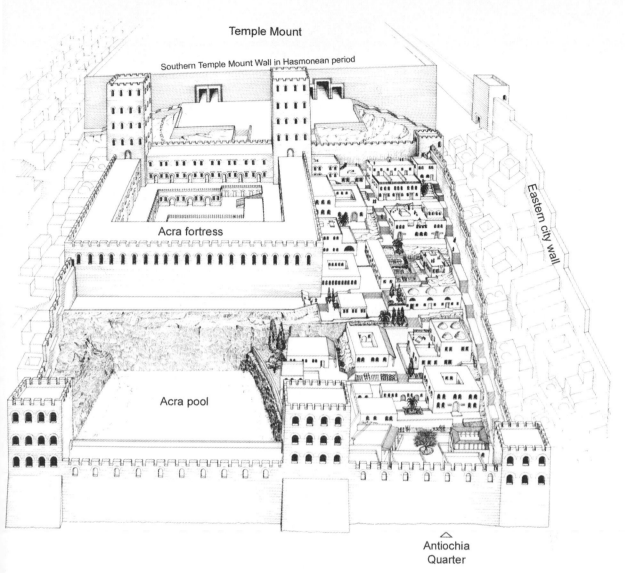

Temple Mount

Southern Temple Mount Wall in Hasmonean period

Acra fortress

Acra pool

Eastern city wall

⌂
Antiochia
Quarter

Reconstruction of the Antiochia quarter of Jerusalem, view from the south. The fortress was built there to supervise the entrances to the Temple Mount; the entire Temple enclosure was visible from the top of its towers. The quarter had its own water supply, based on the collection of rainwater in a large pool.

Magen Broshi have uncovered remains of walls from the Second Temple period, especially in the western part of the upper hill, but they cannot be dated with any precision to one of the Hasmonean kings or to Herod; though various historical conjectures are possible, archaeological considerations are insufficient to associate the construction of the walls with the activities of any specific king.

Mattathias the Hasmonean and his sons were buried in Modi'in, the village of their birth. Seeing themselves as leaders of a popular movement devoted to safeguarding the religion and culture of their ancestors, they eschewed the regal pomp and corruption typical of kings who rule for long periods. The second generation of Hasmonean kings, however, and their descendants were born in royal courts; there they became accustomed to the luxuries of Greek civilization against which their fore-fathers had fought so bravely.

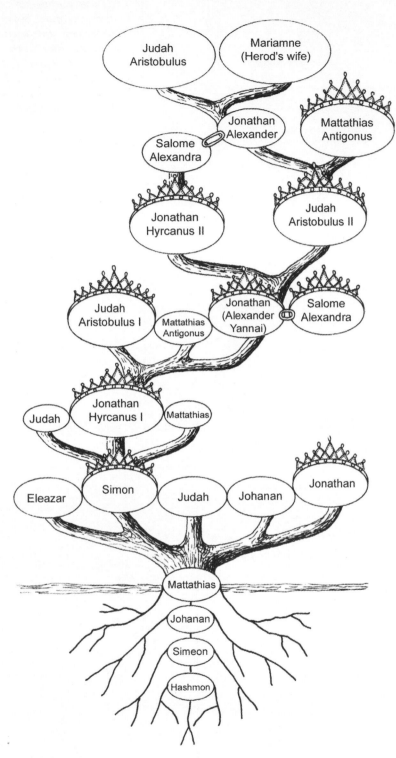

Genealogy of the Hasmonean dynasty.

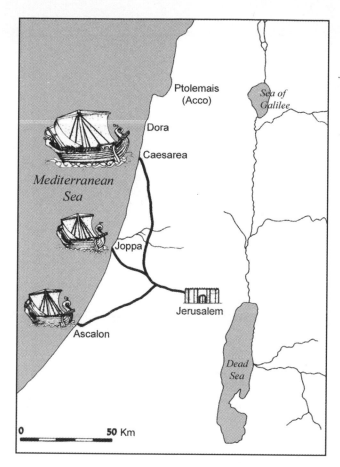

In the north and east of the city they erected magnificent monuments to John Hyrcanus and his son Yannai; at Modi'in they embellished their ancestral tombs with ornate monuments, an extravagance that would certainly not have pleased their ancestors.

Alexander Yannai's many wars aroused considerable popular opposition, particularly on the part of the Pharisees, while his support came from the Sadducees. The reign of his widow, Queen Salome Alexandra, was more peaceful. Some of the laws and customs established at this time left their mark on the people of Israel for generations to come. The queen's brother, Simon ben Shetah, the leader of the Pharisees, promulgated a

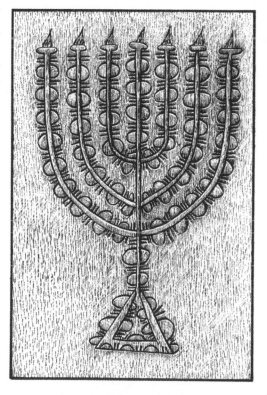

Seven-branched candelabrum incised in plaster in a building in Jerusalem's Upper City.

Portrait of Pompey.

law according to which every Jewish child should receive a proper education—this was the first compulsory education law in history.

After Salome's death, however, Jerusalem's peaceful times were over. The queen's sons, John Hyrcanus and Judah Aristobulus, engaged in a bitter struggle over the succession, which led in 67 BCE to the desecration of the Temple Mount. The strife between the brothers brought about the intervention of Rome. The Roman commander Pompey, on his way to the east in 63 BCE, was called upon by both of the warring brothers to mediate between them. Pompey took advantage of the situation, plundered the Temple treasures and declared Judea under the yoke of Rome.

The penetration of the east by the western power, and its subsequent conquests, justified Antiochus IV's apprehensions a hundred years earlier. The large Roman provinces of Greater Syria and Egypt now arose on the ruins of the Greek kingdoms of the east. The Parthians, still independent after Rome had failed to conquer their kingdom and territories, also annexed some of the Seleucid territories.

In little Judea, which had just lost its independence, two opposing parties struggled against each other. One, headed by Mattathias Antigonus (subsequently the last Hasmonean king), favored looking to the Parthians for help and making an alliance with them, believing that only they could guarantee Judea some autonomy, as in the time of Cyrus or even more so; the other party leaned toward Rome. Mattathias Antigonus thought Rome's presence in the east would be just a passing episode, for Rome was at that time rocked by a power struggle, which, he believed, would split and divide the western power. In the first years of the Roman Empire Mattathias seemed to be right. With the help of the Parthians, he succeeded in capturing the throne of Judea, ruling three years (40–37 BCE) and minting his own coins. Rome, preoccupied with internal affairs, did not intervene. However, when the power struggle ended with the victory of Octavius, renamed Augustus, the single and omnipotent Emperor of Rome, the new administration set about to quell the unrest in the east. Augustus' many talents won the Roman Empire major achievements in many spheres. Rome had almost lost the Land of Israel, but it now again

Coin of Mattathias Antigonus, with a seven-branched candelabrum.

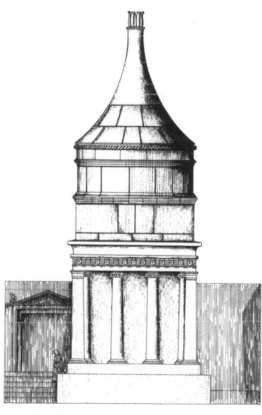

Toward the end of the Second Temple period, several monumental tombs, probably for members of aristocratic and wealthy families, were hewn out of the rock in Jerusalem's traditional burial sites. The most impressive of these tombs are those in the Kidron Valley, known as Absalom's Monument, the Tomb of B'nei (Sons of) Hezir and the Tomb of Zechariah. While some of the tombs are positively identified by inscriptions (such as that of "B'nei Hezir," a priestly family), others have received popular names and the real name of the owner is unknown (e.g., "Absalom's Monument," left).

0 1 2 3 4 5 m

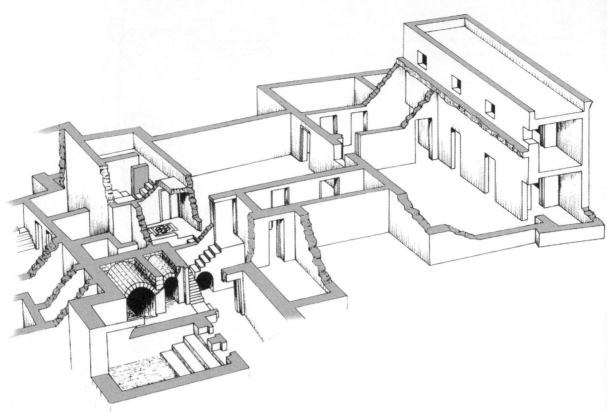

Remains of a large, impressive building were uncovered on the slope of the western hill, southwest of the Temple Mount. On the ground floor were several ritual baths, dressing rooms, courtyards and halls—all built in an opulent style. Some of the rooms have beautiful mosaic floors. These are probably the remains of the Hasmonean palace used by Agrippa II until the Romans destroyed Jerusalem. The diagram shows one of the wings of the palace.

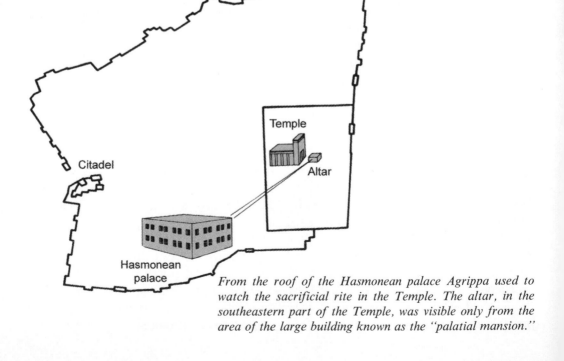

From the roof of the Hasmonean palace Agrippa used to watch the sacrificial rite in the Temple. The altar, in the southeastern part of the Temple, was visible only from the area of the large building known as the "palatial mansion."

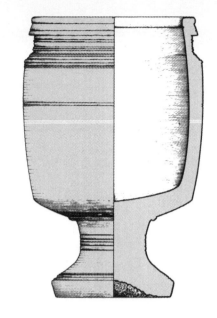

Stone vessel found in Jerusalem. Stone vessels had a special status in Jewish ritual because they cannot become impure according to Jewish law. Thousands of shards from such vessels have been discovered in archaeological excavations near the Temple Mount and in the Upper City.

came under their rule, with no reaction from the Parthians. Mattathias Antigonus was forced to flee, and his dream of an independent Judea under Parthian patronage faded.

The pro-Roman party had prevailed. They were led by the sons of Antipater—an Idumean friend of John Hyrcanus II who achieved a position of prominence under Yannai and Salome—headed by Herod. In reward for his loyalty to Rome during its most difficult hours, Herod was crowned King of Judea in its capital, Jerusalem. Under Herod and his heirs, Jerusalem would know one of its finest periods.

5. JERUSALEM AT THE HEIGHT OF ITS SPLENDOR

FROM HEROD TO AGRIPPA II

JERUSALEM attained her greatest splendor at any time in history during the period of the Herodian dynasty, from the reign of Herod himself, 37–4 BCE, until the destruction of the city and the Temple in 70 CE. As people said then: "Whoever has not seen Jerusalem in her splendor has never seen a beautiful city." This was the view not only of the Jews at that time, but also of Romans who visited it. Jerusalem was outstanding not only for its architectural beauty but also for its Jewish spiritual and cultural life. The city produced the greatest sages, from Hillel and Shammai to Rabban Johanan ben Zakkai and his disciples. Judiciary and educational institutes unprecedented in excellence were established, headed by the Sanhedrin. These achievements were possible due to the personality of King Herod, a gifted ruler who administered his foreign and security policy wisely and was also successful in the economic sphere. Herod brought Judea economic growth and prosperity, creating a firm financial foundation for both spiritual progress and material culture, such as construction.

The city derived its main glory and status from the Temple, around which its life revolved. At that time the Jews were the only people whose religion required them to have a unique religious-cultural center. The Temple therefore became the sole focus of the entire nation; multitudes of pilgrims visited it three times a year—sometimes as many as 100,000 pilgrims at a time. Jerusalem on the eve of its destruction had a population of 150,000 or perhaps even more.

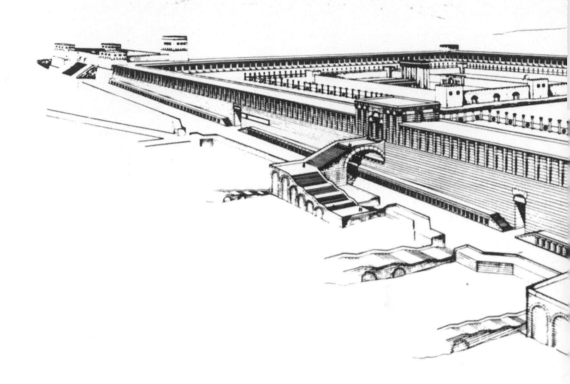

Reconstruction of the Temple Mount, view from the southwest. Herod's enlargement of the Temple Mount made it one of the most magnificent sacred sites in the ancient world.

One of the many stones discovered carved in Herodian style. This stone was originally one of the stones in the wall above the eastern Hulda Gate.

Many stones carved in the decorative style of the Second Temple period were found near the Triple Gate, probably from panels adorning the eastern Hulda Gate in Herod's time.

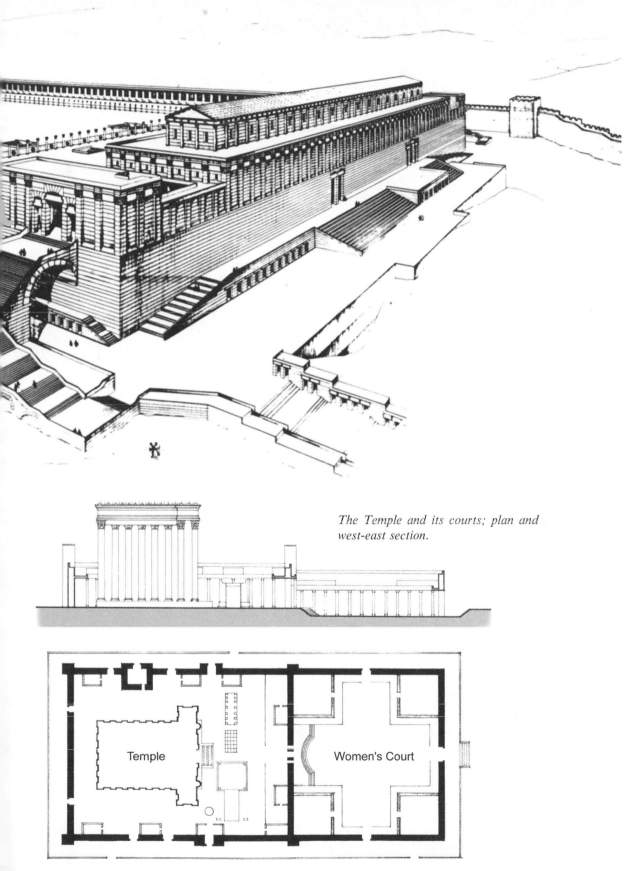

The Temple and its courts; plan and west-east section.

Temple

Women's Court

Façade of Herod's Temple.

The city's art and sport institutions were located outside its walls and—apart from the Temple Mount, the adjacent area and the royal palace—every residential area was densely populated. Tens of thousands of the city's residents and visitors crowded into the Temple courtyards to witness the elaborate ceremonies on the Temple Mount, so that the plaza had to be enlarged considerably—upon completion, it was the largest plaza in the ancient world.

The Temple Mount was famed not only for its size, but also for its engineering and architectural achievements. Among the inventions and innovations introduced were bridges to relieve traffic congestion and underground entry tunnels with ceilings carved by the best stone masons. The gates of the Temple Mount and the structures built on it to serve the pilgrims were among the most impressive of the time. A majestic basilica rose in the southern part of the Temple Mount, covering an area of 10,000 square meters (50 by 200 m).

As the city's population grew, a new quarter was built outside the wall to the north. Herod later enclosed this quarter within a wall, which Josephus called the "Second Wall." As the area of the Temple Mount grew, it encroached on the residential neighborhoods, making it necessary to vacate many homes to the south and west. The people evacuated received financial compensation and alternative land north and west of the Second Wall, and still more residential quarters were built outside the walls. Agrippa I wanted to fortify these quar-

Gatehouse and entrance tunnel to the Temple Mount in the south; western Hulda Gate.

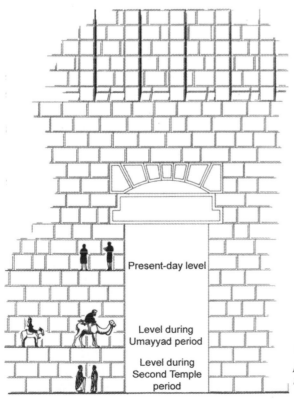

Present-day level

Level during
Umayyad period

Level during
Second Temple
period

Western entrance to the Temple Mount, probably Kiponus' Gate, through which non-Jews could enter and leave.

Interior of the Royal Portico in the south of the Temple Mount—reconstruction.

Supposed image of Herod the Great. This statue, found in Alexandria (Egypt), has been identified by some scholars as representing Herod.

ters with walls, but gave up the idea for fear that the Roman authorities would consider it a sign of rebellion. The fortifications were completed only on the eve of the First Revolt, under Agrippa II, when what Josephus called the "Third Wall" was built.

With the construction activity and expansion of the Temple Mount enclosure, the enlarged and improved fortress became a part of the new north wall of the Temple Mount, and was renamed "Antonia," in honor of Mark Antony, the Roman ruler in the east, with whom Herod was friendly. On completion of the Third Wall, the Antonia became an internal fortress, within the city, while a new fortress was built in the west to defend the city's fortifications. To that end, Herod completed the construction of the fortress begun by John Hyrcanus I, erecting a magnificent structure with three high and sturdy towers named for people close to him: Phasael, for his

The pedestrian bridge of Robinson's Arch, the first "overpass" in the ancient world.

brother; Mariamne, for his beloved wife; and Hippicus, for one of his friends.

Herod's palace, built just south of the city's fortress, had two wings, separated by ornamental gardens. Dissatisfied with even this new palace, the king began building a country residence, as his predecessors the kings of Judah had done. This magnificent palace was built 15 kilometers southeast of the capital, on land which had come into Herod's possession following a military victory

Reconstruction of street under Robinson's Arch—the main street of Jerusalem in the Second Temple period, with shops on either side.

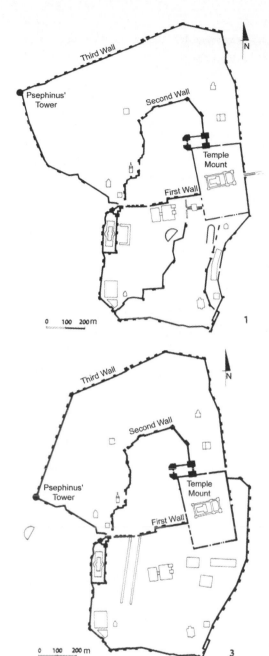

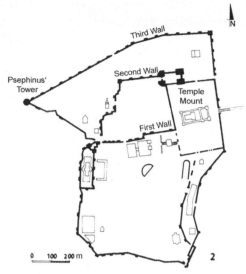

Jerusalem at its largest, toward the end of the Second Temple period; three scholarly views: (1) Avi-Yonah; (2) Kenyon; (3) Ben-Dov.

In the grounds of the Holy Land Hotel in Jerusalem is a model of the city toward the end of the Second Temple period, designed by M. Avi-Yonah. The location of Herod's palace in the model was based on various literary accounts.

there. He also intended the palace to become his burial place and named it for himself, Herodium or Herodis. Water was diverted there from Solomon's Pools through an aqueduct, and the entire desert area around the palace became an oasis, a miniature Garden of Eden. The kingdom was thus now administered from two palaces, in Jerusalem and at Herodium, about one hour away by horse (similar to the distance of the

A large building of the Second Temple period was discovered south of the Temple Mount, containing many ritual baths and mosaic floors. Beneath the floor were large cisterns.

Dozens of ritual baths dating to the Second Temple period have been discovered in excavations in Jerusalem, especially in the Ophel. A Jew had to immerse himself in a ritual bath before entering the Temple Mount enclosure.

Palace of Versailles from the center of Paris).

Jerusalem's appearance and even its character were shaped by the thousands of pilgrims visiting there. The flow of visitors necessitated solutions to many logistical problems, the foremost being sleeping accommodation. A plan was therefore drawn up for the establishment of three encampments outside but near the city: one west of the royal palace (in the area of today's Yemin Moshe quarter and Independence Park); the second, in the upper stretch of the Kidron Valley, northeast of the Temple Mount; and the third, in the area between the Siloam Pool and the spring of En-rogel, in the Kidron Valley south of the Temple Mount.

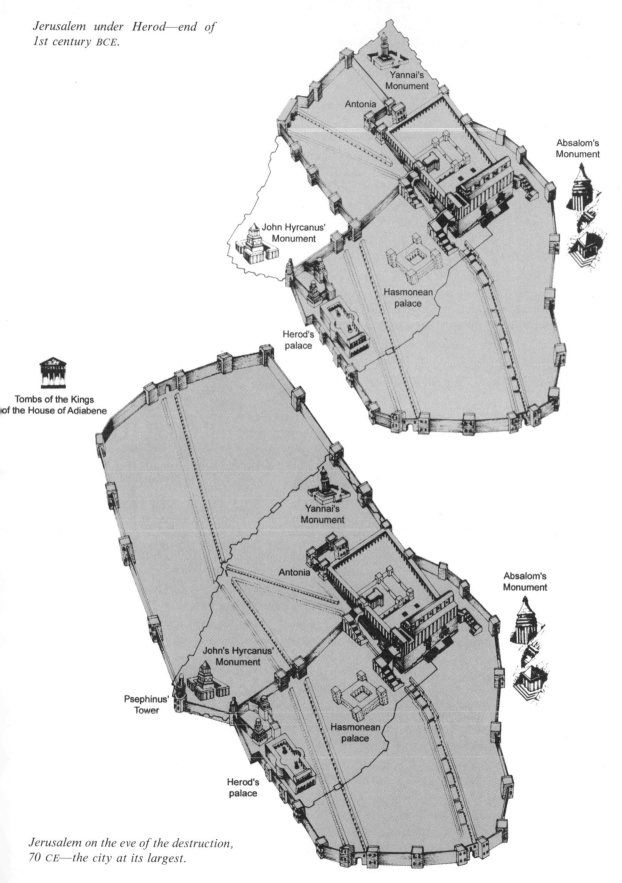

Jerusalem under Herod—end of 1st century BCE.

Yannai's Monument

Antonia

Absalom's Monument

John Hyrcanus' Monument

Hasmonean palace

Herod's palace

Tombs of the Kings of the House of Adiabene

Yannai's Monument

Antonia

Absalom's Monument

John's Hyrcanus' Monument

Psephinus' Tower

Hasmonean palace

Herod's palace

Jerusalem on the eve of the destruction, 70 CE—the city at its largest.

Decorated pottery vessels: Jerusalem royal ware from the 2nd century BCE to the 1st century CE, of a design showing clear Egyptian and Nabatean influence.

Each encampment was set up in a large open space, encircled by a fence with an entrance gate, and near a water reservoir. Pilgrims to Jerusalem would pitch their tents inside the protected area, leaving their animals and equipment there and entering the city with their families to visit the Temple Mount and the city's other sites and markets—much as Muslim pilgrims to Mecca do today. Guards were provided by the city authorities. These encampments had to be established outside the city's built-up and walled area, because Jerusalem was overcrowded even throughout the year; clearly, there was no area available for use only three times a year. Ecological problems created by the presence of humans and livestock also had to be considered. As stated, the encampments had reservoirs and other water sources, both natural and stored in large reservoirs fed by rainwater. In the course of time, when the town expanded and residential quarters were built nearby, these reservoirs were used by the permanent residents, and new pools were built for visitors outside the new residential areas.

In the ancient world it was customary to hold large-scale sports competitions and artistic performances during festivals and pilgrimage seasons, for the pilgrims' entertainment. According to Josephus' account, it appears that in Jerusalem, too, cultural and sports institutions were put up near the encampments, outside the built-up area of the city. A hippodrome, for example, was built near the southern encampment, on the slope leading down to the Kidron Valley (between the Temple Mount and Mount Scopus), and there may have been a theater above the Hinnom Valley, near

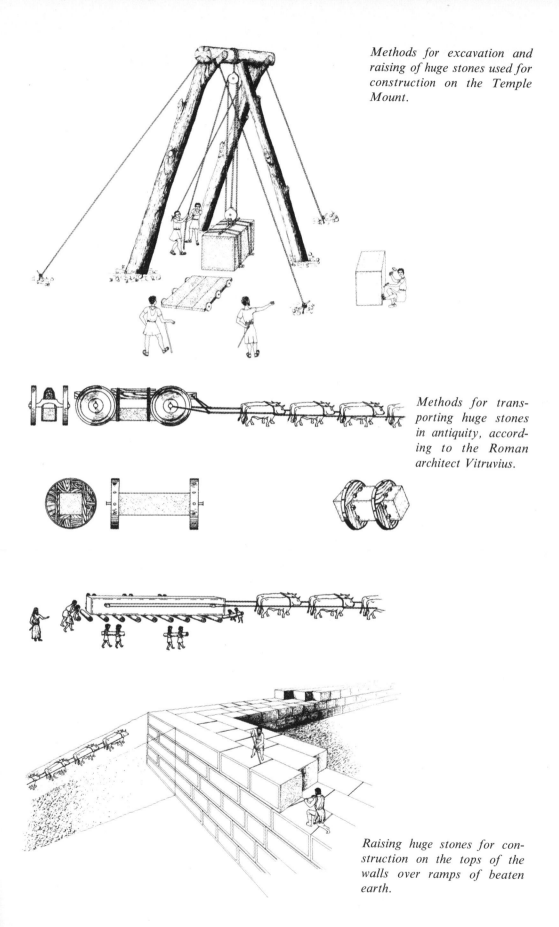

Methods for excavation and raising of huge stones used for construction on the Temple Mount.

Methods for transporting huge stones in antiquity, according to the Roman architect Vitruvius.

Raising huge stones for construction on the tops of the walls over ramps of beaten earth.

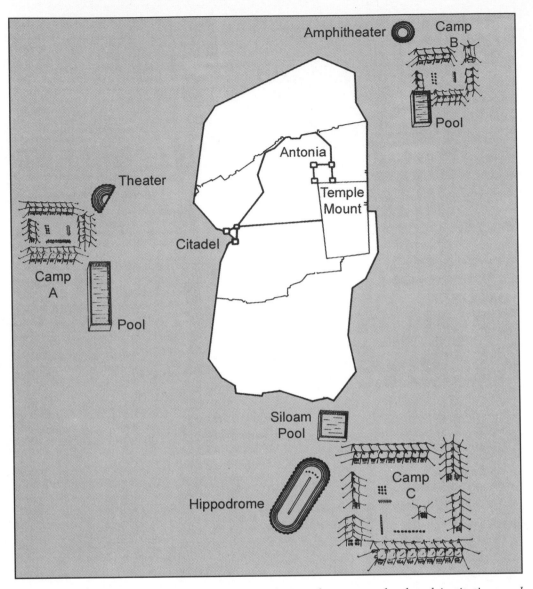

Jerusalem toward the end of the Second Temple period; sports and cultural institutions and encampments for pilgrims were located outside the overcrowded city.

Jerusalem drew multitudes of pilgrims, who were accommodated in three encampments outside the city. They were built close to pools, and near them were entertainment and cultural buildings for the visitors—a theater, an amphitheater and a hippodrome.

the western encampment, or in proximity to the hippodrome. Over the years, scholars have suggested various sites within Jerusalem for a theater, hippodrome and other cultural institutions; however, excavations at these sites have unearthed no evidence to that effect—on the contrary, they have produced remains of residential construction. Archaeology, analysis of Josephus' works and scholarly logic all imply that Jerusalem's cultural and sport institutions must have been located outside the city. Although Jerusalem was a *polis*, planned like other cities of the ancient world, it differed from them in this respect: sports and competitions were foreign to its spirit and ritual.

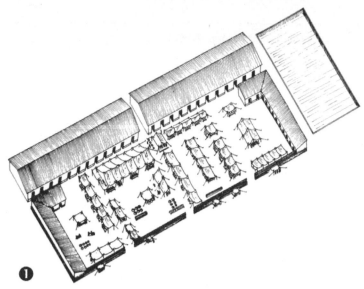

*(1) Encampment —
fenced protected area in
which tents could be
pitched for pilgrims.*

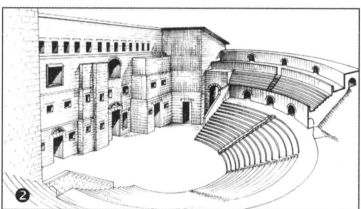

*(2) Theater, built in a
semicircle, with the
benches built in the cir-
cular part. Behind the
stage was an ornate
acoustic wall, against
which the scenery was
placed.*

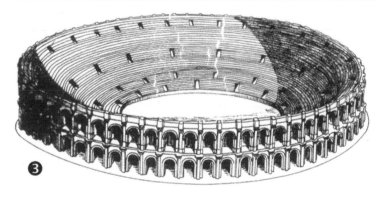

*(3) Amphitheater: two
theaters put together to
create an oval arena in
the center. Usually used
for gladiatorial games.*

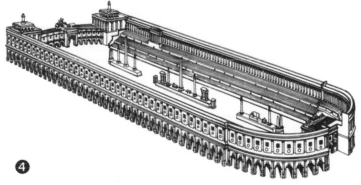

*(4) Hippodrome — a
racecourse for horses
and chariots (from the
Greek); also known in
Latin as a circus.*

117

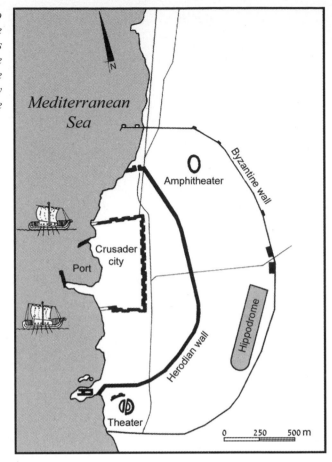

Caesarea, Herod's port city, had no shortage of available land. The planners of Caesarea in Herod's time were thus able to build the city's recreational buildings outside the city walls. Later, when the city expanded, these buildings were surrounded by residential areas.

Pilgrims were able to purchase everything they needed in the city's markets. The Upper Market was built on the slopes of the western hill, in the Upper City, from which it derives its name. It extended from Damascus Gate to a gate built on the bank of the Hinnom Valley southwest of Mount Zion. The Lower Market, which also began at Damascus Gate, extended from there along the old course of the Central Valley, along the western edge of the Temple Mount, reaching Siloam Pool and the Dung Gate of the Second Temple period. Many small shops were built along both sides of the road, roofed with great stone arches. Similar markets operated to the south of the Temple Mount, in the arches upon which the streets leading to the main entrances were built. All the markets near the Temple Mount were the property of the Temple priesthood, and the profits accruing from their rental were used for the upkeep of the Temple.

An impressive structure rose at the southern edge of the Temple Mount, on the extension added by Herod. This was the so-called "royal portico" or "royal basilica," the location of both the money-changers and the law court, all of which were at the pilgrims' disposal. Other institutions, related not to the sacred but to worldly matters, were located in the extension of the Temple Mount, with bridges connecting them to the streets and the foot of the Temple Mount. The city archives, just outside the Temple Mount, played an important role in the economic life of the city and the entire kingdom.

The people of Jerusalem also took care of matters connected with death.

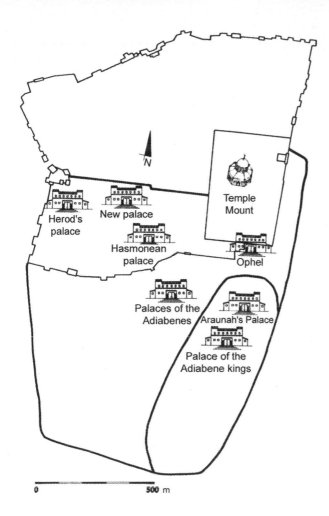

Temple
Mount

Herod's
palace

New palace

Hasmonean
palace

Ophel

Palaces of the
Adiabenes

Araunah's Palace

Palace of the
Adiabene kings

N

0   500 m

During both First and Second Temple periods several royal palaces were built in Jerusalem, as well as fortresses for their protection.

Wealthy families prepared rock-cut family tombs, with niches for coffins—sarcophagi for bodies or ossuaries for bones. Only the wealthy and high-born could afford to have such monumental tombs hewn out of the rock or built. Among these are the so-called "Tombs of the Kings" (actually the tomb of Queen Helena of Adiabene and members of her family), the tombs in the valleys of Kidron and Hinnom, and the tombs in the Sanhedria quarter and on the slopes of Mount Scopus. Besides these monumental tombs, thousands of graves of ordinary Jews have been found. Interestingly, the burial places of the greatest spiritual leaders of the times—Hillel, Shammai and others—are not known; they must have been simple and unpretentious, in the spirit of Jewish law. Ostentatious tombs were considered to

be a sign of foreign influence. The desire to be immortalized is part of human nature; while intellectual or spiritual figures are immortalized by their work, wealthy persons perpetuate themselves in stone and masonry.

After Herod's death, his kingdom was divided up between his three sons. Jerusalem now became the capital of a small state, on the scale of the early days of Hasmonean Judea. Nevertheless, it still retained its exceptional role, as the three states now existing in the boundaries of Herod's former kingdom looked up to one cultural capital: Jerusalem. The division into three states greatly harmed their income and economic viability. In addition, the major perfume and spice industry in the Jordan Valley had been expropriated and its huge income now fed the treasury of the Roman Empire.

 labels: Upper Market, Lower Market, Square of the column, "Damascus Gate" at the end of the Second Temple period

Reconstruction of "Damascus Gate," viewed from the north, toward the end of the Second Temple period. Behind the gate, inside the city, there was a central plaza, with a high column in the center which served as a reference point for the measurement of road distances.

The loss of income greatly impaired Jerusalem's development, and the sound of the stone mason's and builder's tools, heard everywhere during Herod's reign, now ceased almost completely. Compounding the economic difficulties was the fact that Herod's heirs were inept in both foreign and internal affairs, causing great popular resentment. The Roman emperor, Augustus, therefore decided to abolish the Jewish autonomy and place the country under a Roman governor or commissioner—the procurator. This was the form of government in Judea from 10 BCE until the destruction of the Temple in 70 CE, except for five years in which the country was governed by Herod's grand-son Agrippa I, who maintained special ties with the emperor.

During his reign (40–50 CE), Agrippa decided to fortify the city's northern neighborhoods, first settled in the days of his grandfather, Herod the Great. However, fearing he might be suspected of rebellion, he did not implement this decision. This wall, called by Josephus the "Third Wall," was completed by his son Agrippa II shortly before the outbreak of the First Great Revolt. After Agrippa I's death, government by procurator was reinstated; Agrippa's youngest son, Agrippa II, now bore the title of "king" but never actually ruled Judea as his father had done.

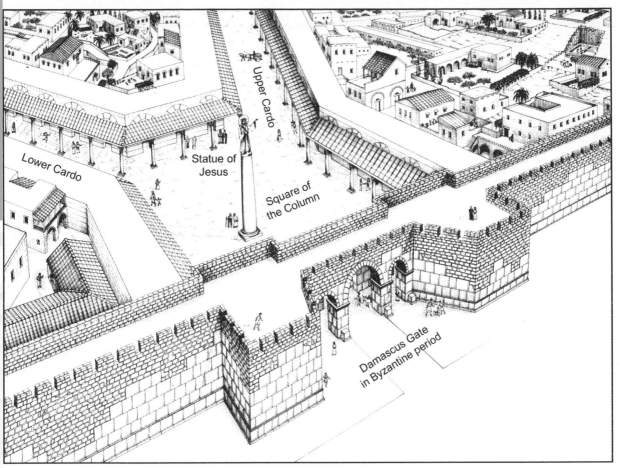

Lower Cardo

Upper Cardo

Statue of Jesus

Square of the Column

Damascus Gate in Byzantine period

Reconstruction of Damascus Gate in the Byzantine period, viewed from the north. Jerusalem regained its important status thanks to its religious status as the site of events in Jesus' life. The gate was rebuilt and the country's road map was redrawn, with all roads fanning out from Jerusalem. This had not been necessary under Roman rule, after the destruction of the Temple, when Caesarea became the capital of the Holy Land.

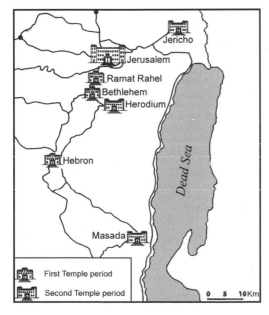

Jericho

Jerusalem

Ramat Rahel

Bethlehem

Herodium

Hebron

Dead Sea

Masada

First Temple period

Second Temple period

0   5   10Km

During the First and Second Temple periods, palaces were built outside but not far from Jerusalem, for the monarch's convenience. Royal palaces outside the city were common in the ancient and modern world, and their construction attested to the monarch's affluence.

121

Another reconstruction of "Damascus Gate" toward the end of the Second Temple period, viewed from the north. One of the outstanding creations of Herod's architects on the eve of the destruction of the Temple.

Remains of an ancient gate discovered beneath the present Damascus Gate—the northern city gate, probably dating to the end of the Second Temple period. Shown in the photograph is the easternmost of the gate's three arches.

Ritual bath from the Second Temple period excavated in Jerusalem. Dozens of ritual baths, built in strict conformity with the rules of Jewish law, have been excavated in Jerusalem.

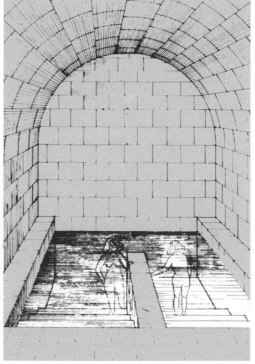

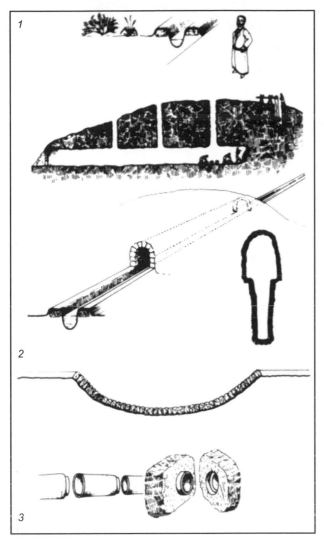

Conveyance of water in antiquity: open channel, the sides coated with plaster to prevent seepage.

(1) Qanat—*tunnel driven into a hillside with abundant groundwater; vertical vents supplied air for the diggers during the excavation work.*

(2) Tunnel cut into the rock where the surface rose above the ground-water level.

(3) Siphon—installation based on the law of gravity: when the water had to be conveyed to another channel or to a lower elevation, it was carried through a closed pipe and reached the other end at the same level in accordance with the law of connected vessels.

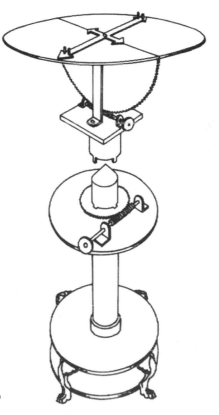

(above) Roman instrument, similar to a modern surveyor's level, for leveling in the construction of aqueducts.

Roman instrument used to calculate measurements in the construction of aqueducts.

The Temple needed large quantities of fresh water. For this purpose springwater was brought to Jerusalem from the south in well-designed aqueducts.

(below) The water supply to the pilgrims' camps in Jerusalem was based on the collection of rainfall in huge pools, usually located outside the city walls. As the city expanded, new pools were dug and the earlier ones remained inside the city for the convenience of its inhabitants. Cisterns were also dug close to the Citadel, to supply water for the garrison. Most of the pools were regularly cleaned and continued to be used during later periods.

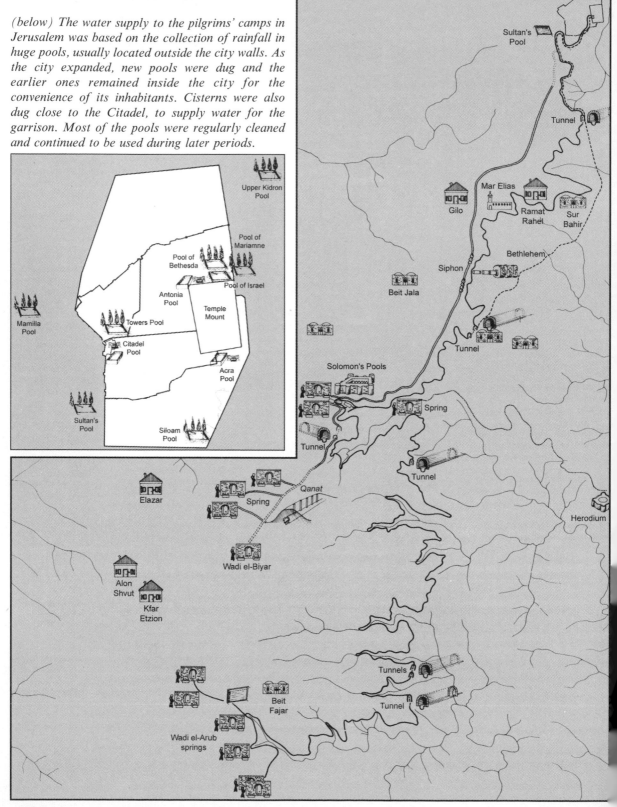

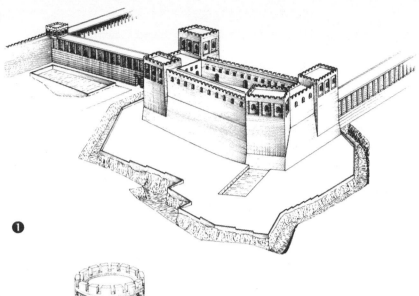

(1) Reconstruction of the fortress originally built north of the Temple Mount, included by Herod in the enlarged Temple Mount. It was strengthened, embellished and renamed "Antonia," in honor of Herod's patron Mark Antony, governor of the eastern provinces of the Roman Empire.

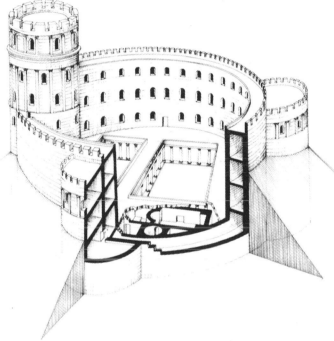

(2) Herod built a magnificent government center about 15 km southeast of Jerusalem, with a residential palace at its center. The land there belonged to him by virtue of a military victory that he had won at the site. This was Herod's palace outside Jerusalem, like the palace of the kings of Judah at Ramat Rahel.

(3) North of Herod's palace the west of Jerusalem was a fortress whose construction had been begun by John Hyrcanus I. Herod enlarged the fortress and built three great towers named for people close to him: Phasael (a brother who died in battle), Hippicus (a personal friend) and Mariamne (the Hasmonean, his beloved wife).

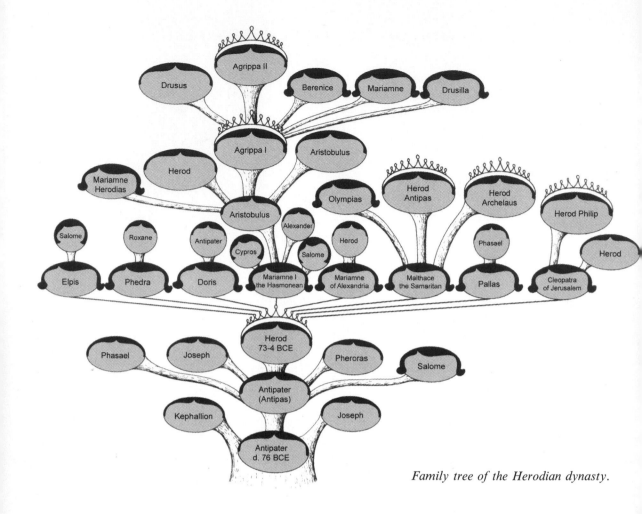

Family tree of the Herodian dynasty.

The procurators of Judea were generally members of the Roman equestrian class (*equites*), who were neither administrators nor intellectuals. Subordinate to the procurator of Syria, their seat of government was in Caesarea, the main port and economic center of the Holy Land, which thus became the real capital of Judea. The status of the two cities is best described by an adage of that time: "When Jerusalem was destroyed, Caesarea ascended; when Caesarea was destroyed, Jerusalem ascended," i.e., when either city gained political ascendancy, the other declined. In any event, Jerusalem continued to be a holy city, the sole cultural capital of the people of Israel, although its development was greatly harmed by its inferior political status.

The Roman procurator would go up to Jerusalem from Caesarea during the three pilgrimage festivals. While his attendance at the festival ceremonies was a form of respect toward the citizens, it was also of military significance: he would be always accompanied by a military force which served as a warning against rebellion, since such large festival gatherings gave the people a feeling of strength. While in Jerusalem, the procurator would reside in Herod's palace, which had become the property of Rome, or in the Antonia fortress, now the headquarters of the military garrison in the city. One procurator who served in Judea and Jerusalem earned immortal fame, or rather notoriety: Pontius Pilate entered the pages of history as the judge who tried Jesus and condemned him to be crucified.

6. JESUS SON OF JOSEPH IN JERUSALEM

THERE was considerable social tension among the so-called "three lands" of Jewish settlement in the Holy Land—Judea, Transjordan and Galilee. Although Jerusalem was the spiritual-religious capital of all three, the Jews of Transjordan and Galilee felt that they were being treated unfairly, since all senior positions on the Temple Mount and in the Temple, including that of the High Priest, were assigned to Judeans. The feeling of discrimination was aggravated by the arrogance of the Judeans, who regarded themselves as the elite, while many of the Jews of Transjordan and Galilee were "new Jews," descendants of converts to Judaism.

Jesus washing his disciples' feet as an expression of equality and humility; artist's conception.

It was no accident, therefore, that the Zealot party emerged in the Galilee, with almost no representatives in Judea and Jerusalem. The Zealots, devoted to the ideal of national freedom, rejected the idea, most typical in Jerusalem, that freedom of religious worship and culture was sufficient. To compete with the Judeans, the Galileans needed an ideology; the ideology that finally developed was a reaction to the corruption and immorality that pervaded Jerusalem society. Many members of the Jewish ruling class, including the priesthood, had

Detail of a relief that shows Jerusalem's art of stone engraving at its best.

Selection of clay perfume vessels from shops that lined a street at the foot of the Temple Mount.

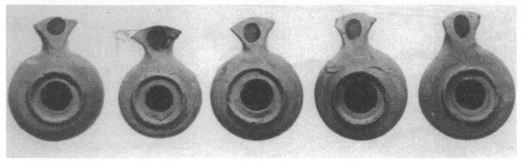

Clay oil lamps were also sold in the shops at the foot of the Temple Mount.

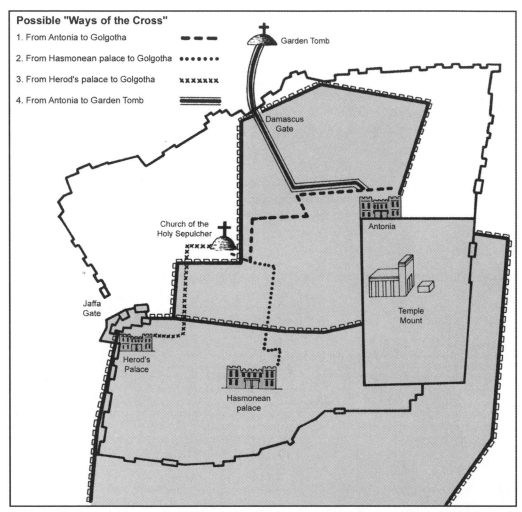

Possible "Ways of the Cross"

1. From Antonia to Golgotha — — —
2. From Hasmonean palace to Golgotha • • • • • •
3. From Herod's palace to Golgotha x x x x x x
4. From Antonia to Garden Tomb ≡≡≡

Garden Tomb

Damascus Gate

Church of the Holy Sepulcher

Antonia

Jaffa Gate

Temple Mount

Herod's Palace

Hasmonean palace

The site of Jesus' trial by the procurator Pontius Pilate was the Praetorium, that is, the seat of the praetor *(procurator or governor). The site of his crucifixion was known as Golgotha or Calvary, just outside the city. Neither of these sites has been positively identified. Some believe that the trial took place at Antonia, some at the Hasmonean palace, while others believe that Herod's palace in the west is the true site. Most scholars identify the site of the crucifixion within the Church of the Holy Sepulcher. Others, however, have proposed a site north of Damascus Gate, now known as the "Garden Tomb."*

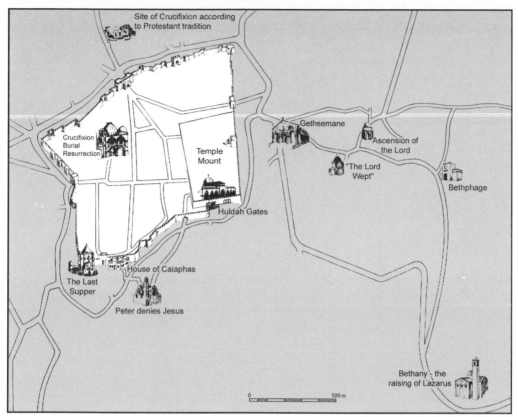

Jerusalem was the center of Jesus' activities. As a Jew, he made a pilgrimage to the Temple; he lived in a house in the village of Bethany, east of the city, where he came from the Mount of Olives. According to tradition, he predicted the destruction of Jerusalem and the Temple in a cave on the Mount of Olives; from there he entered the eastern gate of the city and went south to the Temple Mount, which he entered through the Hulda Gates. It was here that he overturned the tables of the moneychangers sitting in the royal portico. A house on the western hill has been identified as the place of his Last Supper with his disciples, before his arrest. The same place is also traditionally the home of the high priests Ananias and Caiaphas. The generally accepted site of Jesus' crucifixion and burial is in the Church of the Holy Sepulcher, today inside the Old City. According to one Christian tradition, after Jesus was resurrected, he went out to the Mount of Olives and there he taught his doctrines to the twelve apostles. From the top of the Mount of Olives he finally ascended to heaven. All these places were believed sacred by Jesus' followers and disciples, and later, with the spread of Christianity, places of worship were built there.

adopted a licentious, hedonistic life style.

The most prominent proponent of social and religious reform was Jesus, son of Joseph, who was born in the small Jewish town of Nazareth, in Galilee. Through his charisma, Jesus became a popular leader. He preached vigorously against the injustice and corruption that had infected Jerusalem in both sacred and secular areas; he even prophesied the destruction of the city and the Temple. Believing that change and redemption would come only if a messianic figure appeared, his disciples proclaimed Jesus the Messiah. As such he dared to propose religious reforms that were unacceptable to Jewish tradition. Dismayed at his message and his large following, the Jewish leadership and the High Priest tried to persuade him to renounce his ways, which they considered heretical and blasphemous. Having failed, they urged the Roman procurator, Pontius Pilate, to try Jesus for preaching sedition

Archaeological excavation of a tomb from the Roman period in Jerusalem unearthed the skeleton of a crucified person. The method of crucifixion can be reconstructed according to the nails and their location in the skeleton.

and thus endangering Roman rule.

On the Passover festival of about 30 CE, Jesus was indeed brought before Pilate, who condemned him to be crucified, the customary death sentence at that time. This episode was a turning point in the history of the western world and western civilization. A new religion, Christianity, soon ascended the stage of history. In time, it attracted tens of thousands of new adherents, mainly pagans, and eventually changed the face of the western world. Jerusalem thus became the cradle of Christianity.

7. JERUSALEM – SEAT OF JEWISH WISDOM

AT this time Jerusalem was the seat of Jewish wisdom for all facets of the Jewish spiritual world: thought and philosophy, ideas, education, writing, polemics and more. The spiritual leaders of Judaism, known to posterity as the Sages or the Rabbis, had been active in Jerusalem, inspired by its special atmosphere, since the days of Ezra. Over the centuries, they developed institutions which served as beacons and guides for Jewish thought, both theoretical and practical: first the Great Assembly (sometimes called the Great Synagogue), and then the Sanhedrin. One of the most outstanding members of the Great Assembly was Simeon the Just, of Jerusalem, who summed up the Jewish world view of the time in a

Part of the main street at the foot of the southern wall, from the Second Temple period.

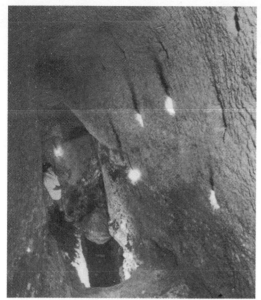

A winding tunnel was carved out of the rock in the southern part of the Temple Mount, to enable priests who had become impure to leave the Temple Mount quickly, without defiling others, and purify themselves in the ritual baths outside.

Jerusalem was the cultural capital of the entire Jewish people, including the large communities of the Babylonian Diaspora. Announcement of the sanctification of the New Moon, which determined the correct time to celebrate the religious festivals, was communicated to the Diaspora from Jerusalem by lighting beacons on the mountaintops. Jerusalem was thus able to maintain its leading religious role for the whole of Jewry.

celebrated saying: "Upon three things the world is based: upon the Torah, upon labor, and upon the practice of charity."

In more modern terms, we might express these thoughts as follows: the Jewish people believe in three supreme ideals. First and foremost is education— represented in this maxim by the Torah. Second is labor—one should not devote all one's efforts to studies, despite their importance, for work and a proper work

The Jewish leaders in Jerusalem on the eve of the destruction of the Temple, as well as their successors in Yavneh and the Galilee were great teachers. Although they recognized the importance of education, they did not deny the need to work for a livelihood. Most of them earned their livings in various free professions and considered their teaching as a sacred calling. Among them were scribes, shoemakers, charcoal burners, blacksmiths and others. Shown below is an artist's conception of three occupations: (left to right) blacksmith, shoemaker, scribe .

ethic are important values; the Sages practiced what they preached and worked for their livings, as well as teaching. The third ideal—a prerequisite for any society—is charity, namely, one's duty to aid the needy, the aged, the widowed, the orphaned and the stranger. The superiority of the Sages' world of values has influenced world civilization ever since. Simeon the Just's teaching heralded the beginnings of compulsory education for the Jewish people, later promulgated as law by Simeon ben Shetah.

Jerusalem radiated its wisdom to all realms of culture and spirit through its institutions—educational, judicial and others. Its position as the cultural capital of all Jewry was established; it would ultimately become a source of light for other peoples and religions as well.

8. FROM JERUSALEM TO YAVNEH

RABBAN JOHANAN BEN ZAKKAI: "GIVE ME YAVNEH AND ITS SAGES"

THE seventies of the first century CE were fateful years for Jerusalem's history. Besides the poor social and economic situation, the city suffered the mostly incompetent administration of the last Roman procurators of Judea. The appearance of a self-styled messiah and the multitudes attracted by his message created fertile ground for rebellion. External-political causes also furthered the imminent uprising: the reign of the emperor Nero in Rome was close to collapse, and a civil war was expected to break out, weakening the empire and perhaps even causing a split. Nevertheless, Rome was still the ruling power in the world; it quickly overcame the turmoil and emerged from the conflict even stronger.

The planners of the Jewish Revolt were increasingly hopeful that the Parthian power would help to overthrow Roman rule in the east because of mutual interests. When minor clashes erupted in Caesarea between Jews and gentiles, the Roman procurator's open intervention in favor of the latter ignited the rebellion. The Zealot leaders, who had come to Jerusalem, decided unilaterally to discontinue the sacrifices that were offered in the Temple for the emperor's welfare,

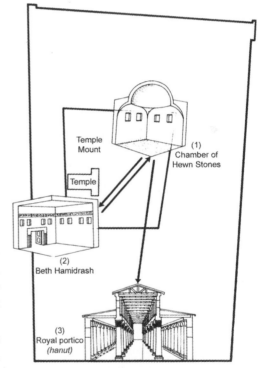

The Sanhedrin convened in the "Chamber of Hewn Stone" in the Temple. During festivals, when overcrowding increased, the Sanhedrin moved to the beth hamidrash *(literally, "house of study") at the western edge of the Temple Mount (near the present-day Wilson's Arch). Later, when the Chamber of Hewn Stone was being repaired, the Sanhedrin moved to the Royal Portico in the south of the Temple Mount—referred to in the Talmud as the* hanut *(literally, "shop").*

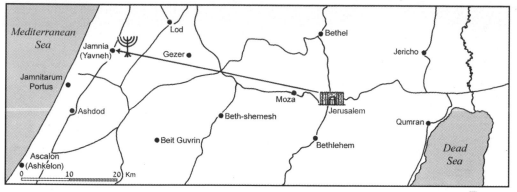

Long before the fall of Jerusalem to Titus, the leader of the Jewish moderates, Rabbi Johanan ben Zakkai, foreseeing the imminent tragedy, surrendered to the Romans and secured the establishment of a new center for the Jewish people, enabling them to survive the loss of their spiritual center. Yavneh thus inherited the unique status of Jerusalem.

The Sanhedrin moved from Yavneh to Galilee, where it successively convened in a sequence of towns, from Usha to Tiberias. These moves may have been made to avoid giving one town the seal of sanctity, and to stress that the situation was temporary until the restoration of Jerusalem's glory.

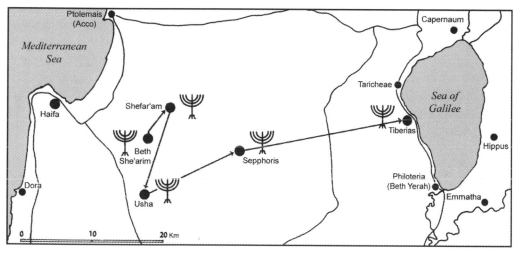

which had symbolized Roman rule. The Galilean Zealots began to organize the rebellion in Jerusalem and to plan the form of the new-old state that would be established when victory came.

The Zealots' success in their first battle with the Roman army raised hopes for an end to Roman rule, which were further bolstered by the bitter wars of succession being fought in Rome after Nero's death—time seemed to be on the rebels' side. In the wake of the first success, the moderates in Jerusalem joined the rebels, taking over most of the important state functions. The rebel state even began to mint its own coins. One of Jerusalem's moderates, the priest Joseph ben Matthias, later known as Josephus Flavius, was appointed commander of the northern front, moved to Galilee and began to fortify it and to organize the available rebel forces.

Eventually, when it transpired that the revolt had been crushed, there was increasing pressure from the moderates to admit failure, apologize to the Romans and open negotiations for surrender. The leaders of the moderates—

In the southwest corner of the Temple Mount there was a tower, where a priest would blow a horn to announce the beginning and end of the Sabbath. An inscription to that effect was found in the debris at the foot of this corner.

Rabban Johanan ben Zakkai, Josephus Flavius and others—were in favor of negotiating in order to save whatever possible of lives, property and, most cherished of all, the Temple itself. However, the extremists—as generally happens—could not be persuaded by logic and appeals to common sense; their leadership, motivated by emotion, was ultimately responsible for the loss and destruction of the city and the Temple. The leaders of the moderates crossed the lines and surrendered to the Romans in order to save what they could: Johanan ben Zakkai escaped from the besieged city, met with the Roman commander Vespasian and predicted that he would most probably take over the imperial throne in Rome. When this assessment proved correct and Rabban Johanan was asked what request he would like to make from the new emperor, he replied: "Give me Yavneh and its Sages."

This request had a profound meaning: even if Jerusalem were laid waste and the Temple destroyed, hope would still exist to save and rebuild the shattered nation and its culture. Few nations could have survived such a catastrophe—the destruction of the Jews' holiest shrine, the abasement of all their values and their sacred law. The Jewish people now had a new spiritual leadership, capable of overcoming the desperate situation and ensuring the eternal survival of the Jewish

The extensive destruction wrought in Jerusalem by Titus' legionnaires left its marks on the pipes and water systems of houses south of the Temple Mount.

Among the public buildings just south of the Temple Mount, shortly before the destruction of the Temple in 70 CE, were palaces built by the royal family of Adiabene, which had converted to Judaism.

people. To maintain the ideology of the Zealots and their allies, exemplified by the call "freedom or death," would have brought annihilation—either physical, as was indeed the fate of the refugees at Masada, or spiritual, through forced apostasy and Hellenism.

Josephus provides a graphic, painful description of the devastation of the magnificent city after its conquest. All its splendid buildings were completely destroyed, apart from the towers of the Citadel in the west. He illustrates the extent of the destruction by comparing the ruined city to a wilderness, where no passing traveler could imagine that a magnificent city had once existed. His much exaggerated account of the destruction attests to his deep pain and sorrow

over the fate of the city of his birth, destroyed because of uncompromising fanaticism.

Thus closes one chapter in the history of Jewish Jerusalem, and a new one now opens, without the participation of the Jews. Jews were barred entry to Jerusalem for several centuries—not only as residents, but even as visitors. The Holy City nevertheless remained embedded in the hearts and thoughts of the nation. It became "celestial Jerusalem," a new model in the history of mankind, an abstract idea that evoked much thought, writing and polemic through the centuries—both when the Jews still dwelt in their own land, but were barred from even entering Jerusalem, and when they were later exiled.

Chapter 5:

JERUSALEM—CITY OF LEGIONS
AELIA CAPITOLINA 70–333 CE

1. JERUSALEM: CITY OF THE TENTH LEGION

JERUSALEM was conquered after a long siege, during which the defenders exhausted the attacking Roman army under Titus (who had replaced his father Vespasian when the latter became emperor). The Roman soldiers vented their anger on the city, robbing and plundering everything they could find, and embarked on its systematic destruction. Not only did the Temple Mount become a heap of ruins, but the other buildings of the city, including the palaces and homes of the nobility, were destroyed. Traders

Roman siege of Jerusalem in 70 CE. Map and calendar of events.

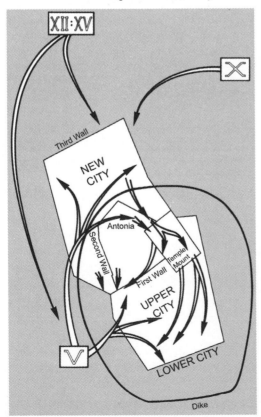

Titus' siege of Jerusalem, 70 CE	
Roman army:	
Legio V	Arrived from Emmaus and set up camp in the west of the city.
Legio X	Arrived from Jericho and set up camp on the Mount of Olives.
Legio XII	Arrived at Mount Scopus and joined the western camp.
Legio XV	Arrived at Mount Scopus and joined the western camp.
Auxiliary units	Scattered among the Legions.
Total: 78,000 soldiers	
Zealot forces:	
John of Gischala	Defense of the Temple Mount
	Defense of the First Wall in the east
Simeon Bar Giora	Defense of the First Wall in the south and west. Defense of the Third Wall in the north
Total: 20,000 soldiers	

Calendar of Events
(according to the Hebrew months)

1. 7th Iyyar	Third Wall breached
2. 16th Iyyar	Second Wall breached
3. 29th Iyyar	Attack on Citadel towers in the west repulsed
4. 1st–7th Sivan	City surrounded by dike
5. 1st–7th Tammuz	Romans renew attack, Bar Giora holds out. Antonia breached
6. 17th Tammuz	Sacrifice of the daily burnt-offering discontinued
7. 24th–26th Tammuz	Temple Mount porticos burned
8. 8th–10th Av	Temple destroyed and burned
9. 1st–10th Av	Lower City taken
10. 8th Elul	Upper City taken

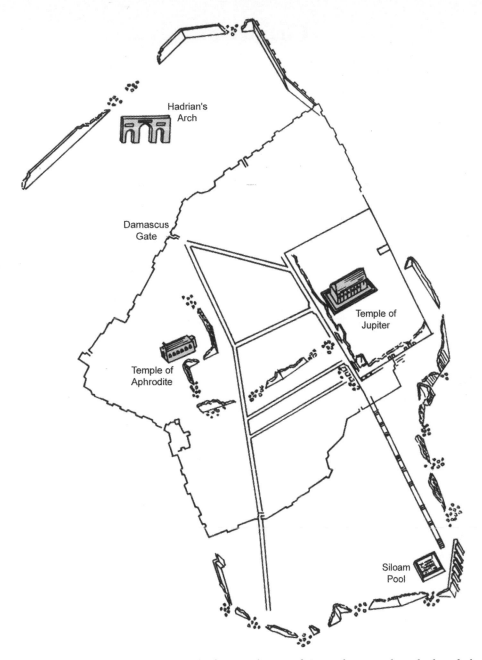

After the revolt had been suppressed, the population of Jerusalem was banished and the city demolished. The Tenth Legion was stationed in the city to guard it and to implement the decree forbidding Jews to return and rebuild it. The legion set up camps in and around the city and the surrounding area. After a few decades, following the Bar Kokhba Revolt, the Roman emperor Hadrian ordered the construction of pagan temples—to Jupiter on the Temple Mount and to Aphrodite at the site of Jesus' crucifixion. A triumphal arch was built outside the city, close to the Third Wall.

in building materials came to the city to buy mosaic stones, paving stones, column capitals and anything that could be reused elsewhere. Every archaeological excavation in strata dating to this period tells of extensive destruction and burning. Nevertheless, Josephus' descriptions were exaggerated, for the public build-

A victory procession was held in Rome, and a grand triumphal arch erected in its honor. The arch was decorated with a relief depicting Jewish prisoners carrying the plundered Temple Mount treasures before the victors. Detail from the relief.

Portrait of Titus, commander of the final stage of the siege of Jerusalem.

(right) The Roman Legion's tents in Jerusalem were lit by pottery oil lamps bearing pornographic engravings.

(below) The legionnaires manufactured clay tiles on which they stamped their seal; a clay tile with the seal of the Tenth Legion, from excavations in the Jerusalem Citadel.

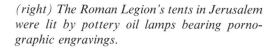

Evidence of the destruction in Jerusalem after its surrender: stones from the Western Wall destroyed by the Roman soldiers, in a pile of debris on a paved street from the Second Temple period.

ings were so strong and large that they could not be completely obliterated. Although the Temple lay in ruins, the Temple Mount still dominated the city.

The Roman emperor Vespasian and his son, Titus, the military commander, used the ruins of the city and its Temple as a warning of the fate awaiting all who ventured to rebel against Rome; the message was reinforced by Jerusalem's former status and international renown. In addition, the Romans issued a decree forbidding any Jew from even visiting the city, let alone living there. The Roman Tenth Legion, under the command of Flavius Silva, was left in the city to enforce this edict. The legionnaires settled in a number of camps built among the ruins, the main one on the slopes of the Upper City. Research and excavations have revealed other camps, both at the foot of the Temple Mount and outside the city—at today's Giv'at Ram, Motza, Ramat Rahel and Abu Ghosh. The role of the latter camps was to guard the roads to Jaffa, Bethlehem and Hebron.

As there were no longer any battles to fight, the soldiers were occupied in various crafts, mainly the preparation of clay bricks and pillars for milestones. The raw material for milestones was available in abundance from the pillars of the porticos on the Temple Mount; these were reworked and engraved with in-

(left) Roman milestone with a Latin inscription mentioning Titus (79–81 CE). The soldiers of one unit of the Tenth Legion stationed close to the Temple Mount made milestones.

(below) The inscription on Titus' Column, with the missing text completed.

IMPCAESAR
VESPASIANVS
AVG IMPTCAE
SARVESPAVG
L FLAVIVS SILVA
AVG PR PR
LEG X FR

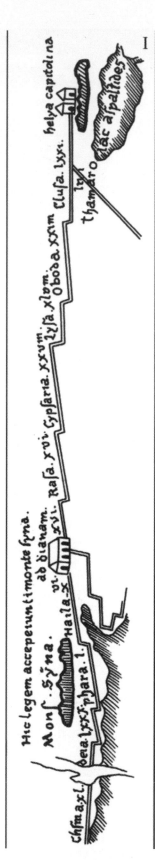

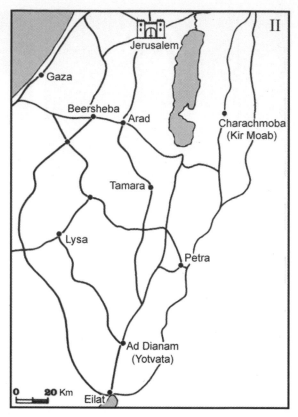

Toward the end of the third century the Tenth Legion was transferred from its post in Jerusalem to Eilat. The road to Eilat passed through various military outposts. These outposts and the distances between them were marked on Roman army road maps. One of these maps, preserved in the crypt of a European monastery for centuries, is known today as the "Peutinger Map."

I—Copy of part of the Peutinger Map, describing the route from "Aelia Capitolina" (Jerusalem) to "Aila" (Eilat).

II—The road from Aelia through southern Palestine to Eilat.

(opposite) Sites in and around Jerusalem where the various units of the Tenth Legion camped along the routes leading to the city, where good raw material for the tile-making industry could be found.

One unit of the Tenth Legion camped close to the Temple Mount. (left) This bronze statuette of a barbarian horseman, probably Celtic, was found in the unit's cult room during the excavations at the foot of the Temple Mount. (right) Bronze mask, also found in the cult room.

scriptions specifying the relevant distances. Two milestones, left in the workshop and not moved to their destination, have been unearthed at the foot of the Temple Mount. The legionnaires' main occupation was the production of clay bricks baked in fire-proof kilns, for use in kitchen ovens and bathhouses. The demand for bricks was great; the products were considered of good quality and were inscribed with the Tenth Legion's emblem and name as a trademark. There is no proof for the assumption that these inscribed bricks were used solely in structures belonging to the legion.

The Tenth Legion remained in Jerusalem for more than two hundred years, until its transfer to Eilat toward the end of the third century CE. During its stay in Jerusalem the legion apparently did not fortify the city, but enclosed the camps with stone fences, as was customary in Roman military camps. Had they needed a real wall, they could have repaired the gaps breached in the walls toward the end of the Second Temple period. However, Jerusalem of the late first and second centuries CE was an unwalled city.

141

2. RENEWED CIVILIAN SETTLEMENT OF JERUSALEM: THE JUDEO-CHRISTIANS

Excavations in Jerusalem uncovered pottery oil lamps decorated with crosses. From its beginning, Christianity adopted the cross on which Jesus was put to death as its chief symbol. However, only much later, after the emperor Constantine established Christianity as the preferred religion, and then the state religion, was public expression of religious feelings permitted, as well as the use of crosses on everyday objects. In the early years of their faith, Christians worshipped in secret and did not display the symbols of their belief in applied art.

EVEN while the Second Temple was still standing, small groups of Jews in Jerusalem had begun to follow the teachings and traditions associated with Jesus. They were the first to ensure the preservation of the locations of the important events of his life, as well as the place of his crucifixion and burial. They regarded themselves as Jews in every way, except for their belief in Jesus as the Messiah. Traditional Judaism disapproved, referring to these "Judeo-Christians" as *minim*, meaning sectarians or heretics. When Jerusalem was conquered by Titus' soldiers, the Judeo-Christians were expelled along with all the other inhabitants. A few years later, however, they asked the Romans to permit their return, asserting that they were not part of the Jewish community, and even welcoming the destruction of the Temple as fulfillment of Jesus' prophecies. The commanders of the Roman Legion, needing civilians to provide services for the army, were presumably glad to enlist enemies of the Jews and Judaism in that capacity. The Judeo-Christians were therefore readmitted to the city, settling in the southern part of the Upper City (today known as Mount Zion). Some of these returnees had actually witnessed the events attendant on the crucifixion of Jesus and were able to point out the sites where they had taken place; hence there was a grain of historical truth to these sites, which were again identified in the Byzantine period. Thus, only a few years after the destruction of the Temple and the expulsion of the Jews from Jerusalem, a civilian population was again living in the city.

3. JERUSALEM IN THE TIME OF BAR KOKHBA AND HADRIAN: AELIA CAPITOLINA

ONLY sixty years after Titus had destroyed Jerusalem and the Temple, Judea, now in the process of recovery, was again in ferment, and relations with the Roman Empire were on the brink of crisis. The Roman emperor at that time was Hadrian (Aelius Hadrianus in Latin), the protégé of his predecessor, the emperor Trajan (both having been born in the city of Italica in Spain). Their reigns were marked by strained relations between the Roman Empire and the Parthian kingdom. In addition, Slavic, Gothic and other tribes on the western borders, resenting Roman rule, were rebelling. Nevertheless, Hadrian's chief fear was of the eastern front and the Parthian Empire. Like Antiochus Epiphanes before him, he believed that all the inhabitants of the Empire, and especially those of the east, should be

Bust of the emperor Hadrian.

A line from one of Bar Kokhba's letters with his exact name in full: Simeon Bar Koseva. Below: coin with a representation of the façade of the Temple.

forced to adopt a single culture and worship—that of Rome, with the emperor at its center. Only such uniformity, he thought, would guarantee a successful solution to the Parthian problem. Hadrian feared that the existence of different ideologies and nations, each aspiring to its own, distinctive, national identity, would arouse Parthian hopes that the conquered peoples would rise against Rome. Hadrian's attempts to impose Roman culture on the Jews evoked a reaction similar to those of his predecessor Antiochus in Hasmonean times. All the Judeans, including their leaders, refused to relinquish their ancestral faith and spiritual heritage. Thus a powerful conflict was ignited, culminating in open revolt against Rome. Hadrian's harsh decrees included a ban on Jewish education and the ordination of educators and

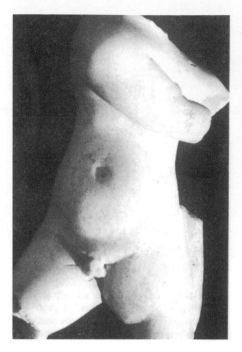

When the emperor Hadrian declared Jerusalem a pagan city and built temples there, statues were erected and houses were decorated with marble statuettes of humans, including nudes. This was a turning point in Jerusalem's history and character.

Two coins dating to the time of Bar Kokhba were discovered in excavations near the Temple Mount. The coin illustrated bears the representation of a date palm, the symbol of Judea.

teachers, and the abolishment of the custom of circumcision. Implementation of all these edicts would have eventually meant the physical and spiritual annihilation of the Jewish people.

A courageous Jewish leader hoisted the banner of rebellion: Simeon bar Koseva (or Koziva) of Judea, nicknamed Bar Kokhba. The revolt erupted when the emperor ordered a temple to Jupiter Capitolinus to be built on the ruins of Jerusalem's Temple. Bar Kokhba was supported by the leaders of the community, including Rabbi Akiva, who at first had been one of the moderates. Having failed in their attempts to secure abolition of the edicts by peaceful means, even the moderates realized that there was no choice but rebellion—religious persecution on such a level demanded the most extreme measures. The people of Judea launched their revolt at a time when Rome was unprepared because of the need to deal with various trouble spots throughout the empire. The revolt succeeded and the rebels established an independent state with all its symbols and institutions, including minting coins, some inscribed with the façade of the

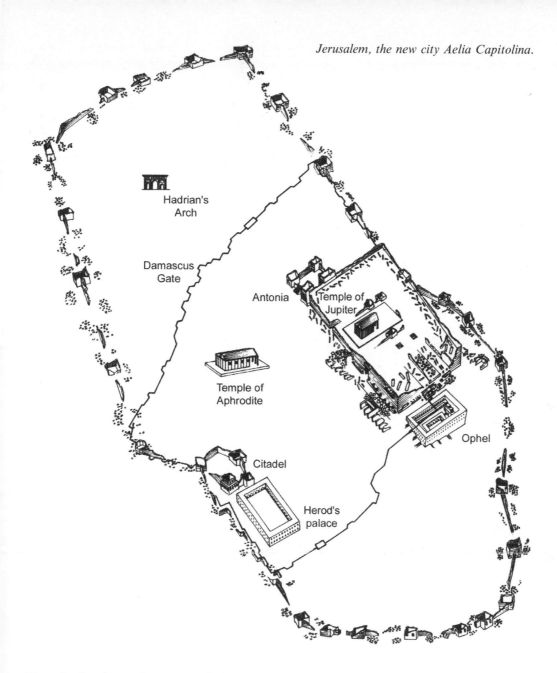

Jerusalem, the new city Aelia Capitolina.

Hadrian's
Arch

Damascus
Gate

Antonia

Temple of
Jupiter

Temple of
Aphrodite

Ophel

Citadel

Herod's
palace

Temple. In the early stages of the revolt they may even have rebuilt the altar on the Temple Mount and offered sacrifices, and were planning to rebuild the Temple.

Hadrian understood that unless he put down the revolt at its outbreak, it might succeed, posing a threat to Roman rule. He therefore brought the best Roman legions from all over the empire to fight in the Holy Land. The revolt was suppressed after bloody battles; both sides had suffered many casualties and a severe blow had been dealt to the power and prestige of mighty Rome. Since the Roman army had suffered such heavy losses in suppressing the revolt, Hadrian opened his report to the Roman senate with a factual account, rather than the customary sentence, "My army and I are well."

Though they paid dearly, the Jews had proved to the entire world their capacity to survive and their power to stand firm in face of a superior opponent: the Jewish world outlook—defined as religion in the language of that time—had survived.

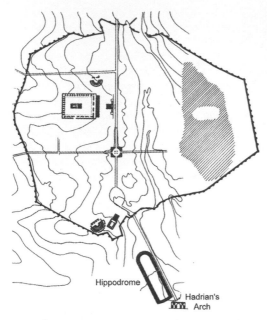

Hippodrome

Hadrian's Arch

Hadrian rebuilt the city of Gerasa (now Jerash, in Jordan). Both there and in Athens he built triumphal arches, as he had done in Jerusalem. Situated outside the city boundaries and not in its ruins, they were intended to indicate the future development of the city. Shown here is a plan of the city of Gerasa and its triumphal arch in Hadrian's time.

was drawn up, based in general on the old plan of the city from the last days of the Second Temple: two main streets running the length of the city from north to south, the Cardines (singular: Cardo; one such street was insufficient), and the Decumanus, crossing the city from west to east. Both Cardines began at the present site of Damascus Gate, one finishing at Mount Zion and the other at the Siloam Pool. The Temple Mount was restored according to the layout of Second Temple days, in preparation for construction of the temple to Jupiter, and accordingly the Decumanus circumvented it, ending up at (today's) Lions' Gate—this clearly implies that the previous town plan was still visible when Hadrian's city was being planned. Our source for Hadrian's projects in Jerusalem are the writings of a seventh-century Christian monk, whose reliability is in some doubt, as his descriptions—especially in connection with the Temple Mount—are strongly colored by Christian beliefs.

Moreover, Rome—and subsequently its successor, the Byzantine Empire—learned a lesson from this revolt and the price paid to suppress it: the Jews could not be coerced into abandoning their religion and laws; Judaism was indestructible. Thus, during the Byzantine period, when the authorities tried to convert entire Jewish communities to Christianity, they did not use violence but compelling enticements.

In retaliation, after suppressing the revolt, Hadrian continued to build the temple to Jupiter Capitolinus on the Temple Mount. Realizing that the Judeo-Christians were objecting to emperor worship, he also began to build a temple to the goddess Aphrodite at the site where, according to Judeo-Christian belief, Jesus had been crucified and buried. In addition, he decided to rebuild Jerusalem as a pagan city. A master plan

Coin of the emperor Hadrian, showing a pair of oxen pulling a plow—in Rome a stone-laying ceremony was accompanied by plowing. This act on the Temple Mount and in Jerusalem, recalling Micah's prophecy of doom, "Therefore shall Zion for your sake be ploughed like a field," was the flame that ignited the Bar Kokhba Revolt.

Latin inscriptions dating to the Aelia Capitolina period have been uncovered in the excavations near the Temple Mount and elsewhere in Jerusalem. Since many of these also feature the adjective "Commodiana," it appears that Jerusalem's return to civilian status and most of its construction were carried out under the emperor Commodus and his successors, not in Hadrian's time.

According to Roman coins and inscriptions found in excavations in Jerusalem, the name Commodiana, in honor of the emperor Commodus, was added to the name Aelia Capitolina. That this was done then provides evidence of extensive planning and construction activity in Jerusalem at that time. There is presumably some connection between the reinstatement of Jerusalem's civilian status and the extensive construction there after Hadrian's reign, perhaps particularly under Commodus.

In accordance with the custom of that time, the emperor erected a triumphal arch, whose remains were still standing in the nineteenth century. The arch was built a few hundred meters outside the present Damascus Gate, to its north, in the open area at the approach to the Sheikh Jarrah quarter. During Hadrian's reign triumphal arches were erected outside other cities as well, including Gerasa and Athens, so that anyone arriving in the city would appreciate the emperor's greatness; alternatively, it has been conjectured that these arches were meant to mark the future boundaries of the city. Remains of two other triumphal arches have been found in Jerusalem: one is the so-called "Ecce Homo" Arch, and the other may be seen today in the Russian Alexander Nievsky Church. To my mind, both of these arches are of a later date, having been erected in the fourth century, during the rule of Constantine the Great.

Above all, Hadrian left his mark on Jerusalem by naming it for himself. It was now no longer Jerusalem, but Aelia Capitolina: Aelia in honor of Aelius, the emperor's family name, and Capitolina because the temple erected on the ruins of the Second Temple was dedicated to the Roman god Jupiter, whose main temple stood on Capitol Hill in Rome. He also changed the name of the country: from Judea to Palaestina (Palestine), as if the Philistines were the first owners of the country—an historical distortion aimed at serving the emperor's political aims.

With Caesarea remaining the country's capital, Hadrian's efforts to rebuild Jerusalem were not very successful. Any attempt to rebuild Jerusalem without its religious and emotional foundation was doomed to failure, because its location did not justify its status as the country's principal city under Roman rule. Thus, Aelia Capitolina never achieved the previous distinction of Jerusalem, despite the considerable resources invested in its development.

The emperors who succeeded Hadrian seem to have been better disposed toward the Jews. The Jewish leaders, who were now living in the Galilee, established good ties with the emperors; Rabbi Judah Hanasi (the Prince), for example, was a friend of the emperor. The relaxation of tension between Judaism and the empire brought about a decline in building activities in Jerusalem, and the city came into its own again only when Christianity became the preferred religion of the Roman Empire.

Chapter 6:

JERUSALEM UNDER THE CROSS
The Byzantine City 333–638 CE

1. THE ROMAN EMPIRE ACCEPTS CHRISTIANITY

A Turning Point in Jerusalem's History—Constantine and Helena

At the beginning of the fourth century, Constantine was crowned emperor of Rome; he was subsequently termed Constantine the Great, a title justified by Roman history. Adept at reading the political map of the world, Constantine understood that the principal danger to Rome's existence lay in the east. Like his predecessors, he realized that a uniform culture, based on religion, would be a unifying force and ensure the continuity of Roman rule. Where he differed from his predecessors, however, was in his realization that he could not fight the new faith, Christianity, that had already gained many adherents all over the empire, especially in the east. The persecution of Christians by earlier Roman emperors had not only failed to harm Christianity, but had even strengthened it and helped its spread.

A man of sharp political wits, Constantine came to terms with the existing situation. Realizing that he could not eradicate Christianity, he pursued his

The emperor Constantine the Great.

After Helena, Constantine's mother, had located the site of Jesus' crucifixion and burial, a church was built there, with a rotunda over the tomb. Plan of the first building.

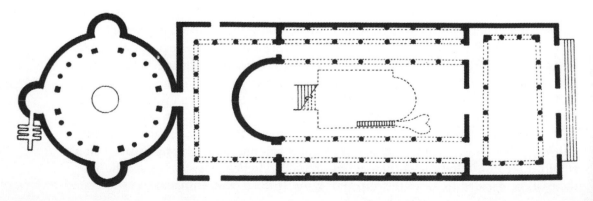

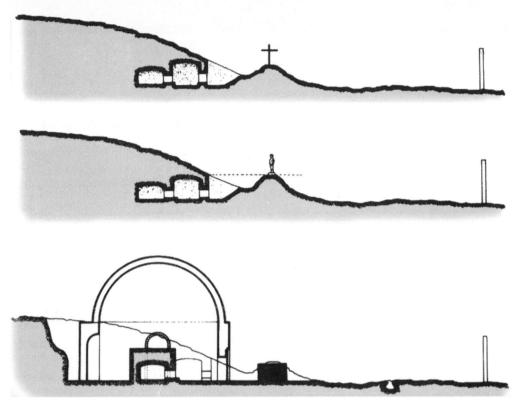

In the modern building, Jesus' tomb itself is in the center of the rotunda. Study of the tomb has shown that it was originally cut in a rocky slope, as was customary for Jewish tombs at the time. At the beginning of the Byzantine period a large statue was placed on the rock of crucifixion (Golgotha) east of the tomb.

goal of making religion and culture uniform in the empire by first permitting the practice of the new faith, and subsequently proclaiming it the empire's principal religion. The emperor thus succeeded where Antiochus Epiphanes and Hadrian had failed: for the first time in world history, a single religion and a uniform culture were constituted throughout the empire, earning Constantine the admiration and respect of Christian leaders. The Roman Empire, at that point of time in a state of decline, was granted another three hundred years of rule in the east—the period known in the history of the Middle East as the Byzantine period.

Another step taken by Constantine also impacted on world history. Since the empire's greatest efforts now focused on the east, he decided to move the imperial court and capital from Rome to the Middle East. A small fishing village named Byzantium at the edge of Europe, far from the previous capital, seemed a suitable location from which to rule the empire's border territories. Byzantium was located on a natural peninsula washed by three bodies of water: the Golden Horn, the Bosporus and the Sea of Marmara. With the transfer there of the capital, the name of the village was changed to Constantinople, that is, "city of Constantine." History nevertheless preserved the name: the new culture that had just come into being—a blend of Rome with eastern civilization and the new religion—would be known from then on as Byzantine culture. Constantine's son and heir, Constantius II, later began to impose restrictions on the Jews as a first step in Christianity's struggle

During Constantine's reign, construction was begun on a new residential neighborhood at the foot of the Temple Mount ruins, to its south. Houses were first built with large spaces between them for courtyards and gardens. However, the buildings gradually became more crowded, and by the end of the Byzantine period (6th–7th centuries) the neighborhood was one of the most densely populated in Jerusalem. (above) The early situation, before the neighborhood was densely populated; (below) the neighborhood toward the end of the Byzantine period.

South of the Temple Mount, on the ruins of large houses from the Second Temple period, a residential neighborhood was built in the Byzantine period, when new residents flocked to Jerusalem.

Pottery storage jar from the Byzantine period, found in excavations of the residential neighborhood south of the Temple Mount. Dozens of such jars were found in every house.

against Judaism. Imperial legislation published in 339 CE was aimed at reinforcing anti-Jewish canons issued by a church council convened earlier in the Spanish town of Elvira, focusing on three subjects: (1) prohibition of marriage between Jews and Christians; (2) increased protection for Jewish converts to Christianity; (3) prohibition of Jews owning Christian or other non-Jewish slaves. These were the first provisions in Byzantine imperial legislation aimed at eradicating Judaism through apostasy and forced conversion.

These ties between the Empire and Christianity had fateful results for Jerusalem's history. Previously, the Roman emperors had barred Jews from Jerusalem in the attempt to sever them from one of their main symbols, an expression of their political and religious freedom.

Now, however, the prohibition was reinforced by religious motives. In Christian theology, the Temple symbolized the old covenant between God and his people Israel. With the coming of Jesus, however, a new covenant had been established, and the revocation of the old one—through the destruction of the Temple—symbolized a turning point, the end of one path and the first step on a

Christian preachers would circulate among the Jews trying to persuade them to convert, berating them for continuing to weep and await the Messiah—he had already arrived, they argued, and everything that had happened was in accordance with God's will. For Jews, therefore, the changes that took place in the Byzantine period were negative, although they had certain positive implications for the history of Jerusalem.

The spread of Christianity focused attention on Jerusalem, where the main events of Jesus' life and death took place: the Last Supper and the events of Easter, his crucifixion, burial and resurrection and his legacy to his disciples. Eager to identify with the stories of Jesus and his disciples, many Christians made pilgrimages to Jerusalem, to visit the new path: the Christians were the "new Israel." In addition, the Christians saw in the destruction of the Temple irrefutable proof and affirmation of Jesus' prophecies, whose validity was still being debated in the early centuries of Christianity. It will be remembered that Jesus publicly prophesied the destruction of the Temple. In keeping with their theology, the Christians permitted Jews to enter the city only once a year, on the Ninth of the Hebrew month of Av—the anniversary of the destruction of the Temple—to mourn its loss. At this time

Helena, the queen mother.

Triumphal arch built by Constantine in Rome near the Arch of Titus and the Colosseum.

historic sites, which were readily accessible. This pilgrim traffic created sources of income in Jerusalem, such as the provision of accommodation and food, a souvenir industry, and so on, and moreover encouraged many Christians to settle in Jerusalem. The emperor realized that he could settle the city and its environs with his supporters from within the empire, thus giving the country a distinctly Christian tone; subsequently, Christians settled in other sacred sites throughout the country. The authorities encouraged this movement as it strengthened their control over the country, although many of these new inhabitants were monks. The promotion of the holy places in Jerusalem and the encouragement of Christian pilgrimage to the city created the model of a Christian holy city, also making it easier to raise funds for its defense and maintenance.

This was the background against which Helena, Constantine's mother, embarked on an important political mission, albeit in a religious guise: she traveled to Jerusalem in order to locate the places in which the events of Jesus' life and death had occurred; wherever some such site was discovered, some structure, such as a church, would be built. The extensive construction provided livelihoods and further accommodation for Christian pilgrims, also creating impressive sites for visitors. Within a short time several magnificent churches were built, some of them among the most impressive in Christendom, such as the Church of the Holy Sepulcher, on the site of Jesus' crucifixion, burial and resurrection; and the church on the Mount of Olives, where he had taught his apostles and spent the night before the crucifixion. These churches were erected where the local

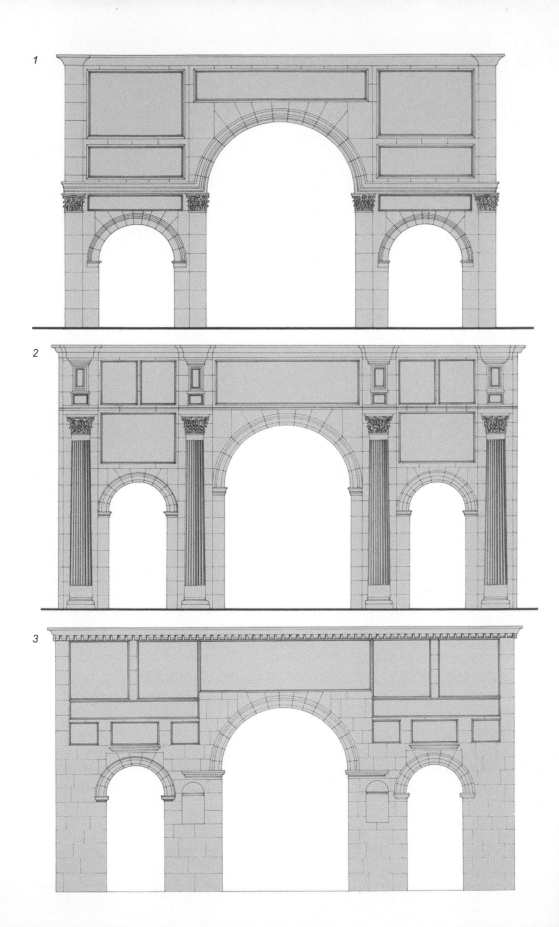

(opposite) Triumphal arches from the time of Constantine the Great.

(1) Triumphal arch near the Church of the Holy Sepulcher. Its remains may now be seen in the crypt of the Russian Alexander Monastery.

(2) Triumphal arch near the Antonia fortress (today in Via Dolorosa), whose remains are now known as the "Ecce Homo" arch—view from the east.

(3) The "Ecce Homo" arch, view from the west.

inhabitants claimed that the events had taken place, according to the traditions handed down from generation to generation.

Jerusalem once again became a pilgrimage center, with all that such a status implied: Christian pilgrimage and tourism gave the city and its inhabitants a firm economic base; new residential quarters were added, with churches, monasteries, hospices and markets. A sturdy protective wall was erected to ensure the security of the inhabitants, and in particular to fortify the city against threats from without, namely, from invasion by the army of the Persian Empire. Jerusalem took on the character of a major religious city, utilized by the Roman emperors to protect the entire east. Once again sacred and secular, spiritual and material, were linked together in Jerusalem.

The newly completed wall was built in the south and west along the same line as the walls of the Second Temple period. In the north the builders used sections of the Second Wall of the Second Temple period, but added a new section. In the east it was convenient for the builders to use the eastern wall of the Temple Mount, which still rose to an impressive height. Farther to the south, the wall followed a route somewhat higher than the Hasmonean and Herodian fortifications, which had been badly damaged during the Great Revolt. This part of the wall was apparently in use throughout the Byzantine period. There is no basis for the opinion that the city's fortifications in the fourth century were limited and that the southwestern hill—today's Mount Zion—was outside the fortified area. This interpretation is based on an inaccurate reading of the diary of the anonymous "Bordeaux Pilgrim."

The victory of Christianity was marked by the erection of two impressive triumphal arches in the center of the city. The remains of one may be seen in (and just outside) the present-day convent of the Sisters of Zion, near the Antonia fortress; the other is visible within the confines of the Russian Alexander Nievsky Church, near the Church of the Holy Sepulcher. Earlier scholars of Jerusalem's history mistakenly identified these arches as those built by Hadrian (as related previously, he built one triumphal arch, which was excavated outside the city wall, north of Damascus Gate). The attribution of the two later arches to Constantine's construction is indicated by their similarity to the arch he erected in Rome, although their level of ornamentation and carving is inferior to that of the Roman arch. Most likely, this particular location was chosen for the arches because, according to tradition, Jesus was tried in the Antonia fortress and the route to the site of his crucifixion passed through streets that led out of the city near the Church of the Holy Sepulcher. The sources of this tradition, which evolved at the time of the Crusaders, are probably ancient, although some authorities have suggested that Jesus' trial took place in the Hasmonean palace and the route to crucifixion began there.

2. From Constantine to Justinian

Christian Jerusalem

THE political idea on which Christian Jerusalem was founded proved successful. Jerusalem became a magnet that drew Christians from all over the empire, who settled both in Jerusalem and in other parts of the country. Following the sack of Rome by Alaric the Goth in 410 CE, many people fled from Italy and the western countries, some going to the conquered Holy Land. Heeding the call of the church father St. Jerome, they settled in Jerusalem. Among these were wealthy women bringing large sums of money, who were warmly welcomed. A period of building and architectural activity now began, since most of this money was used for construction: residential buildings, hospices, monasteries and churches.

A new source of income of the period was the trade in sacred relics (such as bones thought to be those of saints and prophets), which European Christianity,

The empress Eudocia.

(below) Church of the Holy Sepulcher in the days of Emperor Justinian.

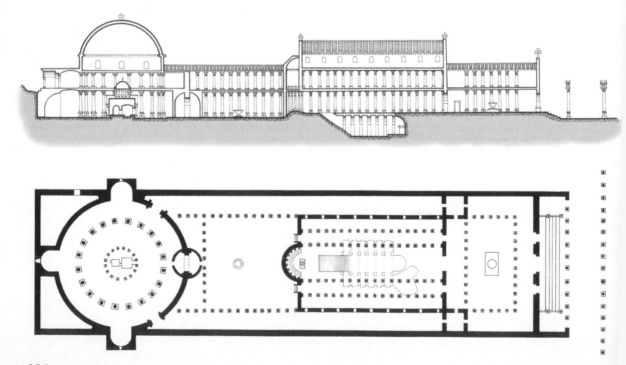

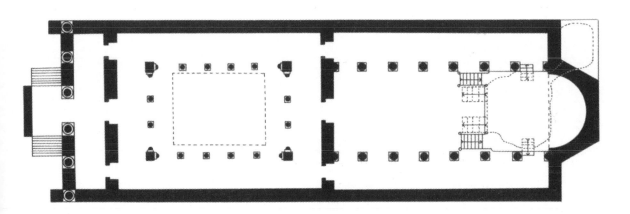

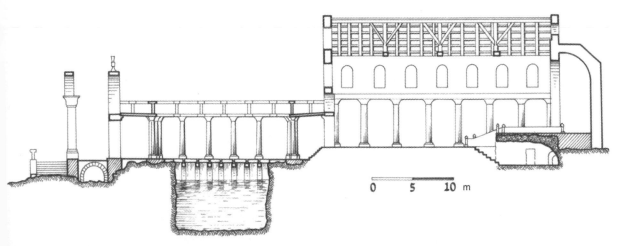

The Eleona Church on the Mount of Olives; (top to bottom) reconstruction, plan, cross section.

now gaining momentum throughout the continent, needed to justify the location of its many churches. Thus, it was reported around this time that the bones of John the Baptist and the Prophet Elisha had been transferred to Egypt and Joseph's mortal remains to the capital, Constantinople. It was also claimed that

Marble capital with leaf design, an outstanding example of Byzantine stone carving, now kept on the Temple Mount. It was probably brought from the Nea Church.

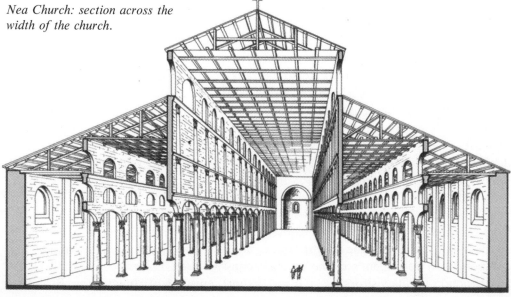

Nea Church—reconstruction of the church and atrium (forecourt); view from the west.

Nea Church: section across the width of the church.

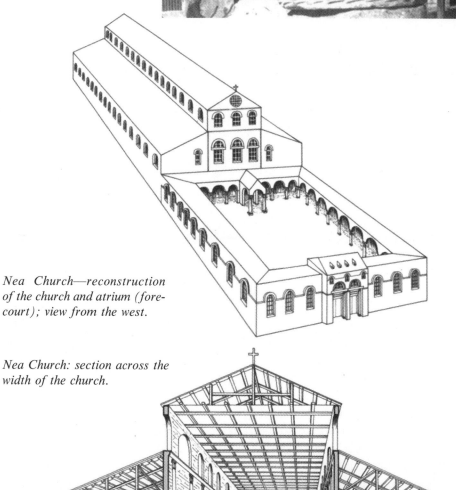

Reconstruction of the covered pavement in the upper Cardo, today in the Jewish Quarter.

the tombs of the prophets Samuel, Habakkuk, Zechariah and others had been discovered, and their supposed bones were taken with due reverence to churches in Europe. On her first journey to the Holy Land, the empress Eudocia discovered the bones of the first Christian martyr, St. Stephen; she took them to Constantinople, where she built a new church in their honor. A church was also built on the remains of the tomb, outside Damascus Gate. There was also a great demand for sacred relics other than bones. Thus, the Virgin Mary's clothes were "discovered" in the home of a young woman in Jerusalem and transferred with great ceremony to the capital. Trade in such relics became an important component in Jerusalem's economy and an attraction for its visitors.

The year 362 CE marks an exceptional episode in the history of the newly Christian city. A new emperor, named Julian (later nicknamed Julian the Apostate), had just ascended the throne. Because of his pagan education, he opposed the dominant status of Christianity and planned to restore paganism to its former glory, centering around the worship of the emperor. In his vain attempt to turn back history, Julian sought allies among the enemies of Christianity, in particular, the Jews. Julian's reign ended after three years, in 365, when he was assassinated by one of his bodyguards. His successor revived the primacy of Christianity, as a means to achieve the unity of his empire and consolidating his rule. Apart from the short episode of Julian, the Byzantine

Section and view towards the Cardo—one of the two main streets in Jerusalem running the length of Jerusalem under Justinian.

Empire in the Holy Land was to continue in Constantine's footsteps.

An important contribution to the status and development of Jerusalem was made by a Byzantine empress named Eudocia. Born Athenais, Eudocia was the daughter of a pagan teacher in the Academy of Athens. In 421 the emperor Theodosius chose her as his empress and she converted to Christianity. In 439 she visited Jerusalem for the first time, bringing the bones of the martyred St. Stephen back to the capital on her return. Banished by Theodosius in 443 after a quarrel, she returned to Jerusalem and settled there permanently. The Jews pinned great homes on the deposed queen; some scholars believe that they were subsequently permitted to settle in Jerusalem. Eudocia contributed greatly to the development and improvement of the city, including its walls. It is with good reason that many scholars refer to the walls of Jerusalem in the Byzantine period as Eudocia's walls.

The most important chapter in the history of Byzantine Jerusalem took place during the reign of one of the greatest Byzantine emperors, Justinian, who took office in 527 CE. Justinian resolved to regain the western provinces, which had been lost to the Roman Empire, and his extensive activity in the west is still visible today; a prominent example is the city of Ravenna, with its churches and mosaics. Understanding the potential of ties between the empire and the church for the stability of his rule, he made considerable efforts to convert the Jews to Christianity. In addition to the external threat of the Persians, Justinian feared the danger of internal divisions in Christianity, which might tear the empire apart. He therefore endeavored to strengthen the mainstream of Christianity by building churches and monasteries throughout the Holy Land, especially in Jerusalem, which he also developed as a

Portrait of the emperor Justinian in the Ravenna mosaic.

Reconstruction of the Cardo, as viewed from the east. Residential housing was across from and above the street.

metropolis. The walls and gates of the city were repaired, streets and markets renovated, new churches built and old ones repaired, sometimes with architectural changes. The sounds of stonemasons' tools were again heard throughout Jerusalem.

The Madaba Map, a mosaic map of the Holy Land uncovered in the town of Madaba, now in Jordan, represents the country in the time of Justinian. Prominent in the center of the map is a detailed representation of Jerusalem. Further details about the buildings of Jerusalem are found in the writings of Procopius, a scribe at the imperial court, who bestowed extravagant praise on Justinian's building projects. Among others, Procopius describes the construction of an immense church, the Church of "Mary, Mother of God," built at the time in Jerusalem and popularly known as the "New Church," or Nea in Greek. This was the first time that a church was built in Jerusalem at a site associated neither with an event nor with a saint's grave. As this huge church was intended to serve as a Christian substitute for the Jewish Temple, it was constructed on a hill

(left) Copper chandelier with glass lamp-holders, probably from the Nea Church.

(below) Bronze vessel discovered in the Byzantine neighborhood south of the Temple Mount. Probably used in the Nea Church.

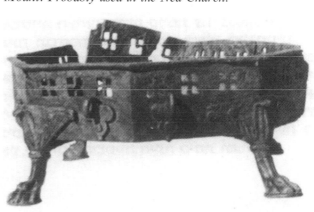

facing the Temple Mount, using stones from the Temple. In addition, a military expedition was dispatched to North Africa to return the Temple treasures and place them in the new church. Building the church with materials from the Temple Mount breached the status quo; the emperor and his representatives responded to irate Jewish complaints with various denials and excuses. However, the Jews were not appeased, and when the opportunity arose they razed the church to the ground. This happened at the beginning of the seventh century, when the Persians conquered the country from the Byzantine emperor Heraclius. It has been argued that the Nea Church was still standing in the ninth century, but this claim is unfounded; the source on which it is based reports a prayer service held near the Nea, but the church had in fact already been destroyed, and the reference was probably to prayers held near or in the ruins, like those held today by Jews at the Western Wall or the destroyed Hurva Synagogue. There is no reason to believe that the church existed and was active.

Jerusalem achieved its greatest glory during the Byzantine period under Justinian. It was then that Constantine's dream of Jerusalem as the focal point of the empire, a unifying magnet for all its communities and nations, became a reality.

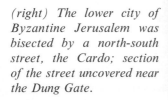

(above) Near the Nea Church, up against the southern wall, a monastery, hostels and hospitals were built. Shown here is a wing of one of those buildings.

(right) The lower city of Byzantine Jerusalem was bisected by a north-south street, the Cardo; section of the street uncovered near the Dung Gate.

3. Jerusalem Under Heraclius

The Beginning of the Decline

THE beginning of the seventh century found both the eastern powers embroiled in a fierce war. The Persians and Byzantines mobilized their best armies and financial resources to achieve final victory. In a short time the Persian army, headed by King Khosrau II, conquered Syria and the Holy Land, reaching the gates of the Byzantine capital Constantinople. In 614 the army of the Byzantine emperor Heraclius suffered a heavy blow in the Holy Land, and Jerusalem was conquered. Khosrau II knew how to exploit Jewish hostility to the Christian authorities; he made extravagant promises to the Jews that Jerusalem would be handed over to them in order to rebuild the Temple, and that they would again enjoy autonomy, as in the time of Cyrus. The Persians were helped by the Jewish population of Galilee; 25,000 young Jews joined the Persian army, and farmers in the many Jewish villages of Galilee gave

Portrait of the emperor Heraclius and his two sons on a coin. On the obverse: the cross that stood on Golgotha (the hill of the Crucifixion) in the Church of the Holy Sepulcher.

Khosrau II, king of Persia.

the army logistic help. Christendom was shocked by the public desecration of the so-called True Cross and the fall of the Holy City. The Persian invaders plundered the churches, and the Jews took the opportunity to vent their anger against the Nea Church, which had been built with stones and pillars appropriated from the Temple Mount ruins, razing it to the ground. Even when the Byzantines later returned to the city, the church was not rebuilt, both because the damage was so severe and because of the lesson learned from its construction (the breach of the

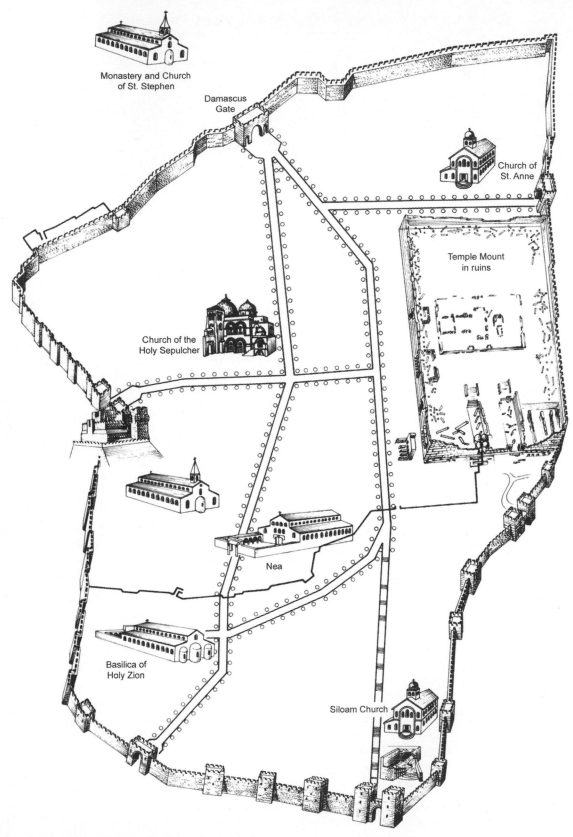

Monastery and Church
of St. Stephen

Damascus
Gate

Church of
St. Anne

Temple Mount
in ruins

Church of the
Holy Sepulcher

Nea

Basilica of
Holy Zion

Siloam Church

Jerusalem in the Byzantine period.

Jug for hot water, a rare piece of pottery from the late Byzantine period (found in excavations by the Temple Mount).

status quo regarding the Temple Mount ruins). Three hundred years of magnificent Christian construction in Jerusalem were thus almost obliterated.

After his victory, which he had achieved with the help of the Jews, the Persian king reneged on his promises: although the Jews were now permitted to enter Jerusalem and settle there, the Temple was not rebuilt and they were not granted national freedom. The Persian ruler had sacrificed his Jewish allies in return for Byzantine recognition of his conquests. Fourteen years later, after Heraclius had rebuilt his army, he invaded Persia through Armenia and soon reconquered all the former Byzantine territory in the east, including Jerusalem. The Christians exacted a terrible revenge, especially from the Jews of the Holy Land, many of whom were killed and many others converted to Christianity, either forcibly or voluntarily, following the terrible crisis and disappointment resulting from the defeat. The hopes brought by the Persian conquest, and the prospect that the God of Israel might now appear in his full glory

and strike at the Christians and Christianity, had not been fulfilled.

Even the leader of the Jews of the Holy Land at that time, Benjamin of Tiberias, converted to Christianity under the influence of the emperor, who promised him that no ill would befall the Jews of Jerusalem. It was an empty promise, however: the Christian rulers strove to obliterate all physical traces of Judaism, for fear of rebellion, and especially in revenge for the destruction of the Nea Church. The first step in this direction was the complete eradication of the ruins on the Temple Mount. Archaeological excavations at the foot of the Temple Mount have unearthed stones thrown down from the upper sections of the southern and western walls. These lie on the ruins of homes dating from the beginning of the seventh century, thus confirming that the worst damage to the walls of the Temple Mount dates from the first half of that century.

While the imperial army and crowds of Christian residents of the city, led by the patriarch, continued the work of destruction on the Temple Mount, and before the ruins left by the Persians had been rebuilt, a new power appeared in the east—the Arabs. The Byzantine Christians, now forced to defend themselves against the invaders from the east, ceased their acts of vengeance and destruction against the Jews. Large sections of the four walls still remained, despite the severe damage to the Temple Mount. Only four years after the appearance of Muhammad, the Arab conquerors' horses entered the gates of Jerusalem.

4. EVERYDAY JEWISH LIFE IN JERUSALEM UNDER BYZANTINE RULE

THE reign of the pagan Byzantine emperor Julian (362–365) aroused Jewish hopes for a return to Jerusalem, the rebuilding of the Temple, and political autonomy and religious freedom. Julian planned a military campaign to conquer the Persian Empire, and sought a way to harness the large Jewish community to his needs: he therefore tried to attract the Jews with various declarations and promises, urging them to go to Jerusalem, restore its ruins and rebuild the Temple. This also accorded with Julian's persecution of the Christians, after the principle "my enemies' enemies are my friends." He also exploited the tensions between Christianity and Judaism for his own ends. First

(right) Relief of a seven-branched candelabrum engraved on a marble slab found in the excavations near the Temple Mount, possibly used for Jewish ritual purposes.

(below) Seven-branched candelabra drawn on a house in the Jewish neighborhood.

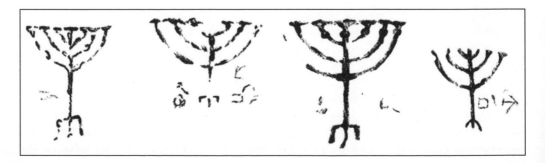

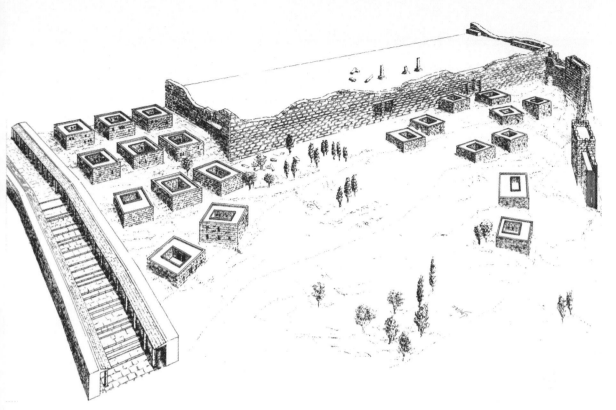

Reconstruction of Jewish neighborhoods south of the Temple Mount. First settled soon after the Persian conquest of Jerusalem (614), and later after the occupation of Jerusalem by Caliph Omar (after 638).

steps were indeed taken to rebuild the Temple: wood was gathered for scaffolding and building materials collected. However, Julian was assassinated after reigning for three years, and his successors restored Christianity to its dominant status in the Byzantine Empire. The scaffolding was removed from the Temple Mount and burned and the Jews were expelled from the city.

Hopes for the renewal of Jewish settlement were rekindled around the time of Queen Eudocia's settlement in the city, beginning in the year 443. Evidence to that effect is provided by a letter that Jewish leaders and priests in Galilee sent to the Jews in the Diaspora: "The time of our people's exile has passed and the day of the ingathering of our tribes has come, because the Roman rulers have commanded that our city Jerusalem should be returned to us. Hurry to Jerusalem for the Festival of Sukkot (The Festival of Booths), because our kingdom will be restored in Jerusalem." It is not known what event or events raised these hopes in the hearts of the Jewish leadership in Eudocia's time. Were the Jews misled by messianic visions? Or perhaps it was the queen who had delusions? In any event, the hopes remained unfulfilled, and the content of the letter itself was the motive for further persecution of the Jews and their institutions.

Even the period of cooperation with the Persian king Khosrau II, at the beginning of the seventh century, brought the Jews nothing but frustration, because he broke his promises. As we have seen, the returning Byzantines wreaked further destruction and damage on the Temple Mount ruins. In comparison, even the Arab conqueror, who repaired the breaches in the walls of the

Hebrew inscription incised on one of the stones of the Western Wall beneath Robinson's Arch, dating to the Byzantine or Early Arab period: "And you shall see, and your heart shall rejoice; your bones shall..." (Isaiah 66:14).

 וראיתם ושש לבכם
ועצמותכ כדש

Temple Mount in order to build a mosque there, seemed like a restorer and rebuilder, according to the testimony of an anonymous Jew of that time found in the Cairo Genizah.

In the centuries that elapsed from the destruction of the Temple to the Arab conquest, the Jews learned to nurture and develop "celestial Jerusalem," while also making every effort to restore earthly Jerusalem. From time to time, sparse evidence that the Jewish leaders were not occupied solely with celestial Jerusalem is uncovered in archaeological excavations in the city.

Pottery oil lamp with a relief of a seven-branched candelabrum, found in excavations at the foot of the Temple Mount—evidence of Jewish residence in the area.

Chapter 7:
JERUSALEM IN THE EMBRACE OF THE MUSLIM CRESCENT
ANCIENT ISLAM 638–1099

1. CALIPH OMAR, CONQUEROR OF JERUSALEM

THE new Arab-Muslim power which now arose on the ruins of the Byzantine and Persian empires was the largest empire the world had yet known. A few years were sufficient for the Arab army to subdue both powers and overrun their territories. Only four years after Heraclius had returned to Syria and the Holy Land with his army, he faced the Arab-Muslim hosts pouring out of the Arabian Peninsula; and ten years after he had marched into Jerusalem at the head of a triumphal victory parade, the city fell to the Arab invaders. The new conquerors were commanded by Omar (or 'Umar), the second of the four first caliphs of the first caliphate, who were known as the "Illustrious Caliphs." Besides his political skills and leadership ability, Omar

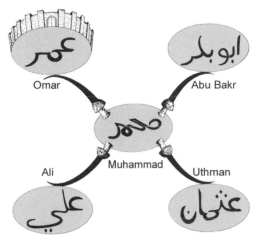

Muhammad and the first four caliphs. The second is Omar, under whose rule Jerusalem was conquered.

Golden Gate—detail from an unfinished relief.

Eastern façade of the Golden Gate (or Gate of Mercy)—a monumental structure dating to the Umayyad dynasty. Possibly intended to commemorate the place where Muhammad entered the Temple Mount enclosure before his ascent to heaven.

was also regarded as one of the leading commanders of the Arab armies.

Omar's entry into Jerusalem was marked by its simplicity. He and his army respected the sanctity of the city, both because of its importance to Christianity and Judaism, and because Muhammad himself had decreed that prayers should be offered facing Jerusalem. (This provision was changed two years later, when Muslims were required to face Mecca in prayer.) While the occupation of Jerusalem was not a great military feat, it had a severe effect on the morale of the Christians and their army. Omar was accompanied by a close adviser named Ka'b al-Akhbar. After visiting sites of the city which were still standing, they toured the devastated courtyard of the Temple; tradition relates that Ka'b, a convert from Judaism, was mocked by Omar for removing his shoes before entering the Temple Mount. If there is a grain of historical truth in this story, it implies that at the time the Temple Mount was not yet sacred to Muslims. We do not know how the visit ended, or whether Omar then ordered a house of prayer to be constructed there. All we know is that the Temple Mount was first consecrated by the Muslims, and a mosque constructed there, during the reign of Mu'awiya, the first Umayyad caliph.

2. FROM AELIA TO MADINAT BAYT AL-MAQDIS

THE SANCTITY OF JERUSALEM IN ISLAM

IT is not known whether Jerusalem was known as Aelia under Byzantine rule. It would be surprising if this were the case: the Christian emperors would hardly name their holy city, the city of Jesus, after the pagan emperor Hadrian, persecutor of Christianity, or after Jupiter Capitoline, the Roman god. In authentic Byzantine inscriptions, such as the Madaba Map, the city is called IEPOY-ΣΑΛΗΜ; in the early days of Arab rule, however, Jerusalem's coins were inscribed with the name *Ilya*. Although the Arabs interpreted this as the name of the prophet Elijah, they apparently found it in the city when they arrived there. Soon after the Arab conquest the name of the city was changed to *Madinat Bayt al-Maqdis*—"City of the Temple," referring to the First and Second Jewish Temples.

Although the Muslim conquerors respected its sanctity from the earliest days of their rule, it was not until the time of the Umayyad dynasty that Jerusalem became one of the major holy cities of Islam. The first Umayyad caliph and founder of the dynasty, Mu'awiya (660–681), expanded the borders of the huge empire. Despite domestic and foreign problems, Mu'awiya was tolerant toward Jews and Christians throughout his empire. The Byzantines, seeking to recoup their losses in the eastern Mediterranean, reinforced their army and navy; but the Arabs had also built up a strong navy and were able to maintain their ascendancy, reaching as far as the shores of Anatolia. Mu'awiya was well aware that the Christian struggle for the Holy Land was based on Jerusalem's sanctity and its special standing for millions of believers; the Christians' political and economic motives were immeasurably

According to tradition, Muhammad arrived in Jerusalem mounted on a wondrous animal with a horse's body, a woman's face and a peacock's tail, called Al-Burak ("Lightning"). Representations of Muhammad on the back of this animal were common in Islamic art throughout the ages.

strengthened by their ideological and religious designs on Jerusalem. To combat this, it was necessary to give Jerusalem the status of a city sacred to Muslims.

Sanctity in Islam was inextricably associated with Muhammad. The Muslims therefore needed to find some episode in Muhammad's life that did not occur in a specifically named place and could therefore be "transferred" to Jerusalem. There was indeed an old tradition that told of a night journey by Muhammad and his ascent to heaven, based on a rather passage verse in the Koran. According to the story, Muhammad was commanded to go out to "the Further Mosque," whose location was not explicitly specified (modern scholars

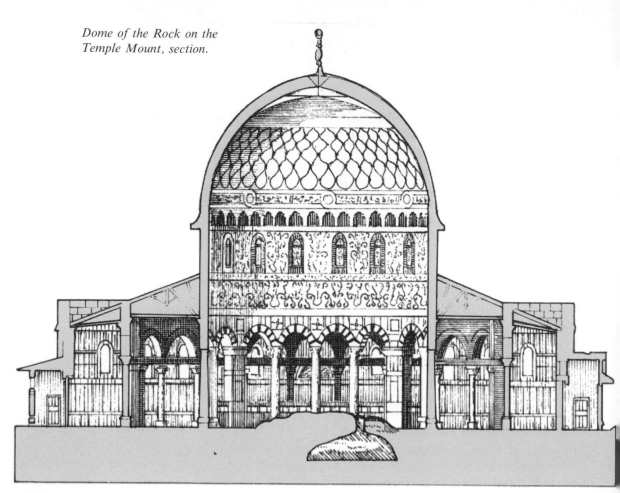

Dome of the Rock on the Temple Mount, section.

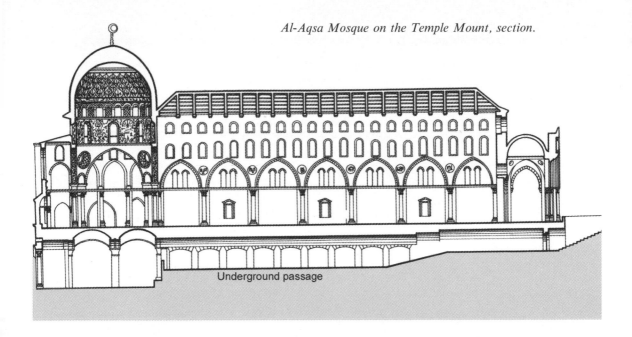

Underground passage

interpret the verse as a reference to Medina). He was carried there on the back of a miraculous winged beast, named Al-Burak ("Lightning"), with a horse's body, a woman's face and a peacock's tail. After Muhammad had tethered his mount near the mosque, he was summoned to heaven to meet with Moses, the prophet Elijah and Jesus—an ascent that the Arabs call *ma'raj*. These leaders of the three monotheistic religions proceeded to discuss various religious subjects, ultimately supporting Muhammad's position. This tradition laid the foundations for various important elements of Islam, and since the episode was not associated with a specific location, it was now interpreted as having taken place in Jerusalem. The fact is that this device was similar to what David and Solomon had done when they sanctified Jerusalem and declared it the capital of their kingdom. The Muslims chose Jerusalem or, more precisely, the Temple Mount, because it already possessed an aura of sanctity; moreover, it was a large, vacant area, whose Jewish owners presented no threat to the huge empire. Finally, such an act, concerned as it was ostensibly with purely spiritual needs, was surely preferable to the acts of destruction perpetrated by the Byzantines.

The Al-Aqsa Mosque and the Dome of the Rock—two of the sites most sacred to Islam. Only the Kaaba in Mecca and the Prophet's Mosque in Medina are more sacred.

In order to build the so-called "Further Mosque"—*Masjid al-Aqsa* in Arabic—the Arabs first had to rebuild the ruined walls around the Temple Mount. While their construction did not resemble the Herodian masonry, the final result was a very large enclosure that they called *Al-Haram al-Sharif* ("the noble enclosure"); on the south there was a large wooden mosque that could accommodate three thousand worshipers. The mosque was described by the French traveler Arculf, who visited the Holy Land in the year 670; this evidence in support of the tradition attributing the construction to Mu'awiya has also been confirmed by modern research. Within a short time the idea of Muslim Jerusalem had become firmly rooted.

Jerusalem had taken on a new character, unprecedented in the history of any other city. It was now sacred to the three monotheistic faiths of western civilization—Judaism, Christianity and Islam.

3. Jerusalem Under the Umayyads

A New Administrative Center

THE Umayyad caliphs ruled over a mighty empire, stretching from the borders of India to Spain. The capital was in Damascus, for Mu'awiya had first served as governor of Blad al-Sham, i.e., Syria and the Holy Land, and administered his domain from Damascus. When he became the omnipotent caliph, Mu'awiya continued to reside in Damascus, as did his successors. They strengthened ties with Jerusalem and invested much money in the city's extensive building projects, so that the sounds of stonemasons' tools were once again heard in the streets of

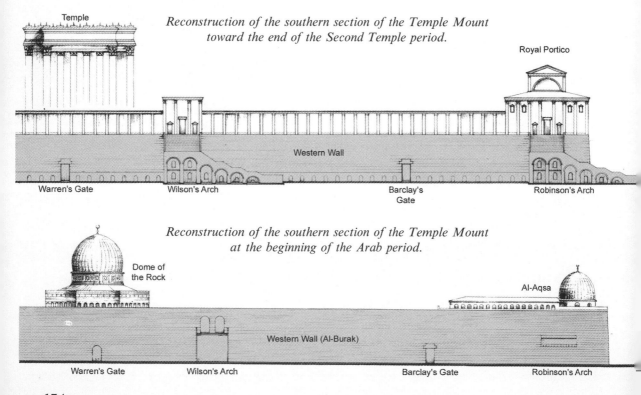

Reconstruction of the southern section of the Temple Mount toward the end of the Second Temple period.

Temple

Royal Portico

Western Wall

Warren's Gate   Wilson's Arch   Barclay's Gate   Robinson's Arch

Reconstruction of the southern section of the Temple Mount at the beginning of the Arab period.

Dome of the Rock

Al-Aqsa

Western Wall (Al-Burak)

Warren's Gate   Wilson's Arch   Barclay's Gate   Robinson's Arch

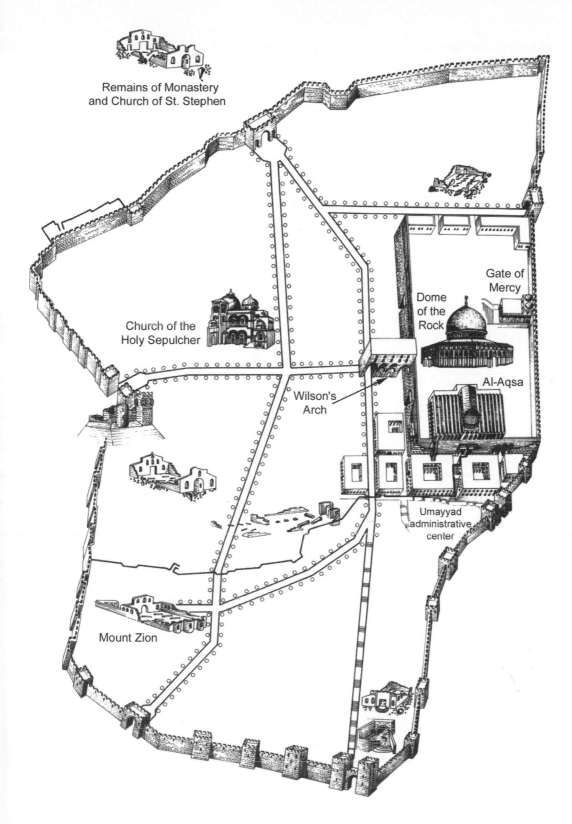

Remains of Monastery
and Church of St. Stephen

Church of the
Holy Sepulcher

Wilson's
Arch

Mount Zion

Dome
of the
Rock

Gate of
Mercy

Al-Aqsa

Umayyad
administrative
center

Jerusalem in the Early Arab period.

175

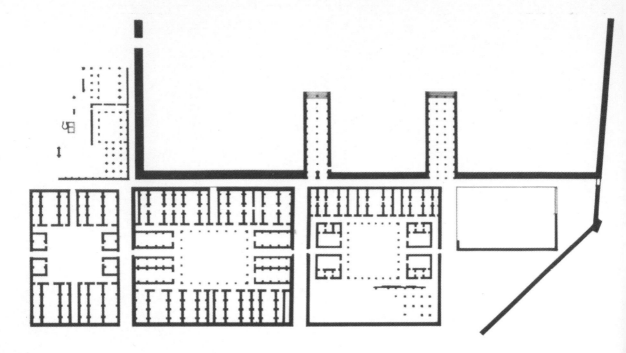

Plan of the Umayyad administrative center southwest of the Temple Mount.

Reconstruction of the Umayyad administrative center, view from the southwest.

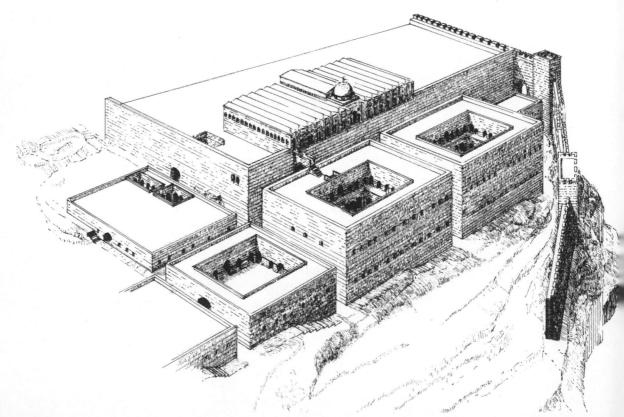

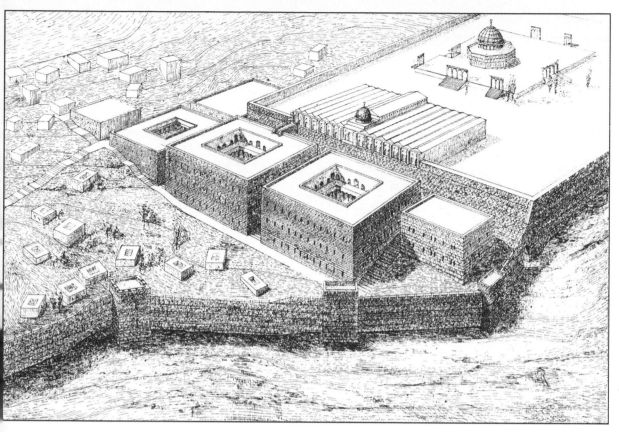

Reconstruction of the Umayyad administrative center, view from the southeast.

Jerusalem. Among the builders in Jerusalem were Armenians and Jews. Needing professionals in the various building trades—stonemasons, engravers and so on, as well as textile workers—the Arab authorities permitted the Jews to make their homes in the city. They lived at first in the Byzantine quarter, south of the Temple Mount, in homes whose occupants had been evacuated.

The Umayyads' first construction project was to repair the breaches in the walls surrounding the Temple Mount. They then went on to build the impressive arches in the southeastern part of the Mount popularly known as Solomon's Stables. Thus the Arabs, like Herod before them, constructed support for the large area of the Temple Mount. This enabled them to build the Al-Aqsa Mosque in the southern part of the Mount—which, as stated above, was originally a huge wooden structure. When Abd al-Malik became the caliph, he decided to construct an impressive building in the center of the Mount, in order to commemorate the place of Muhammad's ascent to heaven. The octagonal building known as the Dome of the Rock, erected in the year 691, one of the most beautiful creations of early Muslim architecture, is still considered one of the world's architectural and artistic wonders. In the year 711, Abd al-Malik's son and successor as caliph, Al-Walid I, replaced the wooden structure of Al-Aqsa with a stone one. After careful planning, at great expense, one of the largest Muslim buildings in Jerusalem was erected—the mosque was originally three times larger than it is today. The Arabs also restored what is known today

Stone and marble carvings and reliefs from the ruins of the Umayyad palace.

as "Wilson's Arch," which had been in ruins since the time of Titus, as well as the Hulda Gates, which were used to enter the Temple Mount area. Another impressive monument erected by the Umayyads in Jerusalem was the Golden Gate (or Gate of Mercy), which was intended to commemorate the place where Muhammad entered the enclosure and tethered his horse Burak. Only in the twentieth century was this site "moved" to the Western Wall, for political reasons.

Archaeological excavations in Jerusalem at the foot of the Temple Mount have uncovered exciting and important finds dating to the Umayyad dynasty, a period for which there is no written testimony and whose records rely mainly on archaeological finds. Among these finds are the remains of a large administrative complex, whose construction was begun by Abd al-Malik's sons, the caliph Al-Walid I and his brothers, the caliphs Suleiman and Hisham. In addition, the Umayyads, following the usual practice of the times, built a palace outside Jerusalem. Like the Hasmoneans, they located it in Jericho; it is known today as "Hisham's Palace." In Jerusalem itself they began to rebuild the Citadel in the west.

The difficult economic and social situation in which the empire found itself in the middle of the eighth century, together with religious aberrations and corruption, caused the Umayyad dynasty to fall. The caliphs' idea of moving the capital of the empire from Damascus to Jerusalem failed on the eve of its implementation, when a violent earthquake shook the Jordan Valley and Jerusalem (747), causing the buildings to collapse before completion. Three years later, in the year 750, a revolution erupted in the Muslim world: the Umayyad dynasty came to an end and the Abbasids took over. The new rulers turned eastward; for reasons of security they settled in the province of Iraq-Persia and made their new capital on the shores of the Tigris River, near the ruins of Ctesiphon, the former capital of Persia. It was the site of a small village, known in Persian as "Baghdad," meaning "village of gardens." The new name of the city, Dar al-Salaam, meaning "House of Peace," failed to take root, and the city—the capital of present-day Iraq—is still known by its Persian name, Baghdad.

The fall of the Umayyad dynasty closes a chapter in the history of the Middle East and of Jerusalem. The caliphs of the dynasty had succeeded in preserving the balance between the three religions in Jerusalem, and in perpetuating the city's sanctity to the new monotheistic religion, Islam.

(left) Capital from a column in the interior courtyard of the Umayyad palace. (right) Fresco from excavations of the Umayyad palace.

Reconstruction of the palace in the Umayyad administrative center, with Al-Aqsa Mosque above.

4. JERUSALEM UNDER THE ABBASIDS

The Umayyad administrative complex was destroyed during the rule of the Abbasid dynasty. Lime manufacturers set up kilns in the ruins, where they burned masonry from the ruins to make lime for construction in Jerusalem.

AFTER the Arab conquest, Iraq and Persia were administered by the family of Abbas, Muhammad's uncle, who established a seat of government at Kufah. The Abbasid governors disapproved of Mu'awiya's seizure of government, and only under duress recognized the new caliph. Opposition to the Umayyad dynasty was continuously flaring up among the Abbasids, and in 750 they declared war on the Umayyads and seized the throne. Although the Abbasids did not view Syria and the Holy Land as the main assets of the territory now under their control and did not invest greatly in their development, they understood the centrality of Jerusalem for Islam. Among other things, it would enable them more easily to deal with the Christian world—both the eastern and the western churches—which was looking covetously toward Jerusalem. The Frankish king Charlemagne, who considered himself the defender of the western world, negotiated with the Abbasid caliph Harun al-Rashid regarding Christianity's claims in Jerusalem. He obtained certain rights in connection with the Church of the Holy Sepulcher in Jerusalem, as well as permission to build a hostel for Christian pilgrims nearby. The Abbasids realized the advantage of concessions to Christianity in Jerusalem; the creation of a commercial center and meeting place for Christian pilgrims, merchants and politicians would both respond to European pressure and benefit their economy.

Harun al-Rashid's son, Abd al-Ma'mun, renovated the Dome of the Rock, which had been damaged in the earthquake of 747. In the course of the work, he erased the name of the builder,

The southern gates of the Temple Mount—the western Hulda Gate—during three periods:
(a) Second Temple; (b) Umayyad dynasty; (c) Abbasid dynasty.

Mediterranean Sea

Tyre

Acre
Haifa
Tiberias

Caesarea
Beth
Shean

Jaffa
Ramla
Jericho

Ashdod
Jerusalem
Gaza

0 10 20 Km

El-Arish

Ramla, founded during the rule of the Umayyad caliphs, was the principal government city in Palestine. Attempts were made at that time to establish Jerusalem as the capital of the entire empire. When the Umayyad dynasty fell, the idea was abandoned, and from then on Ramla became the main seat of government. Under the Abbasids and Fatimids Ramla was more important than Jerusalem.

Abd al-Malik, replacing it with his own name. Nevertheless, through a twist of history, this beautiful and important building was not credited to Abd al-Ma'mun: since he did not bother to read the entire inscription, and so failed to change the date of construction from 691—or the Muslim year 70 AH as recorded in Arabic—the forgery failed to obscure Abd al-Malik's role as builder of the Dome of the Rock.

The Abbasid caliphs also renovated the Al-Aqsa Mosque, which had also been seriously damaged in the earthquake, reducing it to one third of its original size. On the other hand, the Abbasids discontinued work on the administrative complex at the foot of the Temple Mount, which became a heap of ruins. Later, the debris and building remains were handed over to lime manufacturers, who set up kilns and used the masonry to make lime.

During the period of Abbasid rule over the Holy Land, various districts of the caliphate enjoyed a large measure of autonomy when the central government in Baghdad fell into decline. Several local governors and commanders rebelled against the central authorities and set up an autonomous government in the Holy Land, sometimes almost completely independent of Baghdad. The first such rebel, in 868, was a military officer named Ahmad Ibn Tulun, who was stationed in Egypt and built a magnificent mosque in Cairo, renowned in Muslim architectural history. He was followed by Al-Jaysh Humarawi (888), Muhammad Ibn Halanji (905) and Muhammad Ibn Tuag al-Ahshid (924), who set up an autonomous regime in the Holy Land centered at Ramla, which was then an important caravan and trade junction. Jerusalem retained its status as holy city and religious center, but its economic position had greatly weakened and there was almost no progress in public construction. Only in the second half of the tenth century, when the Holy Land was conquered by the caliphs of the North African Fatimid dynasty, did it begin to flourish once more, both materially and spiritually.

5. Jerusalem a Shi'ite City: The Fatimid Dynasty

In 909 a powerful Shi'ite Muslim state was established in North Africa, ruling over today's Morocco, Algeria, Tunisia and Libya. The founder of the dynasty, Sa'id, claimed to be a descendant of Muhammad's daughter Fatima, who was married to Ali, the last of the first four caliphs, and therefore proclaimed that he alone had the right to bear the title of caliph and lead the Muslim world. In the year 969 his heirs began to put his ideas into practice and to gain control of the entire empire. That same year Egypt was conquered by Jawhar al-Sikili, a renowned Fatimid general. His deputy, Ja'far, conquered the Holy Land and its

(right) A Fatimid military barracks was built along the Western Wall, on ruins from the Second Temple and Umayyad periods. Long corridor on the ground floor of the building.

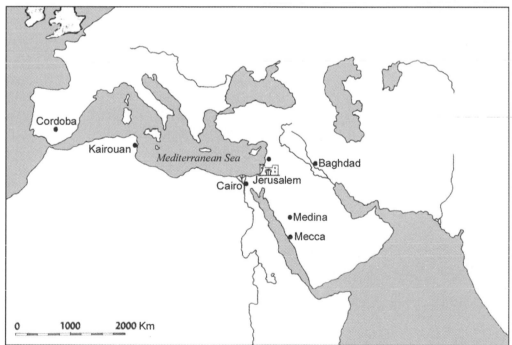

Following the fall of the Umayyads, under the Abbasids and Fatimids, the Arab empire was divided into three main monarchies: the Abbasid eastern kingdom, Fatimid Egypt and North Africa, and Umayyad Spain. Among the more important cities were the holy cities of Mecca, Medina and Jerusalem, as well as the capital cities of Baghdad, Cairo, Kairouan and Cordoba.

Excavations near the Temple Mount uncovered buildings dating to the period of Fatimid rule, in which there were pottery lamps characteristic of the period.

The builders of the Fatimid military barracks erected a system of arches to support the upper sections; they were also used as stables and storehouses. This system utilized Wilson's Arch, part of a structure built by the Umayyads.

"Bar Kalib N. N. R[abbi] Joseph N. N. Mutrah"—a Jew, perhaps a Karaite, who visited Jerusalem in the Fatimid period, carved his name in fulfillment of a vow.

capital Ramla, and reached Jerusalem.

A period of intense political turmoil now began in the Holy Land, and Jerusalem entered one of the most stormy periods of its history. In 974, the country fell to the Karmatians—members of an extremist Muslim sect whose members, like Christian monks, advocated a co-operative life and extreme asceticism. In the same year, the army of the Byzantine emperor John I Tzimisces invaded the Holy Land, and the inhabitants of Ramla and Jerusalem quickly sent him letters of surrender. Eager to realize the dream of the Byzantine emperors and restore Jerusalem to Christianity, Tzimisces began making his way to Jerusalem. Contemporary sources regarding these events are not sufficiently clear, and the history of the period is rather obscure. Only a few months later, the entire country was restored to Fatimid rule (976). Having defeated their enemies, the Fatimids began to organize the administration of the country on a long-term basis.

Jerusalem flourished under Fatimid rule. As a holy city, it now had to hold its own not only against the Christian world, but also against the Muslim holy cities of Mecca and Medina, which were both under the control of the Abbasid-

Sunnite caliphs, rivals of the Shi'ite Fatimids. Jerusalem thus became a center of intense religious activity, which left an indelible mark on construction in the city, as borne out by the remains of many contemporary inscriptions. The Citadel in the west of the city was rebuilt and a

יונה ושבתיה
אשתי מן
קליא חזקו
בחיים

אברהם בר
לולסאחוק

When the Fatimids ruled the Holy Land, many Jews, both Rabbanites and Karaites, came to Jerusalem, to visit the Temple Mount and its environs. Many of them incised their names on the walls as a sign of gratitude for being cured of illness.

"Jeremiah son of Gedaliah son of Rabbi Joseph"—a Jew who visited Jerusalem in the Fatimid period carved his name on a stone of the southern Temple Mount wall.

large military barracks for the Fatimid army erected just west of the Temple Mount, the builders of the latter utilizing the remains of structures from the Second Temple and Umayyad periods (in the area of "Wilson's Arch"). This second citadel was necessary to guard the Temple Mount and defend the Fatimid-Shi'ite army against the city's Sunnite population, as well as to supervise the worshipers on the Mount. In addition to residents of the city, many of the country's Sunnites visited the Temple Mount, and it was feared that disturbances and violence might take place during these pilgrimages.

Jerusalem's spiritual activities flourished even more than its construction.

A special literary genre emerged, known as "Praises of Jerusalem," *Fada'il al-Quds*, which was greatly encouraged by the Fatimid rulers for both internal and external reasons. Court poets and writers described the city's virtues in glowing terms, stating, for example, that two pilgrimages to Jerusalem were equivalent to fulfilling the commandment of Hajj (the pilgrimage to Mecca). On the basis of this extensive literature, some scholars have dated the sanctity of Jerusalem in Islam to the Fatimid period, but that is not the case. What is true is that Fatimid Jerusalem now asserted itself in relation to Mecca and Medina, the competing holy cities under rival Abbasid control; previously, Jerusalem's importance had pitted it against the Byzantine Empire and the Christian world.

One of the most outstanding Fatimid caliphs was Al-Hakim bi-Amr Allah, in short Al-Hakim, who ruled toward the end of the first millennium and the beginning of the second (996–1021). As a zealous Shi'ite Muslim, Al-Hakim dealt harshly with the infidels, both Christians and Jews, even destroying the Church of the Holy Sepulcher in 1009. Toward the end of his life he claimed to be a new Imam, revealed to his nation as the messenger of God. The Druse religion developed on the basis of this teaching.

After Al-Hakim's death, his followers fled to Egypt and the religious fanaticism of his reign gave way to a more tolerant attitude. The new rulers understood that there was no point in confrontation and persecution, which were liable to enflame Christian Europe and ignite a religious war.

Apart from Al-Hakim's brief reign, the Jewish community of Jerusalem flourished under the Fatimid dynasty. The Karaite Jewish community, in particular, enjoyed cooperation and help. The principles of Karaism and those of the Shi'ah were somewhat similar, in that they prescribed literal adherence to the primary written sources (the Bible and the Koran, respectively), rejecting later traditions. Perhaps Anan ben David, the founder of the Karaite sect, gleaned his ideas from his Shi'ite environment.

Many Jews and pseudo-converts served in senior positions in the caliphate and its institutions, such as the ministers Ben-Paltiel, Jacob ben Killis, Manasseh ben Abraham, and others. A great academy (yeshiva), known as *Ge'on Ya'akov*, flourished in Jerusalem at that time, and was a source of prestige and pride for the Jews. The heads of the academy, who held the title of "Gaon," were dedicated guardians of Jewish culture and education right up to the arrival of the Crusaders.

Jerusalem's prosperity under the Fatimids began to decline toward the end of the eleventh century. Struggles between the Fatimids and the Seljuks (see below) had a disastrous effect, and the population decreased significantly. The Crusader conquerors would shortly arrive to find a small and declining city.

6. JERUSALEM – CITY OF SELJUKS AND FATIMIDS

DURING the reign of the Abbasid dynasty the practice of hiring mercenary soldiers spread through the Islamic world and became a cornerstone of Muslim rule. The caliphs, fearing revolts by Arab commanders, began to build an army of mercenary soldiers and commanders, drawn from the subject nations. Although the mercenaries were, of course, converted to Islam, Muslim tradition barred them from serving as caliphs, as they were not "pure" Arabs.

Ruins of the early Byzantine-Arab wall, used as the foundation of the outer wall built by the Fatimids to defend the southern wall of the Temple Mount. Outer walls were built at several points around the city walls.

Eastern wall of Jerusalem: section of the wall near the southeast corner of the Temple Mount. This wall, begun in the Byzantine period, was also used at the beginning of the Arab period.

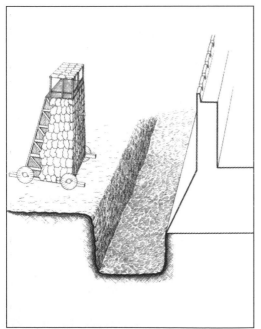

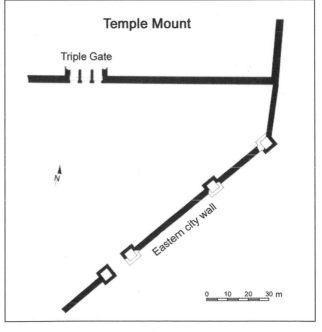

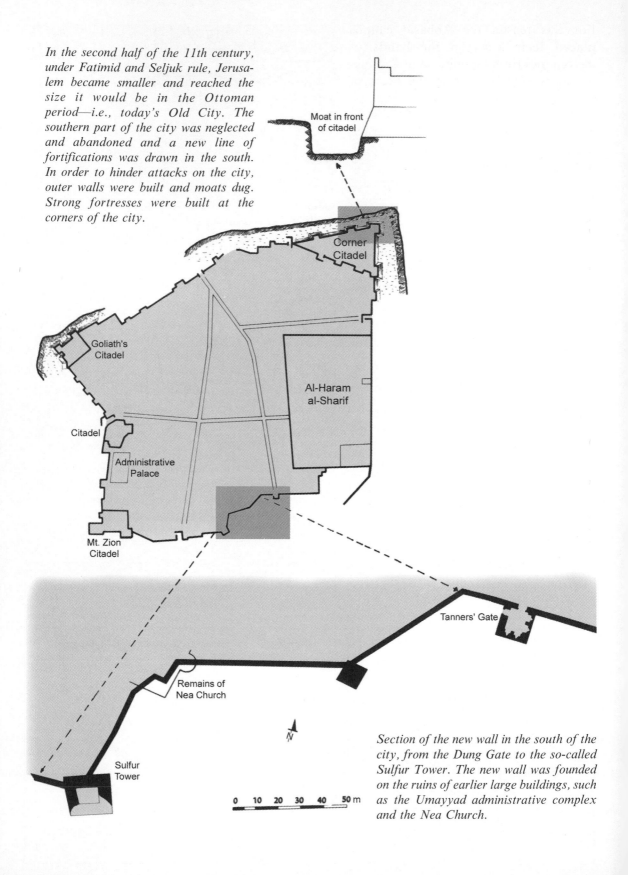

In the second half of the 11th century, under Fatimid and Seljuk rule, Jerusalem became smaller and reached the size it would be in the Ottoman period—i.e., today's Old City. The southern part of the city was neglected and abandoned and a new line of fortifications was drawn in the south. In order to hinder attacks on the city, outer walls were built and moats dug. Strong fortresses were built at the corners of the city.

Moat in front of citadel

Corner Citadel

Goliath's Citadel

Al-Haram al-Sharif

Citadel

Administrative Palace

Mt. Zion Citadel

Tanners' Gate

Remains of Nea Church

N

Sulfur Tower

0 10 20 30 40 50 m

Section of the new wall in the south of the city, from the Dung Gate to the so-called Sulfur Tower. The new wall was founded on the ruins of earlier large buildings, such as the Umayyad administrative complex and the Nea Church.

For this reason the Abbasid caliphs placed their army in the hands of mercenaries from a family named Seljuk, members of a tribe from the heart of Asia, at the empire's farthest reaches.

The Seljuks were converted to Islam and began serving in the Abbasid army. They gradually became skilled soldiers and rose to high military positions. After a few generations, the Seljuks regarded themselves as full-fledged Muslims and, contrary to accepted tradition, soon demanded a part in the government of the empire, particularly in light of the weakness and incompetence of some of the caliphs. The commander of the Seljuk army therefore appointed himself "sul-

(right) Tombstone of a Christian officer (probably a Copt) in the Fatimid army. He served and fell in Jerusalem and was buried together with thirty soldiers in a modest burial field near the southwest corner of the Temple Mount.

Moats were dug in the rock in some places in front of the city wall, in order to prevent siege machines from being brought up close to the city walls.

Additional wall erected in front of and close to the existing walls to obstruct siege machines, where excavation of a moat was either impossible or ineffective.

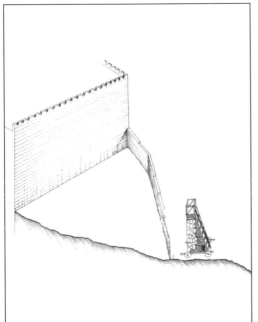

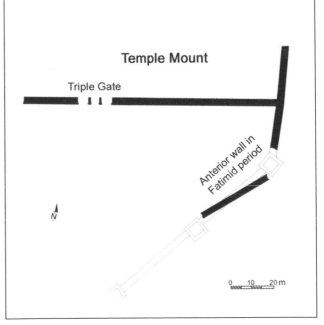

Temple Mount

Triple Gate

Anterior wall in Fatimid period

N

0 10 20 m

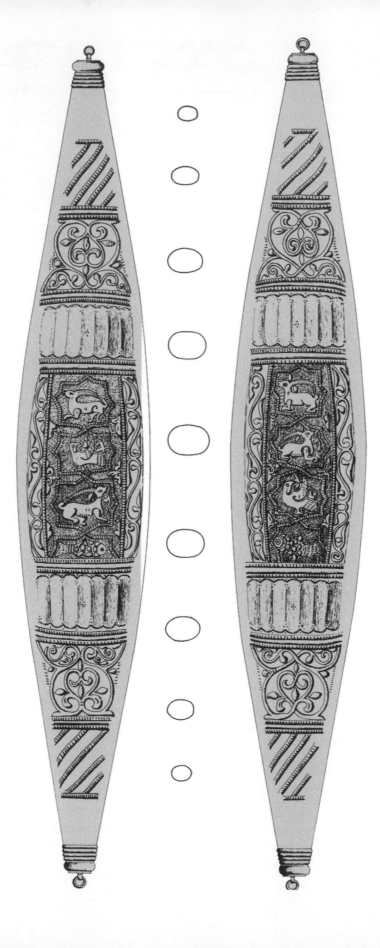

On the eve of the Crusader conquest, soldiers of the Fatimid army hid their property and salaries in the ruins at the foot of the Temple Mount. Shown here are gold coins found in one of these hoards, uncovered in the excavations at the foot of the southern wall.

tan," meaning ruler, and seized power, leaving the caliph only a nominal role, of mainly religious significance. The caliph's name was mentioned in Friday prayers and in the sermon, but in practice it was the sultan who governed all internal and external political affairs, as well as matters of security. The Seljuks, who were devout Sunnite Muslims, soon came into conflict with the Fatimid ambitions to impose the Shi'ite form of Islam on the entire Muslim empire. Besides these religious motives, the Seljuks were also motivated by political rivalry, their main goal being to restore the lands stolen from the empire in Palestine, Egypt and North Africa to their original owners.

(opposite) Silver strips in the best artistic tradition of the Fatimid period, hammered onto metal plates and made into bracelets—an item found in a hoard from the Fatimid period. Similar hoards discovered in excavations by the Temple Mount attest to the population's fear of imminent Crusader conquest.

Naturally, the campaign was launched in the Holy Land: in 1070 , the mercenaries, under the Seljuk commander, Atsiz, previously a mercenary in the Fatimid army, invaded and occupied the Holy Land, including Jerusalem, driving out the Fatimid army. They in fact penetrated Egyptian territory, but were eventually forced to withdraw.

The Holy Land and Jerusalem changed hands several times, from Fatimids to Seljuks and back, until it was difficult to keep up with events. A contemporary Muslim historian, Al-Qalqashandi, described the situation well in his book *Dabh al-A'sha*: "Nobody leaving on a journey could say in advance who might be the Muslim ruler of Jerusalem upon his return."

The city had been hard hit; it was falling into ruin and its population was rapidly dwindling. When the Crusaders later reached Jerusalem, they found walls and fortifications that had been built in haste by the Muslims—apparently under

Two possible interpretations of the description of Jerusalem's walls and gates by the Jerusalem historian Muqaddasi (985): small city with several gates in the southern wall (Y. Tsafrir); large city with eight gates (M. Ben-Dov).

Fatimid rule. The builders must have decided not to invest resources in fortifying the south of the city, which was already as good as lost: the inhabitants had left and their houses lay in ruins. Leaving the walls of the city in the north, west and east in their previous positions, the Fatimid builders built a southern wall along an entirely different course, running along a line north of the present southern wall (which was built later by Sultan Suleiman). Beginning at the southern end of the Al-Aqsa Mosque, it ran south for some 100 meters, then continued westward and climbed the slope of the western hill until it met the western wall of Mount Zion. The builders used the remains of the Umayyad government buildings and of the Nea Church in the foundation courses of the wall. Thus, the City of David, as well as Mount Zion and its slopes, were now left outside the city for the first time since the First Temple period. This created a serious weak point in Jerusalem's defenses, since Mount Zion stood at the same altitude as the city inside the walls, so that siege weapons could be brought up close to the wall. Furthermore, no attempt was made to dig a ditch or moat in front of the wall, as the Muslims believed—wrongly, as it turned out—that the Crusaders had no means of penetrating a fortified city and were ignorant of siege techniques. A few sites excavated outside the present Old City walls have yielded remains of walls and towers of the

Fatimid fortifications, reaching a height of several meters; it was at this time that loopholes for arrows were first used in wall towers. We believe that the construction and repair of the walls took three years, beginning with the first news of the Crusaders' departure from Europe and continuing until their arrival in the Holy Land. This was the same time that was needed to construct Suleiman's wall about five hundred years later.

Jerusalem's Fatimid wall was preceded by the Byzantine wall, which the Arabs repaired. Descriptions of this wall and its gates were provided by the Jerusalem historian Muqaddasi, who wrote in the second half of the tenth century (the beginning of the Fatimid regime). Muqaddasi describes and names eight gates sheathed in iron, each in its own gate tower. By his account, Jerusalem was then as large as it had been in Byzantine times.

Another source relates that Al-Hakim's successors, in the first half of the eleventh century, repaired the city gates, using among other things masonry from the churches destroyed by Al-Hakim. Was this repair also accompanied by a reduction in the city's size and the abandonment of its southern area? This was apparently not the case. A Muslim Persian traveler, Nasir-i Khosrau, who visited Palestine a few years later, in 1046, described the gates in the southern wall of the Temple Mount—the so-called Triple Gate and Double Gate—as being still in use. It necessarily follows that the entire length of the southern wall was still inside the city, because these gates were sealed with stones when the southern parts of the city were left outside. In addition, the remains of a large building, known in Jewish sources of the Fatimid period as "Bathsheba's Courtyard," were found to the south of the above-mentioned gates; this was a hostel, and it is clear from its plan that it was located within the city walls.

Thus, the wall that was standing on the eve of the Crusaders' arrival was the product of construction carried out toward the end of Fatimid rule. In order to place as many obstacles as possible in the way of the invaders, the Fatimid forces added walls in front of the existing walls. Modern excavations have uncovered the remains of some of these walls, and in addition they are described in Crusader accounts of the siege. As already stated, no new moats were dug, but the Fatimids used the old moats in the east and north. Jerusalem was therefore prepared for a crucial war, which would impinge on its future—a war that closed yet another chapter in its history and launched the momentous period of Christian Crusader rule in the city.

Chapter 8:

JERUSALEM, CAPITAL OF THE CRUSADER KINGDOM 1099–1260

1. THE CRUSADERS CONQUER JERUSALEM

GODFREY OF BOUILLON, DEFENDER OF THE HOLY SEPULCHER

THE last quarter of the eleventh century was one of the most tempestuous periods in the Middle East, especially in the Holy Land. The two Muslim powers, Fatimid-Shi'ite Egypt and Sunnite Iraq-Syria, ruled by the Seljuks, fought a bitter war, and their battle arena was the Holy Land; Jerusalem, the city sacred to both factions, found itself in the center of continuous fighting.

The fighting disrupted commerce and international trade routes, creating shortages of the essential goods produced in the east. Perfumes and incense were important for both personal and religious use; spices were indispensable for the food preserve industry serving the re-emerging urban society of Europe.

Above all, the scarcity of medicinal herbs was endangering lives. All these goods, normally brought from the east, were now in short supply in Europe. One of the causes of the Crusades, therefore, was probably the desire to reopen the international trade routes and put an end to the atmosphere of terror that reigned in the Middle East. Supporting evidence to that effect is the participation of the mercantile cities of Italy—Venice, Pisa, Genoa and Naples—in initiating and planning the Crusades, as well as providing military aid. The merchants of these cities were interested, first and foremost, in securing privileges in the ports of the Holy Land; Jerusalem, the holy city, was of only secondary concern. In addition, the pope was determined to divert the constant internecine strife in Christian Europe toward a war against the Muslims, the enemies of Christianity. Given the shortage of land in the European feudal system, due to the continuous redistribution of land to landowners'

Godfrey of Bouillon, one of the leaders of the Crusades, chosen to head the new kingdom with the title "Defender of the Holy Sepulcher."

Siege camps of the Crusaders' besieging forces; directions from which the walls were breached and stages of the battle.

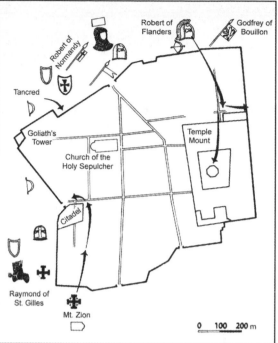

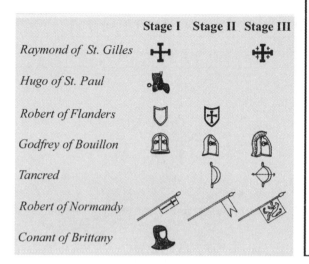

	Stage I	Stage II	Stage III
Raymond of St. Gilles			
Hugo of St. Paul			
Robert of Flanders			
Godfrey of Bouillon			
Tancred			
Robert of Normandy			
Conant of Brittany			

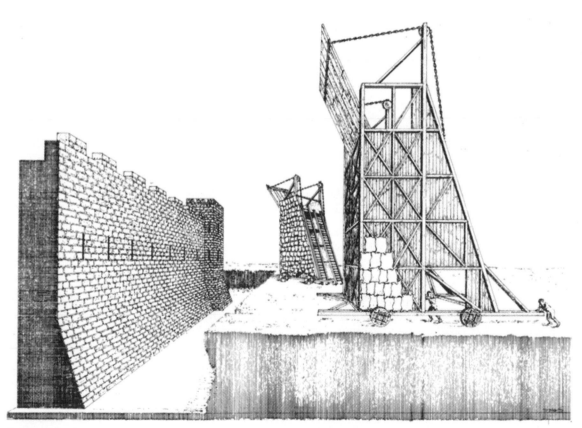

Sophisticated siege engine: mobile tower. The moat was dug to prevent such equipment from being brought up to the walls.

The Ottoman sultan Suleiman built the wall now known by his name mainly on the remains of previous walls—generally Fatimid fortifications which were also used in Crusader times.

and return Jerusalem to the bosom of Christianity.

From northern Syria the Crusaders marched south down the coast to Jaffa. Lacking knowledge of siege warfare, they failed to capture even one fortified city from the Muslims on their way. Over-estimating the Crusaders' ability, the Fatimid garrison fled from Jaffa, so that, for the first time, the Crusaders were able to capture a bridgehead for the continuation of their journey to Jerusalem. The Christians surrounded Jerusalem on all sides, setting up several siege camps. On June 15, 1099, after a two-month siege, the walls of the city were breached and the Crusaders swarmed into the city. The city's defenders, the Egyptian Fatimid army, together with the Muslim and Jewish civilian residents, were mercilessly slaughtered—the cruelty of the Crusaders knew no limits.

The fall to the infidels of what had now become a revered holy city shocked the entire Muslim world. Exploiting the consternation of the Muslims, the Crusaders swept the country, laying the foundations of the Crusader Kingdom of Jerusalem, which was to survive for almost two hundred years.

After the conquest, the Crusaders began to consolidate their rule in Jerusalem as the capital, to rebuild it and restore the splendor of the Christian city from which Christians had been banished for 450 years. Since the proclaimed goal of the Crusade was to liberate the Holy Sepulcher and the other holy places from the Muslims, the Crusaders immediately turned their attention to the structures sacred to Christians, which were either in ruins and/or greatly neglected. The Temple Mount, now consecrated by the

sons and heirs, the Europeans were forced to turn to the east for further sources of arable land. Indeed, after conquering parts of northern Syria, some leaders of the Crusade considered halting their journey to Jerusalem and remaining on the occupied land.

In sum: the Crusaders were motivated by social, economic and political factors—although they bore a religious banner, responding to the call of the leaders of Europe, headed by the pope, to liberate the Holy Sepulcher from Islam

Muslims, had also been captured. Awed by the beauty of the Al-Aqsa Mosque and the Dome of the Rock—triumphs of architectural achievement and construction—the Crusaders refrained from destroying them. They merely removed the Muslim crescents from the buildings and replaced them with crosses.

With the establishment of the Crusader kingdom in Jerusalem, the leaders of the Crusade had to choose a king. Because of internal quarrels and jealousy the choice fell on the weakest among them: Godfrey of Bouillon, who was unsuited to the task, rather than Tancred or Raymond of Saint Gilles. Godfrey was not given the title "King of Jerusalem," because of the envy of the other commanders. The

The Crusader kings were buried in a room east of the main entrance of the Holy Sepulcher Church, at the foot of Golgotha. The tombs disappeared at the beginning of the 19th century, but had been copied by a Franciscan monk named Eleazarus Horn in the 18th century.

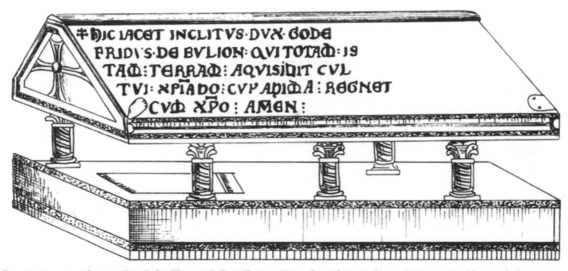

Inscription on the tomb of Godfrey of Bouillon: "Here lies the celebrated Duke Godfrey of Bouillon, who won the whole of this country to the Christian religion. May his soul reign with Christ. Amen."

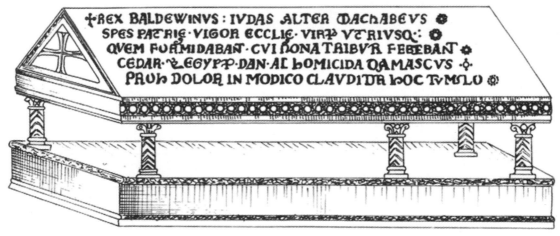

Inscription on the tomb of Baldwin: "King Baldwin, another Judah Maccabee, hope of his homeland, vigor of the church, pride of both. Who was feared by, and to whom tribute was brought by Kedar, Egypt, Dan and murderous Damascus. How great the sorrow that he is enclosed in such a small tomb."

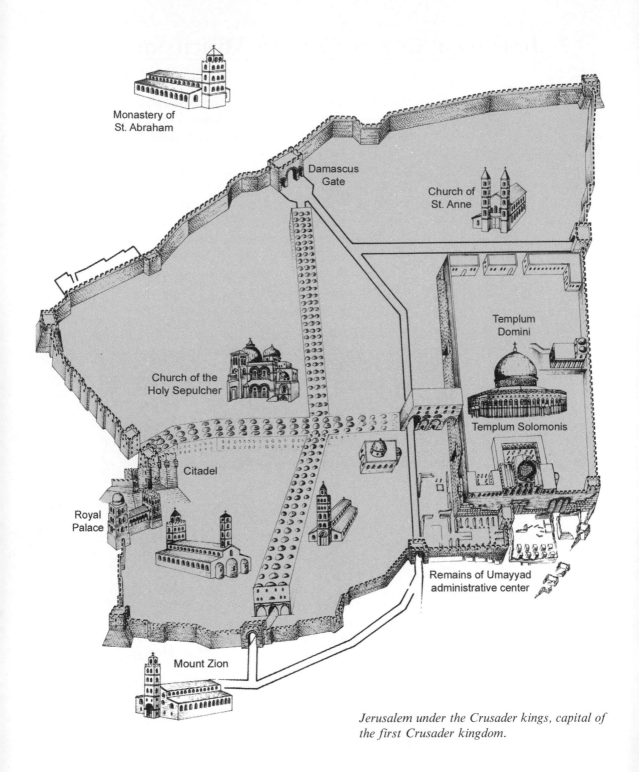

Monastery of
St. Abraham

Damascus
Gate

Church of
St. Anne

Templum
Domini

Church of the
Holy Sepulcher

Templum Solomonis

Citadel

Royal
Palace

Remains of Umayyad
administrative center

Mount Zion

*Jerusalem under the Crusader kings, capital of
the first Crusader kingdom.*

"official" explanation was ideological:
"How can a man born of woman bear
the title 'King of Jerusalem,' where only
one person, Christ the Lord, has
reigned?" So Godfrey was enthroned as
"Defender of the Holy Sepulcher" in a
magnificent ceremony held at the Church
of the Nativity in Bethlehem.

2. JERUSALEM, CITY OF GOD AND MERCHANTS

AFTER serving as "Defender of the Holy Sepulcher" for only one year, Godfrey sickened and died, to be succeeded on the throne by his brother, Baldwin I. The conquerors' envy had already faded, and Baldwin was crowned as "King of Jerusalem." The Crusaders' first efforts in rebuilding Jerusalem were devoted to repairing the breaches in the walls. The Crusaders had found a well fortified city, with a sturdy wall, extra front walls at some vulnerable points and rock-cut ditches at other places. As already men-

tioned, arrow loopholes first appeared in fortifications in the eleventh century, and these had already been used in the Fatimid wall. For the most part, therefore, the Crusaders inherited Jerusalem's fortifications, including the city, from the Fatimids, except for some repairs and improvements. The Crusaders built strong fortresses at the corners of the city, such as the so-called "Goliath's Tower" in the northwest (known in Arabic as *Burj Jalud*). The name of this tower, built of huge stones from the

The Crusaders rebuilt the Church of the Holy Sepulcher. Most of today's structure dates to their time. Shown here is the nave with its cupola and galleries.

The Crusader period in Jerusalem was noted for its vigorous construction, particularly of religious buildings such as churches, convents and monasteries, as well as marketplaces and hospices. The walls and gates were repaired and much effort and funds invested in their reinforcement. The construction took place in all parts of the city and in its environs.

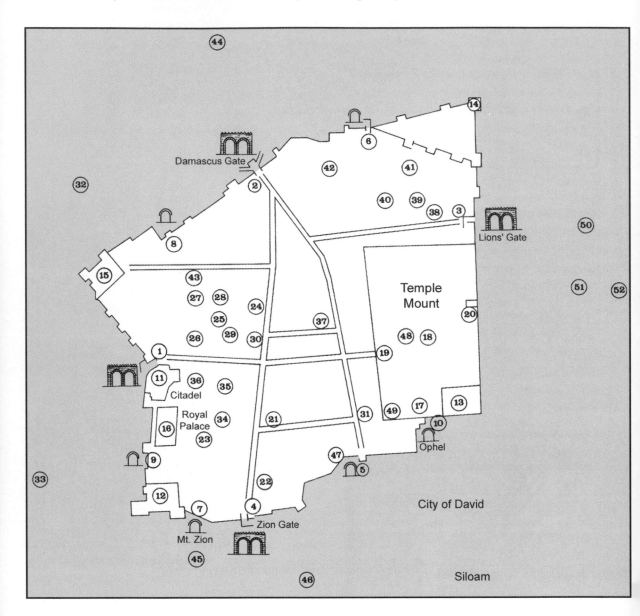

remains of the Psephinus Tower built there by Herod, attests to its Muslim origin. The Crusaders also inherited from the Fatimids the western Citadel, near the Jaffa Gate, and made improvements in it. To the south of the Citadel they built the palace of the Crusader kings, in the area of today's *Kishle.*

The Holy Sepulcher and the church built around it, the objectives of the Crusades, became an architectural challenge for the Kingdom of Jerusalem. Construction of a new church took fifty years, and in 1149 it was dedicated in a magnificent ceremony. It will be recalled that the fanatical Fatimid caliph Al-

The Crusader conquest of Jerusalem was accompanied by brutal slaughter of Muslims and Jews. Many of those who were not put to the sword were condemned to slavery, while others fled or were expelled from the city. The Crusaders began to rebuild Jerusalem as a purely Christian city. Churches and monasteries were built in and around Jerusalem. Jerusalem was designed to be not only a holy city but also a center of international trade. Hospices were built for pilgrims, as well as marketplaces. The Fatimid fortifications were repaired and improved and a royal palace built near the Citadel.

Map of the main buildings (opposite):

1. David's Gate
2. St. Stephen's Gate
3. Jehoshaphat's Gate
4. Zion Gate
5. Tanners' Postern
6. Postern
7. Belcayre's Postern
8. Lazarus' Postern
9. Palace Postern
10. Temple Postern
11. The Citadel
12. Southwest Tower
13. Southeast Tower
14. Stork Tower
15. Tancred's Tower
16. Royal Palace
17. Templum Solomonis
18. Templum Domini
19. Beautiful (Splendid) Gate
20. Golden Gate
21. Venetian Church
22. St. Stephen's Monastery (Armenian)
23. St. James's Cathedral
24. St. Mary la Latine Church
25. St. Mary la Grande Church
26. St. John the Baptist's Church
27. Church of the Holy Sepulcher
28. Monastery of Canons of the Holy Sepulcher
29. Hospitallers' markets
30. Covered markets
31. St. Mary of the Germans' Church
32. Leper Monastery of St. Lazarus
33. St. George's Church
34. Church of St. Thomas
35. St. Mark's Monastery (Syrian)
36. Chapel of St. James the Less
37. St. Julian's Church
38. St. Anne's Church
39. Church of the Sheep's Pool (Probatica)
40. St. Elijah's Church
41. Church of St. Mary Magdalene
42. Church of St. Agnes
43. Patriarch's Palace
44. St. Stephen's Church
45. St. Mary of Mt. Zion Church
46. Church of St. Peter in Gallicantu
47. Cattle market
48. Baptistery
49. Templar Knights' headquarters
50. Church of St. Mary's Tomb
51. Church of Gethsemane
52. Church of the Ascension

Hakim had destroyed the earlier large church, and after his reign, still under Muslim rule, a modest church was erected on the ruins. The Crusaders now built a huge basilica at the site, adjoining the "rotunda" that protected the traditional site of Jesus' tomb. In another corner, the structure of Golgotha, the rock on which the Crucifixion was believed to have taken place, was restored, and in the east a spacious courtyard was renovated, for use as a cloister. The monks who lived there served the entire institution. The best artists of the period decorated the church, paying special attention to car-

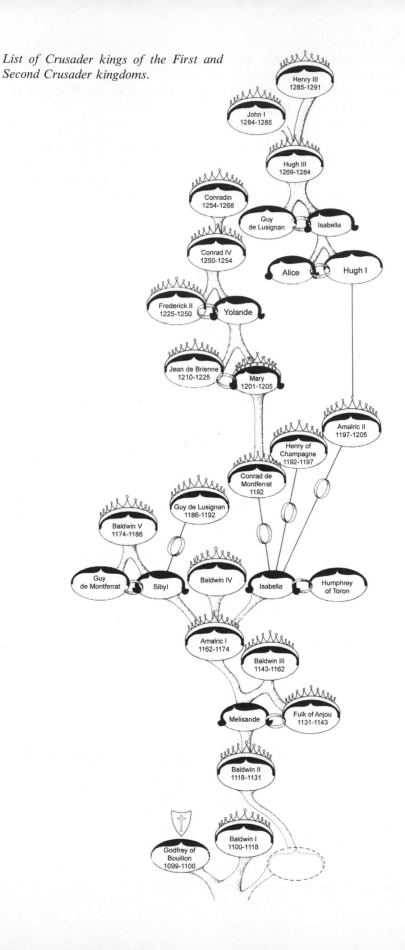

List of Crusader kings of the First and Second Crusader kingdoms.

Henry III
1285-1291

John I
1284-1285

Hugh III
1269-1284

Conradin
1254-1268

Guy
de Lusignan

Isabella

Conrad IV
1250-1254

Alice

Hugh I

Frederick II
1225-1250

Yolande

Jean de Brienne
1210-1225

Mary
1201-1205

Amalric II
1197-1205

Henry of
Champagne
1192-1197

Conrad de
Montferrat
1192

Guy de Lusignan
1186-1192

Baldwin V
1174-1186

Guy
de Montferrat

Sibyl

Baldwin IV

Isabella

Humphrey
of Toron

Amalric I
1162-1174

Baldwin III
1143-1162

Melisande

Fulk of Anjou
1131-1143

Baldwin II
1118-1131

Godfrey of
Bouillon
1099-1100

Baldwin I
1100-1118

202

ving the façade and the lintels of the great double entrance. The kings of Jerusalem were buried in the Church of the Holy Sepulcher, and their tombstones could be seen there until the end of the eighteenth century.

The Church of the Holy Sepulcher was not the only holy site restored by the Crusaders; many other churches were rebuilt and renovated, and dozens of new ones erected, both inside the city and in its environs—on Mount Zion and the Mount of Olives, at Gethsemane, near the Damascus Gate, in the Valley of the Cross and elsewhere.

The shortage of military manpower for the king's army revitalized the Christians socially and culturally. Various religio-military orders were established, whose members took monastic vows, though their principal function was soldiering. Two of these orders were established in the first days of the kingdom: the Knights of St. John of Jerusalem, or the Knights Hospitallers—so called because its primary aim was to provide hospital and other care for pilgrims; and the Knights Templars, named for the Temple Mount in Jerusalem, where their headquarters were located. The Hospitallers' headquarters were in a large complex close to the Church of the Holy Sepulcher, containing monasteries, three churches and many markets.

The Crusaders soon found their place in the international commerce of the Holy Land, which offered considerable potential for profit. Large markets were built in Jerusalem, which also met the needs of the increasing flow of pilgrims. Jerusalem's markets were renowned—

Emblems of the city were often reproduced on the seals of the kings of Jerusalem: the Church of the Holy Sepulcher, the Citadel and the royal palace to its south.

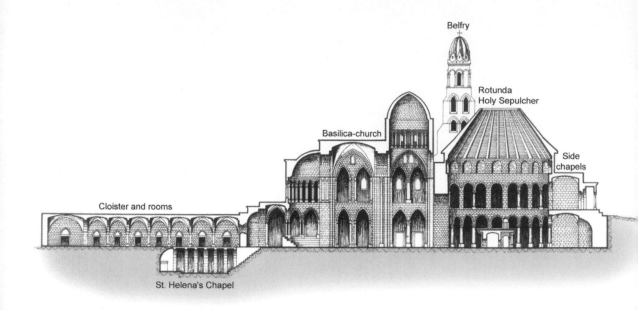

Belfry

Rotunda
Holy Sepulcher

Basilica-church

Side
chapels

Cloister and rooms

St. Helena's Chapel

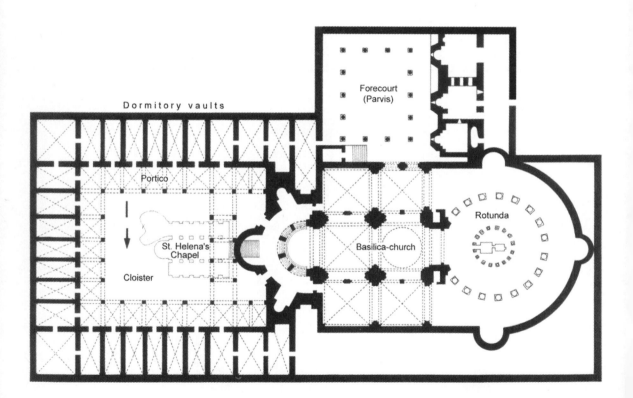

Dormitory vaults

Forecourt
(Parvis)

Portico

Rotunda

St. Helena's
Chapel

Basilica-church

Cloister

The Church of the Holy Sepulcher, which had suffered greatly at the beginning of the 11th century at the hands of the Fatimid caliph Al-Hakim, was the chief target of Crusader hopes. Large sums were invested in rebuilding it and the adjacent monastery. In 1149, fifty years after the conquest of Jerusalem, the magnificent new church was inaugurated with much pomp and circumstance. Most of today's building dates to that time. Shown above: section and plan of the church, the rotunda and the monastery.

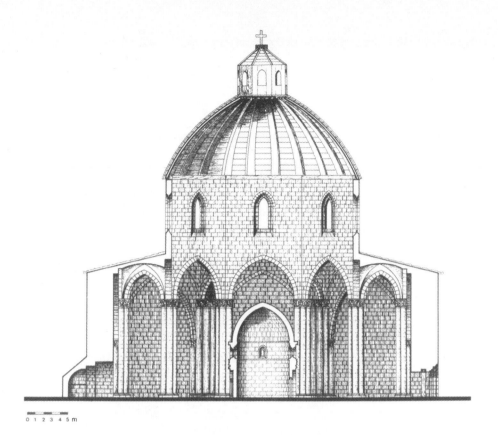

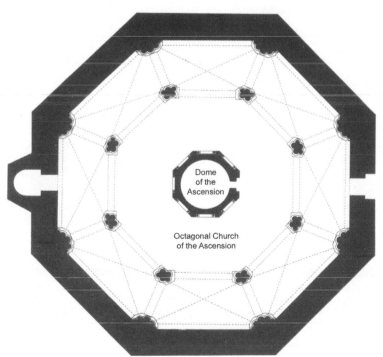

Dome
of the
Ascension

Octagonal Church
of the Ascension

Church of the Ascension on the Mount of Olives, rebuilt by the Crusaders on the ruins of an earlier Byzantine church. It was an octagonal structure supporting a cupola, with an octagonal edicule in the center marking the traditional site of Jesus' ascension to heaven. The building still stands today. Shown here: section and plan of the Church of the Ascension.

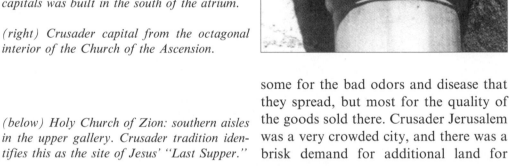

(above) Crusader basket capital from the parvis (forecourt) of the Church of the Holy Sepulcher; a row of columns with basket capitals was built in the south of the atrium.

(right) Crusader capital from the octagonal interior of the Church of the Ascension.

(below) Holy Church of Zion: southern aisles in the upper gallery. Crusader tradition identifies this as the site of Jesus' "Last Supper."

some for the bad odors and disease that they spread, but most for the quality of the goods sold there. Crusader Jerusalem was a very crowded city, and there was a brisk demand for additional land for

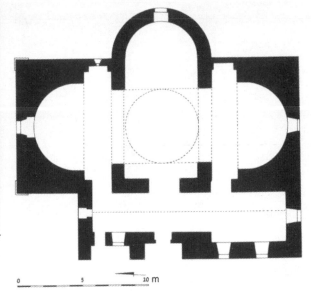

Elbow capital—a characteristic feature of Crusader architecture, from the German Center on the slope of the Jewish Quarter.

(right) The center of the Hospitaller Knights near the Church of the Holy Sepulcher included covered markets and three churches with adjacent hospices. The smallest and most modest of the churches was that named for John the Baptist, the patron of the Order. Shown here: plan and section of St. John the Baptist's Church.

(below) Holy Church of Zion: cloister of the Crusader monastery.

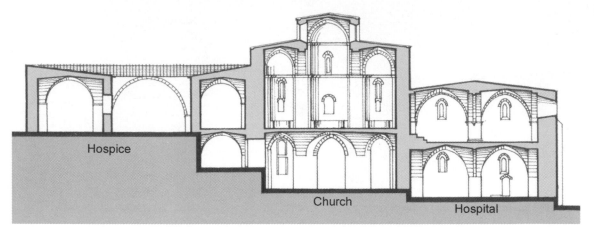

The Hospitaller Order included a group of German knights who wished to establish their own independent order; they succeeded in doing so only in the 13th century, during the reign of Frederick II. While part of the Hospitallers they established a separate center opposite the Temple Mount, on the slopes of today's Jewish Quarter. The center included a hospice, a church and a hospital, which have been uncovered in archaeological excavations. Shown above: section of the German Center (subsequently the Teutonic Center), with the church in the center, the hospital on the right and the hospice on the left.

The German knights built their center on the slope of what is today the Jewish Quarter. In the center of the hostel there was a small courtyard, with a large arch on its west providing access to the street and a stairway to the upper residential floor.

A pair of Crusader capitals from the doorpost of the Gate of the Chain—one of the main gates of the Temple Mount enclosure, on the site of the Crusader Beautiful (or Splendid) Gate.

St. Anne's Church, named for Jesus' grandmother, was built near the Lions' Gate. Its upkeep was paid for with the rent from several shops in Jerusalem's covered markets. Shown here is a section of the church.

Reconstruction of the facade of St. Anne's Church. A bell tower once stood to the right of the entrance.

construction. The city prospered, its inhabitants gaining their livelihoods from commerce, tourism and the pilgrim trade. Evidence of the crowding in the city is the fact that markets reached right up to the city gates. The defensive gate towers were built outside the city to save space for construction; a defensive tower might sometimes occupy an area of 120 square meters, so that locating it outside the city saved a great deal of space. Centuries

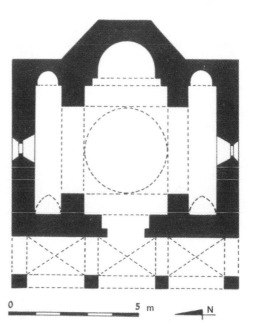

As well as large churches, many small chapels were built in Jerusalem for members of the various small sects active in the capital. One of them is the Church of St. Eli, known today as Deir al-Adas (Monastery of the Lentils).

(opposite) In addition to religious buildings, the Crusaders also built covered markets to serve the increasing pilgrim traffic and the European merchants, especially from the Italian merchant cities.

later, in the thinly populated Ottoman city, the defense towers would be built on the gates, projecting into the city, as can be seen today at the Damascus, Zion and Lions' Gates.

In the course of time the Crusaders permitted the Jews and Muslims to visit the city and even to settle there. This was in order to meet day-to-day needs: the lively trade required professionals in the fields of trade and banking, translators and people well acquainted with the east and able to travel far for commercial purposes. Nevertheless, despite such co-operation in commercial and economic life, the wars between the army of the Kingdom of Jerusalem and various Muslim armies continued. Although on the surface the Muslims seemed to have accepted the status quo, they never really forgot the loss of Jerusalem and eagerly awaited an opportunity for revenge.

3. THE CRESCENT RETURNS TO JERUSALEM

SALADIN, HERO OF ISLAM

THE Crusaders in the Holy Land made every possible mistake in their relations with the Muslim world surrounding them. From time to time, when political relations between the Muslims and the Crusaders seemed to have stabilized and peaceful relations seemed possible, one of the kings or barons would launch a military adventure. The Crusaders also mismanaged their internal politics and social life. Rather than absorb the local Christians and assimilate with them, they curtailed their rights in the holy places and discriminated against them economically. The local Christians, members of the eastern churches, were not accepted into European colonial society. They suffered abuse, scorn and humiliation from the Crusaders, and eventually even preferred to return to Muslim rule just to throw off the yoke of the Crusader "liberators."

The Crusaders failed to understand the legitimate interests of the Muslims in Jerusalem, a city sacred to them as well, the location of some of their most important holy sites: upon the Temple Mount stood the third holiest mosque in

The Ayyubid sultan Saladin, who united Egypt and Syria.

Islam, as well as the Dome of the Rock, symbol of Muhammad's ascent to heaven. Since the Muslims were in any case permitted to live in the city, the Crusaders could have compromised and re-

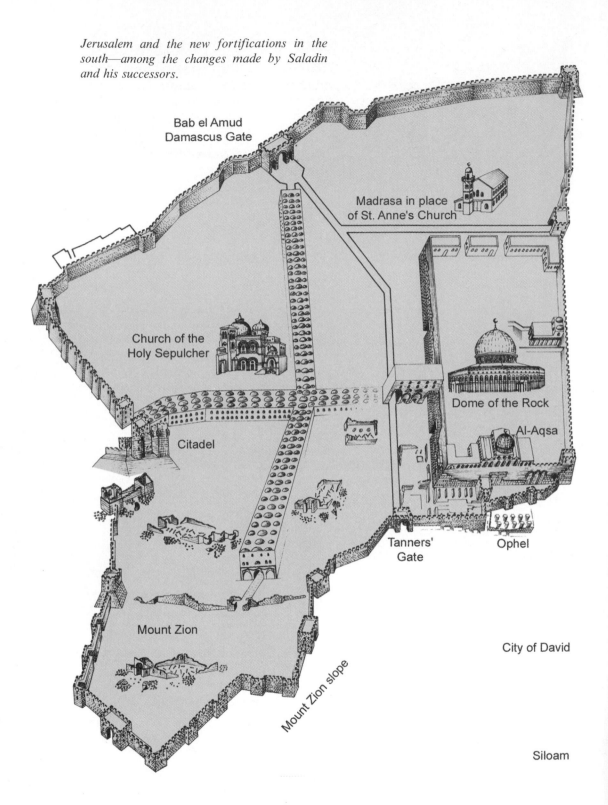

Jerusalem and the new fortifications in the south—among the changes made by Saladin and his successors.

Bab el Amud
Damascus Gate

Madrasa in place
of St. Anne's Church

Church of the
Holy Sepulcher

Dome of the Rock

Al-Aqsa

Citadel

Tanners'
Gate

Ophel

Mount Zion

City of David

Mount Zion slope

Siloam

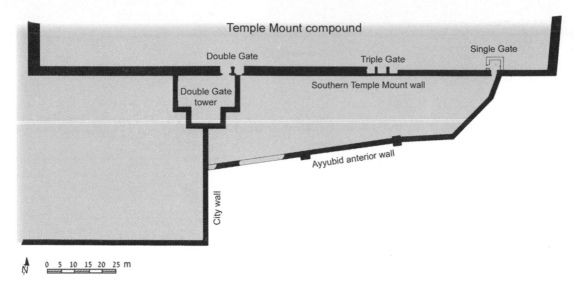

Temple Mount compound

Double Gate

Triple Gate

Single Gate

Double Gate tower

Southern Temple Mount wall

Ayyubid anterior wall

City wall

N

0 5 10 15 20 25 m

Saladin and his first successors improved and expanded Jerusalem's fortifications. Mount Zion was now included in the boundaries of the city, and a strong outer wall was built in the southeast to protect the southern wall of the Temple Mount, a vulnerable point of Jerusalem's defenses. Shown here is the plan of the outer wall that Saladin built in the southeast of the city. Later, the Ayyubid ruler of Damascus, Al-Malik al-Mu'azzam 'Isa, destroyed the fortifications of the city in the fear that the Crusaders might capture the city and would then easily entrench themselves there.

turned these sites to Muslim institutions. But the Crusaders compounded their errors, establishing the headquarters of the Templar Order on the Temple Mount and converting many buildings sacred to Islam into churches. These actions were serious affronts to Muslim pride, and the liberation of Jerusalem from the Crusaders emerged as a pan-Muslim dream.

For several generations, as we have seen, the Muslim rulers had manned their armies with mercenaries who, they believed, would not endanger their own power. In the twelfth century many officers and soldiers at the courts of the Fatimid caliphs in Egypt were members of the Kurdish-Sunnite communities, brought from Persia and Anatolia. In 1169, taking advantage of the regime's weakness, one of these Kurdish mercenaries seized power from the sultan and crowned himself Sultan of Egypt. His name was Saladin or, in Arabic, Salah al-Din Yusuf el-Ayyub—the dynasty that he founded is therefore known as the

Ayyubid dynasty. The new sultan's primary goal was the expulsion of the Crusaders from Jerusalem. To that end he took two preliminary steps: he united Syria and Egypt, and trained an army in

After Saladin conquered Jerusalem, some churches were destroyed and others converted into Muslim religious institutions. Human figures and statues adorning Christian buildings in the city were also destroyed, including the capitals of the Gate of the Chain, which depicted Daniel in the lions' den.

Coastal campaign
Jordan Valley campaign
Central campaign
Saladin's forces
Al-Adil's forces
Other forces

0 10 20 Km

In July 1187 Saladin trounced the Crusader armies at the Horns of Hittin, overlooking Tiberias and the Sea of Galilee. Eager to take advantage of his stunning victory, the sultan split his army and sent forces to various Crusader strongholds throughout the country. Naturally, an important force was sent to Jerusalem, which quickly surrendered to the Muslim forces.

isolated Christian enclave, which the Muslim troops surrounded and besieged upon reaching it on September 17, 1187. One of the Muslim camps was set up on Mount Zion, exactly where the Crusaders had camped when they had besieged the city eighty-eight years before. After exhausting negotiations, Sala-din received the keys to the city on October 2, 1187, and the besieged Crusaders were allowed to leave the city in return for a large ransom. The large golden cross on the Al-Aqsa Mosque, which had been converted into a church by the Templars, was removed by Saladin's soldiers and dragged through the streets. The Temple Mount was again a Muslim place of worship, and on Friday, October 9, the traditional Friday services were held there once again before a large crowd. The qadi (Muslim religious judge) of Damascus, who had come especially to Jerusalem, delivered a fervent sermon on the significance of Jerusalem's conquest for the Islamic world.

Saladin lost no time in putting the Islamic imprint on the city. Churches were converted into mosques, the bells were removed from church towers, crosses and other Christian symbols disappeared and buildings were purged with special rose oil brought from Teheran. The sultan established Islamic religious schools or colleges (Arabic: madrasas) in Jerusalem; among others, St. Anne's Church near the Lions' Gate (the traditional site of the home of Anne and Joachim, the Virgin Mary's parents)

tactics for which the Crusaders would be unprepared. Saladin was successful on both fronts; his efforts hastened the end of the Kingdom of Jerusalem, whose institutions and leadership were in any case riddled with corruption and decay.

On July 4, 1187, Saladin's army won a decisive victory against the Crusaders at the foot of a hill near Tiberias known as the Horns of Hittin. Exploiting the shock of their victory, the Muslim sultan's army invaded the Crusader kingdom from several directions, and quickly overran it almost entirely. Jerusalem was now an was converted into one of these colleges. In time these religious colleges became the representatives of Islam in Jerusalem. A magnificent walnut pulpit—made in anticipation of the "liberation"—was brought to Al-Aqsa Mosque. It stood in the mosque for almost eight hundred years, until it was destroyed in 1968 in a fire set by a mentally ill Christian, named Dennis Rohan, from Australia.

Knowing that the Christians would not take the fall of their kingdom and its capital Jerusalem lightly, Saladin began to prepare the city for a long siege. The experience of previous wars had taught him that the weakest point in the city's defenses was Mount Zion, outside the walls to the south. He therefore began to build a new wall, with a ditch just beyond, all around Mount Zion, to include that area within the walled area of Jerusalem. His successors continued the construction of this wall.

Having celebrated his victory, the conquering sultan also turned his attention to the few remaining pockets of Crusader resistance in the rest of the country. At the same time, he continued to fortify Jerusalem against the anticipated Christian avenging onslaught.

4. FREDERICK II, GERMAN EMPEROR AND KING OF JERUSALEM

SPURRED on by the loss of the Kingdom of Jerusalem, the Christians in Europe indeed launched a new crusade to restore the Holy Land to Christendom and recapture Jerusalem from the Muslims. This campaign, the Third Crusade (1189–1192), was headed by Emperor Frederick I of Germany (nicknamed "Barbarossa" = Red-beard), Philip II Augustus, king of France, and Richard I the Lion-heart, king of England. Frederick Barbarossa drowned on the way, in an attempt to swim a stream in Anatolia, and the journey continued in an atmosphere of anarchy and lack of leadership. Upon reaching Palestine, the Crusaders engaged the Muslims in a series of battles in the coastal region. The battle for the road to Jerusalem, which took place on the Ramla-Latrun plain, was one of the longest and most bitter: the fortresses at Latrun and Ramla changed hands several times until a cease-fire was declared. Under the cease-fire agreement, Jerusa-

Silver coins from a hoard discovered in excavations near the Temple Mount. Minted in Poland in the 13th century, they were buried in the debris to save them from plunder by the Khwarizmian Turks attacking Jerusalem.

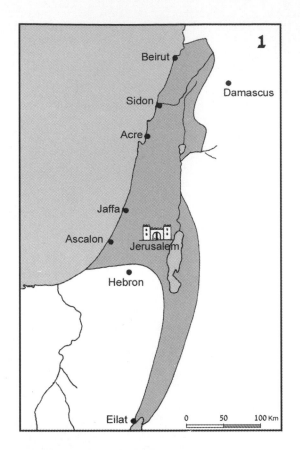

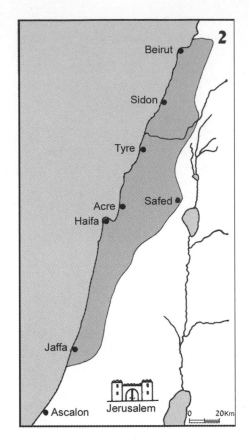

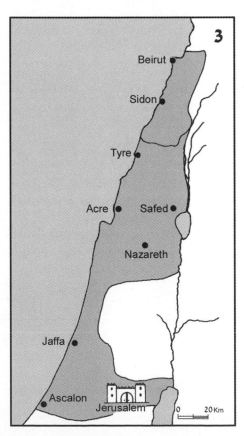

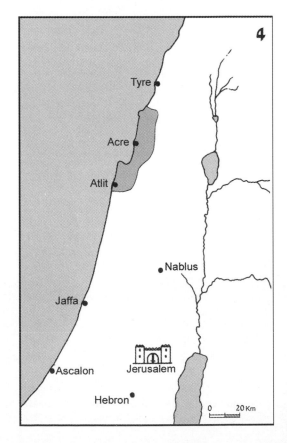

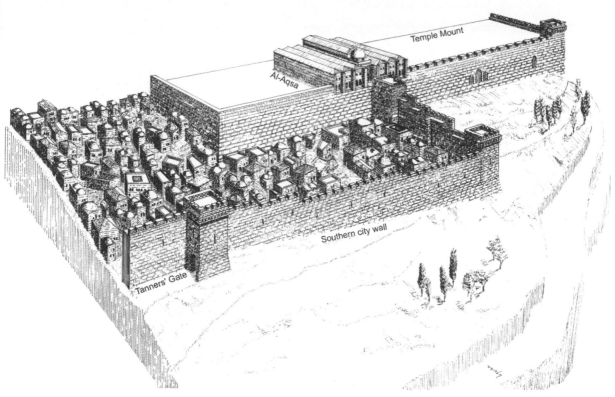

Reconstruction of the southern end of the Temple Mount in the second quarter of the 13th century. The Temple Mount was controlled by the Muslims, while the city was ruled by the Christian Crusaders. Until the Khwarizmian conquest (1244), the densely populated residential neighborhoods flourished, including those at the foot of the Temple Mount.

(opposite) The Crusader kingdom was called the "Kingdom of Jerusalem" and its king "the King of Jerusalem," even when Acre was capital and not Jerusalem, and when the King lived in Cyprus and there was no Crusader force in Palestine.

Four stages in the development of the Crusader Kingdom of Jerusalem:

(1) The First Kingdom at the height of its expansion—c. 1160.

(2) The Second Kingdom of Jerusalem, after Frederick II, according to the agreements concluded by Thibaut of Champagne and Richard of Cornwall in 1241.

(3) The kingdom after the voyage of Louis IX (St. Louis), in 1254.

(4) The Kingdom of Jerusalem after the extensive conquests of Sultan Baybars, during the decline of the Crusader kingdom, c. 1270.

lem remained in Muslim hands, and the second Crusader Kingdom of Jerusalem was confined to a narrow strip of the coast, with its capital at Acre.

After Saladin's death his heirs divided up his territory among themselves. The unification of Syria and Egypt, which had been a decisive factor in opposition to the Crusader conquest, collapsed. Although the heads of both states were descendants of Saladin, their relations were marred by constant hatred and tension. At times the Muslim rulers made common cause with the Crusaders.

At the beginning of the thirteenth century, fearing a new Crusade to reconquer the kingdom, the Syrian sultans decided to prepare the defense of the Holy Land and Jerusalem. A great deal of money was invested in fortifying Jerusalem: gate towers were constructed

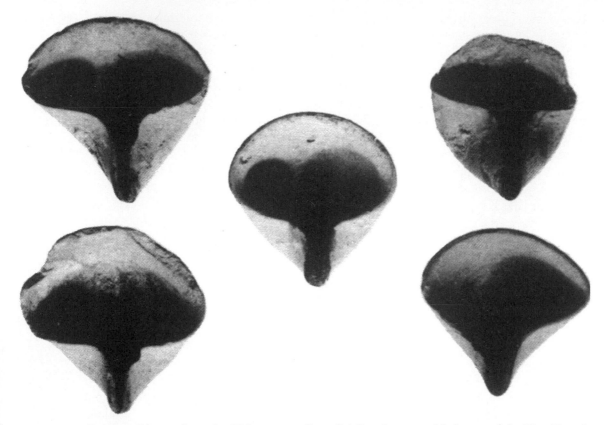

Pottery oil lamps from the 13th century. Superficially, they resemble lamps of the First Temple period, but are actually quite different in size and method of manufacture. These lamps were found in cisterns in the Church of St. Mary of the Germans on the slope of the present-day Jewish Quarter.

and the Citadel strengthened. As was their custom, the Ayyubids recorded their undertakings in monumental inscriptions. However, the Ayyubid sultan Al-Malik al-Mu'azzam 'Isa, upon ascending the throne in Damascus, adopted a new doctrine with regard to the fortification of Palestine: although he had been involved in the construction of fortifications during his father's reign, he came to the conclusion that these fortifications should be dismantled and destroyed. According to his strategic concept, since the Crusaders were experienced in holding fortresses or fortified cities and in withstanding siege warfare, all the existing fortresses should be destroyed, lest the Crusaders later use them to their own advantage. The Muslims therefore de-

stroyed abandoned fortresses standing throughout the country, including some that had been built previously by the Ayyubids themselves, such as the Mount Tabor fortress and the walls of Jerusalem. The Muslims now went back to Saladin's original strategy: fighting in the open field, without reliance on stone walls, ditches or glacis.

The vicissitudes of Jerusalem's fate in the thirteenth century had not ended: the German king, Frederick II, was crowned Holy Roman Emperor, and on June 28, 1228, he led a fleet of forty vessels that set sail from Italy for the Holy Land (the Sixth Crusade). The Ayyubid rulers were in turmoil: they quickly violated the various agreements they had signed, and an atmosphere of profound mistrust prevailed. There ultimately ensued an amazing agreement between the Ayyubid sultan of Egypt, Al-Malik al-Kamil, and Emperor Frederick II, signed in French and Arabic early in 1229. Jerusalem was ceded to the Christian emperor without a battle. Known as the Tel 'Ajjul–Jaffa agreement (for the place where it was negotiated), it made considerable concessions to the Christians. It stated, in part: "The Sultan cedes Jerusalem to the Emperor or his representatives. The Emperor may do as he desires regarding the fortification of the city and other matters. Al-Aqsa Mosque, known to the Christians as the Temple of Solomon, and the Dome of the Rock or the Mosque of Omar, known as the Temple of the Lord, and all the area of *Haram al-Sharif*, that is, the Temple Mount area, will remain in the hands of Muslim authorities, who will worship there in accordance with their laws, including the muezzins' call to prayer. The keys of the gates of *Haram al-Sharif* will also remain in Muslim hands. A Christian desiring to go up to the *Haram* to pray will be permitted to do so, provided he obeys the laws of the place and the Muslim authorities and behaves in accordance with its spirit, removing his shoes on entry. The Christians will permit any Muslim who so desires to go to Bethlehem and pray there. Adjudication of Muslims in Jerusalem will be carried out by Muslims."

After the signing of the Tel 'Ajjul–Jaffa agreement, Frederick II entered Jerusalem. At the Church of the Holy Sepulcher, in the presence of the Teutonic knights, the crown of the Kingdom of Jerusalem was placed on his head. Jerusalem would remain under Christian control for fifteen years (1229–1244).

A new situation had now been created in Jerusalem, previously unknown in the city's history. Under the agreement, Jerusalem was transferred to the control of the Christians, who would be permitted to fortify and develop it. The sites on the Temple Mount sacred to both Christians and Muslims would be open to all—under exclusive supervision of the Muslims. The agreement reflects the wisdom of Frederick II, who preferred achievements gained peacefully and through compromise, rather than war.

Frederick II's expedition to the Holy Land had thus yielded remarkable political gains. These could have been even greater, had it not been for strong opposition from the local Christians, who feared that his main objective was to establish a vassal kingdom in Palestine, directly under his crown. Significantly, Frederick II had set out to the east at a time of serious discord with the Church—just one year before, he had been excommunicated by the pope. Nevertheless, the German emperor achieved unprecedented gains in Jerusalem, which could have opened a new period in its history. However, other powers, waiting as it were in the wings, were about to change the entire balance in the region.

5. THE KHWARIZMIAN TURKS, DESTROYERS OF JERUSALEM; THE TATARS

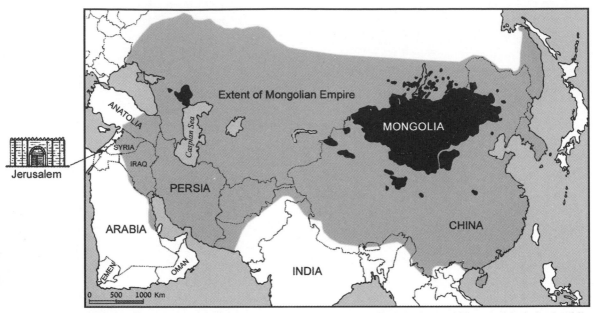

From the heart of Central Asia, the Mongol hosts reached the heart of Europe and the Middle East. Palestine and Jerusalem were not spared.

THE new power that stepped onto the stage of history in the first half of the thirteenth century, almost causing a world revolution and an upheaval of the power structure, were the Mongols. Temujin, ruler of a Mongolian tribe—later known as Genghis Khan (Mongolian for "mighty ruler")—was a military genius and superb fighter who terrorized Europe after subduing China. The Khan, his sons and military commanders swept across Europe like a storm. After Kiev and Moscow had been defeated, followed by all of Russia, Hungary, Poland, Bohemia and Germany fell into his hands like ripe fruit. However, his momentum was halted in the Holy Land, and his commanders were badly beaten by the Mamluks from Egypt (see below). Europe could now breathe a sigh of relief.

The Mongol campaigns, however, also impinged indirectly on the history of Jerusalem. Certain Turkish tribes living in Central Asia: Ottomans, Seljuks and Khwarizmians, had fled in fear of the Mongols and found sanctuary in Egypt, where they served in the sultan's Ayyubid army. When the Khwarizmians were sent to the Holy Land on a military campaign in 1244, the Crusaders in Jerusalem appealed for help from the Muslim leaders in Damascus, who were their allies. In September of that year the Khwarizmians broke through the walls of Jerusalem and rampaged through the city. To the previous devastation brought on Jerusalem by the Egyptians, Canaanites, Amorites, Hittites, Jebusites, Babylonians and Arabs was now added that of the Khwarizmians. The Jews of Jerusalem, also terrorized by the conquerors, smuggled their sacred books to Nablus for safe-keeping by the Jews there.

Devastation and slaughter swept Jeru-

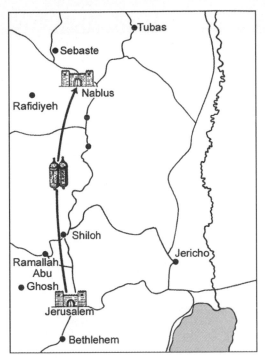

The Khwarizmian conquerors rained fear and terror; their rule was marked by religious persecution and oppression in all areas. The Jewish community smuggled its Torah scrolls out of Jerusalem, for protection, to the Jewish community of Shechem (Nablus).

salem once more, and much of the city was destroyed. The Mamluks, the commanders of the new Egyptian army, also ruled over Jerusalem for a time, but were soon driven out by a new Mongolian invasion, headed by Genghis Khan's grandson Hulagu. With the city once more under heavy attack, the Jewish community—which had only just began getting organized—again smuggled their sacred books to Nablus. Jerusalem became abandoned and deserted.

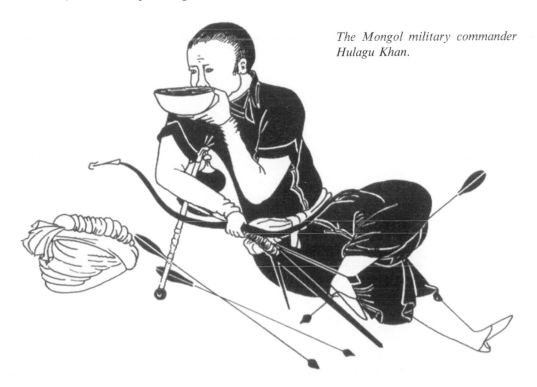

The Mongol military commander Hulagu Khan.

6. BAYBARS THE MAMLUK IN JERUSALEM; JEWISH COMMUNITY RESTORED BY NAHMANIDES

IN 1260, in the course of just one year, the Holy Land was the scene of momentous upheavals. In order to ward off the danger of the Mongolian invasion approaching Egypt, the Egyptian sultans sent their armies to the Holy Land. The ensuing battle, which took place near Ma'yan Harod, earned the victorious commander, Baybars, great renown; he subsequently became sultan of Egypt.

The Egyptian Ayyubid sultans, in keeping with Islamic tradition, had based their army on loyal mercenaries: first the Turkish Khwarizmians and afterwards slaves of Turkish or Caucasian extraction, purchased in Asia and meticulously trained for their military role. This is the source of the name Mamluk, an Arabic word meaning "slave." The Mamluk mercenaries, who rose to senior positions in the army, were released after a certain time in order to prevent them from amassing military power and possibly rebelling. In order to pacify them, the sultans gave them land and property and ensured their economic future. The Mamluks rose to the sultanate in Egypt by peaceful means, when one of their commanders, Iz al-Din Aybak, married Shajar-Adur, widow of the last Ayyubid sultan, Al-Malik al-Salih Ayyub. The sultanate was thus taken over by the Mamluks; the succession was not hereditary, but based on election of the most suitable person for the role.

In 1260, encouraged by his success in the battle at Ma'yan Harod, Baybars murdered the ruling Mamluk sultan, Qutuz, and appointed himself in his place. Baybars aspired to build a huge Muslim empire in the east and to defeat the remains of the Crusader kingdom of Jerusalem. For this purpose he laid roads for his army, built bridges and rebuilt the

Seal of Nahmanides: "R. Moses son of Nahman...," found in the 1920s in the Acre valley and now on display in the Israel Museum, Jerusalem.

(opposite, above) Scholars have long identified the synagogue in the Jewish Quarter described by Rabbi Obadiah of Bertinoro in the late 15th century as the synagogue of Nahmanides. The present author recently suggested that the building designated by Nahmanides for his congregation was a building close to Zion Gate, abandoned by the Crusaders when they left Jerusalem.

(opposite, below) Reconstruction of the Crusader hall (with four pillars and a dome) designated by Nahmanides as a synagogue. A ritual bath was also found nearby, as well as a bathhouse.

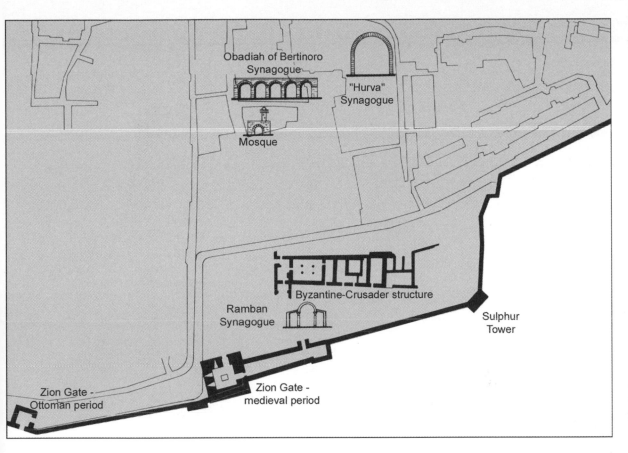

Obadiah of Bertinoro Synagogue

"Hurva" Synagogue

Mosque

Byzantine-Crusader structure

Ramban Synagogue

Sulphur Tower

Zion Gate - Ottoman period

Zion Gate - medieval period

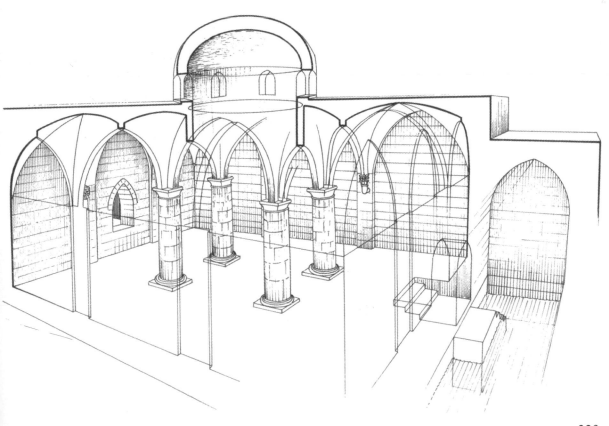

These leopards or lions adorn the so-called Lions' Gate (known to Christians as St. Stephen's Gate), which was built by the Ottomans. It has been suggested that the sultan Baybars' heraldic insignia were carved on the gate that he built at the site, and the Ottoman builders reused them when they rebuilt the gate.

(above) Sultan Baybars' heraldic emblem was a leopard or lion. Carved on the Jindas Bridge near Lydda (Lod), alongside an inscription in praise of the sultan, who built the bridge, are reliefs of a leopard preying upon a mouse, representing the Crusader enemy.

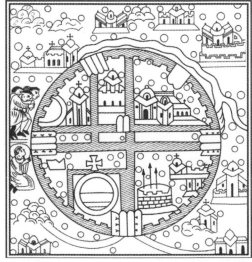

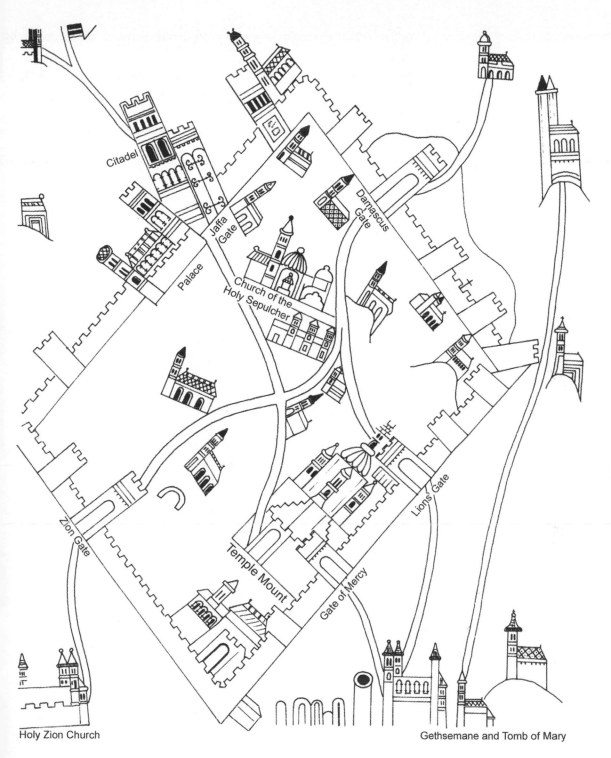

Citadel

Jaffa Gate

Damascus Gate

Palace

Church of the Holy Sepulcher

Zion Gate

Temple Mount

Lions' Gate

Gate of Mercy

Holy Zion Church

Gethsemane and Tomb of Mary

(left and above) Several maps of Jerusalem date to the 12th–13th centuries. While some of these maps were relatively accurate, depicting the city as a quadrilateral, others were primarily symbolic and depicted the city as a circle. While the grounds for this idea are unknown, comparison of the names appearing on these maps with archaeological discoveries and surveys have proved that the details of the maps are quite accurate. The maps thus provide important information about the city's appearance and fortifications, and especially about its buildings and street names.

abandoned Crusader fortresses; in addition, he rebuilt the citadel of Damascus and improved that city's fortifications. In Jerusalem, Baybars established law and order, encouraged settlement in the city, and apparently fortified its walls. Baybars' emblem, a lion, was engraved on many of his building projects, bridges and fortifications. It is probable that the lions that gave their name to the Ottoman "Lions' Gate" were originally placed there by Baybars when, together with the Jerusalem wall, he rebuilt the earlier gate at the site; the Ottomans probably incorporated them in the new gate that they built. By 1266, Baybars had succeeded in reducing the Crusader kingdom to a small bridgehead—a strip of coast stretching from the capital, Acre, in the north, to Atlit, farther south.

Jerusalem was important to Baybars as a city sacred to Islam. To further his political aims, he often appealed to the religious sentiments of the inhabitants of Palestine and built many mosques. As part of his policy of resettling Jerusalem, Baybars encouraged the Jews to return. In 1267 Rabbi Moses ben Nahman (or "Ramban"), also known as Nahmanides, who had been forced to flee Spain after he had bested the heads of the Christian church in a public disputation, arrived in the Holy Land. On the 9th of the Hebrew month of *Elul* (in the late summer), Nahmanides came to the devastated city and immediately set about rebuilding what was then—and is still today—the Jewish Quarter. In a letter to his son in Spain, he described the extent of the devastation in the city and his first attempts at reconstruction, in the course of which he took over an abandoned Christian building and converted it into a community center and synagogue. The building, which has been uncovered in archaeological excavations between Mount Zion and the Jewish Quarter, was originally a wing of a Crusader monastery and church.

Nahmanides' synagogue was eventually confiscated, and by the close of the Mamluk period the Jews were worshiping in a more modest building. Nevertheless, Nahmanides' activities laid the foundations for the Jewish presence in Jerusalem, which has continued uninterrupted ever since. It was apparently in his time that it became customary to hold prayers by the western wall of the Temple Mount—long known as the Wailing Wall or simply the Western Wall.

Chapter 9:

JERUSALEM RESTORED TO ISLAM
THE MAMLUKS 1260–1515

1. UNDER THE SHADOW OF THE CRUSADER THREAT

WHILE Baybars was still consolidating his authority, news began arriving that the Mongols were organizing for another invasion of the Middle East. To meet the threat, the sultan expanded and strength-ened his army and went to the Holy Land to await the Mongol hordes, like a tiger awaiting its prey. A surprise awaited Baybars, however: the Mongolian leader canceled his planned invasion of the Holy

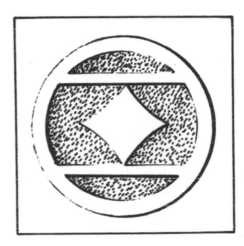

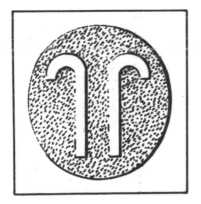

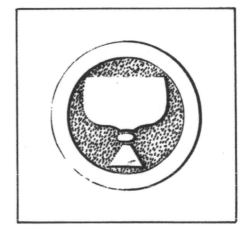

Symbols, originally on the armored shields of the Mamluk emirs, carved in stone on buildings in Jerusalem.

Land. Baybars, a professional soldier thirsting for battle, decided to use the opportunity to attack the Crusader "Kingdom of Jerusalem." Although the entire kingdom consisted of a narrow strip along the coastal plain—except for an area around Nazareth and Safed—its economy, which was based on international trade, was strong and its many port cities, especially Acre, brought in considerable revenues. Within a short time, Baybars had captured most of the Crusaders' towns and fortresses, leaving them only a tiny enclave between Acre and Atlit.

The sultan, to avert any attempt by invading Crusaders from Cyprus, which they were holding as a bridgehead to recapture the abandoned coastal fortresses, set about devastating all the conquered areas, with the help of a specially trained demolition unit. Baybars himself, after the capture of Arsuf-Apollonia, exchanged his uniform for work clothes and joined his soldiers in the destruction as an example. Despite this policy, Baybars built fortresses for his own army at various inland locations—Subeibeh, Kerak (Kir-moab), Hunin and elsewhere. Only fortresses in the coastal area were destroyed, as the maintenance of such strongholds formed the traditional basis of Crusader military strategy.

Since the Via Maris was an important international trade route, Baybars built strongholds along it, which would also help him direct trade to Egypt and its port at Alexandria. He established protected khans—hostels or caravan inns for merchants. At vulnerable places he built massive stone bridges to transport advanced war equipment and other necessities. Along the Via Maris in the Sharon Plain, from Aphek (today Rosh ha-Ayin) to Nahal Iron, the Egyptian military commanders were awarded captured Crusader properties (such as Qalansuwa, Qaqun, Taiybeh, etc.). They were thus able to exploit the agricultural potential of these areas, as well as to protect the road.

The sultan gave Jerusalem his special attention. Clearly, any Crusader attempt to regain Jerusalem and expand the Christian foothold there would be based on its sanctity to Christianity and the need to liberate it from the enemies of Christendom. He therefore encouraged resettlement of the neglected and sparsely populated city, even supporting the Jews who wanted to resettle there. As already related, Nahmanides took advantage of this propitious moment. Like many previous rulers, Baybars too used religion for political purposes, and therefore promoted construction of mosques and encouraged any activity that would enhance the Islamic character of the city. He also repaired Jerusalem's fortifications and rebuilt the Citadel at its entrance. His building activity is also evident in other cities that played a role in controlling the travel routes, such as Ramla, Lydda, Beit Guvrin and others.

2. JERUSALEM OF RELIGIOUS COLLEGES, HOSTELS, MARKETS AND TOMBS

Important Muslim religious buildings were built in Mamluk Jerusalem. Some Christian buildings were converted into Muslim religious buildings, while others were destroyed.

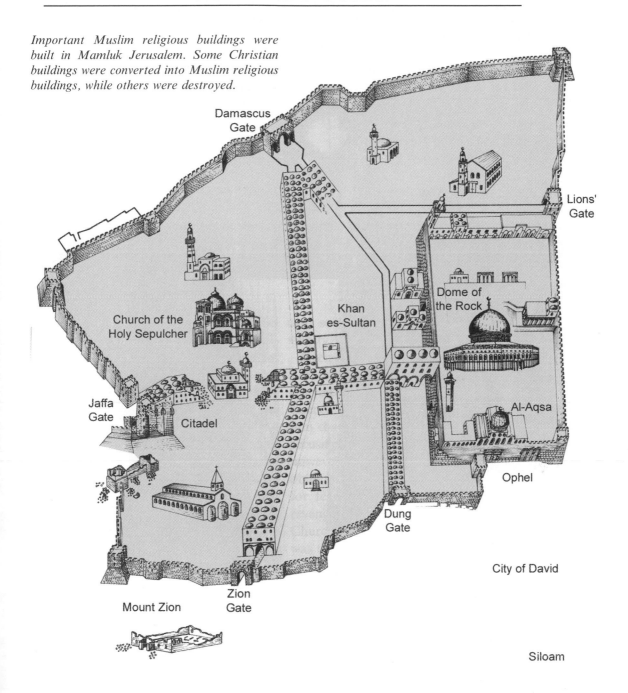

Damascus Gate

Lions' Gate

Dome of the Rock

Khan es-Sultan

Church of the Holy Sepulcher

Jaffa Gate

Citadel

Al-Aqsa

Ophel

Dung Gate

City of David

Mount Zion

Zion Gate

Siloam

BAYBARS' successors, the first Mamluk sultans, continued their uncompromising struggle against the Crusaders. Toward the end of the thirteenth century, they conquered Acre, the capital, and the knights of Atlit fled by sea to Cyprus. Christian rule over the Holy Land ended in 1293. Despite the presence of Crusaders in the Mediterranean area (Cyprus, and subsequently coastal areas of Anatolia and Rhodes and later Malta), they no longer posed a threat to the Holy

Most Mamluk construction in Jerusalem dates to the years 1260–1516. Much of it was carried out on the Temple Mount and in the immediate vicinity.

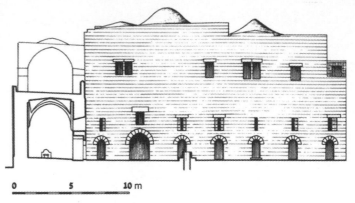

0   5   10 m

Courtyard of a zawiya *(hospice).*

Mamluk tomb.

View into the study hall of a madrasa *(religious college).*

Courtyard of a khan (caravan inn).

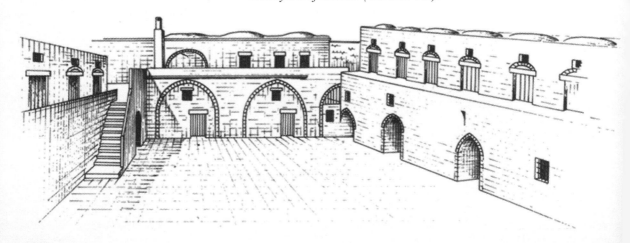

230

Section of a bathhouse in Jerusalem.

Sabil *(drinking fountain).*   Muezzin's *minaret from the Mamluk period.*

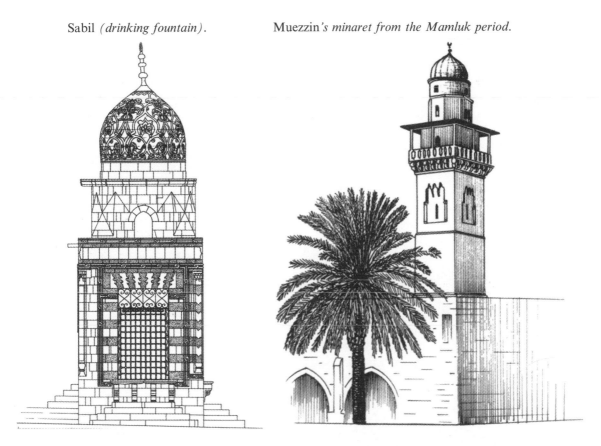

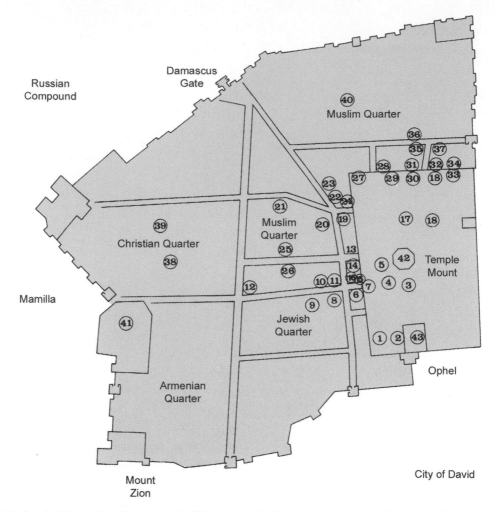

Under the Mamluk rulers, many buildings were built in Jerusalem, mostly west and north of the Temple Mount, in the streets and alleys leading to the gates of the enclosure. Religious institutions were also built on the Temple Mount itself and near surviving Christian religious sites, in order to belittle them.

Land and in fact made no further attempt to conquer it. All that remained were thoughts, dreams and reflections about the Holy Land. It became a destination for spies and other seekers of information, disguised as pilgrims; it figured prominently in maps and in sermons delivered by priests and other religious functionaries.

Throughout their rule the Mamluks respected Jerusalem's sanctity to the Christians and, guided by the lessons of the past, refrained from imposing excessive restrictions on Christians in the Holy City. The Church of the Holy Sepulcher continued to serve as a sacred Christian site, although its keys were kept by Muslim guards, in accordance with a tradition dating to Saladin's time. The Mamluks endeavored not to harm the Christians' many religious buildings and did not expropriate them for their own needs. Furthermore, they permitted visits by Christian pilgrims and the establishment of monasteries and hostels for their use. At the same time, the Mamluks encouraged Muslim pilgrimage to Jerusalem and reinforced its Muslim character. They built inns and markets, such as Khan es-Sultan near the covered (opposite) Map of the main Mamluk buildings in Jerusalem:

1. Al-Fakhriyya
2. Al-Fakhriyya minaret
3. Summer pulpit
4. Arcades of the platform
5. Qa'itbay drinking fountain
6. Al-Tankiziyya
7. Al-Ashrafiyya
8. Turbat Barka Khan
9. Al-Tashtamuriyya
10. Al-Qilaniyya
11. Al-Taziyya
12. Khan es-Sultan
13. Cotton Market
14. Ribat Zammani
15. Al-Uthmaniyya
16. Turkan Khatun
17. Western arcade
18. Eastern arcade
19. Al-Arghuniyya
20. Al-Muzhiriyya
21. Al-Hanbaliyya
22. Ribat al-Mansuri
23. Ribat 'Ala al-Din
24. Al-Manjaqiyya
25. Tomb of Sitt Tunshuq
26. House of Sitt Tunshuq
27. Manarat Bani Ghawanima
28. Al-Jawaliyya
29. Al-Subeibiyya
30. Al-Farisiyya
31. Al-Malukiyya
32. Al-Karimiyya
33. Manarat Bab al-Asbat (= Minaret of Gate of the Tribes)
34. Al-Ghadariyya
35. Al-Dawadariyya
36. Al-Salamiyya
37. Ribat al-Mardini
38. Manarat 'Umar (= Minaret of Omar)
39. Manarat Salih
40. Al-Bistamiyya
41. Al-Qal'a (= Citadel)
42. Dome of the Rock
43. Al-Aqsa

markets at the top of the Street of the Chain, and the so-called Cotton Market and the adjacent khans near the western entrances to the Temple Mount. Two luxurious bathhouses were built nearby, to serve both the local population and pilgrims.

Above all, the mosques and religious colleges (*madrasas*) gave Jerusalem its thoroughly Muslim character. The central Mamluk government encouraged its emirs and other notables to build in the city, offering donors various benefits and concessions, as well as the opportunity to immortalize their names. *Madrasas* built with donors' contributions were named in their honor and engraved with their names in large decorative inscriptions, sometimes also bearing their emblems. The donor was also granted the right to be buried in Jerusalem—a singular honor —usually in a special room in a wing of "his" *madrasa*, where the students would occasionally pray for his soul. Thus, many wealthy Muslims were persuaded to invest in the city, and dozens of buildings they built in the fourteenth and fifteenth centuries still grace the streets of Jerusalem's Old City. Various domed monuments and religious memorials were built on the Temple Mount during this period, all contributing to the enhanced Muslim character of the city, while its sanctity for Christians was preserved.

The Mamluks encouraged the Coptic Christians, granting the heads of the community certain privileges in the Church of the Holy Sepulcher, the most important Christian site in Jerusalem.

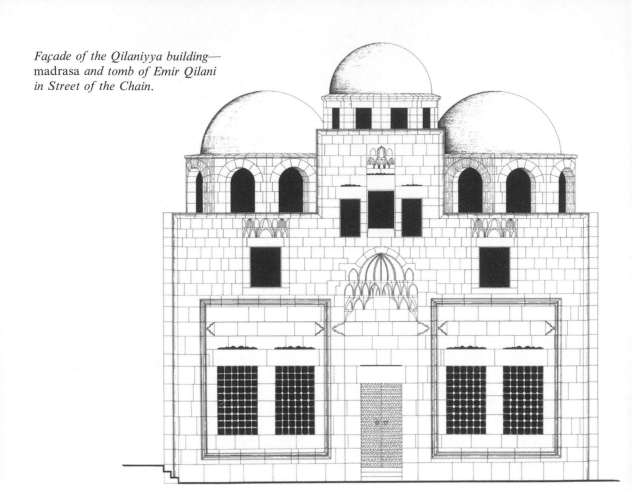

Façade of the Qilaniyya building— madrasa *and tomb of Emir Qilani in Street of the Chain.*

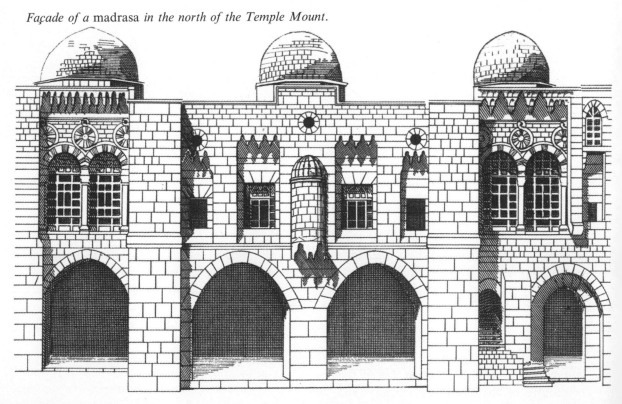

Façade of a madrasa *in the north of the Temple Mount.*

Cotton Gate to the Temple Mount—a typical example of Mamluk architecture.

The Copts, including the patriarch of the Coptic church, were Egyptian citizens and subjects of the sultan; hence they were dependent on his good will, among other things, with regard to religious appointments.

Despite the considerable emphasis on construction for religious purposes in Mamluk Jerusalem, one should not think that the city was unwalled and defenseless. For most of the Mamluk period it was probably protected to a certain degree by the Citadel and by walls. This is also apparent from various contemporary reports and, in particular, maps. Older scholarly theories that Mamluk Jerusalem was an unwalled city were based on two factors. One was the destruction of the walls by the Ayyubid sultan Al-Malik al-Mu'azzam 'Isa at the beginning of the thirteenth century; the other was an account written by the noted Italian Rabbi Obadiah of Bertinoro toward the close of the fifteenth century. However, after the Tel 'Ajjul–Jaffa agreement had been signed, restoring the city to the Crusaders, the latter were permitted to rebuild the walls, which they no doubt did. Rabbi Obadiah's account reflects a much later period, when the walls had apparently been dismantled for repairs. Our information about the period preceding Suleiman's wall refers to walls and gates in the city. We have a report, for example, that the gate near Mount Zion was known as "Gate of the Jews" and was locked at night, the keys being handed over to Jews living in the Jewish Quarter. Obviously, if there was a locked gate, there must have been a wall around the city.

3. Sultan Qa'itbay and His Dream of Jerusalem

Window and cupola in a Mamluk madrasa *in the north of the Temple Mount.*

ALTHOUGH Mamluk rule was not hereditary, it had became the exclusive province of a small self-appointed group, which led to corruption. Toward the end of more than two centuries of Mamluk rule, their government institutions were in a state of decay. Corruption and oppression were rife, and international ties were grossly neglected. Government control became weak, and a complete breakdown was only a matter of time. In the second half of the fifteenth century, Bedouin nomads from the desert, disdaining the rule of law, made frequent incursions into the rest of the country, once even storming Jerusalem through Lions' Gate—further evidence, incidentally, of the existence of walls and gates at the time. The Mamluk governor of Jerusalem fled and hid on the Temple Mount, and merchants and passersby were left to the marauders' mercy. Robberies and poor security on the roads damaged international trade. Added to this were the errors of the central government, which imposed excessive taxes on exports— spice, perfume and medicinal herbs, although representatives of European rulers and merchants were able to exempt themselves. The unstable situation recalled conditions on the eve of the First Crusade, and it was feared that history might repeat itself.

Sultan Qa'itbay, recognizing Jerusalem's importance, arrested the decline and successfully restored its economy and religious life. In addition to rebuilding the city and the religious sites and curbing the lawless behavior of the desert nomads, the sultan repaired the water-supply system that brought spring water into the city. A Swiss traveler named Felix Fabri, then touring the Holy Land, described this activity. He reported that rumors were circulating among the public that the Egyptian government was considering the transfer of its capital from Cairo to Jerusalem. This reflects the real

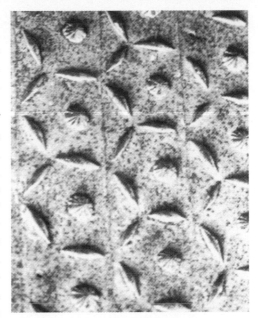

Mamluk madrasas *and tombs had ornate, opulent doors, usually with an iron covering. Detail from the door of the Qilaniyya building: seashells surrounded by barley seeds.*

danger that existed of Europeans penetrating the east, and the fear of a renewal of the crusades. The great discoveries in the west, which were first thought to provide a sea route to India that would bypass the Middle East, somewhat halted the European *Drang nach Osten*. Later, however, when it turned out that the new route was too long and would greatly increase the cost of the already expensive products, the Europeans returned to Jerusalem and the east as the main travel route. By that time, however, Jerusalem and the Holy Land were already under Ottoman rule.

Goblet and part of an inscription on the building of the tomb of Emir Tiz in Street of the Chain.

Arabic	Transliteration	Designation	Origin and meaning
خان	khan	Government-protected inn	Mongolian word meaning "ruler"
خانكة	khanka	Small inn for Dervishes	Diminutive of khan
زاوية	zawiya	Dervishes' inn or small mosque	Corner, humble or hidden place
رباط	ribat	Monastery of the Sufi order	Tethering place; barracks
ربع	rab'	Military camp; barracks	Walled quadrangle of a camp
قيسارية	qaysariyya	Governent-protected inn	From the Latin *caesar* = emperor
برج	burj	Wall tower	From the Aramaic *burgin* = fort
مسجد	masjid	Mosque	Place for prostrating oneself
مكان مبارك	makan mubarrak	Blessed place	
منارة	manara	Minaret of mosque	Original meaning: "lighthouse"
ماذنة	ma'thana	Minaret of mosque	From the Arabic *mu'athin* = *muezzin*
مدرسة	madrasa	College for study of the Koran	Place of study
حمام	<u>h</u>ammam	Bathhouse	Place of hot water
حوض	<u>h</u>aw<u>d</u>	Pool	
سبيل	sabil	Public drinking fountain	Place suitable for walking
سقاية	saqaya	Pool	From verb meaning "to irrigate"
مجاري المياء	majari al-miya'	Water channel	
قبر	qubar	Tomb, grave	
تربة	turba	Tomb, mausoleum	From Arabic *turab* = dust, earth
ضريح	dari<u>h</u>	Tomb, mausoleum	Minaret

Glossary of terms used in commemorative inscriptions on Mamluk buildings in Jerusalem.

4. JERUSALEM, PILGRIMAGE CITY: JEWS, MUSLIMS AND CHRISTIANS

MANY years before David conquered Jerusalem, a traveler on his way to the Hills of Ephraim, bringing his concubine home from Bethlehem, passed near Jerusalem. Despite the late hour, he decided not to spend the night there. Since then, a considerable quantity of flood water has flowed through the Kidron Valley, and Jerusalem has been visited by many people—Crusaders, pilgrims, tourists and travelers. This change began at the time of the First Temple and intensified during the Second Temple period, when

(right) Illustration from a medieval travel book written by a Christian pilgrim on his way to Jerusalem.

(below) Members of the eastern community ("Saracens") in Jerusalem; illustration from a travel book by B. von Breydenbach (1483–1484).

Page from a pilgrim's guidebook to the Holy Land and Jerusalem, by Arnold von Hartz (1498–1499). Guidebooks often included a Hebrew glossary, indicating the prominent place of the Jewish population of Jerusalem in hostelry and guiding.

Jerusalem became the most famous pilgrimage city. Historical upheavals, as well as the conversion of Jerusalem into a city holy to Christians and Muslims as well as Jews, brought new waves of pilgrimage. The Jews, who in their times of distress envisaged the city as "Celestial Jerusalem," never renounced the earthly city and continued to visit it, sometimes risking their lives to do so. A pilgrimage to Jerusalem and a visit to the city were intense emotional experiences, as the writings of many pilgrims show. The first written records of such visitors were engraved in stone by builders or visitors. Even the walls of the Temple Mount bore such inscriptions, some of which have survived till the present, perpetuating the names of Jewish pilgrims. They deal mainly with the fulfillment of vows undertaken during the pilgrimage to assure the pilgrim or his or her family of good health. For example: "Jonah and his wife Shabbatia from Sicily, may you be well," and similar messages.

Most impressions of the visit, however, were committed to writing by travelers. Some even wrote books that were passed from hand to hand among would-be visitors unable actually to visit Jerusalem, who could thus somewhat slake their thirst for the sanctity of the city. The extensive literature written by pilgrims— Jews, Christians and Muslims—is an invaluable resource for the history of Jerusalem, for it constitutes first-hand evidence of people reporting spontaneously on what they saw. Nevertheless, care must be taken to separate imagination from reality in travelers' descriptions: pilgrims did not come to the city as scholars, and the guides accompanying them sometimes told imaginary tales. Hence, any description rendered by a pilgrim should be examined closely and its value and importance to our understanding of Jerusalem's past weighed carefully. A Muslim historian from Algeria, Ibn Khaldun, who made a pilgrimage to the city in the fourteenth century,

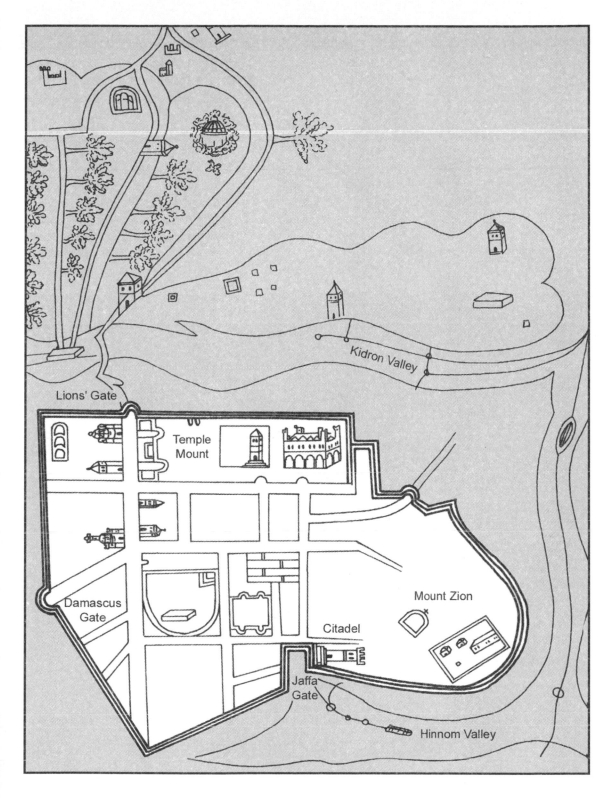

The Marino Sanuto map, c. 1320. This map was given to the pope as a source of information prior to launching a new Crusade to conquer Jerusalem. It shows the city completely surrounded by a wall, including the area of Mount Zion. Some scholars believe it to be largely imaginary, but it nevertheless warrants attention.

later wrote an important book entitled *Introduction to the Science of History* (*Muqaddimah*), in which he also reported what he had seen in Jerusalem. His standard is obviously much higher than that of the anonymous "Traveler of Bordeaux," who was concerned primarily with sites connected with the lives of Jesus and the prophets.

Works written by pilgrims of all three religions during the Crusader, Mamluk and Ottoman periods are particularly numerous. Without this literature, Jerusalem's history would have been incomplete, for it describes all aspects of life: the city's appearance, the inhabitants' daily life, their food and clothing, their way of life and stories about their rulers.

There are few cities in the world for which such invaluable data are available. The present book has also benefited considerably from the descriptions of such travelers.

Even under the Crusaders and the Mamluks, and particularly in Ottoman Jerusalem, many of the writers provided their books with illustrations, including maps and drawings of buildings and people. Our reservations about the accuracy of travelers' reports should also be extended to drawings and maps which were supposedly made by eyewitnesses. Nevertheless, although these too are sometimes less fact than fiction, they are an invaluable source for Jerusalem research.

Chapter 10:
JERUSALEM UNDER OTTOMAN RULE 1515–1917

1. SELIM THE GRIM AND SULEIMAN THE MAGNIFICENT

AT the beginning of the sixteenth century, Jerusalem underwent a major political upheaval: the city passed from the hands of the Mamluk Egyptian sultans to the Ottoman Turks. Like their predecessors, the Ottoman Turks were Sunnite Muslims hailing not from the Arabian Peninsula but from Central Asia. Since the eleventh century, Turkish tribes to the east of Anatolia had been coveting the Byzantine Empire. Gradually moving west from Central Asia, they slowly encroached on Christian Byzantine territory. The most prominent of these tribes in the fourteenth and fifteenth centuries were the Ottomans. In 1453 the Ottoman sultan Mehmet II succeeded in capturing the Byzantine capital Constantinople, ending 1,100 years of Byzantine rule in the east. Mehmet's superior fighting tactics attested to military ability, resourcefulness and guile; taking advantage of a young army, he exhibited a fresh military

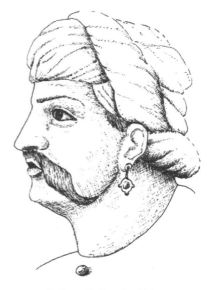

Sultan Selim the Grim.

approach that would play an important historical role.

The Ottoman sultan set up his capital in the conquered city, which became known in Turkish, via a series of

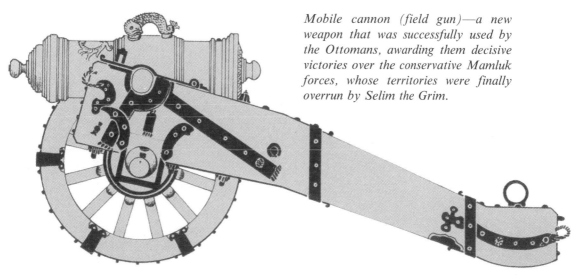

Mobile cannon (field gun)—a new weapon that was successfully used by the Ottomans, awarding them decisive victories over the conservative Mamluk forces, whose territories were finally overrun by Selim the Grim.

Sultan Suleiman the Magnificent.

control over the holy places, for no one could lead the Muslim world without possessing Mecca, Medina and Jerusalem. Jerusalem was even more important than the two other cities because, in addition to its sanctity, it lay at the crossroads of Syria and the Holy Land with their international routes and ports.

At the beginning of the sixteenth century, the Ottoman sultan Selim the Grim began to realize his ancestors' dreams: mustering an army, he engaged the Mamluk regiments in battle. After defeating them in a major encounter in northern Syria, Selim continued to pursue the Mamluk forces as they retreated southward. Damascus fell into their hands, but the Ottomans continued their southward push to Egypt. Despite the storm of battle and the importance of maintaining his momentum, Selim made a slight detour while coming through Palestine and went to Jerusalem to visit the holy places, thus demonstrating his religious goals and proclaiming the Ottoman vocation.

Exploiting his military power and using

mispronunciations in Arabic, as Istanbul. The transfer of the capital to the European part of the new kingdom and the border area indicated that Ottoman policy was now oriented toward Europe. The conquerors were eager to replace the Byzantines in international trade with Europe, but soon realized that they would first have to deal with the Middle East, where the Egyptian Mamluks were still in power. Despite the decay and political, social and military corruption due to 250 years of rule, the rotten fruit of Mamluk power still hung on the tree, though only a slight wind was needed to bring it down.

The new Ottoman policies were guided by the desire to centralize all international trade with its enormous revenues. This would ensure a monopoly, fill the sultan's treasury and perhaps fulfill the dream of a worldwide empire in the style of the ancient Arab Umayyad empire. To achieve this, however, the Ottomans first had to become the sole Muslim empire, which meant gaining control over Persia, Syria, Palestine and Egypt. Furthermore, conquest of the Islamic lands implied

The Citadel of Jerusalem, known popularly as "David's Tower."

revolutionary modern fighting methods (such as field guns), Selim defeated the Egyptians and conquered their capital, Cairo. He thus began to realize the Ottoman sultans' dream of ruling the entire east. The fruits of his victory were harvested by his son and heir, the most famous of all the Ottoman sultans, known to his people as Suleiman al-Qanuni ("the Lawmaker"), and to the Europeans as Suleiman the Magnificent. Suleiman expanded the borders of his empire toward North Africa and the Arabian Peninsula, but without neglecting his old dream—the conquest of Europe.

Suleiman considered Jerusalem of paramount importance as a holy city which would help to maintain the unity of his empire. His development and construction activities here earned him world renown. It is something of a historical curiosity that Jerusalem, whose ancient name was "Shalem," was conquered by the Ottoman sultan Selim, whose name means "peace," while his son Suleiman, or Solomon, was responsible for much of its architectural splendor.

2. SULEIMAN'S PROJECTS IN JERUSALEM AND THEIR PURPOSE

THE famous military commander who conquered Jerusalem for Selim the Grim was named Sinan, which was also the name of Suleiman the Magnificent's court architect, although there was no connection between the two. Suleiman's projects in Jerusalem and his architect's planning are still standing today, among the choicest jewels of Jerusalem architecture. To mention just a few: the construction and repair of the city walls and gates; work done on the Temple Mount, especially the Dome of the Rock, which was faced with porcelain tiles; installation

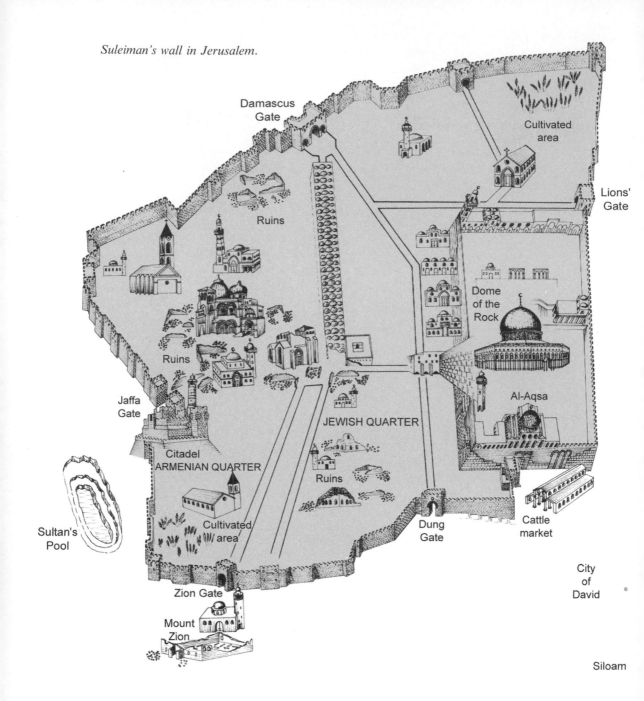

Suleiman's wall in Jerusalem.

Damascus Gate

Cultivated area

Lions' Gate

Ruins

Dome of the Rock

Al-Aqsa

Jaffa Gate

JEWISH QUARTER

Citadel

ARMENIAN QUARTER

Ruins

Ruins

Cattle market

Dung Gate

Sultan's Pool

Cultivated area

City of David

Zion Gate

Mount Zion

Siloam

of the water-supply systems, including numerous *sabils*—roadside drinking fountains; restoration of the Western Wall as a site for Jewish prayer; and more. Such manifold activities require an explanation, as to their goals and the degree to which they were achieved.

The wall Suleiman built in Jerusalem is the most complete and finest city wall built anywhere in the world in the sixteenth century. Its total length along the top is 3,800 meters; if the towers are taken into account, the figure is 4,325 meters. There are now nine gates in the wall, including the Golden Gate and the Excavations (Ben-Dov) Gate; the original wall contained only four gates and two posterns. Thirty-five towers, of which only seventeen were completed, were built into the wall, containing 344

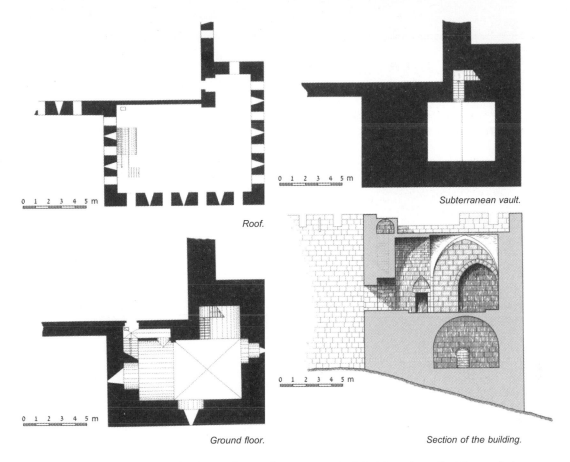

Roof.

Subterranean vault.

Ground floor.

Section of the building.

*The Stork Tower (*Burj Laqlaq*), at the northeast corner of Suleiman's wall. Plans of the different stories and section.*

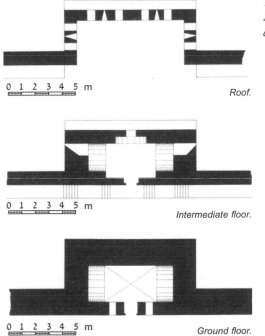

Roof.

Intermediate floor.

Ground floor.

The "Nea" Tower in the northern side of Suleiman's wall. Plans of the different stories and section.

Section of the building.

Architectural elements in Suleiman's wall: (clockwise, from above) ornamentation; inscription; battlements; loophole; machicolation.

loopholes. On the top of the gate towers Suleiman built seventeen machicolations, and the wall is decorated with inscriptions commemorating the sultan's achievement. An unusual aspect of the wall is the large amount of decorative carving in the stone, featuring both floral and geometrical motifs and giving the huge walls outstanding charm and beauty. Three years of income from taxes collected throughout Egypt were needed to build the wall. On completion of the wall it was found that Mount Zion, Jerusalem's most militarily vulnerable

(left) Floral and geometrical carvings on Suleiman's wall.

point, was not included inside the walled area; those responsible for this omission paid with their lives.

The great effort devoted to financing and constructing the wall was the result of the sultan's initiative and planning. Suleiman had received information that the Holy Roman Emperor Charles V, King of Spain, Archduke of Austria and defender of western Europe, planned to launch a new crusade to the east; of course, the liberation of Jerusalem and the Holy Sepulcher from the Muslims would again be the central motif. He therefore believed it necessary to fortify Jerusalem and prepare it for war and siege. Indeed, one of Charles's titles—included in the Spanish ambassador's letter of appointment to the sultan's court—was "King of Jerusalem." Although the title was purely symbolic (Spanish monarchs still bear to this day), the sultan was incensed. It is not clear, however, whether Charles actually intended to go to war in the east, or whether it was just a deterrent tactic, to relieve Ottoman pressure on the Austrian borders. At the same time, it was by then already evident that Columbus had not discovered a new route to India bypassing the Middle East, but a new continent, so the old routes remained just as important for Europe as they had been in the past. Whatever the case, the need to invest money and equipment in Jerusalem did in fact force the Ottomans to relax their military pressure in the west. Previous theories that Suleiman's wall was intended to halt a Bedouin attack on Jerusalem are therefore untenable; that objective could have been achieved at minimal cost by stationing an Ottoman cavalry unit in Jerusalem.

The ornamentation of the wall and gates, expressing an artistic conception of

Jaffa Gate.

Damascus Gate.

military construction, were evidence of Suleiman's emphasis on the religious significance of Jerusalem for Muslim believers. This was not just another city, but a holy city, and he wanted everyone—Europeans as well as his Muslim subjects—to know that he would spare no expense to glorify it.

Overseeing the planning of the wall was Suleiman's court architect Sinan, who himself designed the Damascus Gate. His inspired work contained the embryo of modern architecture, as he based his design on the original plan of the gate during the Second Temple period rather than its form under the Fatimids, the Crusaders or the Mamluks. But Sinan's main achievement in Jerusalem was the renovation of the Dome of the Rock. Here, too, Jerusalem's religious importance to Muslims was demonstrated for the Europeans, who were waving the

*(above) Public drinking fountain—*sabil; *one of five built by Suleiman in Jerusalem.*

(left) Damascus Gate was designed by Sinan, Suleiman's court architect. Detail from façade.

banner of its sanctity to Christendom. In addition to repairs inside the building, which restored the splendor and beauty of the interior, Sinan also redesigned the exterior. The mosaics previously adorning the outside of the building had become worn and damaged, and Sinan replaced them with glazed porcelain tiles, then considered a triumph of cultural progress and showing influence of the Far East and China. The tiles were ordered from the royal atelier at Iznik,

Zion Gate—façade and plan.

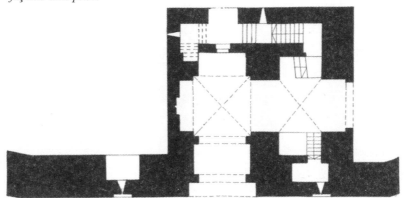

Lions' Gate—façade and plan.

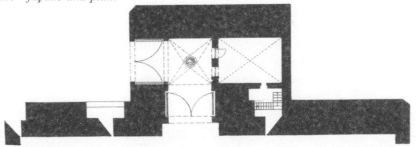

Façade of the postern known as the Dung Gate.

Anatolia, in a wide range of colors against a blue background. As usual in Islamic art, the Muslim artists used Arabic script as a major artistic motif, with prominent inscriptions in praise of Islam and Allah. The tiles were restored in the twentieth century by the late King Hussein of Jordan.

Sinan was given another small task in the field of religious architecture: planning repairs to the Western Wall and preparing it for Jewish worship. Suleiman's grandfather, Sultan Bayezid II, had established ties with the Jews at the end of the fifteenth century, at the time the Jews were expelled from Spain. Recognizing the Jews' talents in economy, banking and administration, as well as in the cultural and academic spheres, he opened the gates of his kingdom to them. Jews expelled from Spain were successfully absorbed into the Ottoman Empire and made a great contribution. In time, many of the Jews expelled from Portugal also reached the Ottoman Empire. Bayezid's grandson, Suleiman the Magnificent, presumed that augmenting the population of Jerusalem with settlers from his own territories would enhance their loyalty. He therefore encouraged both Muslims from distant lands (like Morocco) and Jews to settle there, as a way to restrict the local community and provide balance. The Jewish community in Jerusalem was subsequently greatly strengthened and Suleiman took care to provide it with a convenient living area at the foot of the Temple Mount, close to the Western Wall, which had been a Jewish place of worship since Nahmanides' time.

Suleiman's care for the city's water-

The ruins of Jaffa were rebuilt around the beginning of the Ottoman period, and it once more became Jerusalem's port city. The Ottomans also restored Acre, hoping to take a part in the international trade through Alexandria (Egypt).

Postern of Herod's Gate.

Unfinished tower in the southern wall.

supply system also added to its people's comfort. Reservoirs were cleaned and repaired, including the so-called Sultan's Pool, and several public drinking fountains (*sabils*) were erected.

To thwart hostile Christian criticism of Muslim rule over Jerusalem, Christians were granted freedom of worship and extensive rights at their sacred sites in Jerusalem, especially at the Church of the Holy Sepulcher. Suleiman shrewdly abrogated the rights of the Roman Catholics, whose center was in western Europe, and transferred them to the eastern churches—Greek Orthodox and Armenians—who enjoyed his protection in the Balkans and Armenia.

In sum, Jerusalem at this time lived in the shadow of the discovery of America and the continued importance of routes to the east. Suleiman was at pains to disabuse the European Christians of any thought that Islam might relinquish Jerusalem; at the same time, he demonstrated for Muslims throughout his empire the sultans' regard for the values and traditions of Islam as embodied in Jerusalem.

3. JERUSALEM'S FOUR QUARTERS AND THE TEMPLE MOUNT

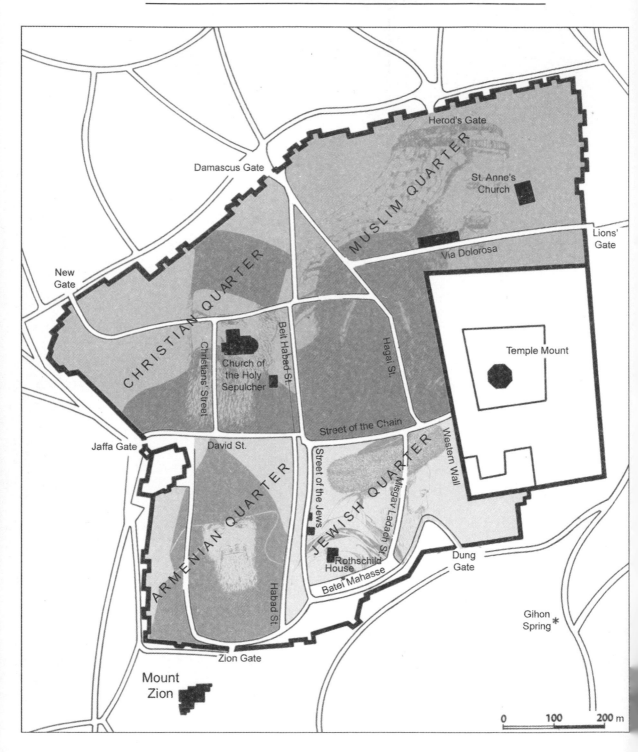

Herod's Gate

Damascus Gate

MUSLIM QUARTER

St. Anne's Church

Lions' Gate

Via Dolorosa

New Gate

CHRISTIAN QUARTER

Christians' Street

Beit Habad St.

Church of the Holy Sepulcher

Hagai St.

Temple Mount

Street of the Chain

Jaffa Gate

David St.

ARMENIAN QUARTER

Street of the Jews

JEWISH QUARTER

Misgav Ladach St.

Western Wall

Rothschild House

Dung Gate

Habad St.

Batei Mahasse

Gihon Spring *

Zion Gate

Mount Zion

0   100   200 m

The four quarters of Jerusalem and the "fifth quarter"—the Temple Mount. The ethnic divisions of the quarters were not observed: from time to time, as one community increased, members moved into a neighboring quarter whose population had decreased.

Arab peasant woman

The population of the Old City of Jerusalem has always consisted of members of different religions and nationalities. These differ from one another in dress and appearance and give the city its special character.

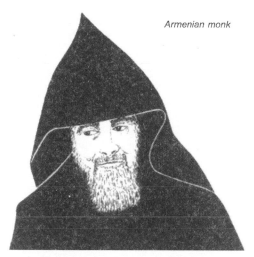

Armenian monk

Yemenite Jew blowing a shofar

THERE are four neighborhoods, or quarters in Jerusalem, differing in their areas and populations: Muslim, Christian, Armenian and Jewish. The Christian Quarter is in the northwest corner of the city; the Muslim, to its east; the Armenian Quarter is in the southwest, the Jewish Quarter to its east. This now traditional subdivision of the Old City dates to the early days of Ottoman rule in Jerusalem, and perhaps even to the time of the Mamluks. Although the city had already been divided into quarters before then, the division was not based on ethnic identities.

In those days a city "quarter" comprised about a quarter of the total area, both in Jerusalem and in many other cities. The subdivision of Jerusalem and the term "quarter" derived from city

Pravoslav monk

Pravoslav nun

Muslim woman

planning, probably influenced by the camps of the Roman Legion. Roman cities were planned with two streets, one running across its length and the other across its width, meeting in the center. Each street would begin and finish at a gate in the city walls. Such a town plan was convenient and made for easy defense, because it needed few gates. The streets crossed at the city's central square or forum, where there might be water fountains. This was basically how Jerusalem was planned, but because of its special topography, built on a low hill and a higher one, there were two length-wise streets. Both began at the northern gate—the present-day Damascus Gate. One crossed the Lower City to the Dung Gate, and the second crossed the Upper City from Mount Zion. This had been the basic plan of Jerusalem since Second Temple times, and it was retained in the Ottoman period.

Under the Ottomans, the southern wall ran along a different line and the city became smaller, but the southern Dung and Zion Gates remained. The four quarters were determined more or less by the above-mentioned city plan, although the lengthwise streets were

Ethiopian monk

Muslim cleric

Catholic nun

not, of course, exact borders. The street across the width of the city—David Street and its continuation, the Street of the Chain—separated (as it still does) the Armenian and Jewish Quarters in the south from the Christian and Muslim Quarters in the north. Even in Suleiman's time the names of the quarters did not accurately reflect the makeup of the population. With Suleiman's encouragement, the Jewish population increased and the Muslim population declined. Jews therefore rented houses at the edge of the Muslim Quarter, where it bordered on their own quarter. Today, too, many Christians are leaving the Old City, either for better and more comfortable accommodation outside the city walls or for other countries, and Muslims are settling in the Christian Quarter.

Even when the first divisions were established, there were enclaves of other people within the Jewish Quarter. Muslims from North Africa—known in Arabic as *Mughrabis*, meaning "westerners"—lived in a poor neighborhood adjoining the Western Wall. Later, refugees from Africa—black Muslims who had fled from Chad, Sudan and Nigeria for various reasons—settled in the heart

Franciscan monk

Muslim "Qawas"

Hasidic Jew from Eastern Europe

of the Muslim Quarter, close to the Temple Mount. The Christian Quarter included members of various Christian communities and denominations, such as Greek Orthodox, Greek Catholic and others. Within the Armenian Quarter there were also Maronite and Assyrian (Syrian) Christians. From the beginning of the Ottoman period until close to the end of the nineteenth century an area within the walls, south of the Jewish Quarter, was reserved for a leper neighborhood, later moved outside the walls. Gypsies also lived in a separate part of the Muslim Quarter; they were promi-

nent in a number of special professions, such as blacksmiths and in zincing copper utensils, or in magic shows or street performances during festivals and holidays. Within the quarters there was an additional division into groups of buildings bearing the names of Arab families, usually of the contractors and builders of the premises. It should be added that Ottoman Jerusalem contained many open spaces, some used for agriculture and others for fruit gardens. This is still the situation today, although to a lesser extent.

The character and use of the buildings

Greek Orthodox monk

Arab peasant

Orthodox Ashkenazi Jew

differed from quarter to quarter. The Christian Quarter was the site of several monasteries, where the heads of the various Christian communities lived. There were also many churches, the most important being the Church of the Holy Sepulcher. From the beginning of the Ottoman period until the mid-nineteenth century, the Hospitaller complex of Crusader times remained in ruins in the heart of the Christian Quarter. Only in the second half of the nineteenth century was it rebuilt by the Greek Orthodox Church, as what is now known as the "Muristan."

Jerusalem was unique in also having a fifth "quarter," the Temple Mount, which under Muslim rule was called, as we have already noted, *Al-Haram al-Sharif* ("the noble enclosure"). It covered some 36 acres, about one fifth of the entire area of the Old City. At the south of the Temple Mount area, close to its southwest corner, there was a cattle market in an open and largely unbuilt area. The original names of Jerusalem's quarters have survived from Ottoman times, although their populations have changed in accordance with the development of the city.

4. Ibn Farukh, Ruler of Jerusalem

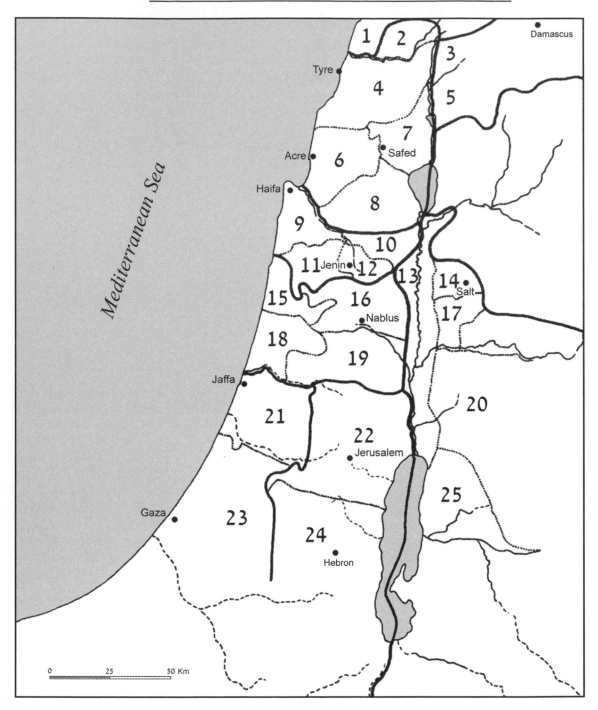

The Ottoman Empire was divided into provinces (eyalets or vilayets); these were divided into districts, or sanjaqs. The number and size of districts in each province varied.

This division also applied to Jerusalem, which was not classified as a province but only as a district. The Jerusalem district was divided into two equal subdistricts—Jerusalem and Hebron; similarly, the Gaza district was divided into the Gaza and Ramla subdistricts.

Despite its prominent status as a holy city in Islam, Jerusalem's political status was no higher than that of numerous other towns throughout the empire.

UNDER Suleiman's successors the Ottoman Empire began to decline. The sultans were preoccupied with internal intrigues and women, and the royal court was full of princes and other pretenders to the throne. Despite the corruption, however, the empire continued to exist, thanks to the foundations laid by its early founders, especially Suleiman, and thanks to the general lessening of the Europeans' designs on the east, due to their own wars. The Europeans were troubled by the Balkans, while the Holy Land and Jerusalem were not a cause of any dissension. The Ottomans, too, devoted more attention to their conquests in Europe than to the east.

The main decline set in during the reign of Sultan Murad III (1574–1595). As the central government deteriorated, the Jews of Jerusalem took advantage of the disorder and corruption to increase their presence in Jerusalem, and theirs became the largest community. As we read in a contemporary Jewish source: "In the days of Sultan Murad...more of our people inhabit the city of our God than have dwelt there since Israel was exiled from its land. . . . Many have purchased houses and fields and rebuilt the ruins...and the streets of the city are

The excavations by the Temple Mount uncovered a garbage dump of the Al-Aqsa Mosque. Among the broken items found was a pottery sherd from the 18th century, one of the costly products of Iznik, the sultan's ceramics manufacturing center.

filled with boys and girls..." (*Memoirs of a Jerusalemite*, pp. 385–387).

The relative calm reigning in the Middle East inspired some of the local governors to rebel and establish autonomies, sometimes almost completely independent of Istanbul. According to the administrative division of the empire, the region of Syria and Palestine was divided into two provinces (Turkish: *eyalets*): Sidon and Damascus. These provinces were divided into districts (*sanjaqs*), each headed by a governor who answered to the pasha of the *eyalet*. The administrative divisions gave Jerusalem a subordinate status, as the *sanjaq* of Jerusalem was equal in size to the districts of Nablus, Ramla or the Lebanese Shuf Mountains. Despite Jerusalem's supreme importance to the Islamic world, the sultans could not establish their capital there, as they considered their links with Europe to be of prime

Legend to map:	
1. Iqlim al-Shumer	13. Ghor
2. Qal'at al-Shaqif	14. Kura
3. Iqlim al-Balan	15. Qaqun
4. Tibnin	16. Jebel Shami
5. Hula	17. 'Ajlun
6. Acre	18. Bani Sa'b
7. Jira	19. Jebel Qibli
8. Tiberias	20. Salt
9. Atlit	21. Ramla
10. Shafa	22. Jerusalem
11. Sha'ra	23. Gaza
12. Jenin	24. Hebron
	25. Shaubak

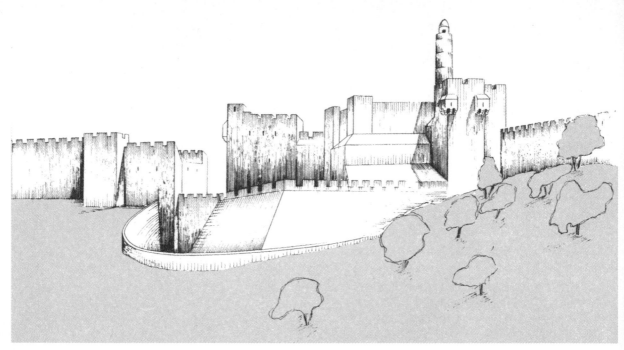

The Citadel of Jerusalem, restored by the Ottomans and used by the governor Muhammad Ibn Farukh.

importance. Furthermore, the Ottomans also feared that establishing Jerusalem as the capital of the Muslim empire would create continuous friction with the Christian European states. Nevertheless, Jerusalem's administrative inferiority was only apparent, and it in fact enjoyed preferential treatment because of its religious character as a holy city. In order to correct this discrepancy, Jerusalem was granted status equal to that of Istanbul, not as a political but as a religious center; as in the past, Jerusalem's sanctity was again tied in with political needs, with a concomitant effect on its position and development. As long as the European powers evinced little interest in the east, the sultans' investments in the development of Jerusalem also declined; but when the west looked toward the east, construction activity increased.

In the Ottoman period the walls of the city were rebuilt along the previous line of the walls. However, as the population was small in relation to the size of the city, many areas were left in ruins, including the Muristan near the Church of the Holy Sepulcher. Other areas in the corners of the city remained unoccupied and were used for cultivation. Near the Stork Tower there is a large area which was still being cultivated in 1980 by the owner, who grew wheat there.

As the central government weakened and the sultan's power declined, powerful individuals, such as the heads of strong and well-established families throughout the empire, began to assert themselves in opposition to the central government in Istanbul. Among such rebellious notables were Fakhr al-Din of Lebanon, members of the Turabey family from Nablus, Daher al-Omar of Galilee, and others. The most outstanding of these was the seventeenth-century Muhammad ibn Farukh, son of a senior Circassian officer serving under the governor of Gaza. His father had begun to promote himself following the governor's death, and in 1603 he became governor (*sanjaq bey*) of Jerusalem and later also of Nablus. He had also held the important position of *Amir el-Hajj*, whose prestigious and very lucrative task was to protect caravans making the annual Hajj pilgrimage to Mecca. Muhammad, known to his contemporaries as simply Ibn Farukh, inherited the position upon his father's death in 1621.

The sultan put Ibn Farukh in charge of suppressing the Bedouin tribes in the Holy Land, who had been flouting the rule of law, robbing caravans, raiding villages and even besieging Jerusalem. Robbery of pilgrims and visitors to Jerusalem, carried out in broad daylight, elicited many protests from the Europeans. Ibn Farukh overcame the Bedouin and succeeded in other undertakings as well, accumulating great wealth. Eventually, he felt strong enough to try and impose his will on the city's people. In his overriding greed, he levied heavy taxes on Jerusalem's inhabitants, which his soldiers collected by force. He especially tyrannized the Jews, whom he saw as an inexhaustible source of funds. Ibn Farukh's policy led many Jews and others to flee from the city and the neighboring villages to other districts. As a result, Jerusalem's development regressed in the first half of the seventeenth century, in contrast to the prosperity of other *sanjaqs* whose governors also exercised independence. Ibn Farukh of Jerusalem is not remembered favorably in the history of Jerusalem. Jerusalem's annals contain both people who advanced the city's development, and those who caused its decline. Ibn Farukh is counted among the latter.

5. Jerusalem Advances Toward the Nineteenth Century

Toward the end of the eighteenth century, several European countries were vying for economic and political supremacy in the world. The main contenders were Britain and France, both of whom recognized the importance of the Middle East as a crossroads of international trade. In 1794, the French consul in Alexandria wrote to his minister: "In order to interfere with British trade in India, it would be sufficient to establish commercial agencies in Cairo, Alexandria and Marseilles." Four years later, the French government decided to take decisive action and conquer the east. In charge of the campaign was a brilliant young officer named Napoleon Bonaparte. After conquering Egypt, Napoleon turned his attention to Palestine, in order to avert encirclement by the Ottomans and the British. Napoleon's march from south to north was aimed at the coastal cities of Jaffa and Acre. The latter succeeded in holding him off, and he

Muslim tombstone from the Mamilla cemetery. Up to the 19th century there were only a few graves in the area of the Mamilla Pool. Burials were resumed there toward the end of the century, over a large area, on orders from the local Muslim authorities, for fear that the Ottoman government might sell the area to a European country or to Jewish investors, who would build another residential neighborhood between Yemin Moshe and Nahalat Shiv'a, or a pilgrim center like the Russian Compound. Once more a religious measure was taken for political motives, as has long been the case in Jerusalem.

Many years later the Mufti Hajj Amin al-Husseini built a magnificent hotel on part of the cemetery's land in order to obstruct Jewish settlement in the area.

tried to expand his conquests in the Galilee mountains as a kind of bridgehead to Acre.

Napoleon's political strategy led him to seek help from various minorities in the east, among them the Jews. He believed, for example, that the establishment of a Jewish state in the Holy Land, which would be strongly dependent on France, might help him in his designs to gain a foothold in the east. Thus, after occupying Malta, he permitted the Jews to build a synagogue there, which they had long been forbidden to do. In Egypt he appointed qualified Jews to his military administration; throughout the Middle East he enlisted Jews to his help in gathering intelligence. In the newspaper *Moniteur* of May 22, 1799, Napoleon published a manifesto calling upon the Jews of Asia and Africa to join him in rebuilding Jerusalem and restoring it to its former glory. Jews in the Galilean villages indeed assisted the French army with food supplies; in return, the French army chased off bandits who had been troubling them. However, not everyone considered Napoleon a savior; Hayyim Farhi, adviser to Ahmad al-Jazzar Pasha, governor of the province of Sidon, was an active partner in planning the defense of Acre and the conduct of the war against Napoleon.

Apart from the plan to conquer Jerusalem and a failed military campaign launched in the direction of the city by one of Napoleon's commanders, Jerusalem did not play a central role in the French army's interests in the Middle East. Eventually, the French and their commander were defeated and they left Palestine in 1799. Peace reigned once again, but not for long. Napoleon's campaign signified the reawakening of European interest in the Holy Land and the European powers' renewed designs on the territory of "the sick man on the shore of the Bosphorus." It was around this time that the leaders of the Orthodox and Armenian churches destroyed the tombstones of the Crusader kings of Jerusalem in the Church of the Holy Sepulcher, wishing to erase all memory of Western-Catholic European glory and power in the holy places.

6. EUROPEAN ENTRY INTO JERUSALEM

Jerusalem on the eve of the 20th century. European penetration was already visible in many buildings in the city and its environs.

Many public buildings were built in Jerusalem in the 19th century under the auspices of various European countries. Each country aspired to bring its own architectural style to Jerusalem. The Ottoman architectural style was used in particular in buildings built by Jews, such as synagogues in the Jewish Quarter, although the builders were generally from the Ashkenazi (European) communities. The money for these synagogues was donated by rich Jews from India, a sign of British influence "behind the scenes."

Tiferet Yisra'el Synagogue

German Augusta Victoria Hospital

NAPOLEON recognized the importance of Jerusalem for the control of the Holy Land and routes of the entire Middle East, but failed to achieve his goal. Jerusalem's time-honored status made it a unifying factor for all parts of the country. Clearly, a ruler who demonstrated deep social and religious sensitivity toward the city would enjoy the support of its citizens, all the more so if he took steps to advance its economic development by construction and in-

Hurva Synagogue

Italian Hospital in Musrara

creased employment. Such a ruler would also receive financial aid and moral and other support in his own country. At the same time, any European foothold gained in Jerusalem would invite strong pressure from the Ottoman sultans. However, the sultan's weakness prevented him from opposing European presence in Jerusalem based on religious motivation.

As we have stated, beginning with Napoleon, and especially from the sec-

Russian Church of Mary Magdalene on the Mount of Olives

Neighborhood mosque in Sheikh Jarrah

Ethiopian Church on Ethiopia Street, Jerusalem

Spanish monastery in Ein Kerem

Notre Dame de France, French monastery and hospice

Russian Church of the Ascension on the Mount of Olives

ond half of the nineteenth century till the beginning of World War I (1914), European governments once more sought to establish a presence in the Holy Land and Jerusalem. Both large and small countries tried to obtain some kind of foothold in Jerusalem. Societies were established in various European countries to promote the Christian heritage and historical research of the Holy Land. Religious orders and monks were given permission to build monasteries and churches con-

(right) German Catholic Dormition Church and bell tower, built on the ruins of the Crusader "Church of Holy Zion" on Mount Zion.

(below) German (Lutheran) Church of the Redeemer with its high bell tower. It was built on the ruins of a Crusader church not far from the Church of the Holy Sepulcher.

nected with events in the life of Jesus and his family in and around Jerusalem. Russians, French, Italians, Germans and Spaniards competed with each other as to who would erect more buildings and purchase more land. The construction provided employment for the country's inhabitants, who were grateful for the initiatives.

Every country that built in Jerusalem tried to stress the unique features of its own architecture. Thus, the Russians

Jaffa

Jaffa Gate, Jerusalem

Haifa

Acre

The Ottomans built clock towers throughout the country, including Jerusalem, in order to demonstrate their superiority to Europe. Clock towers in Jaffa, Jerusalem, Haifa and Acre.

built the Church of Mary Magdalene with its onion-shaped cupolas, and the Germans designed the towers of the Augusta Victoria Hospital, the *Erlöserkirche* (Church of the Redeemer) and the Dormition Church in typical German style. The last two were built in response to the demand of the German emperor, who maintained good relations with the Ottoman sultans, to allocate land to his country's two religious denominations, the Protestants and the Catholics. The Protestants built the *Erlöserkirche* in the heart of the Christian Quarter, and the Catholics (Benedictines) received Mount Zion, where they built the Dormition Church and its bell tower, commemorating the place where Mary, the mother of Jesus, fell into eternal sleep. The Italians built a bell tower in the Florentine style, and the Spaniards built in their own finest architectural style.

Hostels had to be built to take proper care of the growing number of Christian pilgrims, who brought large sums to the country's treasury and revitalized Jerusalem. Freedom of religious travel blunted any propaganda in favor of another crusade to free the holy places. Many hostels were built in Jerusalem at that time—the Russians, the French, the Germans, the Austrians and the Americans built hostels with accommodation for many people, each in their own typical architectural style. Large sums of money were invested in this construction, providing a great deal of employment. The Russians and the French even persuaded the Ottoman government to breach the Old City wall and build a new gate in the walls of Jerusalem to facilitate the entry of pilgrims. First called the Abd al-Hamid Gate, after the reigning sultan, it later became known as the New Gate.

The extensive construction and the conspicuous towers of Christian Europe rising above the skyline spurred the sultan to prove to the people of Jerusalem that he, too, could provide work and

Jerusalem, the Holy City. Two scenes of Jews praying at the Western Wall; a procession of Christian pilgrims through Via Dolorosa.

275

erect monuments. He therefore decided to erect a clock tower on Jaffa Gate, and others in Jaffa, Acre, Haifa, Safed and elsewhere. Because of the anti-religious ideas then beginning to spread in Turkey—eventually leading to Ataturk's revolution—additional mosque minarets would not have been sympathetically received, while the clock represented European progress. The clock tower on Jaffa Gate was removed by the British when they conquered the city in 1917, as it served as an Ottoman symbol.

7. THE JEWISH QUARTER OF JERUSALEM AT ITS ZENITH

DURING those years, in the second half of the nineteenth century, the Jewish Quarter of Jerusalem reached its peak. As the European powers increased their influence in Jerusalem, they opened consulates to help their citizens. It thus became easier for Jews from various European countries to settle in Jerusalem; whereas they had previously been subject to the arbitrary dictates of the Ottoman governor, they now had an address to turn to for protection and assure them proper treatment. European countries, even those practicing antisemitism at home, favored settlement of their Jewish citizens in Jerusalem, as a way of further reinforcing their presence.

The Jews of Holland and Germany, as well as the Rothschilds, donated large sums of money to build housing for needy Jewish inhabitants of the Jewish Quarter. Rothschild House was erected with a shelter for the poor beside it. Several synagogues were built: the "Hurva" Synagogue, whose construction had begun in 1700 when Yehuda he-Hassid came to Jerusalem, was completed with the help of a donation from a rich Iraqi Jew; the Tiferet Yisra'el (or Nissan Beck) Synagogue was built with a donation from a Jew from Bombay. The British government also welcomed the increased Jewish settlement; it was in keeping with Britain's interests and the wave of romanticism then sweeping British society, based on nostalgia for the past and the liberation of ancient and persecuted peoples like those of Judea and Greece—as evidenced, for example, by Lord Byron's personal participation in the Greeks' struggle for independence.

When the Jewish Quarter no longer had room for all its inhabitants, Jews rented premises in the nearby Muslim Quarter. To this day, the entrances of many Muslim houses still bear evidence of the *mezuzot* that the Jewish residents had affixed to their doorposts in fulfillment of the biblical commandment (Deut. 6:9). It is even more surprising to find wine cellars that the Jews built quite openly in the Muslim Quarter. One of these, known after its owner as "Miriam's Cellar," just north of the Cotton Market, was still operating toward the end of World War II. This attests to the tolerance of the Muslim residents toward their Jewish neighbors, as wine production is strictly forbidden to Muslims, all the more so in close proximity to the Temple Mount. Toward the end of the nineteenth century the number of Jewish residents of Jerusalem reached 11,000 or more. As at the beginning of the seventeenth century, the Jewish community was again the largest in the city.

(opposite) Aerial view of the heart of the Jewish Quarter. In the center is Rothschild House, and on the left, "Batei Mahasse"—a communal housing complex built with money donated by the Rothschilds and the Jewish communities of Germany and the Netherlands for needy members of the Ashkenazi community in the Old City.

277

8. THE BEGINNINGS OF HISTORICAL AND ARCHAEOLOGICAL RESEARCH IN JERUSALEM

THIS chapter does not aim to review research into Jerusalem's past, but to demonstrate the contribution made by the research and the researchers to the advancement of European political goals and hence to the growth of European influence in Jerusalem. The nineteenth century is known as the era that stimulated organized study of the history of the Holy Land, and of Jerusalem in particular. The first steps in this field were taken by Christian clergymen in order to refute politically motivated publications challenging the truth of the Old and New Testaments. Such publications, which rapidly gained currency, claimed that the texts were written after their historical time, with a specific objective, and lacked any historical truth. These politically motivated claims were directed against the government and clergy of various countries. In reaction, studies supporting the truth of the Bible began to appear. Obviously, proving these hypotheses through actual finds in the area—such as an inscribed coffin ascribable to Jesus or to one or other of his disciples—would be of inestimable

Among the Christians who left the confines of the Old City walls were merchants who built their shops in the area that would later become Jaffa Road. Above: shops built by the Greek Orthodox Patriarchate for Greek Orthodox merchants.

(opposite) The delegation of the British Palestine Exploration Fund (1867–1870) included junior officers and sergeants from the Engineering Corps and Intelligence Corps of the British army. The study of Jerusalem's past has benefited greatly from their skills, and some of their conclusions still apply today. The delegation also excavated in the environs of the city, examining its water sources and fortifications, as well as the mood of the inhabitants and the Ottoman government officials. This information later helped the British army in the First World War and facilitated their conquest of Jerusalem.

The delegation was accompanied by artists, draftsmen and photographers, whose work served as a basis for the work of artists, some of whom never visited the Holy Land. An example of this is the drawing of Robinson's Arch, as reproduced in Picturesque Palestine, Sinai and Egypt, *ed. Colonel C. W. Wilson.*

Some building took place outside the walls of Jerusalem in all periods of history. Until the end of the 19th century, however, no residential housing was built there, but only palaces, guard posts, mausoleums or monasteries. The Monastery of the Cross, 2.5 kilometers west of the Old City, first built in the Byzantine period, was destroyed and rebuilt a number of times during various periods of history. In the 19th century the Greek Patriarchate rebuilt it as a religious seminary.

value. These early efforts spawned a large body of serious research, which sought to discover the past and to understand the events of Jerusalem's history.

The earliest and one of the foremost researchers of Jerusalem was an American clergyman named Edward Robinson, who visited Jerusalem in the second quarter of the nineteenth century and published the results of his research. Robinson uncovered important finds in Jerusalem and revolutionized the understanding of Jerusalem's past. Yehosef Schwarz, a Jewish contemporary of Robinson and native of Jerusalem, wrote a Hebrew book entitled *Tevu'ot ha-Aretz* ("The Produce of the Land"); through his knowledge of Jewish religious literature (such as the Mishnah, the Talmud and the Midrashim) he made an important contribution to Robinson's work. Some researchers of Jerusalem were casual visitors who became amateur archaeologists, or people who had come to the city to fill civil positions, such as city engineers and planners. Outstanding among these was the Italian Pierotti and the Swiss Conrad Schick, whose profession helped them to appreciate the importance of archaeological remains.

The researchers also included missionaries and doctors, such as the American Dr. James Thomas Barclay, who was fascinated by the search for the past and is credited with some important discoveries. There were also adventurers, such as Montague Parker, who headed a group which dreamed of discovering hidden treasures. Parker found neither gold nor silver, but enriched our knowledge of Jerusalem's past.

The greatest contribution was made by the British Palestine Exploration Fund (PEF), whose earliest activities date to 1867. Discoveries made by expeditions initiated by the PEF are still important to Jerusalem research today, over 140 years later. The PEF was unique for its political-military background: since many civilian explorers had failed in their efforts for fear of the local Arabs, the PEF established ties with the British army, which agreed to assign them young intelligence and engineering officers to help advance the research. These officers knew how to defend themselves, spoke Arabic and were also familiar with architectural research. The results of their expeditions are outstanding; these members of the Intelligence Corps, under the

Rabbi Yehosef Schwarz, a Jew from Hungary, immigrated to the Holy Land and lived in the Old City of Jerusalem until his death (1865). He studied the past of the Land of Israel and recorded his research in a book entitled Tevu'ot ha-Aretz *("The Produce of the Land").*

guise of researchers, also explored the country and mapped out its roads, settlements and water sources—preparing a superb intelligence infrastructure for the British army in readiness for the future invasion. The members of the PEF were closely acquainted with Jerusalem and drew up very accurate maps of it. Among them were Charles Wilson, Claude Conder, H. Kitchener and Charles Warren. While they were in Palestine they were only junior officers, lieutenants or captains, but by the time they had completed their military service they had risen high in the ranks: Charles Warren, for example, finished his service as a general, Commander of the Royal Engineers. The contribution of this group was immense; it added yet another layer of information—especially archaeological—to the political and military interests of the powers in Jerusalem.

9. BEYOND THE WALLS

THE BOOM IN CONSTRUCTION MOMENTUM AND THE GROWTH OF JERUSALEM'S POPULATION

THE European powers' increasing interest in Jerusalem and extensive building activity brought the city economic prosperity. Hundreds of unemployed Arabs from the villages of the Hebron Hills arrived in Jerusalem seeking work, and many remained and raised families there. The protection provided by the European consulates also encouraged Jews to come to the city. The monasteries and ecclesiastic centers, including hostels, became a magnet for Christians, whether visitors, religious functionaries or those providing them with services. With the great increase in population, Jerusalem had become too small; health and sanitary services within the city walls could no longer cope with the situation. Thus, the crowded conditions and lack of hygiene within the Old City encouraged increasing numbers of residents to make their homes beyond the walls. New neighborhoods began to spring up outside the walls, launching a process that would ultimately change the appearance of Jerusalem. The move to settle outside the walls was helped, among other things, by the stable security situation, which made it possible to live outside the walls without fear of robbery or violence.

Among the new neighborhoods built outside the Old City walls, to the west, was the Jewish neighborhood of Yemin Moshe, not far from Mishkenot Sha'ananim. Its houses were built with red-tiled roofs in a typically European style.

(right) In order to help the residents of the Mishkenot Sha'ananim neighborhood, Sir Moses Montefiore built a windmill there.

The departure from the enclosed built-up area seemed to make the walls superfluous, and Jerusalem's Ottoman governor, who was notorious for his greed, began to negotiate for the sale of the wall to building contractors, who would dismantle them and make a profit from selling the stones for building. However, sense and sensitivity overcame the greed for money, and pressure from Europeans not to destroy such a major architectural treasure saved Jerusalem's walls. The walls remained in place, and the first people to leave began building houses against it, using it as a fourth strong wall for their buildings. Some of the first houses and

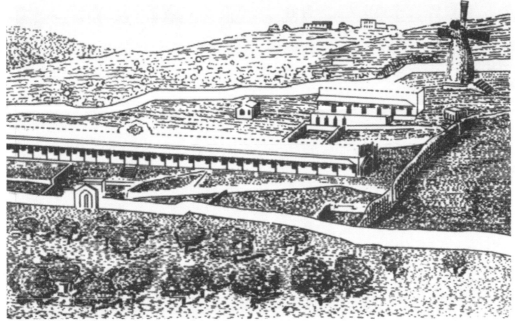

The Jewish Quarter of the Old City was very crowded—it was small in area and had more inhabitants than any other population group in Jerusalem. Encouraged by the favorable security conditions, Jews were the first to leave for residential neighborhoods built outside the walls. Mishkenot Sha'ananim was one of the first neighborhoods to be built and inhabited outside the walls.

(clockwise, from right):
Sir Moses Montefiore, a wealthy Jew, investor and philanthropist from England.

Sir Moses Montefiore's coat of arms.

A windmill was built to provide a livelihood for the residents of Yemin Moshe and the nearby Mishkenot Sha'ananim.

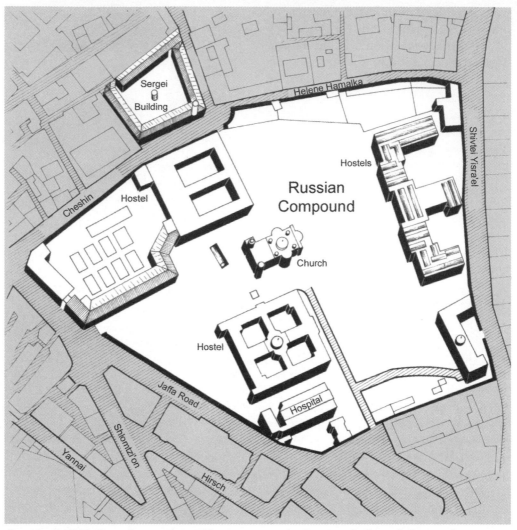

Outside the Old City, close to the northwest corner, the Russians built a whole complex to serve Russian pilgrims: hospices and a hospital built around a church in the center. Today most of these buildings are used by the government of Israel.

shops built in Jaffa Road, which led from Jaffa Gate toward the port of Jaffa, abutted the wall and in fact concealed part of it.

The existence of satellite Arab villages around and near Jerusalem was based on the supply of their produce to the city. Arab laborers who arrived in Jerusalem in the wake of the increasing economic prosperity made their homes in the villages of Silwan (Siloam), Beit Safafa, Lifta, Malha, Ein Kerem, El-Azariya, Beit Hanina and Shu'afat. Silwan, on a hill to the southeast of the Old City, was especially popular because of its proximity to the city and its rich source of water—the Gihon Spring. Thus, the ancient burial field, dating from the First Temple period (eighth to sixth centuries BCE), now became a residential area.

The Christians, who wanted to build monasteries and hostels, purchased land outside the Old City, close to the walls. Thus the Russians bought their property in the area later known as the Russian Compound, and the French built the Notre Dame hostel. But the first people to make an organized move beyond the walls were Jews. The Jewish Quarter was one of the smallest in the Old City, although its population was the largest. The crowded conditions left only one option—to leave the Old City. Mishkenot Sha'ananim, Yemin Moshe, Nahalat Shiv'a, Sha'arei Hesed, Me'a She'arim, the Bukharan Quarter and Mahaneh Yehuda were the first Jewish neighborhoods, widely spaced to the west of the Old City. The Christians also built residential neighborhoods outside the Old City: the German Colony, southeast of the Old City, built by German Christians who had seceded from their church and come to Palestine; the American Colony, built to the north of the city. The buildings in these neighborhoods were of modern design and of high standard; one of their characteristics was the roof of imported red tiles—a revolutionary innovation in the scenery of Palestine and Jerusalem.

The city's wealthy Muslims, envious of the standard of living of their Jewish and Christian neighbors (who were poorer than they were), also began to emerge from the Old City. They built comfortable residential neighborhoods of spa-

After Mishkenot Sha'ananim, another neighborhood was established outside the walls close to the Russian Compound. It was called Nahalat Shiv'a ("Inheritance of the Seven") in honor of its seven founders, headed by Rabbi Joel Moses Salomon.

cious houses in a superb, modern architectural style, with large gardens, in various locations: the present Emek Refa'im Street, near the Germany Col-

One of the first Arab neighborhoods outside the Old City walls was in the north of the city, in the Sheikh Jarrah area; it was built by wealthy Jerusalemites, who had the means to build magnificent, red-roofed houses in the neo-classical style.

The heart of the Jewish Quarter—an aerial photograph taken in 1976.

Abraham Moses Luncz, one of the leading scholars of new Jewish Jerusalem toward the end of the 19th century and the beginning of the 20th, published Luah Eretz Yisra'el, *an almanac devoted to Land of Israel studies. He died in Jerusalem in 1918.*

ony; Abu Tor, a spectacular observation point to the south of the Old City; Musrara in the north; Sheikh Jarrah and Wadi Joz overlooking the Kidron Valley.

Many buildings in the Muslim Quarter of the Old City were abandoned because their occupants preferred the new buildings, which represented a marked improvement in their living standards. New inhabitants from the surrounding villages soon rented the abandoned buildings. Each house now accommodated several families, and the Muslim Quarter of the Old City became a slum.

With the move outside the walls Jerusalem began to grow quickly. By World War I, Jerusalem was already the country's largest city, both in area and in population. The competition for Jerusalem brought it considerable prosperity. Employment in the building trades attracted thousands of Arabs, canceling out the numerical ascendancy of the Jews

toward the close of the nineteenth century. Jerusalem expanded both beyond the watershed line and westward. Naturally, no neighborhoods were built east of the watershed line, not even Arab neighborhoods. There were only two small villages in that area—El-Azariya and Abu Dis; beyond that, on the edge of the desert, the Bedouin nomads of the Judean Desert made their homes in tents.

This was the shape of Jerusalem on the eve of the British conquest.

Chapter 11:
JERUSALEM UNDER THE BRITISH MANDATE 1917–1948

1. JERUSALEM SURRENDERS TO GENERAL ALLENBY

DURING World War I, the Holy Land once more became an arena of international conflict, as it had been so often in the past. Less than one hundred years after the struggle between France, England, Turkey and Russia over control in the area, the gateway to the Middle East was again embroiled in war.

At the turn of the century, the European powers reached the conclusion that the decadent Ottoman government was a danger to world peace, and that the "sick man on the shore of the Bosphorus" had to be destroyed. Shortly after the outbreak of World War I, while the fighting was still raging, the great powers divided up the Ottoman Middle East between them. Under a secret agreement negotiated by British and French diplomats Sir Mark Sykes and Georges Picot in 1916, the region was to be divided up into areas administered directly by France or Britain, or areas under the influence of one or the other, which would be a confederation of Arab states. Palestine would be ruled by an international condominium, whose character would be established in consultation with Russia and the other allies and with the agreement of Sharif Husein of Mecca. This caution and territorial indefiniteness was dictated by the sensitive issue of the Holy Land and the status of Jerusalem.

The Zionist movement did not stand idly aside; it again raised the question of the Jewish people, Palestine and Jerusalem in various political circles in Britain. Zionist activity and Britain's declared interests in the Middle East eventually led to a declaration recognizing the Jews'

right to a national home in Palestine.

On October 31, 1917, the wording of a declaration prepared by the British foreign secretary, Arthur James Balfour, was approved; this would later become known as the Balfour Declaration. Some saw this as partly motivated by the Bible-based religious sentiments of a group of influential British politicians, including Jews like Herbert Samuel—a kind of romanticism, envisaging the renewal of the glorious historic past of states and peoples, such as the Greeks and the Jews, which had influenced the growth of western civilization. However, political considerations were the decisive factor: the Zionist movement and the renewed Jewish settlement in Palestine were seen as serving the interests of Great Britain, the new rulers of the Middle East.

Out of support for the Jews and the Zionist enterprise, the British tried to alter the terms of the Sykes-Picot agreement and to receive the areas in which the Jewish National Home was to be established as a protectorate. As early as May 1917, a few months before the final approval of the Balfour Declaration and before the British occupation of Palestine, the British prime minister David Lloyd George told General Edmund Allenby, commander of the Egyptian Expeditionary Forces, that he expected him to take "Jerusalem before Christmas." A month later Allenby was appointed to succeed General Archibald Murray as commander of the British forces in Egypt and Palestine. Infused with energy and the desire to fulfill his superiors' hopes, Allenby broke through

Europe was thrilled by the news that General Allenby had captured Jerusalem. Church bells rang out joyfully to mark the return of Jesus' city to Christian hands.

the Turkish-German defenses in Sinai and captured Beersheba. Taking immediate advantage of the enemy's surprise, he set out with his forces for Jerusalem. Allenby was fully aware of the importance of the city and the momentous consequences of its conquest. The first attempt to capture Jerusalem failed because of the army's fatigue and the difficult winter conditions, but a month later the British attacked with renewed energy, storming the outskirts of Jerusalem on December 8. The next day, the last Turkish soldiers retreated from the city and a letter of surrender was sent to Allenby. On December 11, 1917, 401 years after the Ottoman sultan, Selim the Grim, had entered the gates of the city, Ottoman rule over Jerusalem came to an end.

Allenby, with ceremony suited to the occasion, entered the historic holy city through Jaffa Gate and received the keys to the city. Out of a sense of the importance of the occasion, the general descended from his horse and entered on foot, signifying his humility before the greatness of Jerusalem. This act left a deep impression on all those present, and Allenby's biographer, Brian Gardner, wrote: "... [I]n a simple but impressive ceremony, Allenby made his official entry into Jerusalem. French and Italian representatives walked on either side of him. They were followed by Chetwode and twenty officers. Next to Colonel Wavell,

just behind Allenby, was Major Lawrence.... A Guard of Honour picked from all the countries represented in the campaign was drawn up. Allenby walked under the gate, betraying no sign of emotion; aloof, apparently unmoved, and without dawdling. Thus did the Christian nations return to Jerusalem after 730 years. . . . The General entered the city on foot, and left it on foot...."

As Gardner remarks, less than twenty years before, the German Kaiser Wilhelm had entered the place on horseback; the British general, by contrast, entered humbly, expressing his profound respect for the city of Jesus.

The fact that Jerusalem had been wrested from Muslim hands and was now subject to Christian rule was received with considerable excitement. In Gardner's words:

"The great bell of Westminster Cathedral rang for the first time for three years. The bells of every church in Rome rang for an hour. In Paris there was a special service in Notre Dame. . . . It was, after years of wretchedness and misery, an event which captured and held the imagination of the world."

Once the celebrations of the conquest and victory were over, Jerusalem's real problems rose to the surface. The struggle over its fate and that of Palestine in general was to dog the British Mandate throughout its existence.

2. JERUSALEM BETWEEN JEWS AND ARABS

IN the years preceding the conquest of Palestine, the British negotiated with all the parties in the area in order to advance their aims. They ignited the nationalistic hopes of the Arabs in the Ottoman Empire, but also held talks with the Jews in general and especially the Zionists, as well as with the United States, France and their other European allies. When the war was over and the Ottoman Empire had collapsed, the time arrived for the British to fulfill their promises. Naturally, the conflicting interests in the area could not all be satisfied.

In 1920, Sir Herbert Samuel, a Jew and one of the architects of the Balfour Declaration, was appointed high commissioner of Palestine. Until the completion of Government House on a hill southeast of Jerusalem, in 1927, the high commissioner had his seat in the Augusta Victoria Hospital on the Mount of Olives, which had been confiscated from the Germans. Government House was purposely located outside the city and outside both Arab and Jewish residential areas, as a symbol of neutrality in the struggle between the two peoples. As in the time of the ancient kings of Jerusalem, the seat of government was again located outside the city boundaries—on a hill offering an impressive view toward the Dead Sea and Transjordan, up to Mount Nebo, from where Moses had seen the Promised Land. To the north lay the Old City with its church spires and

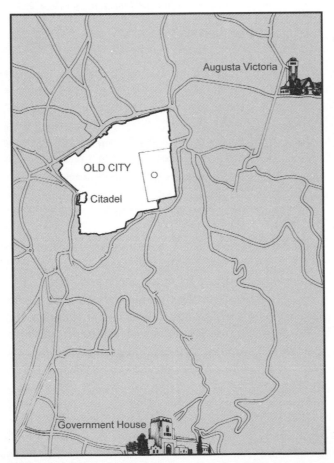

The British government appointed a High Commissioner for Palestine, whose seat of office was in Jerusalem. At first he resided in the German Augusta Victoria Hospital on the Mount of Olives. A new residence was built in the southeast of the city, overlooking the Old City. Was the choice made out of a desire to escape the noise of the city? or was it an expression of respect for the Holy City, the city of the Prophets and Jesus? or perhaps he was guided by political wisdom, preferring not to emphasize Britain's exclusive rule over the city holy to so many?

The Augusta Victoria Hospital on the Mount of Olives served as the high commissioner's residence and seat of government until the completion of Government House in the East Talpiot neighborhood.

towers, as well as the Temple Mount; while to the west were the new neighborhoods then beginning to spring up.

From his residence high up in the Augusta Victoria building, the high commissioner began to maneuver between the conflicting demands of the Jews and the Arabs. Since fulfillment of these demands would have entangled the British government, it adopted a policy of preserving the status quo. Only naturally, however, each party tried to advance its own aim and achieve its national goals.

In 1921 Samuel denied that the British government intended to establish a Jewish government in Palestine that would rule over a Muslim and Christian majority. This was his reaction to Arab unrest and acts of rioting, terror and murder of Jews.

Several distinguished Arab families, whose status had been preserved throughout the years of Ottoman rule, were then living in Jerusalem; some of them held key government posts, especially in the religious administration (accountable to Sheikh al-Islam in Istanbul). These included the Dajani, Nashashibi, Khaledi, Nusseibeh and Husseini families. They traced their lineage to members of the families of officers in Saladin's army who had settled in Jerusalem after its conquest and received special privileges. Some of them even claimed to trace their ancestries as far back as the commanders of Omar's army during the first Muslim conquest of Jerusalem. Personal relations within and among these families were riven with hate. Their constant rivalry for posts and leadership roles sometimes led them to extreme measures in order to gain popular support.

Prominent among the leaders of the disturbances that began in the early days

The hallowed site of the Temple Mount was used by the Mufti as the center of his political power. He carried out his struggle against the Jews and the British from his offices on and around the Temple Mount, and exploited the sanctity of the place to shelter and protect him.

of British rule was a young red-bearded man, a graduate in theology from the Al-Azhar College in Egypt: Hajj Amin of the Al-Husseini family, who had been arrested for his part in the disturbances and later released. After the death of the Mufti of Jerusalem, Kamel al-Husseini, the high commissioner appointed Hajj Amin in his place—an appointment that had grave consequences for the future. Sir Herbert Samuel had assumed that the appointment would appease Hajj Amin and encourage moderation. This was a miscalculation. Only one year later, Husseini seized the chairmanship of the Supreme Muslim Council, combining the religious prestige of his post with the administrative and financial power of the council, which also controlled the *waqf* (Muslim religious endowments).

Over the years the Mufti of Jerusalem became the key figure in the Arab struggle against Zionism, the symbol of Palestinian Arab nationalism. He was an unscrupulous fighter for his cause, being involved in murder, violence and terror; he later maintained close ties with the Nazis and Hitler, supporting and assisting the Nazi program for the extermination of the Jewish people. The Mufti's implacable war against Zionism led him to neglect Muslim religious interests, although he controlled huge resources: many Muslim buildings that were almost in ruins were not repaired; no investments were made in Muslim education, and so on. Only later did other Arab leaders, such as King Farouk of Egypt, understand that love and respect for Jerusalem as the crown of Islamic glory had to find expression in investment and actions. It might be said to Hajj Amin's credit that he made some attempts to emulate Jewish efforts and methods. One example of this was his establishment of a political body known as the Arab Higher Committee, parallel to the Zionist Executive in Palestine.

Opposing these efforts was the Zionist movement, headed by Chaim Weizmann. Immediately after the end of World War I Weizmann took steps to ensure the implementation of the Balfour Declaration. The Jewish Committee of Representatives changed its name to the Zionist Executive in Palestine and moved its headquarters to Jerusalem.

The debate about the location of the Jewish state had already been settled in Herzl's time, in the early days of political Zionism: it could only be in Palestine, not in Uganda as some had suggested at the time. Clearly, Jerusalem occupied a unique position in the Jewish world, second to none; no other city could be capital of the Jewish state. The Zionist movement now did everything in its power to ensure this position, in practice as well as in theory. At the same time, it was fully realized that Jerusalem was of importance to other religions and peoples, so that a suitable way had to be found to preserve their share in the city. The Zionists developed Jerusalem outside the walls, while neglecting the Jewish Quarter in the Old City—perhaps in recognition of the fact that the interests of the three monotheistic religions (Judaism, Christianity and Islam) would focus on the Old City, while political goals would be fulfilled outside the walls.

Weizmann's demands from the British government at the end of the war included the three basic points of Zionist policy: to direct the military government

Hajj Amin al-Husseini, Mufti of Jerusalem, leader of the Arabs of Palestine.

in Palestine to rehabilitate the status of the Jews, which had been severely affected by the war; to secure agreement to cooperation with the Arab nationalist movement; and to broaden international recognition for the rights of Zionism in the country through the League of Nations. This shrewd basic policy attested to long-term vision and humanism, recognizing the rights and needs of others.

In parallel to their declaration of intentions, the Zionists began to view Jerusalem as the capital of the nascent state. The institutions of the Zionist Executive were moved to Jerusalem, plans were made to establish cultural institutions there, and the Western Wall once again became a focus for religious yearnings.

3. THE WESTERN WALL AND THE STRUGGLE OVER ITS CHARACTER AND STATUS

SINCE the Jews returned to Jerusalem in Nahmanides' time, the Western Wall has been the most sacred Jewish site in Jerusalem. The importance of the wall was further enhanced after the Ottoman conquest thanks to Suleiman the Magnificent who, eager to attract Jews to Jerusalem, made the wall more accessible as a place of Jewish worship of unprecedented scope.

Christian pilgrims came to Jerusalem throughout the entire period of Ottoman

rule; when they visited the Western Wall, they saw Jews weeping over its stones. Many of the pilgrims committed their impressions to writing and described the Jews mourning the destruction of the Temple. Not infrequently, the writers expressed their joy at what they regarded as fit punishment for the Jews' refusal to accept Christianity, and the Western Wall was designated contemptuously as the "Wailing Wall." But Christian contempt and mockery actually strengthened the Jews' tie with the wall, which became a symbol of remembrance and hope that the Temple would soon be rebuilt.

Halacha (Jewish religious law)—at least, since the Arab period, and that is still the prevailing view today—forbids entry to the Temple Mount area because at present all Jews are considered potentially unclean through contact with the dead; such ritual impurity can be purged with the ashes of a red heifer (see Numbers 19), which is not available. Jewish law thus created a kind of theoretical structure, founded on realistic considerations: since the Temple Mount was in the custody of non-Jews and Jews were in any case barred entry, it was more convenient to say that entry was forbidden for religious reasons than because it was prevented by Gentiles.

But another consideration was at work here, concerning the very idea of the Temple as an expression of the tangible versus the spiritual. The great Jewish sage Maimonides (1135–1204) wrote that, essentially, the Temple, with its sacrificial rites, was first built as a compromise. Although the invisible and intangible God who can be neither seen nor even conceived of requires no "home" or other structure, in contrast to pagan gods' temples, the ancient Jews needed a tangible place where they could pray to the invisible God. But even though the Temple was built, the Holy of Holies was left empty. Maimonides therefore considered prayer far superior to the physical sacrificial rite. The same applies to the rebuilding of the Temple. Thus, according to the mainstream of Jewish thought throughout the two thousand years since the destruction of the Temple, a perfectly full religious life is possible without the

The Western Wall also served as a focus of the Jews' national hopes, although it was essentially a sacred site and place of Jewish prayer.

rites surrounding the Temple Mount. In fact, those rites were a cause of corruption in the First Temple period, inspiring the Prophets to prophesy the destruction of the Temple; and history repeated itself, in that respect, in the Second Temple period.

All this having been said, it was—and still is—impossible to expunge the thoughts and hopes of its restoration from Jewish minds. It is perhaps this duality that produced the above-mentioned ruling, as well as the idea that the Temple would be rebuilt only in the days of the Messiah, and by divine agency. Even that would not take place without the solution of a number of problems: the exact location of the "Holy of Holies" must be found; people must be purified with the ashes of a red heifer mixed with a small amount of the original ash from the Temple, which is not available; and there are further conditions.

However, the need for something concrete is a human weakness, and so throughout the generations Jews have needed a physical symbol—and what better symbol of the nation's hope to "renew its days as of old" than the Temple Mount? Thus the Western Wall and the Dome of the Rock beyond came to symbolize national and religious rebirth.

Jewish art in many contexts has frequently utilized the Dome of the Rock, and sometimes also the Al-Aqsa Mosque, as religious symbols. The same symbols were also used in seals and emblems of various associations, both Zionist and non-Zionist, national-religious and secular. The nationalist awakening that adopted the Temple and the Western Wall as symbols brought angry reactions from the Muslims: they believed it to be a sign of the Jews' intention to destroy the Muslim holy sites and replace them with the Jewish Temple.

This subject became the focus of attention for Muslims in Jerusalem and the rest of the world—continuing even today—and they began to create obstacles for the Jews. At the beginning of the nineteenth century, for example, the Muslim tradition that Muhammad had tethered his miraculous horse Al-Burak at the eastern wall of the Temple Mount—which was logical, given the direction from which he had presumably come—when he ascended to heaven was transferred to the Western Wall. The Mufti Hajj Amin al-Husseini purposely moved his offices and the Muslim religious high court to the "Tankiziyya" building, built by the Mamluks close to the Western Wall, from which he could inspect the Jews coming there and sometimes also provoke them.

In the nineteenth century Sir Moses Montefiore, and later also Baron Edmond de Rothschild, made attempts to purchase the Western Wall and the area in front of it. In 1913 another such attempt was made by the directors of the Anglo-Palestine Bank. However, the administration of the *waqf*, the Muslim religious trust, refused.

During the period of the British Mandate, Muslims and Jews clashed time and time again over the control of the Western Wall. Hajj Amin and his representatives brought up a variety of complaints. They demanded that no benches be allowed into the area to seat the elderly during prayer; that the *shofar* (ram's horn) should not be blown at the Western Wall on the New Year festival; that no barrier should be put up to separate women from men; and so on. The Mufti frequently instigated disturbances, with stones and feces thrown at the worshipers. The British government established a parliamentary committee to examine such complaints and suggest solutions. An international commission was set up to reach an agreed solution, and its three members arrived in Jerusalem in 1930. Having heard evidence from twenty-one Jews, thirty Muslims and one

Briton, they tried to propose a compromise decision, but the Mufti rejected all proposals. Finally the British government passed a law in 1931 confirming the status quo. Nevertheless, the Western Wall continued to be a focus of struggle and conflict throughout the Mandate. The British authorities strictly imposed the restrictive regulations, especially where they applied to the Jews.

The Mufti claimed that he was opposing the Jews and their tradition of the Western Wall because they intended to destroy the mosques on the Temple Mount and rebuild the Temple. However, he surely knew quite well that Christians would not welcome the rebuilding of the Temple, and moreover that the Jewish religion would not permit any such endeavor before the advent of the Messiah. His struggle was therefore one more chapter in the Arab national struggle against Jewish aspirations for political independence in Palestine.

4. CONSTRUCTION IN MANDATORY JERUSALEM

The British made their mark on construction in Jerusalem through their attempt to combine European and oriental architecture. The results are still visible in several public buildings in Jerusalem, among them Government House, the Rockefeller Museum, and the Scottish Church and hospice (illustrated here).

JERUSALEM owed much of its growth during the nineteenth century to the great powers' competition for influence there. Construction on an impressive scale was initiated in the Old City and in the increasingly many new neighborhoods outside the walls. The competitive atmosphere continued under the British Mandate as well. Although there was now less building by foreign powers, the British

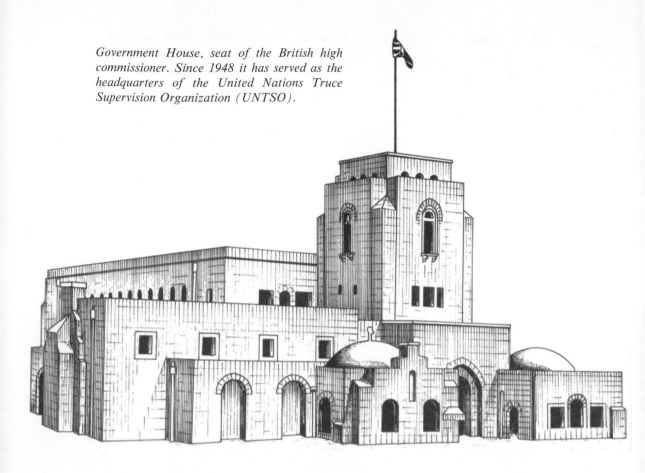

Government House, seat of the British high commissioner. Since 1948 it has served as the headquarters of the United Nations Truce Supervision Organization (UNTSO).

Government House and the Rockefeller Museum are good examples of the attempt to combine European and oriental architecture and create a new Jerusalem style.

Rockefeller Museum

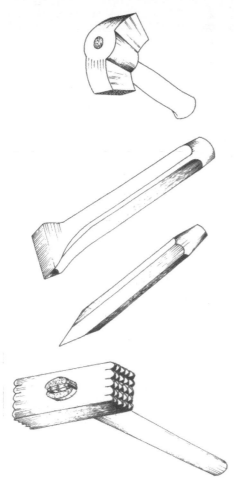

Chisels and hammer used by Jerusalem stonemasons.

above all, private homes, were built all over the new city. Many new Jewish neighborhoods went up, mainly in the west of the city and in empty spaces between the previous neighborhoods, such as Rehavia, Kiryat Shmu'el, Mekor Baruch, Kerem Avraham, Sanhedria, Ge'ula, Romema, Beit Hakerem and Bayit Vegan; neighborhoods were also built in the south of the city—Talpiot, Arnona and Kibbutz Ramat Rahel. Such intensive development was unprecedented in Jerusalem's history. The Arabs also built new residential quarters, especially wealthy neighborhoods and villas for affluent Arabs who had left the Old City: the Greek Colony and Katamon for former residents of the Christian Quarter, and small neighborhoods like Abu Tor, Mamilla and Jurat al-'Anab in the Hinnom Valley. The Supreme Muslim Council built a large hotel—the Palace—on land belonging to the Muslim cemetery in the Mamilla neighborhood, for which purpose they destroyed many graves, including an impressive Mamluk tomb. However, the Arabs built almost no public buildings, relying on the Muslim holy sites in Jerusalem to guarantee their continued presence.

The mandatory administration built a number of buildings in Jerusalem, the foremost being Government House. With government agreement and support, the Rockefeller family erected the Palestine Archaeological Museum on a hill facing the city's northern wall. The Scottish Church received permission to construct a church and hostel near the railway station, St. Andrew's Church. The large King David Hotel was built in imperial style, and opposite it the headquarters of the YMCA (Young Men's Christian Association). The two last-named buildings are of original and interesting architectural design, integrating eastern and Byzantine elements with western design in a new architectural style.

The British mandatory government

authorities, the Arabs and especially the Jews began extensive construction, vying with one another to leave their mark on the character of the city. The Jews were the most successful, because of their fervor, organizational skill and ability to raise both manpower and money. Jewish construction was marked by a sense of mission; the Jews felt that they were building the capital of their future state. Many public and administrative buildings sprang up, such as the Jewish Agency compound, which was a notable architectural achievement. In 1925 the Hebrew University was dedicated on Mount Scopus, a major event in the city's history. Schools and *yeshivot* (talmudic colleges), hotels and hospitals and,

An Arab stonemason at work.

(drinking fountain) that had been placed close to the western tower of the Citadel. These were dismantled as being symbols of late nineteenth-century Ottoman construction, of which the British wanted to erase all memory.

One important regulation introduced by the British mandatory government has dictated the character of Jerusalem until the present day. In the 1920s, Sir Ronald Storrs, the first military governor of the city and later the district commissioner, issued a ban on the construction of outer walls faced with plaster, clay, tin and the like. Since concrete was unavailable at that time, the preferred building material was Jerusalem stone. This has given the city a distinctive appearance—

established municipal authorities to care for the inhabitants' needs, in fact opening up the modern era of Jerusalem's administration. The British drew up master plans and outline plans for Jerusalem, laid out public parks and improved the city's water-supply system. Various steps were taken to enhance the appearance of the Old City, especially of public buildings. The Ottoman walls, which had deteriorated over the years, were repaired and maintained, especially the top of the wall and the crenellations. Some of the gates were also repaired or rebuilt, to provide access to motor vehicles. The walls were restored more or less to their original state, in the time of Suleiman the Magnificent. Thus the British removed a gate tower that that had been built outside the Dung Gate two hundred years after the wall, as well as the clock tower over the Jaffa Gate and a *sabil*

although the regulation was not introduced for aesthetic reasons, but to achieve a balance between the Jews and the Arabs. The British had seen that the large number of Jews moving to the city was quickly upsetting the demographic balance. Since construction with stone is more expensive and requires skilled stonecutters—not a popular profession among the Jews—Jewish building would be reduced, they believed, by requiring the use of stone. Unintentionally, this ruling has enhanced the city's appearance and done much to create its unique character.

At a later stage, the use of other building materials was permitted, provided that the walls were faced with Jerusalem stone. Still visible in the Rehavia neighborhood are a few fine concrete buildings that were built before the regulation was introduced.

Chapter 12:
JERUSALEM DIVIDED AND REUNITED
1948–1989

1. THE UN RESOLUTION: JEWISH STATE AND ARAB STATE, INTERNATIONAL JERUSALEM

GREAT difficulties had to be overcome in order to establish a Jewish state in the Holy Land. On the one hand, tens of thousands of Arabs lived in areas suitable for Jewish settlement. Some of them had lived there for many generations—perhaps Jews and Christians who had been converted to Islam over the centuries; others were more recently arrived Muslims from North Africa and Egypt. The Zionist movement paid large sums of money to purchase land from the Arabs; the Jewish settlements were concentrated in limited areas, some of it swampland. On the other hand, the only way to solve the problem of antisemitism and absorb the masses of displaced persons who had survived the Holocaust was to establish a state in the Jews' historic homeland in the Holy Land. There was thus a conflict of interests between the Jews' desire and need to establish a state in Palestine and the Muslim Arabs living in the same stretch of territory.

The conflict between the two peoples had escalated since the 1920s, and a variety of suggestions for a mutually agreed solution failed, such as the idea of a binational state, similar to Belgium or, as then existed, in Czechoslovakia and in Yugoslavia. The differences between Arabs and Jews in the country were greater than between the peoples of those other countries: they practiced different religions, the situation was further complicated by the presence of a Christian-Arab minority, and so on. The Muslim-Arab community, recalling the inferior status of the Jews under Muslim

David Ben-Gurion, Israel's prime minister and minister of defense in the War of Independence. His establishment of Israel's capital in Jerusalem was the decisive factor in shaping the city's destiny. Apparently, the decision to give up the Old City was unavoidable at that time.

rule for hundreds of years, could not accept the idea of members of that race gaining their own state at Arab expense. The Jewish-Arab conflict was brought before various international organizations, which concluded that the only solution was to partition the country into two states, based on the principle that property of disputed ownership should be divided. Neither side favored these proposals, and some Jews even wished to extend the borders of the

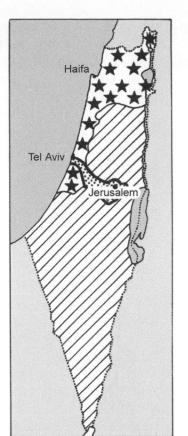

Peel
Commission
— 1937

Haifa

Tel Aviv

Jerusalem

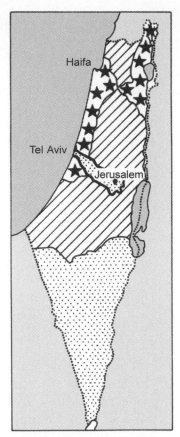

Woodhead
Commission
— 1938

Haifa

Tel Aviv

Jerusalem

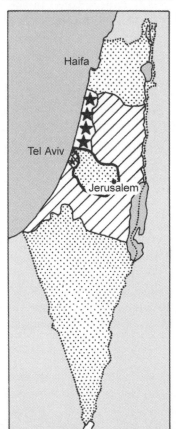

Morrison Plan
— 1946

Haifa

Tel Aviv

Jerusalem

UNSCOP Plan
— 1947

Haifa

Tel Aviv

Jerusalem

⭐ Jewish zone

▨ Arab zone

▦ British zone

☐ International zone

········ International border

future state to the east bank of the Jordan.

At the conclusion of World War II, the establishment of a Jewish state as a solution for the Jewish problem became an urgent necessity. The desire to atone for the Holocaust—the most terrible wrong inflicted in human history—and the guilt felt by many of the world's leaders placed the problem high on the international agenda. The United Nations, which had been established in the wake of the war, appointed a committee that went to Palestine to draw up a plan for partition, dividing the country into two states, one Jewish and one Arab. This idea of partition, which contained at least the kernel of Zionist aspirations for an independent state, even if the proposed territory was small, was accepted by a majority vote of the Jewish Agency. The idea won the support of the new postwar Great Powers, the Soviet Union and the United States, who wished to weaken the British Empire and its international political influence—a development also favored by France and other countries opposing Britain. The pressure exerted on Britain by the various Jewish resistance movements in Palestine and their determined opposition to the British army and government aroused British public opinion, which demanded an early solution to the problem. On November 29, 1947, two and a half years after the end of World War II, the United Nations General Assembly convened and, by a considerable majority, adopted a resolution calling for the establishment of two states in Palestine—a Jewish state and an Arab state.

Jerusalem was the most difficult problem to be solved, for there was no solution that could possibly meet the demands of each party. The problem had been raised as far back as 1937, when the so-called Peel Commission, appointed by the British government, proposed to leave Jerusalem in British hands, with a corridor linking it with Jaffa port. Ten years later, with complete British evacuation of the area planned, it was proposed to include Jerusalem in the area of the Arab state, but under international supervision. A counterproposal by the Jewish Agency called for Jerusalem to be connected to the territory of the Jewish state, to the west—the Jewish population was concentrated in the western part of the New City, the eastern part consisting only of Arab neighborhoods. The Arabs rejected the proposals out of hand: they would neither agree to the establishment of two states, nor to the plan for Jerusalem; immediately after the UN resolution had been adopted, the first battles of Israel's War of Independence broke out.

(opposite) It was clear that, in any solution to the Jewish-Arab conflict over Palestine, the status of Jerusalem would arouse difficulties. The various partition proposals contained special steps to isolate Jerusalem from the political imbroglio, but without success.

The 1947 partition plan—the UNSCOP plan—separated Jerusalem and declared it an international city but with an Arab area in the center. This solution was impractical.

2. JERUSALEM IN 1948

THE first Arab attacks following the UN General Assembly vote were by loosely organized bands of local Arabs. After the British withdrawal and the declaration of the Jewish State of Israel, the Arab states invaded the country.

From the very beginning of the war, the Arabs recognized the historical importance of subduing Jewish Jerusalem. This was clearly expressed by David Ben-Gurion in a speech before the Zionist Executive Committee on April 6, 1948: "The value of Jerusalem cannot be measured, weighed or counted, for *if a country has a soul, then Jerusalem is the soul of the Land of Israel.* The battle for Jerusalem is crucial, and not merely from a military point of view. We must not only secure the road to Jerusalem and defend our positions inside the city—but also strengthen Jerusalem's position in general...Jerusalem demands and has the right to our defense. That oath by the waters of Babylon is as binding today as it was then; otherwise we will not be worthy of being called the People of Israel....Our enemies know that the fall of Jerusalem would be a mortal blow for all the Jewish people. We must enable Jerusalem to withstand even a long siege...."

Immediately after the UN resolution had been adopted, most of the road linking Jerusalem with the rest of the country was already under Arab control.

Until Jaffa was taken, it was even difficult to reach Jerusalem from Tel Aviv; the road to Mikveh Israel passed through the Hatikva Quarter, continuing through Arab villages—only at Beit Dajan (now the Jewish village of Beit Dagan) was there a lone Jewish position. The road then continued to Rehovot, from which several

In 1968, at the age of eighty-two, David Ben-Gurion visited the archaeological excavations at the foot of the Temple Mount. He insisted on descending the ladders into the depths of the excavations to see the discoveries from the First Temple period (tombs) and the Second Temple period (ritual baths). His declaration that Jerusalem was the soul of the Land of Israel accompanied him throughout the visit, and he expressed great interest in all the findings.

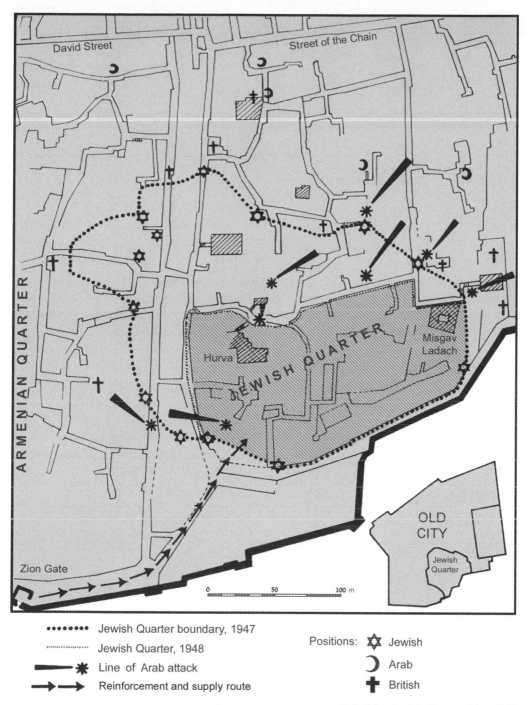

David Street

Street of the Chain

ARMENIAN QUARTER

JEWISH QUARTER

Hurva

Misgav
Ladach

Zion Gate

0   50   100 m

OLD
CITY

Jewish
Quarter

●●●●●●● Jewish Quarter boundary, 1947

············· Jewish Quarter, 1948

━━━✳ Line of Arab attack

━▶━▶ Reinforcement and supply route

Positions: ✡ Jewish

☾ Arab

✝ British

Fall of the Jewish Quarter, May 1948

A bitter battle was fought in the Jewish Quarter between a small group of defenders and thousands of Arab attackers. In the first stage the defenders retreated to the heart of the Quarter and entrenched themselves in a small area. However, this area also fell. The fall of the Quarter was the result of many years of neglect and apathy on the residents' part. No great effort was made, apparently, to hold on to the Quarter, perhaps because for fear that if the Old City fell to the Jews the plan to internationalize the city would be implemented. At that time, partition of the city was perhaps the best solution.

routes branched off to bypass the Arab town of Ramla. However, even this bypass road again passed through Arab villages, such as Kubab, whose inhabitants frequently attacked Jewish traffic. The traffic was thus forced to take yet another detour, through the village of Hulda; but there, too, the Arab villagers of 'Aqir also attacked Jewish travelers. There was no Jewish outpost between Hulda and Neveh Ilan, near Abu Ghosh in the Jerusalem Hills. The road ran through a winding valley where it was very easy to attack passing vehicles. Traffic was exposed to continuous Arab attack for six kilometers, from the mouth of the valley, Bab al-Wad (now known as Sha'ar Hagai) to the Arab village of Saris (now Shoresh). At the exit from the valley, a few kilometers on, there was another Arab obstacle—the small village of Kastel, and farther on the village of Colonia, opposite the Jewish village of Motza. This was the sole road to besieged Jerusalem, along which supplies of food and arms were sent in armored convoys with military escort. On all other sides, Jerusalem was sealed off by Arab settlements.

The British support for the Arabs was an open secret. Prior to the establishment of the state, the British authorities obstructed Jewish travel in various ways: they conducted searches, confiscated arms and did everything possible to prevent units of the Jewish defense forces, the Haganah, from taking control of Arab villages along the road. The convoys traveled under very difficult conditions and the battles along the route to Jerusalem were among the bitterest in the war. Essentially, until May 15 the Arabs had the upper hand in the battle for the road to Jerusalem.

With the departure of the British forces, the Transjordanian Arab Legion entered the war; a large Legion force captured the Latrun area and threatened to cut off Jerusalem. Three young men

(opposite) At the end of the War of Independence, Jerusalem was divided between Israel and Transjordan. The cease-fire line, which gradually became the border, cut through neighborhoods, sometimes even through houses. It left Mount Scopus in Israeli hands—an enclave that could be reached only through Transjordanian territory in accordance with special agreements.

who made their way from Jerusalem to Hulda discovered a route that would avoid Latrun, reach Sha'ar Hagai and continue to Jerusalem. This route was later nicknamed the Burma Road. The heavy fighting over Latrun ended in defeat for the Jewish forces, but they were able to secure the newly opened Burma Road—from Rehovot to Hulda, then to Beit Shemesh and Sha'ar Hagai to Jerusalem. This was achieved by a long military campaign, known as "Operation Nahshon," beginning in April 1948, before the departure of the British forces, and ending in the summer of that year. The hostile Arab villages that had been attacking Jewish travel were occupied, and the villagers fled.

In Jerusalem itself, heavy fighting raged between the Jewish forces, on the one hand, and the regular forces of the Arab Legion and heavily armed Arab irregulars, on the other. In the process, most of the Arab neighborhoods and villages to the west of Jerusalem were captured, but Jewish settlements north and east of Jerusalem, such as Atarot and Beit Ha'arava, were evacuated. Kibbutz Ramat Rahel, south of the city, changed hands several times and was eventually recaptured by Israeli forces in a battle which also involved the invading Egyptian army.

The Jewish Quarter of the Old City, however, fell to Transjordan. This was the price paid for the neglect of previous years; during the years of the British

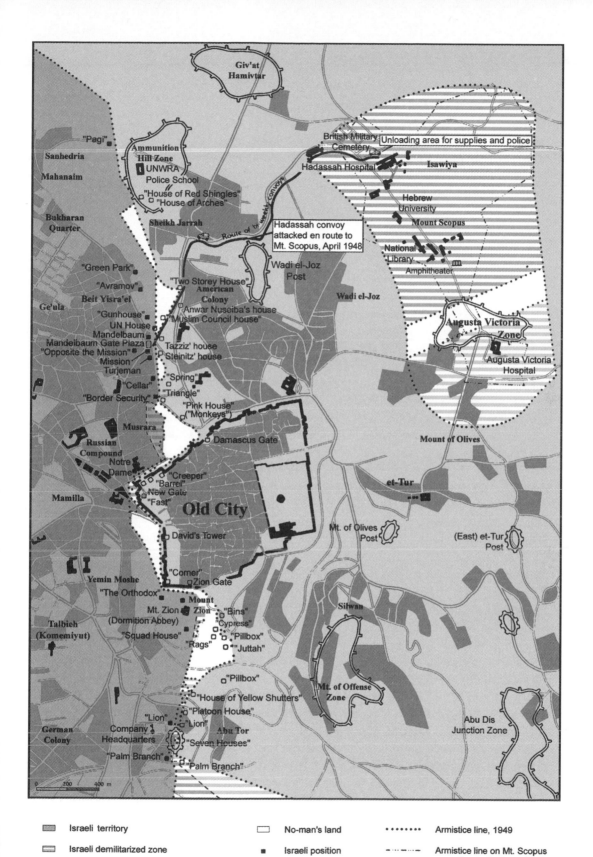

Giv'at Hamivtar

"Pagi"

Sanhedria

Mahanaim

Ammunition Hill Zone
UNWRA Police School
"House of Red Shingles"
"House of Arches"

Sheikh Jarrah

British Military Cemetery

Unloading area for supplies and police

Hadassah Hospital

Isawiya

Hebrew University

Mount Scopus

National Library

Amphitheater

Route of bi-weekly convoy

Hadassah convoy attacked en route to Mt. Scopus, April 1948

Wadi el-Joz Post

Wadi el-Joz

Bukharan Quarter

"Green Park"

"Avramov"

Beit Yisra'el

Ge'ula

"Two Storey House"
American Colony
Anwar Nuseiba's house
"Muslim Council house"

"Gunhouse"
UN House
Mandelbaum
Mandelbaum Gate Plaza
"Opposite the Mission"
Mission
Turjeman

Tazziz' house
Steinitz' house

Augusta Victoria Zone

Augusta Victoria Hospital

"Cellar"

"Border Security"

"Spring"
"Triangle"

"Pink House"
("Monkeys")

Mount of Olives

Musrara

Russian Compound
Notre Dame

Damascus Gate

et-Tur

Mamilla

"Creeper"
"Barrel"
New Gate
"Fast"

Old City

Mt. of Olives Post

(East) et-Tur Post

David's Tower

"Corner"
Zion Gate

Yemin Moshe

"The Orthodox"

Mount Zion
Mt. Zion
(Dormition Abbey)

"Bins"
"Cypress"

Silwan

Talbieh
(Komemiyut)

"Squad House"

"Pillbox"

"Rags"

"Juttah"

German Colony

"Pillbox"

"House of Yellow Shutters"

"Platoon House"

"Lion"
Company Headquarters
"Lion"

Abu Tor

"Seven Houses"

Mt. of Offense Zone

Abu Dis Junction Zone

"Palm Branch"
"Palm Branch"

0   200   400 m

Israeli territory

Israeli demilitarized zone

Jordanian territory

Jordanian demilitarized zone

No-man's land

Israeli position

Jordanian position

•••••••• Armistice line, 1949

—·—·—·— Armistice line on Mt. Scopus according to Jordan and UN

Divided Jerusalem, 1949–1967

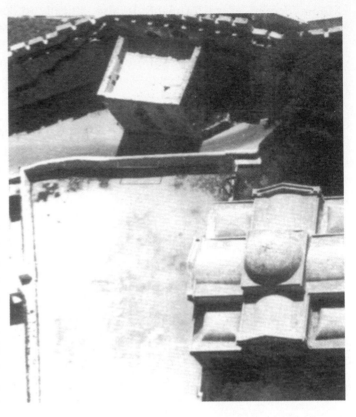

View of Zion Gate from above; the elderly, women and children were evacuated through this gate after the fall of the Jewish Quarter.

Mandate, the Quarter had become a slum, most of whose residents were ultra-Orthodox Jews, mostly poor, whose only desire was to live near the site of the Temple. Small units sent by the Haganah to help defend the Jewish Quarter were unsuccessful. The Jordanians surrounded the walled Old City and Haganah attempts to break in failed. Immediately after the establishment of the state, the Jewish Quarter fell. The elderly, women and children were evacuated; the defenders were taken prisoner and incarcerated in Transjordan.

On April 3, 1949, a cease-fire agreement was signed between Israel and Transjordan. The armistice line passed east of Ramat Rahel and then ran north behind the houses of the Talpiot neighborhood, cutting the Abu Tor neighborhood into two, with the top section going to the Jews and the bottom section to the Arabs. It then descended to the Hinnom Valley and climbed to Mount Zion, which was also divided between Israel and Transjordan. From that point on the line followed the Old City wall for some distance, going down the slope of the Hinnom Valley to Beit Taunus, and from there to "Notre Dame," northwest of the Old City wall. It then ran north, crossing the Musrara (now Morasha) neighborhood toward "Mandelbaum Gate" (not a real gate, but the official crossing point between Israel and Jordan until 1967)

and on to Shmu'el Hanavi Street, the Pagi neighborhood and the tombs of the Sanhedrin.

Jerusalem was thus cut in half from north to south by a winding line that essentially preserved the state of war. The entire Old City came under Transjordanian (later Jordanian) rule, while the western city was held by Israel. At key points, great concrete walls were built as barriers against sudden attack. Barbed wire was stretched along the line, mines were planted, and military positions were built on both sides. The division also created human tragedies: in the southwest of the city the small Arab village of Beit Safafa was cut in two in order to leave the railway line to Jerusalem in Israel's hands. Mount Scopus, with the buildings of Hebrew University and Hadassah Hospital, remained in Israeli hands, but was surrounded on all sides by Arab territory, forming a kind of Israeli enclave. The cease-fire agreement permitted Israel to change its guards on

Mount Scopus every fortnight. It also permitted Jews to pray at the Western Wall, but this part of the agreement was never honored. After the capture of the Jewish Quarter, the Arabs began system- atically to destroy the synagogues there, in an effort to obliterate the long Jewish past of the Old City. Thus began one of the most difficult periods in Jerusalem's history—a divided city.

3. DIVIDED JERUSALEM

FOR nineteen years Jerusalem remained divided, the east under Jordanian control and the west under the Israelis. The eastern city seemed to have frozen in time. Jordan and the other Arab nations, who had glorified Jerusalem and insisted on its status and importance, in fact did nothing for the city: only two new tourist hotels were built and most of the construction carried out during those years was of military camps. During the Mandate, the Citadel at Jaffa Gate had been used as a museum, but now all the exhibits were removed by the Jordanians and lost, and it became a military fortress. Military positions were built on the Old City walls, damaging this in- estimable architectural treasure. Camps were built for the Arab Legion on the slopes of the Mount of Olives and for this purpose—as well as to improve the Jericho-Jerusalem road—the Jordanians desecrated the ancient Jewish cemetery on the mount, using the tombstones for building. The Muslim cemetery on Ma- milla Road in West Jerusalem, now in Jewish territory, was also slightly damaged by the need to broaden a road, but most of it was preserved and re- stored. It should be recalled that the first damage to this cemetery was done by the Supreme Muslim Council, when it built the Palace Hotel on a large part of its land. However, this was not a desecration: according to Is- lamic religious law, the sanc- tity of a cemetery expires after forty years.

An exceptional event took place in Jerusalem in 1964, when it received perhaps the most famous pilgrim in its

Paulus PP. VI —

Pope Paul VI at the time of his visit to Jerusalem. The first pope to visit the holy city where Jesus had lived and worked, the site of his crucifixion and burial.

After the War of Independence the Church also resumed building in Jerusalem. On the slope of the Mount of Olives, which Christian tradition identifies as the spot where Jesus wept and predicted the destruction of Jerusalem and the Temple, a small church was built, called Dominus Flevit *("the Lord wept")*.

past few hundred years of history—Pope Paul VI. No other pope had ever visited Jerusalem, despite its paramount significance as a focus of Christian pilgrimage and a symbol of Christian values. The real reason for Pope Paul's unprecedented visit is unknown; perhaps contacts were underway regarding the fate of the city and its international status. The Jordanians were aware of the importance of the visit. As soon as the details were known and preparations began, some two years in advance, King Hussein began to demonstrate his regard for Muslim Jerusalem; he launched rebuilding and preservation work in the Temple Mount area, among other things facing the Dome of the Rock with gilt aluminum and replacing the porcelain tiles that had adorned the exterior since the time of Suleiman. The new tiles, like the original ones, were also ordered in Turkey, from Kütahya, considered to be the successor of the old Iznik workshops. The dome of Al-Aqsa Mosque was also replaced, by a new dome faced with silvered aluminum. In 1963, around the same time, Hussein planned to plant a large public garden in what had been the Jewish Quarter and began to evacuate the Arab squatters. The king had two objectives: to obliterate any trace of Jewish activity and existence in the Old City during the seven preceding centuries, and to beautify that part of Jerusalem between the Temple Mount and the Church of the Holy Sepulcher, in order to show the pope and the entire world Jerusalem's importance and sanctity to the Muslims. These measures were discontinued after the pope's departure.

Apart from this, the years of Jordanian rule over Jerusalem added nothing to the city's development. Although King Hussein began to build a small palace atop the tel (archaeological mound) of Giv'at Sha'ul for his visits to Jerusalem, most of Jordan's development efforts were invested in government, educational and cultural institutions, and especially in economic projects, on the east bank of the Jordan.

While the eastern side of Jerusalem slumbered, the Israeli side was throbbing with construction activity. David Ben-Gurion turned his vision into reality and established Jerusalem as the capital of the new state, thus raising its status in the world. The most urgent need was housing for the thousands of new immigrants who flocked to Jerusalem—as to the country as a whole—mainly Holocaust survivors and Jewish refugees from Arab countries. The first arrivals occupied abandoned homes in areas like Mamilla, Katamon, Musrara and Jurat al-'Anab, formerly Arab neighborhoods whose inhabitants had fled in the storm of war. New neighborhoods were built for later waves of immigrants, who were first accommodated in tents and huts in temporary transit camps.

Great effort was invested in transferring the state's government institutions to Jerusalem. The first sessions of Israel's parliament, the Knesset, took place in Tel Aviv, but once the fighting ceased a modest building (now housing the Ministry of Tourism) was acquired in King George Street and the Knesset moved to Jerusalem. Many government offices,

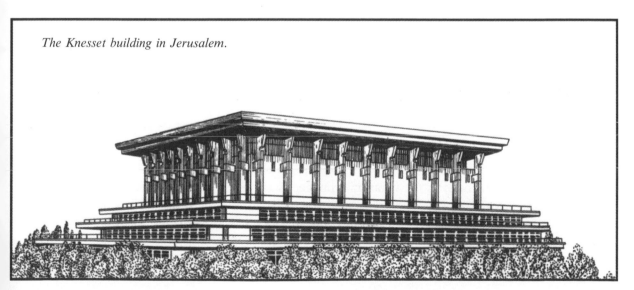

The Knesset building in Jerusalem.

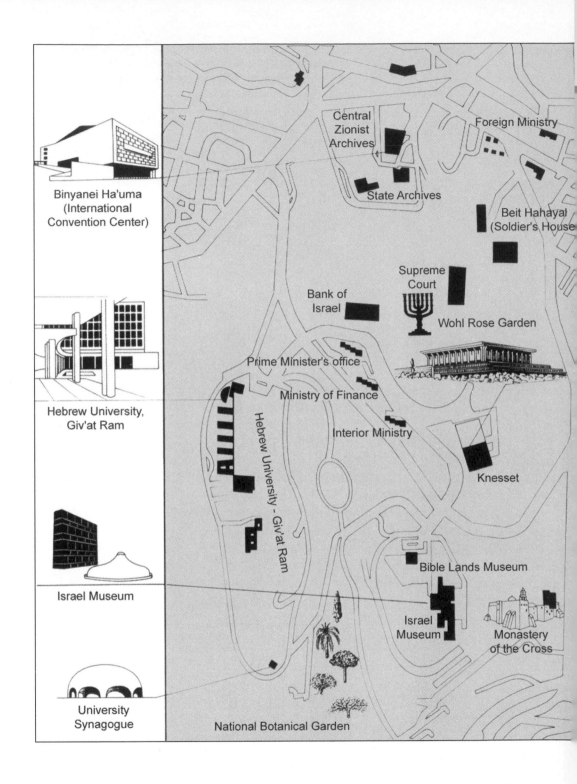

Binyanei Ha'uma (International Convention Center)

Hebrew University, Giv'at Ram

Israel Museum

University Synagogue

Central Zionist Archives

Foreign Ministry

State Archives

Beit Hahayal (Soldier's House)

Supreme Court

Bank of Israel

Wohl Rose Garden

Prime Minister's office

Ministry of Finance

Interior Ministry

Hebrew University - Giv'at Ram

Knesset

Bible Lands Museum

Israel Museum

Monastery of the Cross

National Botanical Garden

including the Prime Minister's Office, also moved to Jerusalem, and construction of a government complex began on Giv'at Ram, a barren hill in the heart of the city. Some years later a new building was constructed for the Knesset on the same hill. The first president of Israel, Chaim Weizmann, lived in his own house in Rehovot. His successor, Izhak Ben-Zvi, was a long-time resident of Jerusalem and his home became the presidential residence. Some years later an official

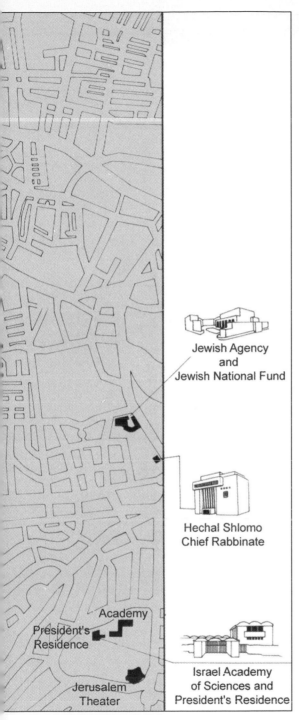

Jewish Agency
and
Jewish National Fund

Hechal Shlomo
Chief Rabbinate

Academy

President's
Residence

Jerusalem
Theater

Israel Academy
of Sciences and
President's Residence

In the difficult first years of Israel's existence, the government under David Ben-Gurion made great efforts to gain recognition for Jerusalem's status as capital. A large area was allocated for the construction of a new government center, and cultural and educational institutions were built. The center of the judiciary system was also established in Jerusalem.

presidential residence was built in the Talbieh neighborhood, near the Israel Academy of Sciences.

After Mount Scopus had been cut off from the city, the faculties of the Hebrew University were scattered in various public buildings throughout the city. In the 1950s work commenced on a university campus close to the government complex, which would house the National Library, also exiled from Mount Scopus. Magnificent new premises for

Hadassah Hospital, also originally located on Mount Scopus, were later built at Ein Kerem, a former Arab village on the outskirts of Jerusalem.

As a nation respecting its past, Israel set up its central museum in Jerusalem, the Israel Museum, which at first concentrated on archaeological exhibits relating to the country's past, and on Judaica, preserving the traditions of all the Jewish communities. Wings for a wide variety of exhibits were later added to this museum. Among the other museums established in the city was "Yad Vashem," the Martyrs' and Heroes' Remembrance Authority, which is dedicated to documenting the Holocaust and commemorating its victims. It was constructed on a slope of Mount Herzl, close to the tomb of Theodor Herzl, the father of modern Zionism, and the military cemetery. Each year, Independence Day

celebrations are officially opened on this hill, which has brought together three basic elements: the resting place of the visionary and founder of the Zionist movement; a memorial to the Holocaust, which contributed to the establishment of the state; and a testimony to the heavy price that the Jewish people have had to pay for their independence.

Israeli Jerusalem in the west of the city functioned for nineteen years as the capital of the state of Israel, while its sacred sites—the Temple Mount and the Western Wall—were held by the Jordanians. To express yearning for the city's past throughout those years, people would go up to Mount Zion and, with a heavy heart, look down from the heights of the traditional site of King David's tomb toward the Temple Mount and the Western Wall, barely visible among the homes of a residential district.

4. JERUSALEM REUNITED

IN 1967, on the eve of Israel's nineteenth Independence Day, President Gamal Abdel Nasser of Egypt announced the closing of the Tiran Straits to Israeli shipping. The Egyptians, interpreting the absence of an immediate Israeli reaction as weakness, increased their demands and pressure on Israel. When no other alternative remained, the Six-Day War broke out. The armies of several Arab countries, including Jordan, participated in the war. Despite a message from the Israeli government asking him not to intervene, King Hussein decided to join in the attack, assuming that the anticipated Israeli defeat would transfer parts of the Jewish State into his hands. West Jerusalem was shelled, and Government House was captured from the UN observers stationed there. Within two days, however, the tables were turned. Egypt suffered a crushing defeat, and the

Jordanian army's debacle changed the face of Jerusalem and the West Bank of the Jordan River. Within three days, the Jordanians had been driven from all their positions on the West Bank and the Old City of Jerusalem was surrounded. The city holy to the three monotheistic religions, with its many religious and sacred buildings, was now about to surrender to the army of the State of

(opposite) After Jordan joined the Egyptians and Syrians and its forces overran Government House, the Israeli government, headed by Levi Eshkol, gave orders to fight back and to conquer Jerusalem. It was a fateful decision. The difficulties stemmed mainly from the large number of holy places whose integrity and safety had to be protected during the fighting. Lines and methods of attack were planned subject to these constraints, generally with success.

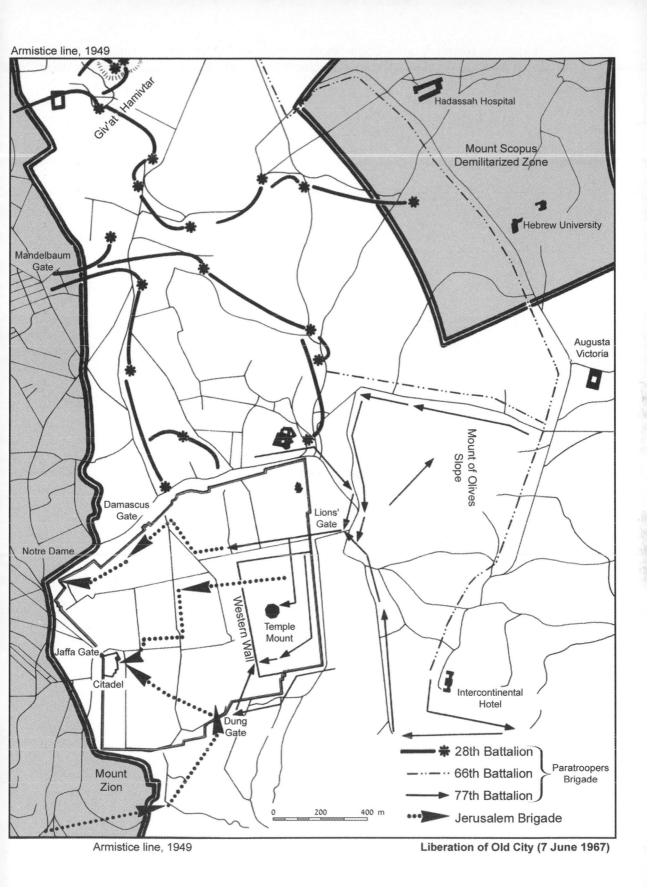

Armistice line, 1949

Giv'at Hamivtar

Hadassah Hospital

Mount Scopus
Demilitarized Zone

Hebrew University

Mandelbaum
Gate

Augusta
Victoria

Mount of Olives Slope

Damascus
Gate

Lions'
Gate

Notre Dame

Western Wall

Temple
Mount

Intercontinental
Hotel

Jaffa Gate

Citadel

Dung
Gate

Mount
Zion

0   200   400 m

28th Battalion

66th Battalion

Paratroopers
Brigade

77th Battalion

Jerusalem Brigade

Armistice line, 1949

Liberation of Old City (7 June 1967)

Since the Six-Day War the Western Wall Plaza has become a focus of national expression. Swearing-in ceremonies for army recruits are sometimes held there.

Israel. The decision to conquer East Jerusalem was a difficult one because of its political implications, and it was clearly necessary to ensure that no sacred sites would be damaged in the heat of battle. Israel's prime minister, Levi Eshkol, made the decision: the need of the hour was to unite Jerusalem. There would no longer be two cities, but one united one. The Israeli government assumed that the fall of East Jerusalem would promote peace negotiations between Israel and its neighbors, and the shock of the loss might bring results. The battle for Jerusalem was a short one, and the soldiers of the Israel Defense Forces (IDF), led by paratroopers and the Jerusalem Brigade, entered the Old City through the Lions' Gate and the Dung Gate. As the cry "The Temple Mount is in our hands" rang out, the first Israeli paratroopers hurried to the most sacred site of all, the Western Wall. A new chapter had opened in the history of Jerusalem: it was now a united city.

The shock of the battle for Jerusalem brought far-reaching results. Nobody had foreseen Jordan's participation in the war, and nobody could have reasonably anticipated Israeli actions under attack. Many feared that Israel would be unable to maintain the holy places, while others were convinced that the advent of the Messiah was imminent. The Jordanians and their king, as well as the Arab population of Jerusalem and the rest of the country, were overwhelmed—as were many of Israel's citizens. The first to come to his senses was David Ben-Gurion, the 80-year-old former leader, who declared that the occupied territories should be returned, except for the Golan Heights and Jerusalem, and a peace agreement signed. The "Old Man," as he was known, had again proved his political insight and historical perspective. As prime minister and minister of defense during the War of Independence, who considered the borders secured then as the basis for a peace

Immediately after the Six-Day War, Prime Minister Levi Eshkol ordered that the Jewish Quarter be rebuilt and Jews be enabled to live there again. Shown here is one of the rebuilding projects, at the corner of Misgav Ladach and Tiferet Yisra'el Streets.

agreement, Ben-Gurion realized that the victory of the Six-Day War offered an opportunity not to be missed. The 1948 cease-fire lines could now be established as permanent borders, with international recognition and the agreement of the Arab countries. As for Jerusalem, in 1948 Ben-Gurion had not believed that the world would agree to Israel's control over the Old City, and so had not invested much effort in winning that battle. Now that the world had already recognized Israel's existence, he believed, control of Jerusalem by the Jews—as the third party which would permit Muslims and Christians free access to their holy sites—might be more acceptable. Ben-Gurion was motivated by a feeling of historic justice and the assumption that both Muslims and Christians revere the prophets of Israel. He even suggested destroying the Old City walls, which he believed to be a symbol of the divided city. By now, however, Ben-Gurion held no official post and responsibility. Prime Minister Eshkol and his government rejected the proposal and, lacking a practical solution, trusted that time would bring its own solution.

In the meanwhile, a number of modest steps were taken. The Mughrabi neighborhood beside the Western Wall was evacuated and pulled down, in order to permit preparation of a large open space before the Western Wall for the crowds of people expected to visit there. Instructions were also issued to rebuild the Jewish Quarter and populate it with Jews. Repairs were begun at the cemetery on the slopes of the Mount of Olives, and the barbed-wire fences, concrete walls and mines that had marked the borders between Jewish and Jordanian Jerusalem were removed. When peace failed to materialize, and the shock of Israeli rule over Jerusalem did not bring the Arabs to the conference table, it was decided to unite the city on a unilateral basis and proclaim it an integral part of the state of Israel. The large Arab population of East

Jerusalem would be considered "citizens" of Jerusalem but not of Israel. They remained Jordanian citizens, with the right to vote only in Jerusalem's municipal elections. The government and the municipality began to take practical steps to unite Jerusalem.

Levi Eshkol, Israel's prime minister during the Six-Day War. It fell to him to make the fateful decision regarding the unification of Jerusalem.

5. CHANGES AND TRENDS SINCE JERUSALEM'S REUNIFICATION

FORTUITOUSLY, the mayor of Jerusalem at the time of its reunification was just the right man for the job, a man of political insight and experience—Teddy Kollek. His heart was open and his ears attuned to the feelings of all the citizens, despite opposing interests. Under government guidance, and with the advice of his aides and advisers, Kollek conducted Israeli policy with considerable flexibility, with the judicious help of all Israel's governments, who recognized the importance of the grave and special responsibility that had been placed in their hands. Nevertheless, at times the actions of the nation's leaders regarding Jerusalem fell short of their declared intentions.

There have been many episodes during the years of Jerusalem's reunification, some of which will now be described, together with the basic trends that characterized this period. As a result of

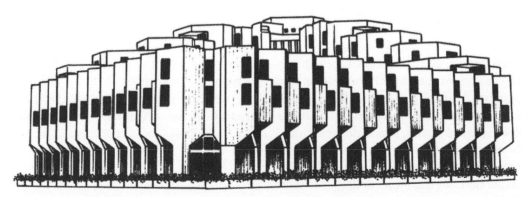

After the Six-Day War the question of high-rise building in Jerusalem was hotly debated. In some instances advocates of low building were successful, resulting in a number of low buildings which look like severed towers, such as the Laromme Hotel (now the Inbal Hotel).

the government's decision to strengthen the city, expand its borders and enlarge its Jewish population, many new neighborhoods were built in Jerusalem: in the west, north and south the area of the city was expanded with the construction of Gilo, East Talpiot, Ramot Eshkol, Ramot and Giv'at Shapira (popularly known as "French Hill") and other neighborhoods, and the number of Jewish citizens was almost doubled. In the first few years, no new Jewish residential neighborhoods were built in East Jerusalem, leaving an eastern corridor to Jerusalem in case Jordan should receive any status in the city under a peace agreement. Eventually, there was strong government support for an open declaration rejecting any such option. A satellite city was then constructed—Ma'aleh Adumim. In continuation of these plans, the northern neighborhoods were also expanded. The large-scale Jewish construction aroused a vigorous Arab response, and many residential neighborhoods were built in north Jerusalem, between the city and Ramallah. The Arab buildings are particularly large, as this population is accustomed to separate family units surrounded by gardens. The accelerated construction raised aesthetic questions: a voluntary movement called "Beautiful Israel" was established, with the objective of preserving the character of construction in the city. The debate centered on high-rise buildings and construction on hilltops, and later on the preservation of residential buildings and neighborhoods. After a long struggle by the movement, the East Talpiot neighborhood was built on the slope of a hill in such a way that the view of the desert was preserved. High-rise construction was forbidden in the low-lying areas facing the Old City. For that reason, two hotels, the Laromme and the Hyatt, were built with a relatively low number of stories and therefore look incomplete, like truncated bases of towers. There is no absolute solution to the debate about high-rise construction, for quality and beauty depend not on height but on pleasant appearance—a low building may also be quite ugly. Nostalgic preservation is not a value in itself; Jerusa-

(overleaf) At the conclusion of the war extensive building activities began in Jerusalem, at a pace and to a degree unprecedented since Jews first began to settle outside the Old City walls.

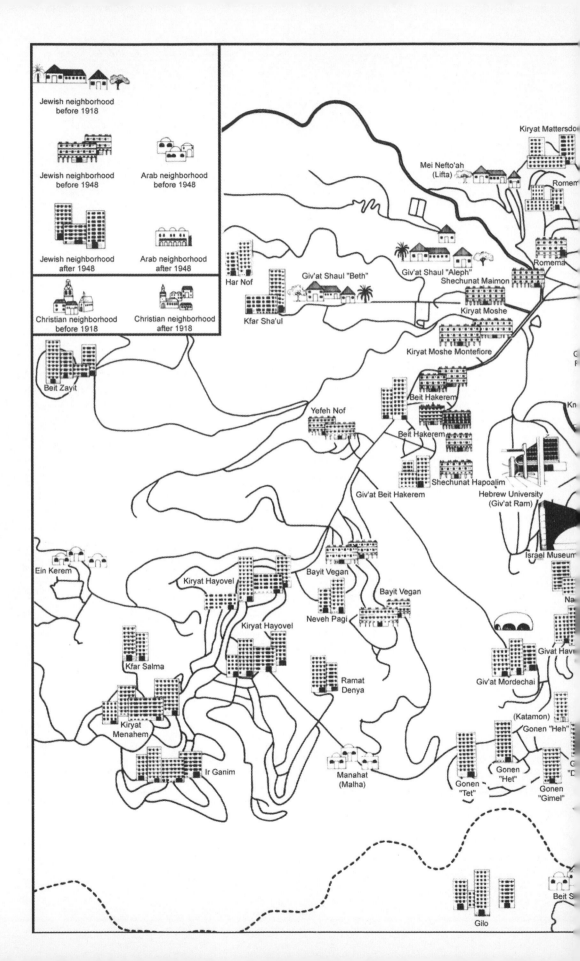

**Jewish neighborhood
before 1918**

**Jewish neighborhood
before 1948**

**Arab neighborhood
before 1948**

**Jewish neighborhood
after 1948**

**Arab neighborhood
after 1948**

**Christian neighborhood
before 1918**

**Christian neighborhood
after 1918**

Kiryat Mattersdo

Mei Nefto'ah
(Lifta)

Romem

Har Nof

Giv'at Shaul "Beth"

Giv'at Shaul "Aleph"
Shechunat Maimon

Romema

Kfar Sha'ul

Kiryat Moshe

Kiryat Moshe Montefiore

Beit Zayit

Yefeh Nof

Beit Hakerem

Beit Hakerem

Shechunat Hapoalim

Giv'at Beit Hakerem

Hebrew University
(Giv'at Ram)

Kn

Israel Museum

Ein Kerem

Kiryat Hayovel

Bayit Vegan

Bayit Vegan

Na

Neveh Pagi

Kiryat Hayovel

Givat Hav

Kfar Salma

Ramat
Denya

Giv'at Mordechai

(Katamon)

Gonen "Heh"

Kiryat
Menahem

Manahat
(Malha)

Gonen
"Het"

G

"D

Ir Ganim

Gonen
"Tet"

Gonen
"Gimel"

Beit S

Gilo

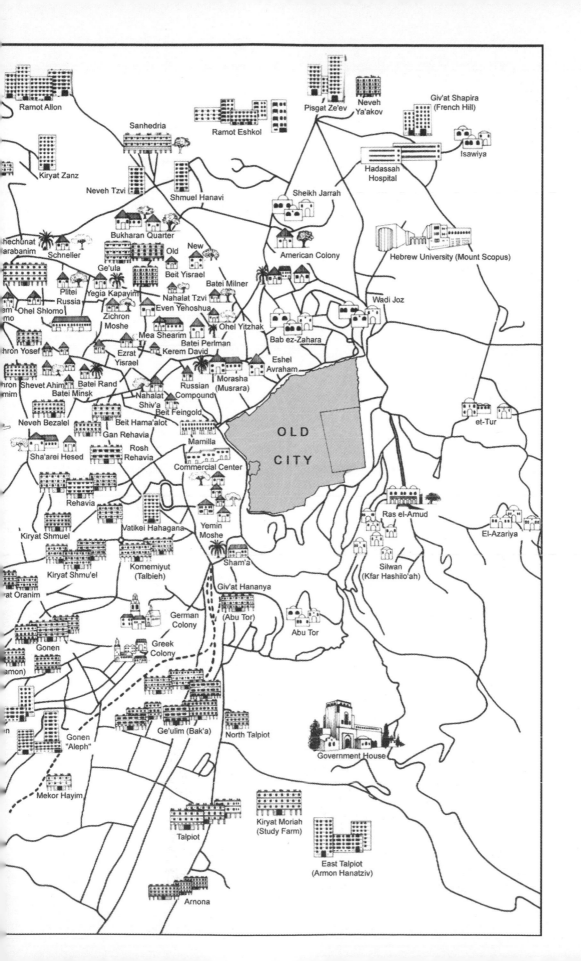

Ramot Allon

Kiryat Zanz

Sanhedria

Neveh Tzvi

Shmuel Hanavi

Ramot Eshkol

Pisgat Ze'ev

Neveh Ya'akov

Giv'at Shapira (French Hill)

Isawiya

Hadassah Hospital

Sheikh Jarrah

American Colony

Hebrew University (Mount Scopus)

shechunat arabanim

Schneller

Ge'ula

Old

New

Beit Yisrael

Wadi Joz

Plitei Russia

Yegia Kapayim

Nahalat Tzvi

Batei Milner

em mo

Zichron Moshe

Even Yehoshua

Ohel Yitzhak

Ohel Shlomo

Mea Shearim

Batei Perlman

Bab ez-Zahara

hron Yosef

Ezrat Yisrael

Kerem David

hron Shevet Ahim

Batei Rand

Eshel Avraham

et-Tur

imim

Batei Minsk

Nahalat Shiv'a

Russian Compound

Morasha (Musrara)

Neveh Bezalel

Beit Hama'alot

Beit Feingold

Gan Rehavia

Sha'arei Hesed

Rosh Rehavia

Mamilla

OLD CITY

Ras el-Amud

Commercial Center

Rehavia

Kiryat Shmuel

Vatikei Hahagana

Yemin Moshe

El-Azariya

Komemiyut (Talbieh)

Kiryat Shmu'el

Sham'a

Silwan (Kfar Hashilo'ah)

at Oranim

Giv'at Hananya

German Colony

(Abu Tor)

Gonen

Greek Colony

Abu Tor

amon)

Gonen "Aleph"

Ge'ulim (Bak'a)

North Talpiot

Government House

Mekor Hayim

Kiryat Moriah (Study Farm)

Talpiot

East Talpiot (Armon Hanatziv)

Arnona

The Western Wall Plaza has become symbolic of the desire to open up a new era in Jerusalem's history. The Israeli government invited the internationally renowned Israeli architect, Moshe Safdie, to design the plaza and he submitted a preliminary plan which was placed before a committee of experts. However, internal political battles made its implementation well-nigh impossible.

lem is marching into the twenty-first century and should not be preserved as a shabby nineteenth- or early twentieth-century town.

Two important focuses of the new planning of the city were the Western Wall Plaza, in the heart of the Old City, and the Mamilla neighborhood in west Jerusalem, close to the walls. These two projects were placed in the hands of one of Israel's most important architects, the internationally renowned Moshe Safdie. He submitted plans that imaginatively combined the ancient remains with the demands of modern construction. The Western Wall Plaza was examined by a committee of experts which also heard evidence from the public, and a master plan for the development of the plaza was finally approved. As of the time of writing, however (2001), neither of these plans has been fully implemented.

The years since the Six-Day War have also been a glorious period for archaeology. Many archaeological excavations have been carried out and more knowledge of the city's history has been acquired than in the preceding one hundred years. The city's appearance has changed over the generations, as I have tried to explain in this book. Following the extensive archaeological excavations, great progress has also been made in the preservation and restoration of ancient sites. This writer had the honor of initiating, planning and carrying out the first restoration work after the Six-Day War: the German Crusader church in the Jewish Quarter and the Beit Shalom Park at the foot of the southern wall.

In Jerusalem, however, archaeology has a political aspect. Despite the importance of the finds uncovered in the excavations, as well as the fact that they related to all periods of Jerusalem's history, the Muslim authorities could not reconcile themselves to the fact that these exciting discoveries were made by Israeli Jews. These include the Umayyad administrative complex, the Byzantine Nea Church and its secrets, and important remains from the periods of the Fatimid sultanate and the Crusaders. The Muslim authorities in Jerusalem attacked every archaeological project and complained to the United Nations Educational, Scientific, and Cultural Organization (UNESCO) that Israel was obliterating the non-Jewish chapters in the city's history. Moreover, excavations at the foot of the Temple Mount, they accused, were designed to bring down the walls of the Temple Mount and destroy its mosques in order to build the Jewish Temple. Despite the transparent nonsense of these accusations UNESCO decided to appoint a representative to examine them. The UNESCO representative praised the excavators'

Another important focus of Jerusalem's modern history following the Six-Day War was the borderline between the Old City and the new city—the Mamilla neighborhood. Here, too, a plan was requested from architect Moshe Safdie, and political conflict between various committees and groups has prevented its implementation. Shown below, the Safdie plan for Mamilla: model of park and boulevard.

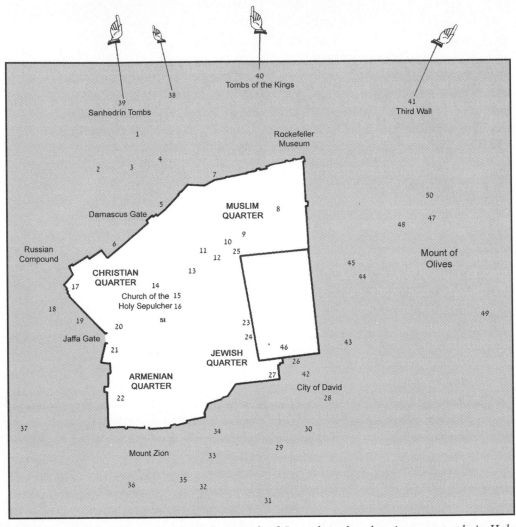

Until the Six-Day War archaeological research of Jerusalem played an important role in Holy Land studies. Despite objective difficulties and relatively poor finds, many excavations took place in the city and knowledge of its past was enhanced.

Jerusalem has been the focus of archaeological activity in the Holy Land since excavations and surveys to study the country's history first began. In no other city or archaeological site in the world has so much research been carried out. Before 1967, many excavations were carried out in the City of David on the lower hill, as well as in other open areas around and within the Old City. However, most such activities were carried out after the Six-Day War. Shown above is a map of the principal excavations carried out in Jerusalem prior to 1967.

	Archaeologists	Years	Principal Discoveries
1	Sukenik and Mayer	1925–1927	The Third Wall
2	Bliss	1894	"Orpheus" Mosaic
3	Schick	1881	Tombs
4	Warren, Wilson	1867	Tombs
5	Hamilton	1937–1938	Ancient gate and fortifications
5	Hennessy	1960–1964	Ancient gates
6	Hamilton	1937	Walls and fortifications
7	Hamilton	1938	Walls and fortifications

8	Mauss	1863–1876	Remains: Second Temple, Byzantine, Crusader
9	Warren	1867–1870	Second Temple, Roman
10	Warren	1867–1870	Struthion Pool
11	Clermont-Ganneau	1873	Byzantine structures
12	Clermont-Ganneau	1874	Arch, Second Temple, Roman, Byzantine
13	Greek archaeologists	1895	Medieval remains
14	Corbo	1961–1963	Holy Sepulcher Church—Middle Ages
15	Pierotti	1857–1860	Second Temple, Roman, Middle Ages
16	German archaeologists	1895	Middle Ages, buildings
17	Vincent	1912	Remains of buildings from Second Temple period and Middle Ages
18	Merrill	1902	Remains of buildings from Second Temple period and Middle Ages
19	Schick	1878	Ancient walls
20	Merrill	1902	Remains of Second Temple period
21	Johns	1934–1940	Second Temple, Ottoman
22	Kenyon	1960–1966	Byzantine, Middle Ages
23	Warren and Wilson	1867	Second Temple, Middle Ages
24	Warren	1867–1870	Second Temple, Middle Ages
25	Pierotti	1857	Rock-cut tunnel
26	Warren	1867	Tunnels, Second Temple, Middle Ages
27	Kenyon	1960–1967	Roman remains (?)
28	Parker	1909–1911	Tunnels and rock-cuttings
29	Bliss and Dickie	1891-1897	Second Temple, pools, water conduits
30	Weill	1913–1914	Fortifications, rock-cut caves, First and Second Temple periods
31	Kenyon	1960–1967	Fortifications and trenches
32	Germer-Durand	1882–1912	Byzantine mosaics, houses
33	Kenyon	1960–1967	Trenches, pottery
34	Kenyon	1960–1967	Masonry
35	Bliss and Dickie	1894–1897	Masonry
36	Maudslay	1871–1874	Ancient gates, fortifications
37	Schick	1891	"Herod's Family Tomb"
38	Dominicans	1881	Tombs
39	Palmer	1898	"Tombs of the Sanhedrin," Second Temple period tombs
40	De Saulcy	1863	"Tombs of the Kings"
41	Sukenik	1928–1929	Tombs, Second Temple period
42	Clermont-Ganneau	1873–1874	Remains of fortifications
43	Slouschz	1924	Tombs
44	Johns	1930	Remains from Middle Ages
45	Orfali	1909	Second Temple, Middle Ages
46	Hamilton	1947	Early Arab period
47	Corbo	1959	Tombs, Second Temple, Byzantine
48	Russian archaeologists	1870–1893	Tombs, Second Temple, Byzantine
49	Various archaeologists	1890	Armenian mosaics
50	Various archaeologists	1890–1947	Tombs, Second Temple

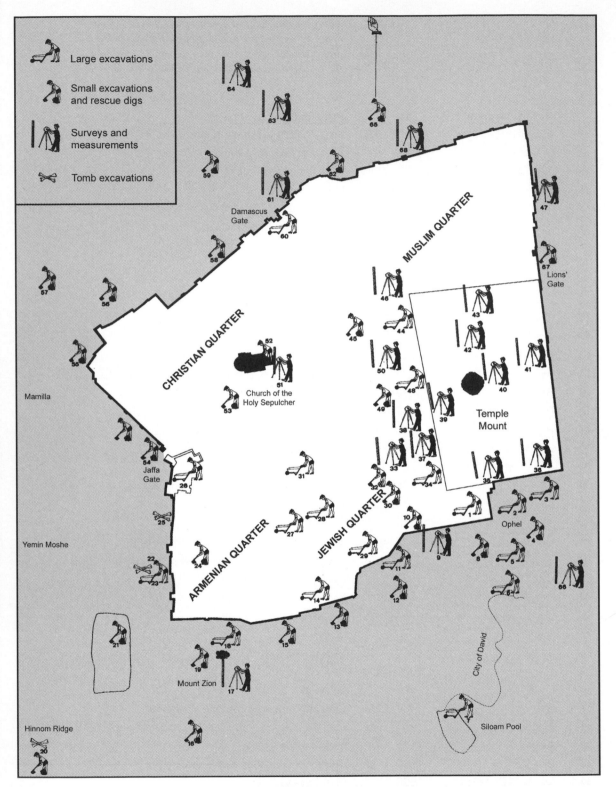

Legend:
- Large excavations
- Small excavations and rescue digs
- Surveys and measurements
- Tomb excavations

CHRISTIAN QUARTER

MUSLIM QUARTER

ARMENIAN QUARTER

JEWISH QUARTER

Temple Mount

Church of the Holy Sepulcher

Damascus Gate

Lions' Gate

Jaffa Gate

Mamilla

Yemin Moshe

Hinnom Ridge

Mount Zion

Ophel

City of David

Siloam Pool

After the Six-Day War in June 1967, archaeological and architectural research in Jerusalem increased at a dazzling rate. In addition to officially planned major projects, numerous rescue digs and random excavations were conducted, as well as extensive surveys and measurements. Within twenty years our picture of Jerusalem's past changed. The information accumulated in those twenty years far exceeds that of the preceding hundred years.

After the Six-Day War of 1967, extensive excavations began in and around the Old City. Some were planned in advance as major projects, but most were small excavations and rescue digs. These were accompanied by extensive surveys and measurements that have provided invaluable information on Jerusalem's history. Below are the principal excavations and surveys carried out from 1968 to 1989.

	Archaeologists	**Years**	**Principal Discoveries**
1	Mazar & Ben-Dov	1968–1977	First Temple to Ottoman
2	Mazar & Ben-Dov	1969–1977	First Temple to Fatimid
3	Ben-Dov	1977–1985	First Temple to Fatimid
4	Ben-Dov	1973	Medieval tombs
5	Shiloh	1982	Late Bronze to Second Temple
6	Shiloh	1980–1986	Early Bronze to Byzantine
7	Shiloh	1980	Second Temple period
8	Ben-Dov	1972	Byzantine, dwellings
9	Ben-Dov	1975–1980	Survey of southern wall
10	Ben-Dov	1977–1981	Byzantine, Umayyad, Middle Ages
11	Ben-Dov	1975–1977	Second Temple, Byzantine, Middle Ages
12	Edelstein	1976	Byzantine mosaic
13	Margovski	1970	Byzantine neighborhood
14	Avigad	1976	Second Temple, Byzantine, Middle Ages
15	Broshi	1972–1975	Byzantine, Middle Ages
16	Pixner & Margalit	1982–1989	First Temple to Middle Ages
17	Pinkerfeld	1949–1950	Survey of Mount Zion structures
18	Broshi	1969–1971	Second Temple, Byzantine
19	Eisenberg & Hess	1985	Byzantine
20	Barkay	1978–1985	First Temple, Second Temple, Byzantine
21	Kloner	1974	Middle Ages, Ottoman
22	Kloner & M. Magen	1973	First Temple
23	Broshi	1972–1975	Second Temple, Byzantine, Middle Ages
24	Broshi & Bahat	1970	Second Temple, Byzantine, Middle Ages
25	Broshi	1971	First Temple, Second Temple
26	Amiran & Eitan	1969–1970	First Temple to Ottoman
	Geva, Sivan, Solar	1980–1988	First Temple to Ottoman
27	Avigad	1970	Byzantine
28	Avigad	1970–1980	Second Temple, Byzantine
29	Avigad	1970–1980	Second Temple, Byzantine
30	Ovadiah	1969	Crusader
	Ben-Dov	1970–1974	Second Temple, Byzantine, Crusader
31	Avigad	1970–1977	First Temple, Second Temple, Middle Ages
32	Avigad	1975	Middle Ages
33	Ben-Dov	1980–1982	Survey of Crusader structures
34	Mazar & Ben-Dov	1968–1977	First Temple to Ottoman
35	Ben-Dov	1972	Survey of western Hulda Gates
36	Ben-Dov	1972–1973	Survey of eastern Hulda Gates and King Solomon's Stables
37	Ben-Dov	1970–1975	Survey of Western Wall plaza

(continued) ☞

(continued from previous page)

	Archaeologists	Years	Principal Discoveries
38	Ben-Dov	1969–1986	Survey of underground structures, Second Temple to Middle Ages
39	Tamari	1969–1970	Survey of Mamluk building
40	Rosen-Ayalon	1970–1973	Survey of domed structures on Temple Mount
41	Ben-Dov	1972	Survey of Golden Gate
42	Burgoyne	1970–1985	Survey of Mamluk buildings
43	Burgoyne	1970–1985	Survey of Mamluk buildings
44	Ben-Dov	1969–1987	Ministry of Religious Affairs excavations
45	M. Magen	1978	Byzantine to Middle Ages
46	Bahat	1988–1989	Survey of rock-cut tunnel
47	Ben-Dov	1975–1982	Survey of walls and gates in the east
48	Ben-Dov	1969–1987	Ministry of Religious Affairs: Second Temple to Middle Ages
49	M. Magen	1978–1980	Second Temple, Byzantine
	Bahat & Solar	1975	Crusader, church
50	Burgoyne	1970–1984	Monumental research of Mamluk buildings
51	Corbo	1967–1980	Survey of Church of the Holy Sepulcher
52	Broshi	1972–1975	First Temple, Second Temple, Byzantine, Middle Ages
53	Kloner	1975	Byzantine
54	Goldfuss	1985	Byzantine, Middle Ages
55	Bahat & Ben-Ari	1970	Middle Ages
56	Bahat	1981	Middle Ages
57	Maeir	1988	Second Temple, Middle Ages
58	Solar	1979	Middle Ages
59	Netzer & Ben-Arieh	1973	Second Temple, Byzantine
60	M. Magen	1982–1985	Second Temple, Byzantine, Middle Ages
61	Ben-Dov	1975–1980	Survey of Ottoman walls
62	Mazor	1983	Middle Ages
63	Barkay	1975	First Temple, Second Temple
64	Barkay, Mazar & Kloner	1974	First Temple
65	Netzer & Ben-Arieh	1973	Second Temple
66	Ussishkin	1969–1971	Survey of tombs
67	M. Magen	1984	Middle Ages
68	M. Magen	1985	Ottoman
69	Maeir	1989	Second Temple, Byzantine, Middle Ages

(left) Besides excavations and surveys, much work has been done in preserving and reconstructing archaeological findings, and more sites have been opened to the public.

(below) The field of archaeological research expanded to include not only excavations but also surveys and measurements, which have been extraordinarily fruitful.

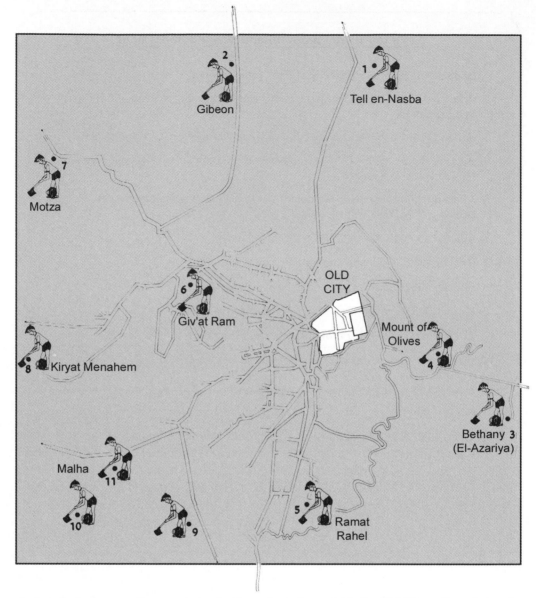

Archaeological excavations carried out at important sites outside the Old City walls and close by have made important contributions to research into Jerusalem's past.

work in private, but wrote politically motivated reports intended to please his superiors. This approach is surely deplorable; it is not the task of an ostensibly cultural organization to solve political problems, even if they relate to a sensitive site like the Temple Mount.

Another project that changed the face of united Jerusalem was a major fundraising organization set up by Mayor Teddy Kollek—the Jerusalem Founda-tion. The Foundation has initiated and financed various development projects with the help of donations from Jews and non-Jews abroad. It has established a wide range of social welfare institutions, public parks and cultural institutions, and placed many sculptures in squares and streets, changing the face and char-acter of the city.

Mention should be made of a few small but conspicuous movements established

Selected Excavations in and Around Jerusalem

1. **Badè** 1926–1935: Fortified city of First Temple period.

2. **Pritchard** 1955–1962: Dwellings, fortifications and water systems from First Temple period.

3. **Saller** 1954: Church and monastery of Byzantine and Crusader periods.

4. **Bagatti, Corbo** 1953–1955: Tombs of Second Temple and Byzantine periods. Mosaic floors of a church.

5. **Aharoni** 1955–1963: Israelite palace. Byzantine monastery and church. Roman bathhouse. Second Temple period tombs.

6. **Avi-Yonah** 1949: Camp of Roman Tenth Legion.

7. **Bacchi** 1962: Byzantine church and monastery.

8. **Amiran** 1953: Barrows from First Temple period.

9. **Mazar** 1978: Fortified farm from First Temple period.

10. **Edelstein** 1980–1988: Farm, mosaics from Roman-Byzantine period.

11. **Eisenberg** 1987: Dwellings from the Middle Bronze Age.

in Jerusalem. The "Temple Mount Faithful" demand permission to recite Jewish prayers on the Temple Mount; the so-called "Women in Black" demonstrate regularly near the home of the prime minister, demanding an immediate peace agreement with the Arabs and return of all territories occupied since the Six-Day

Michael Avi-Yonah, a leading scholar of Jerusalem history. Avi-Yonah directed a modest excavation of the Roman Legion camp at Giv'at Ram (1949); he had previously dug at Ramat Rahel (1927) together with Moshe Stekelis (1927). However, his principal importance in the field and his special status in the scholarly world are due to his research into the topography and historical geography of Jerusalem. He was renowned for his scientific integrity, broad perception and ability to analyze archaeological discoveries and link them with written sources.

Jerusalem's appearance underwent a great change with the placement of sculptures in its streets, squares and public buildings. This began modestly in the new campus of the Hebrew University at Giv'at Ram (1958). The sculptures, in abstract and modest lines, became more numerous especially after the Six-Day War, and today there are works of art scattered throughout all parts of the city. When the Israel Museum and the Billy Rose Sculpture Garden were opened, figurative sculptures also began to be placed around the city. At first, ultra-religious circles held demonstrations in protest, sometimes accompanied by violence. However, they gradually adjusted to the idea that this was art and not idol worship, and modest figurative sculptures can now be found in the city's squares and gardens. This change has improved Jerusalem's appearance in a way unknown in its history.

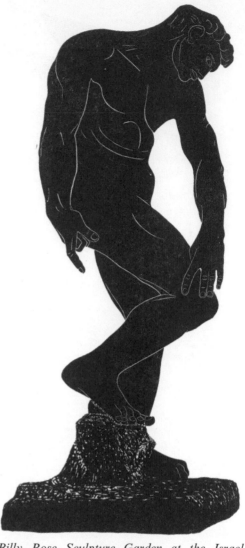

Liberty Bell Garden, near Yemin Moshe: "Ass's Foal" by Yuval Rimon (1988).

Billy Rose Sculpture Garden at the Israel Museum: "Adam" by Auguste Rodin (1880).

Holland Square, near Mount Herzl: "Jerusalem Stabile," by the sculptor Alexander Calder (1977).

In the square of the Hebrew University campus at Giv'at Ram: sculptures by Yitshak Danziger based on biblical motifs.

(above) Chopin Street, near the Jerusalem Theater: "Noah's Dove," by François Lalanne (1978).

(right) Following the war widespread archaeological excavations began, to an unprecedented extent. Major and smaller excavation projects and rescue digs took place both inside and outside the Old City.

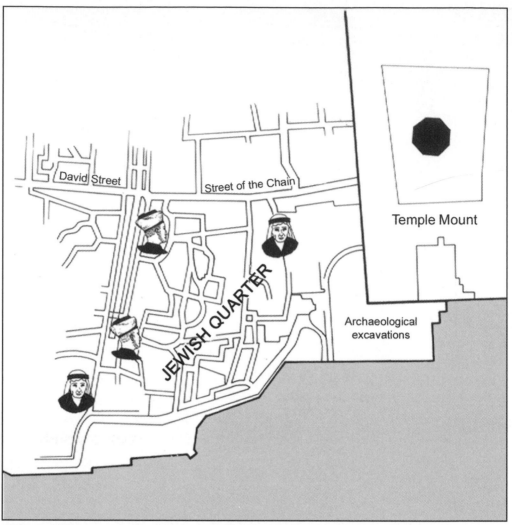

After the Six-Day War, work began on rebuilding the Jewish Quarter. Arab families who had lived there before 1948 and refugees who had come after the War of Independence were evacuated in return for compensation. With two exceptions, the squatters left voluntarily, with no need for legal action. By 1990, about twenty Muslim families and businesses remained in the Jewish Quarter.

War; ultra-Orthodox (*haredi*) Jews would like to enforce Sabbath observance, as they understand it, in Jerusalem's streets and cultural institutions, not to speak of their objection to the construction of sports facilities; and clashes among the various Christian churches and denominations. Alongside this wide range of human activity, other significant activities are restoration and preservation work being done by the Muslims on the Temple Mount and extensive restoration undertaken at the Church of the Holy Sepulcher. On a more mundane plane, immense efforts have gone into constructing a modern infrastructure for sewage, electricity, telephone and television in all parts of the Old City, greatly improving living conditions there while preserving its unique character. All these activities, and others too numerous to describe here, are making their own contribution to Jerusalem's history.

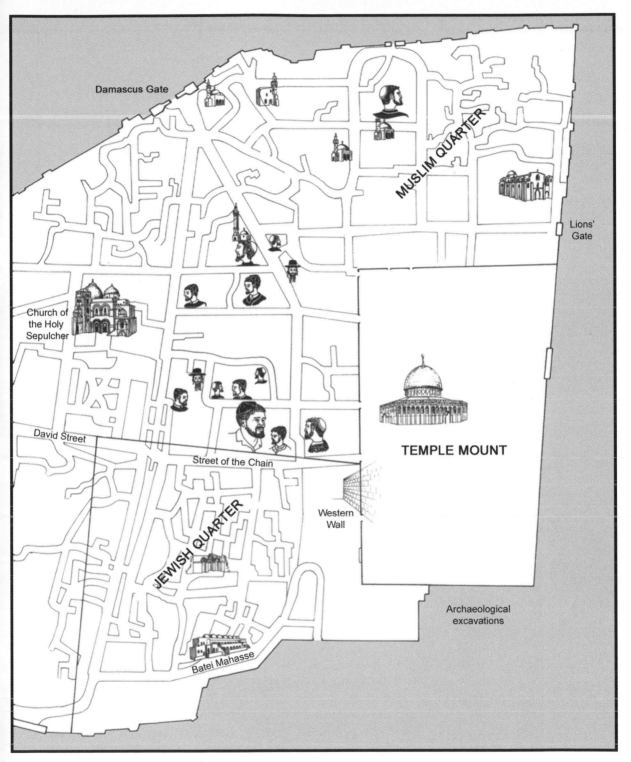

After the Six-Day War several Jewish associations were founded with the aim of purchasing buildings in the Muslim Quarter. They purchased formerly Jewish property, but later bought any available property. By 1990, Jews owned about twenty buildings in the Muslim Quarter.

6. TOWARD THE FUTURE

A FEW months after the Six-Day War, once the Palestinian Arabs had recovered from the first shock of defeat, they began to reactivate the terrorist organizations they had established some years before. They launched a cruel and continuous war in many parts of Israel against innocent civilians, including women, children and the aged. An ancient Jewish source states "Of the ten measures of beauty given to the world, nine were taken by Jerusalem." By analogy, one might say that, of ten measures of terror, nine were taken by Jerusalem. Explosive devices were set off in the Zion Cinema, in the Mahaneh Yehuda market, in public buses, and more, not to speak of dozens of terrorist acts that have been prevented. Once the Israeli security forces found ways to cope with the problem and contain it, the Palestinians turned to acts of terror within and around the Old City, directed against Israelis and tourists. This local terrorism was intended to demonstrate Arab anger over the reunification of Jerusalem and its initial success—a kind of announcement to the world that the Palestinians refuse to accept the new situation. Nevertheless, time sometimes creates its own solutions, and for a while

(left) Jerusalem's history is a magnet for thousands of people—not only members of the three monotheistic faiths, for whom Jerusalem is central, but also visitors from afar, like those of the East. Shown here: Thai princesses visiting the archaeological excavations near the Temple Mount.

(opposite) A row of houses with red roofs in the Sha'arei Hesed neighborhood. Such roofs were characteristic of construction outside the walls in the 19th and 20th centuries. Today's architects are trying to restore their part in Jerusalem's landscape and entire neighborhoods now have red roofs.

Building with stone-faced concrete has been used for all construction in Jerusalem since the Six-Day War. In order to preserve Jerusalem's eastern character, architects have much use of decorative arches. In additions, diagonal lines are utilized in some buildings, solely in order to preserve something of the appearance of older houses with their gabled tiled roofs.

The entry of the European powers into the Holy Land, especially Jerusalem, was accompanied by extensive building. It was they who introduced the red tile roofing familiar to them. Such red-tiled roofs could be seen in all parts of the city, even in exclusively Arab areas. Jerusalem has in fact undergone radical changes in its character and appearance. In the Byzantine period, for example, tiles were used only in church roofs. During the Mandate, tiled roofs gave way to flat concrete roofs on which water storage tanks were placed.

Following the Six-Day War, Jerusalem architects returned to the use of tiled roofs in many buildings, out of a desire to preserve the city's special character. However, it should be stressed that this feature dates from the 19th century and not earlier.

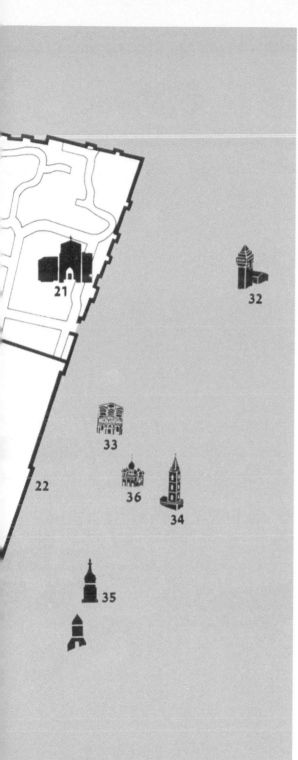

The Old City of Jerusalem and its environs are a living museum, a magnet for visitors from both within and outside the country.

1. Jaffa Gate
2. Citadel
3. St. James's Church
4. Dormition Church
5. New Gate
6. Franciscan Monastery
7. Church of the Holy Sepulcher
8. Muristan
9. Hezekiah's Pool
10. Damascus Gate
11. Hurva Synagogue
12. Zion Gate
13. Nea Church
14. Herod's Gate
15. Antonia
16. Dome of the Rock
17. Western Wall
18. Robinson's Arch
19. Temple Mount excavations
20. Dung Gate
21. St. Anne's Church
22. Golden Gate
23. Al-Aqsa Mosque
24. Solomon's Stables
25. Triple Gate
26. Double Gate
27. Acra
28. Gihon Spring
29. Hezekiah's Tunnel
30. Siloam Pool
31. St. Peter in Gallicantu Church
32. Augusta Victoria Hospital
33. Gethsemane
34. Church of the Ascension
35. Absalom's Monument
36. St. Mary Magdalene Church

Since the lower hill of the city was first inhabited and called "Jerusalem," it has developed and grown. Until the 19th century, any growth was confined within walls and fortifications. Nine specific stages in Jerusalem's development and growth can be identified throughout the ages: (1) Canaanite and Jebusite; (2) City of David and Solomon; (3) Jerusalem in the period of the United Kingdom and the Restoration; (4) Herodian period; (5) end of Second Temple period; (6) Byzantine and Early Arab periods; (7) Fatimid and Crusader periods; (8) first Ayyubid rulers; (9) the Ottoman city, successor to the Mamluk city.

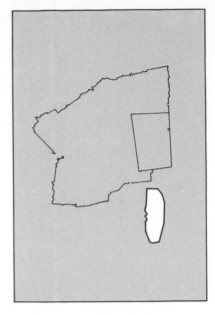

(1) Canaanite and Jebusite city

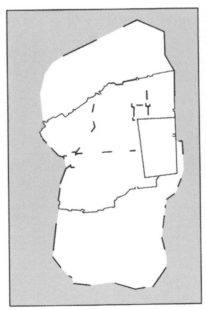

(5) Aelia Capitolina

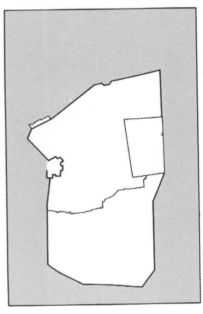

(6) City under Byzantine and Early Arab rule

it seemed that Jerusalem had entered a new phase in its history—a united city under Jewish rule, allowing freedom of worship and thought for all religions. In the struggle between the competing claims of Christianity and Islam to Jerusalem, it was thought that perhaps the present compromise is the best and most practical, with the keys of the city held by the believers in the most ancient

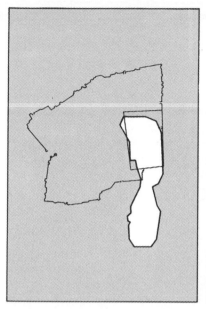
(2) City of David and Solomon

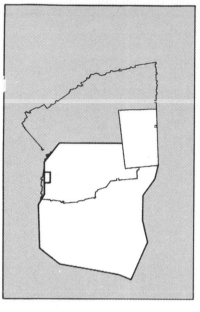
(3) Jerusalem in the time of the United Kingdom and the Restoration

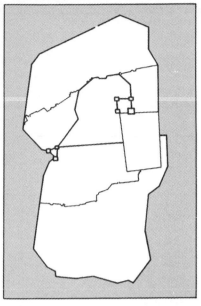
(4) Jerusalem at the end of the Second Temple period

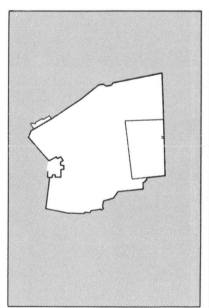
(7) City under Fatimid and Crusader rule

(8) Jerusalem at the beginning of Ayyubid rule

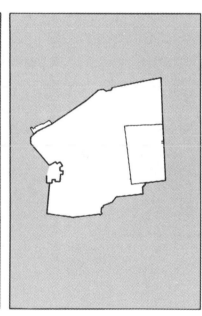
(9) The Ottoman city

and smallest monotheistic religion.

However, the de facto compromise that had been maintained for almost twenty years was later undermined. In the late 1980s a popular Palestinian opposition movement, the *intifada*, began in the Gaza Strip and spread like wildfire throughout the West Bank, soon reaching the gates of Jerusalem. Initially peaceful protests, involving commercial

Muslims and Christians, no less than Jews, keenly await a settlement of the Arab-Jewish conflict and a solution to the thorny issue of Jerusalem. The core question is whether a bridge can be built between the different populations, enabling them to live together in the city in whose name is intertwined with the word shalom—*"peace"—but whose history has been fraught with wars.*

strikes and the closure of shops and markets—often achieved by threats and terror, were accompanied by increasing violence, with riots in the Old City squares and streets. The growing violence evoked the response it apparently sought, as the news media impatiently awaited pictures of the dispersal of demonstrations with tear gas and bullets. Such news reports discouraged visits to Jerusalem by foreign tourists—and even by Israelis from the rest of the country. Jerusalem was essentially redivided by the *intifada*: fewer Jews visited the Old City markets, out of both fear and anger at the continuing conflict.

United Jerusalem is now at the crossroads. If our generation were to produce a truly great leader, would he realize—like the prophets and the sages on the eve

of the destruction of the Second Temple—that the glory and ultimate fate of Jerusalem depend on human efforts? Jerusalem's future will not be determined by material achievement alone, but by a society living in peace, making mutual concessions in a spirit of neighborly love. As the Jewish sage Hillel said: "What is hateful to you, do not unto your fellow man; that is the entire Torah."

(overleaf) Toward the end of the Ottoman period, the municipal limits of Jerusalem were expanded. The area was further enlarged as the city grew and developed during the British Mandate and following the establishment of the State of Israel, even before the Six-Day War, reaching a peak in 1990. Even today (2001–2002) plans are afoot to add more territory to the municipal area of Jerusalem, especially in the west.

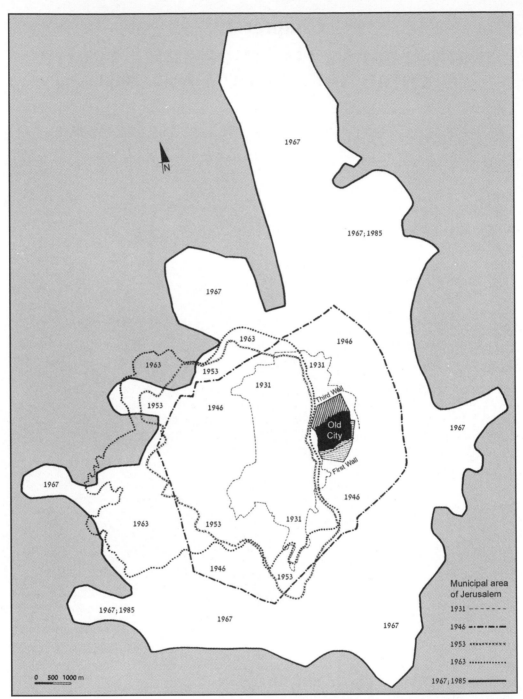

The city reached its peak size in antiquity toward the end of the Second Temple period, but shrank over the next two thousand years. Only in the last few decades has the area of the city increased once more. Under the British Mandate, there were two increases in the area under Jerusalem municipal jurisdiction, in 1931 and 1946. The increase in 1946 added more Arab urban-type areas in the east. After the War of Independence, the Jewish area of Jerusalem expanded to the west, while the eastern side of the city expanded northward and eastward. The municipal limits of the Jewish city were increased twice, in 1953 and 1963. The big change came after the Six-Day War (1967). The municipal area of united Jerusalem, as determined on June 28, 1967, was greatly increased to the north, west and south, and slightly to the east, with further slight adjustments in 1985. In 1991 further discussion began on expanding the area of the city, this time to the west.

344

Chapter 13:

JERUSALEM AT THE THRESHOLD OF THE THIRD MILLENNIUM 1989–2000

1. PEACE AGREEMENTS BETWEEN ISRAEL AND THE PALESTINIANS

FOR more than fifty years, Israelis and Palestinians have been embroiled in a bitter armed struggle. Nevertheless, within the past three decades, two Arab states, Egypt and Jordan, signed peace treaties with Israel; the borders were opened, and it was hoped that the abysmal hatred would soon ebb. Indeed, the first fruits of peace were already visible: increased tourism, economic investment and reduction in military spending. However, the main points of contention between Israel and the Palestinians have not been removed.

In 1992, after fifteen years of right-wing government, Israel's left wing again came to power. The new prime minister was Yitzhak Rabin, a native of Jerusalem, who had taken part in all the battles for the city. In 1948 he had commanded the Har'el Brigade, which fought bitterly to keep the road to Jerusalem from the coastal plain open, and in 1967 he commanded the Israel Defense Forces as chief-of-staff in the Six-Day War, which culminated in the occupation of East Jerusalem and the reunification of Jerusalem.

The new government, led by Rabin and his foreign minister Shimon Peres, paved the way to a reconciliation between the two warring peoples, Israelis and Pales-

General chief-of-staff Yitzhak Rabin (right) with defense minister Moshe Dayan (center) and the commander of the central area forces Uzi Narkiss, entering Jerusalem through the Lions' Gate on June 7, 1967.

tinians. It was clear that unless the conflict was resolved, the Middle East would be in constant danger of war, a keg of gunpowder ready to explode at any minute. In talks held secretly in Oslo, the capital of Norway, certain under-

Yitzhak Rabin (1922–1995), the prime minister who worked for reconciliation between Israel and the Palestinians. The process that he helped to set in motion will have to include an agreement on the status and fate of Jerusalem.

would be a peaceful one, with an end to warfare. At the same time, it was clear to them that one problem presented enormous difficulties—the status of Jerusalem. In the preceding twelve chapters, I have tried to show how Jerusalem, over the centuries, has found a place in the hearts of millions—Jews, Christians and Muslims. The Oslo Agreements were to have led to the establishment of a Palestinian state alongside Israel. This condition had in fact been proposed in 1947, but the Arabs had rejected it out of hand. The central question outstanding once the Oslo "Declaration of Principles" had been signed was, would Jerusalem remain unified when a final agreement was secured and a territorial compromise reached? And in that event, how could it serve simultaneously as the capital of both states, Israel and Palestine?

Since this issue was of enormous complexity, it was decided to postpone its discussion until the very last stage of peace negotiations. Until then—this was the prevailing thought in the peace camp—the two sides would be accustomed to peaceful relations by the facts of life, the mere force of day-to-day contact; what could not be done by conscious effort would be accomplished by time, and Jerusalem would ultimately find its place in a peaceful Middle East.

standings and agreements were reached between the two sides on many of the outstanding issues. Both sides seemed convinced that the only viable solution

2. POLITICALLY MOTIVATED DEVELOPMENT PROJECTS

THERE are extremists on both sides, Israelis and Palestinians, who refuse to compromise; their ideology may be summed up by the slogan, "All or nothing," essentially expressing a preference for war over any solution involving partition or cooperation. Each of the extremist movements has of course enlisted God in support of its stand.

Jewish extremist circles enjoy the support of certain wealthy individuals who have contributed lavishly for the purchase of land and property from the Palestinians. An old Arab proverb says, "Money is like a salve; place it on a wound and it will heal." Thus, Jews have been able to buy Arab property despite the danger incurred by the sellers, who risk death at the hands of their own brethren.

A street scene in the Muslim Quarter of the Old City.

Arab property has been bought up, for considerable sums, by Israelis in the Muslim Quarter of the Old City. In addition, there has been at least one large-scale acquisition in the Christian Quarter—St. John's Hospice, near the Church of the Holy Sepulcher, was leased to a group of Israeli extremists.

The same circles have also tried to acquire the Muslim neighborhood of Wadi Hilweh, in the area of the historic City of David, just south of the present walls of the Old City. The idea underlying this project is to interrupt direct contact between Arab-inhabited areas and Jerusalem, especially the Old City. The motives of the builders of the Har Homa neighborhood southeast of Jerusalem are similar: to cut off the Arab-populated areas of Judea, including Bethlehem, from Jerusalem.

The Palestinian majority in East Jerusalem is also aware of the importance of establishing ethnic facts "on the ground." There has therefore been a considerable amount of building, without legal permits or proper planning, in various parts of East Jerusalem, and new neighborhoods—sometimes lacking the most basic urban necessities—have sprung up in various locations, such as Al-Za'im, east of Mount Scopus and the Mount of Olives, on the road to the Jewish town of Ma'aleh Adumim.

Within the Old City itself, momentous changes are taking place. Many Christian-Palestinian families have sold their property—both residences and commercial establishments—to Muslims and left the city and even the country. It is relatively easy for a Christian to emigrate to a western country, such as the United States, where the religious environment is similar to his own and there already exist communities of Arab émigrés. Thus, most of the stores in the Christian Quarter are now in the possession of Muslim Palestinians.

Quite naturally, development of this kind, which is undertaken with an eye to political bargaining and improving each side's positions, has had a detrimental effect on the highly complex social texture of the city and the hitherto stable character of the Old City, as well as leading to construction of inferior quality. Jerusalem's appearance is changing as a consequence of unrestrained competition.

3. THE TEMPLE MOUNT AND THE VICINITY

ONE important focus of the struggle for control in Jerusalem is the Temple Mount, together with its immediate vicinity. As far as Jewish religious law— halacha—is concerned, the position adopted by some circles is well-nigh absurd. As already noted previously, mainstream halacha forbids any Jew

entry to most of the area of the Temple Mount, on the grounds that at present every Jew is considered ritually unclean or impure because of possible contact with the dead. Such impurity can be purged only by using the ashes of a red heifer, necessarily mixed with at least some of the ashes of a red heifer from the

(above) Interior of the Dome of the Rock. According to Islamic tradition, this is the rock from which Muhammad ascended to heaven. According to Jewish tradition, this is the "Foundation Stone" which was in the Holy of Holies of the Temple. In all likelihood, the reference was neither to a rock nor a large cornerstone, but to a small stone. The mistake in identification was made in the Crusader period, no earlier than the 11th century.

(left) An early aerial photograph of the Temple Mount, looking east.

Second Temple period—which is of course unobtainable.

The question of actually building the Temple is similar; it cannot be done under the present conditions. Among other things, a new Temple would have to be erected in the exact location of the two previous Temples, which is not known. In sum, Jewish religious law allows nothing of any religious import

Aerial view, looking east, of the large-scale excavations at the foot of the Temple Mount after 1967, which uncovered the remains of the Umayyad administrative complex.

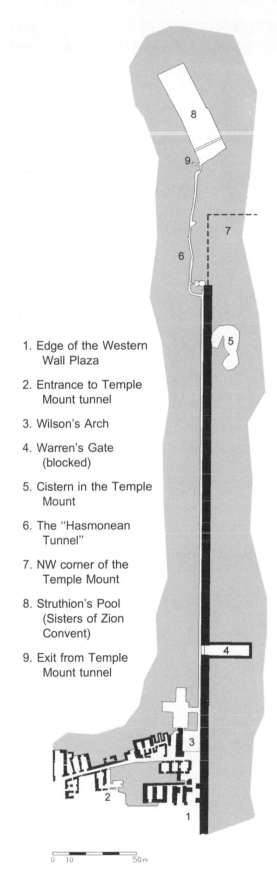

1. Edge of the Western Wall Plaza

2. Entrance to Temple Mount tunnel

3. Wilson's Arch

4. Warren's Gate (blocked)

5. Cistern in the Temple Mount

6. The "Hasmonean Tunnel"

7. NW corner of the Temple Mount

8. Struthion's Pool (Sisters of Zion Convent)

9. Exit from Temple Mount tunnel

to be done on the Temple Mount. Small fringe groups, such as the "Temple Mount Faithful" and others, have no Jewish leg to stand on; they are seen by the great majority of religiously observant Jews as annoying and exceptional.

With the exception of demonstrations by such groups, which are of no practical significance and merely attract journalists' attention, most work has been done outside, though close to, the Temple Mount. Even such ostensibly scientific research as has been undertaken in the vicinity is sometimes seen as politically motivated.

Tension in the area was perhaps somewhat alleviated by the large-scale excavations at the foot of the Temple Mount after 1967, which uncovered extensive non-Jewish remains, such as a Byzantine residential neighborhood and the great Umayyad administrative complex. The systematic excavation of these remains, since made accessible to the public and preserved, did much to silence objections. Nevertheless, later incompetence, including the removal of many remains and the neglect of some sites, has reversed the tide, once again undermining the very fragile relations of trust carefully built up over the years.

Muslim authorities are particularly sensitive to activity taking place beneath the surface, far from the public eye, in the course of which Jewish designations have been given to various structures of indisputably Christian or Muslim origin. Thus, in 1996, a new tunnel, some 25 meters long, was opened on instructions from the Israeli government. The purpose was to permit exit from a tunnel that had been dug by the Ministry of Religious Affairs under the Old City houses, for the length of the Western

Plan of the tunnel along the western wall of the Temple Mount. It was dug under the auspices of the Ministry of Religious Affairs.

The Hasmonean aqueduct near the northwestern corner of the Temple Mount.

(below) The tunnel along the western wall of the Temple Mount, north of Wilson's Arch.

"Solomon's Stables," probably from the 7th century.

Wall. The work, done in 1968, was intended to facilitate access to visitors. As it happened, the exit was at Via Dolorosa, in the heart of the Muslim Quarter. The Arabs considered this undertaking a violation of the Jerusalem status quo and riots broke out on a large scale, not only in Jerusalem but elsewhere in the occupied territories. An uneasy calm was ultimately restored, but only after more than one hundred Israelis and Palestinians had been killed.

The Palestinians harbor a constant fear that certain Jewish groups wish to establish a synagogue on the Temple Mount or in its underground parts, despite the halachic prohibition. These groups point to the example of the Cave of Machpelah in Hebron, part of which has been set aside for Jewish prayers. However, the position of the Cave of Machpelah in Islamic theology cannot be compared with that of the Temple Mount. Any infringement on that position is liable to have disastrous consequences on an unpredictable scale. Indeed, all past Israeli governments have studiously avoided any such development. The riots that broke out because of the opening of the tunnel—outside the Temple Mount! —have only sharpened awareness of the possible calamitous effects of Jewish activity on the Temple Mount itself.

In order to avert any chance of Jewish groups attempting to build a synagogue in the area, the Muslim authorities in charge of the Temple Mount—the *waqf* administration—are building Muslim prayer sites all over the enclosure. Paved prayer areas, marked by a *mihrab* (prayer niche indicating the direction of Mecca), are being prepared in various places, thus "officially" converting them into mosques.

With the space above ground unavailable, Jewish fanatics proposed to build a

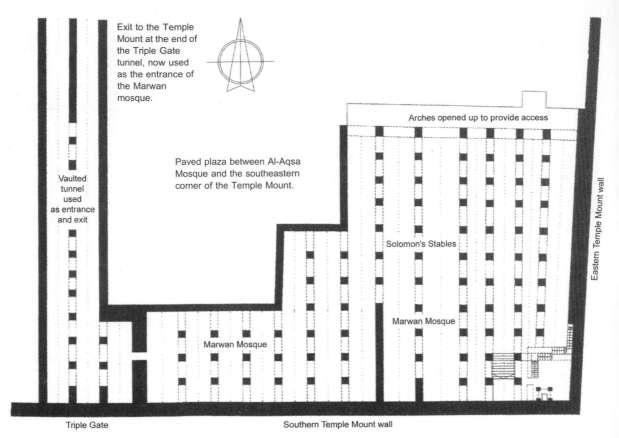

Exit to the Temple Mount at the end of the Triple Gate tunnel, now used as the entrance of the Marwan mosque.

Vaulted tunnel used as entrance and exit

Paved plaza between Al-Aqsa Mosque and the southeastern corner of the Temple Mount.

Arches opened up to provide access

Solomon's Stables

Marwan Mosque

Eastern Temple Mount wall

Marwan Mosque

Triple Gate

Southern Temple Mount wall

"Solomon's Stables"—plan. This expansive underground space was built by the Umayyad caliphs when they repaired the Temple Mount before building the Al-Aqsa Mosque. It may have been used as a mosque before the latter was completed.

synagogue beneath the Temple Mount. A particularly appropriate site to that end would have been the tremendous underground space known as "Solomon's Stables." The use of such underground facilities, they believed, would solve the halachic problems, since prayer there would not involve entry to the actual area of the Temple Mount.

In apprehension of such actions, the *waqf* authorities have begun to open up the underground areas, converting them into mosques. "Solomon's Stables" are an ancient Muslim structure. Before the Al-Aqsa Mosque and the Dome of the Rock could be built, the Muslims had to reinforce the enclosure; to that end, they emulated Herod's example, building a great vaulted structure to support the pavement of the Temple Mount plaza.

Later, this underground area was used by the Crusaders. The Templar Knights, who had their headquarters, known as the "Temple of Solomon," on the Temple Mount, used it as stables, hence the name, "Solomon's Stables." After Saladin's conquest of Jerusalem in 1187, he sealed off access to the space and it fell into disuse, until it was later used as a central storehouse for the Temple Mount. There are grounds for the view that Muslims used to pray in these underground halls before Al-Aqsa was built. They were therefore known in Arabic as the prayer house of Marwan—father of Caliph 'Abd al-Malik, who built the Dome of the Rock in 691.

In 1998 the underground structure was renovated and converted into a mosque named for Marwan. The structure was

(above) Two of the seven arches in "Solomon's Stables," looking south. They were blocked up by Saladin in 1187 and re-opened in 2000 by the Waqf *in order to gain access to the Marwan mosque.*

(right) One of the vaults in "Solomon's Stables," cleaned and restored by the Waqf *authorities.*

considerably improved and carefully preserved: during the carefully executed work, no damage was done. Groups of visitors, of different religions, have been permitted access after prior coordination. In December 1999, in order to facilitate visits by large groups, the Muslims began to breach the openings sealed up by Saladin, in order to adapt them to their function in the renovated structure, as emergency exits. Even before that, restoration work was done in an open space just below Al-Aqsa, known as the "Double Gate" area, or *Al-Aqsa al-*

Qadima, that is, "Ancient al-Aqsa." This space is essentially a tunnel through which pilgrims could leave the Temple Mount in Second Temple times, known as the "Western Hulda Gate"; it was repaired as an entrance to the Temple Mount by the Umayyad caliphs, the restorers and builders of the Muslim Temple Mount, who called it the "Prophet's Gate."

A further cause of Israeli-Palestinian tension are the activities in the archaeological park at the foot of the Temple Mount. At one time, the present author was in charge of the restoration work there, with an eye to putting on display remains of all the periods that had been exposed, in order to give the visitor information about the past of this part of Jerusalem, at the foot of the Temple Mount—the story of Jerusalem with its builders, its conquerors and destroyers through the generations.

One of the most remarkable finds of the excavations near the Temple Mount was the Umayyad administrative complex (see above, Chapter 7, for details). Today, no serious study of Early Muslim Jerusalem can ignore this discovery, which should have been given a prominent place in the archaeological park.

However, without consulting the qualified personnel who excavated the site

Jerusalem is a city rich in history—five thousand years of continuous history. As it was always an important city, there are a great many archaeological remains. Road building and other construction work require careful study and documentation of such remains before work can begin. The discovery of ancient tombs has been particularly problematic, arousing sometimes violent protests by ultra-Orthodox groups. Dealing with such problems occasionally requires changes in the planned course of a road or recourse to complicated halachic solutions. Road-building in Jerusalem is as difficult as the rock it has to cut through, needing patience, mutual tolerance and respect.

and determined its nature, the responsible authorities dealt with it in a disgraceful manner. The central Umayyad palace was built around an open courtyard;

instead of leaving this intact, a strange, heavy metal structure was built there, completely out of context. In addition, the residential rooms around the courtyard in the south wing were filled with soil and gardens were planted. Plants have a way of growing, and sooner or later these rooms will become a veritable jungle, to the detriment of the original nature of the site. "The world's upside-down!" as the Muslim Mufti of the Temple Mount remarked to me.

Whether these measures were taken deliberately or inadvertently, out of sheer ignorance, the results are deplorable. Whatever the case, here is yet another case in which Jerusalem's antiquities have taken an active part in the political struggle over the character and future of the city.

4. NEW DISCOVERIES

IN the ten years before the start of the third millennium, there was little serious archaeological work in the Old City of Jerusalem. Previous excavations, especially those at the foot of the Temple Mount, were conceived and initiated by archaeologists; they were not chance discoveries accompanying construction work. Such discoveries have indeed been made, particularly in the Jewish Quarter, but archaeological initiative has lost much of its previous glitter and now plays second fiddle to contractors and developers. Consequently, archaeological interest in Jerusalem has largely shifted to the periphery of the new city, where new neighborhoods are being built quite distant from the heart of the Old City, the cradle of Jerusalem's culture and history.

What emerges from the few recent excavations that have been published is that, dotted around Jerusalem, there were farmsteads and small villages which subsisted mainly on the production of olive oil and wine, as well as terrace agriculture. The discoveries relate to different periods: the time of the Patriarchs, First and Second Temple periods, Byzantine and Arab periods, Crusader times, and so on right up to the Ottoman period. A further conclusion from the recent discoveries is that, when there was an influx of visitors, including of course pilgrims, to the Holy City, and more food was needed, these needs were supplied by livestock bred in the vicinity and by farms that produced food such as wheat, barley, fruit and vegetables.

Some archaeological work has been done inside the Old City in the wake of construction and development work. Taken together, these have fleshed out our knowledge of the city's past. Thus, buildings from the Byzantine and Crusader periods were uncovered in the crypts of the Coptic Church near the Church of the Holy Sepulcher. Sewage work by the municipal authorities in the Kidron Valley unearthed the remains of a Crusader monastery whose church was excavated in the Mandatory period; among the remains were exquisite frescoes and Latin inscriptions. Development operations in the area of the Muristan is gradually revealing ruins that were visible there in the nineteenth century before it was built up—remains of the churches of the Hospitaller quarter, dating to the Crusader period.

Another focus of archaeological activity is the area of the Kidron Valley and the slopes of the City of David. As already mentioned, Jewish organizations have purchased Arab-owned property there for political motives. In the course of their development work, some remains of the past have come to light. However, these discoveries are of marginal significance, both because the area concerned is small and because of the political motivation. It is unfortunate that in these cases, too, discovery of the past is inextricably bound up with politics. While Jewish settlers report Jewish remains, the other side identifies them as Canaanite. Thus, serious research is supplanted and distorted by politics.

5. ROADS AND TUNNELS AROUND JERUSALEM

IN the feverish development activities that seized Jerusalem after the Six-Day War (1967), tens of thousands of residential apartments were built and a similar number of people have made their homes there. Within a short time, the population of Jerusalem increased to more than 600,000—three times the prewar figure. The capital is now the largest city in Israel. New neighborhoods have sprung up around a single urban center, which has consequently become badly congested. Further complicating the situation is the considerable traffic passing through Jerusalem from the Jordan Valley and the Dead Sea region on its way to the west and the coastal region. The ensuing traffic jams create an intolerable situation.

After Ehud Olmert was elected mayor of Jerusalem, various contingency plans for Jerusalem traffic were put into action and a large-scale traffic project is in progress. The hilly topography of the city and complicated problems of land ownership present enormous difficulties in this context. The situation is aggravated by the archaeological remains, especially ancient tombs, scattered around sites earmarked for road build-

(below, opposite) Jerusalem is a city built on hills, valleys and watercourses. The construction of modern roads has required innovative solutions, including the excavation of tunnels beneath blocks of buildings and residential neighborhoods. On occasion, extensive public building projects have been planned above tunnels, in order to exploit land reserves that might otherwise be lost. The value of land in Jerusalem is immeasurably higher than it is elsewhere in Israel.

ing. Nevertheless, several important roads have been built and tunnels dug, and further plans are in the making. Even now, at the opening of the new millennium, traffic in Jerusalem has been somewhat eased; completion of the whole project should solve some of the problems that still trouble Jerusalemites in this area. One still unsolved problem, for which as yet no plans have been made, is that of traffic in the general area around and inside the Old City—both for the residents and for tourists and visitors.

The basic idea of an overall solution for Jerusalem's traffic problems is to create a peripheral ring road, with roads branch-

Jerusalem has grown in recent years to be the largest city in Israel (population, c. 600,000). As a result, the building of a complex transportation network is underway to meet the needs of the city's residents. The system is made up of peripheral ring roads, double- and multiple-lane highways, and tunnels. A light railroad is also planned to run between the city center and the outlying neighborhoods. The network has already begun to be implemented and should be completed in large part in the early years of the third millennium.

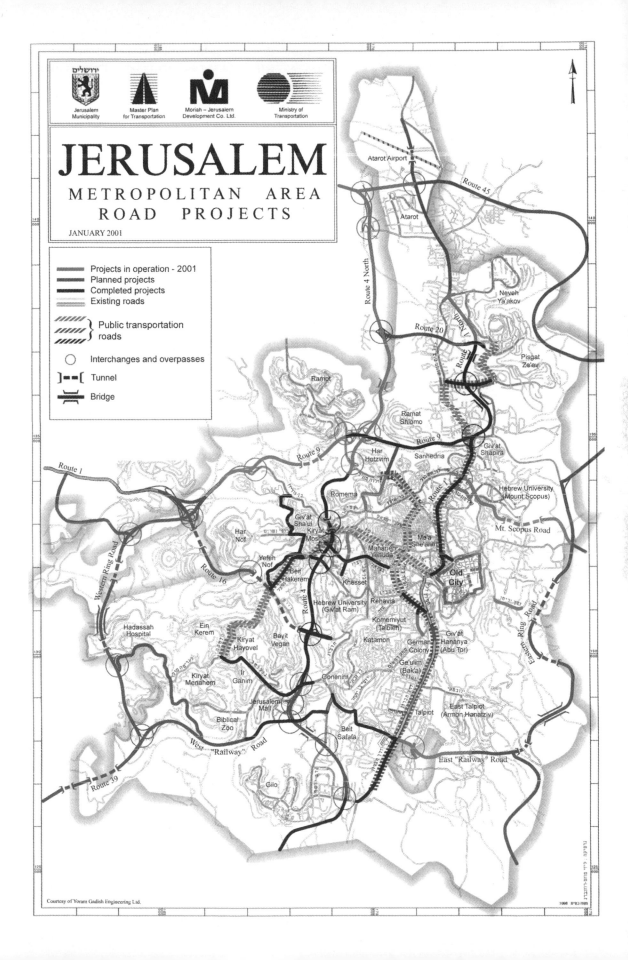

ing off to various neighborhoods and to interurban routes, obviating the need to drive through the city center. Separate public transportation systems for each neighborhood or cluster of neighborhoods will also lessen traffic congestion in the center. Plans are also underway for a light railroad, to serve as the major means of transportation in the busy city center. In sum, Jerusalem's traffic problems have already been somewhat alleviated; it is to be hoped that completion of the master plan will bring further relief.

6. Isaiah's Vision: "All the Nations Shall Flow to It"

At the beginning of the third millennium, the entire Middle East is yearning for better days. One would like to believe that people who scoff at the idea of a "New Middle East" will have to eat their words; but the path to that goal is strewn with obstacles. One of the problems is the status of Jerusalem. The two peoples, of different faiths, find it difficult to accept one another's demands, but once they

Jewish worshipers by the Western Wall.

Muslim worshipers around the Dome of the Rock.

reach the conclusion that the best solution is peace, they will have come much closer together. In March 2000, Jerusalem was the scene of a momentous visit by a distinguished tourist—Pope John Paul II. Of the over 265 popes who have ruled the Catholic Church, only two had come to Jerusalem before him. The first was St. Peter, the first pope, Jesus' senior disciple, who was at his Master's side throughout his active life and so naturally was with him in Jerusalem. From Peter to Paul VI, no pope had ever set foot in Jerusalem.

Such visits are bound up with a weighty theological problem: a pope is not an ordinary tourist or pilgrim. As we have already noted, Paul VI's visit took place against some as yet undivulged political background. Whatever the case, it generated a flurry of Muslim activities in the Old City, initiated by the late King Hussein. Most probably, the visit was connected with efforts to reach some internationally agreed conclusion in regard to the Jerusalem issue. Was John Paul's visit at the start of the third millennium an indication that the three parties have come to some agreement about Jerusalem? Only time will tell. The distinguished visitor was certainly treated with the utmost respect, as befits a reigning pope.

The five thousand years of Jerusalem's history tell us that since David chose it as his royal capital, and since his son

Pope John Paul II praying at the Western Wall during his visit in March 2000.

Pope John Paul II attending a conference of the three monotheistic religions at the Notre Dame of Jerusalem Center, during his visit to Israel in March 2000. On his right, Israel's Ashkenazi Chief Rabbi Yisrael Meir Lau, and on his left, Sheikh Taysir Tamimi, head of religious courts in the Palestinian-ruled territories of the West Bank.

Solomon built the Temple there, the city has enjoyed a status unrivaled by any other city on earth. Its position was further consolidated when it became holy to the two great monotheistic religions, Christianity and Islam, whose roots lie in the earliest monotheistic faith, Judaism.

The experience of the past two thousand years proves that all attempts on the part of one religion to "purge" Jerusalem of the presence of one of its rivals have failed, either immediately or after the passage of time. The creation of a city in which the believers of one faith or the members of one nation possess exclusive rights is doomed to failure. Saladin, who conquered Jerusalem from his hated foes the Crusaders, understood this very well, and therefore let them keep their holy places, in particular the Church of the Holy Sepulcher. Foresight is not a question of special wisdom; it is only necessary to look at the past and understand it. In any case, we can do nothing but

leave things to the course of history, awaiting developments in the coming years.

One point must be made here: for the world, and for Jerusalem's own inhabitants, "Jerusalem" proper is the Old City and its environs. If King David were to visit Jerusalem today and were invited to visit the Knesset, he would surely ask in surprise whether he was in Jerusalem. A visitor from antiquity coming to the villages of Abu Dis or El-Azariya would surely have a similar reaction.

This point, incidentally, was understood many decades ago by Eri Jabotinsky, son of the leader of the Revisionist Party (a predecessor of the Israeli right wing), Ze'ev Jabotinsky. Eri Jabotinsky wrote a letter to a friend, Eliyahu Meridor, who lived in the Rehavia neighborhood of Jerusalem, only half a kilometer away from the Old City walls. He addressed the envelope as follows: "Eliyahu Meridor, 17 Ben Maimon

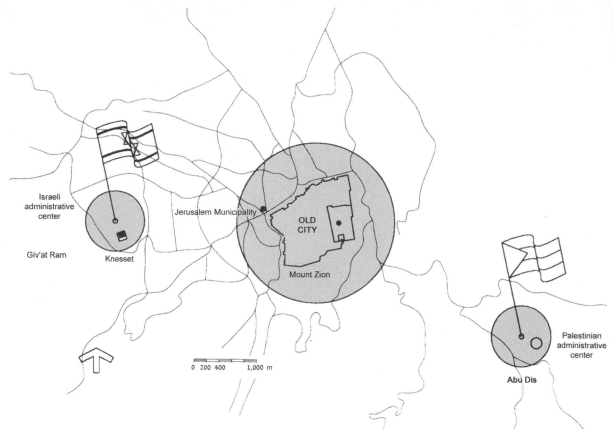

Jerusalem—a capital for two nations?
1. The Israeli government buildings on Giv'at Ram and the village of Abu Dis, which has been proposed as a site for the seat of the Palestinian Government, are approximately the same distance from the Old City.
2. The Old City and a circular area around it would be under joint administration. This small area in the heart of Jerusalem, and its immediate vicinity, contain almost all the buildings and sites sacred to the three monotheistic religions.

Street, *near Jerusalem*." On the other side of the political map, David Ben-Gurion, one of the most prominent leaders of the activist left wing, envisaged a solution to the Jerusalem problem that would be negotiated and agreed by all parties with interests in the city. For him, too, "Jerusalem" was the Old City and its immediate vicinity. A solution along these lines might save Jerusalem, as well as the entire Middle East and indeed the world, from further wars and present it, for the first time in its history, as a real "city of peace," fulfilling the psalmist's words, "Peace be within your walls, and

security within your towers!" (Psalms 122:7).

Both nations' parliaments could continue to exist—the Knesset at its present site on Giv'at Ram, and the Palestinian parliament in the region of Abu Dis–Azariya. In between there would be a single, free city—the Old City and its environs—in which a mayor might be elected in turn, say for four-year terms, from each of the four quarters, to govern the Old City as a separate unit.

Jerusalem could thus become a real abode of peace and a cherished ideal for all civilized peoples. It would then be justified to call upon various international institutions to move to Jerusalem: the United Nations Headquarters, including the UN General Assembly, from New York; the International Red Cross from Geneva; UNESCO from Paris; the International Atomic Energy Agency from Vienna; and many others. There would be room for all these around the Old City, as there would be for the embassies of all countries of the world to Israel and the Palestinian state.

Utopia? — Indeed! But without dreams we cannot hope for a better future. Perhaps we should quote a few lines here from the prophecy of one of the greatest utopists of all times, the prophet Isaiah (2:1–4):

The word which Isaiah the son of Amoz
* saw concerning Judah and Jerusalem.*
It shall come to pass in the latter days
That the mountain of the house of the Lord
Shall be established as the highest of the
* mountains,*

And shall be raised above the hills;
And all the nations shall flow to it,
And many peoples shall come, and say:
"Come, let us go up to the mountain of the
* Lord,*
To the house of the God of Jacob;
That he may teach us his ways,
And that we may walk in his paths."
For out of Zion shall go forth the law,
And the word of the Lord from Jerusalem.
He shall judge between the nations,
And shall decide for many peoples;
And they shall beat their swords into
* plowshares,*
And their spears into pruning hooks;
Nation shall not lift up sword against
* nation,*
Neither shall they learn war any more.

Perhaps, 2,700 years after Isaiah uttered this prophecy, the time has come for his stirring words to be fulfilled, and Jerusalem will welcome home its lost sons and daughters, of all nations and all faiths.

BIBLIOGRAPHY AND SOURCES

Aharoni, Y. — *Excavations at Ramat Rahel: Seasons 1961–1962.* Rome, 1964.

Aharoni, Y. — *The Land of the Bible: A Historical Geography.* London, 1967.

Aharoni, Y. and M. Avi-Yonah — *The Macmillan Bible Atlas.* New York, 1974.

Amiran, D., A. Shachar and I. Kimhi (eds.) — *Urban Geography of Jerusalem.* Berlin and New York, 1973.

Amiran, R. — "The Tumuli West of Jerusalem Survey and Excavations 1953." In *Israel Exploration Journal,* vol. 8, no. 4: 205. Jerusalem, 1958.

Amiran, R. — "The Water Supply of Israelite Jerusalem." In *Jerusalem Revealed.* Jerusalem, 1975.

Aslanapa, O. — *Turkish Art and Architecture.* London, 1971.

Avigad, N. — "Excavations in the Jewish Quarter of the Old City, 1969–1971." In *Jerusalem Revealed.* Jerusalem, 1975.

Avi-Yonah, M. (ed.) — *Encyclopedia of Archaeological Excavations in the Holy Land.* 4 vols. Jerusalem, 1976.

Avi-Yonah, M. — "Jerusalem of the Second Temple Period." In *Israel Exploration Journal,* vol. 18, 1968.

Avi-Yonah, M. — "The Third and Second Walls of Jerusalem." In *Israel Exploration Journal,* vol. 18, 1968.

Avi-Yonah, M. — "The Walls of Nehemiah: A Minimalist View." In *Israel Exploration Journal,* vol. 4, 1954.

Bahat, D. and M. Ben-Ari — "Excavations at Tancred's Tower." In *Jerusalem Revealed.* Jerusalem, 1975.

Barag, D. — "Owners of Multiple Seals in Judea During the Eighth to Early Sixth Century BCE" (Hebrew). In *Eretz Israel,* 26:35–38. Jerusalem, 1995.

Barclay, J. T. — *The City of the Great King, or, Jerusalem as it was, as it is, as it is to be.* Philadelphia, 1858.

Barkay, G. and A. Kloner — "Burial Caves North of Damascus Gate, Jerusalem." In *Israel Exploration Journal,* vol. 26, 1976.

Ben-Arieh, S. — "The Third Wall of Jerusalem." In *Jerusalem Revealed.* Jerusalem, 1975.

Ben-Dov, M. — *In the Shadow of the Temple.* Jerusalem, 1982.

Ben-Dov, M. — "The Area South of the Temple Mount in the Early Islamic Period." In *Jerusalem Revealed.* Jerusalem, 1975.

Ben-Dov, M. — "The Restoration of St. Mary's Church of the German Knights in Jerusalem." In *Ancient Churches Revealed,* 140–142. Jerusalem, 1993.

Benoit, P. — "Praetorium, Lithostroton, and Gabbatha." In *Jesus and the Gospel,* vol. I. London, 1973.

Benvenisti, M. — *The Crusaders in the Holy Land.* Jerusalem, 1970.

Berchem, Max van — *Matériaux pour un Corpus Inscriptionum Arabicarum.* Deuxiéme Partie: *Syrie de Sud, I–III, Jérusalem.* Cairo, 1927.

Bliss, F. J. and A. C. Dickie — *Excavations at Jerusalem, 1894–1897.* London, 1898.

Blomme, Y. — "Faut-il Revenir sur la Datation de l'Arc de l'Ecce Homo?" In *Revue Biblique*, no. 2. Paris, 1979.

Boëthius, A. and Ward-Perkins — *Etruscan and Roman Architecture.* London, 1970.

Breydenbach, B. von — *Die Fart oder Reyss uber Mere zu dem Heiligen Grab unseres Herren Jesu Cristi Gen Jerusalem.* 1670.

Broshi, M. — "The Expansion of Jerusalem in the Reigns of Hezekiah and Manasseh." In *Israel Exploration Journal*, vol. 29, 1979.

Broshi, M. and Y. Tsafrir — "Excavations at the Zion Gate, Jerusalem." In *Israel Exploration Journal*, vol. 27, 1977.

Burgoyne, M. H. — *Mamluk Jerusalem.* London, 1987.

Busink — *Der Tempel von Jerusalem.* Leiden, 1970.

Cahill, J. M. — "Rosette Stamp Seal Impressions from Ancient Judah." In *Israel Exploration Journal*, 45:230–252. Jerusalem, 1995.

Cole, D. — "How Water Tunnels Worked." In *Biblical Archaeology Review*, vol. VI, no. 2. 1980.

Conder, C. R. — *The City of Jerusalem.* London, 1909.

Corbo, V. C. — *Il Santo Sepolcro di Gerusalemme.* Vols. 1–3. Jerusalem, 1981.

Coüasnon, C. — *The Church of the Holy Sepulchre, Jerusalem.* The Schweich Lectures 1972. London, 1974.

Creswell, K. A. C. — *Early Muslim Architecture.* Vol. I, Part II. Oxford, 1969.

Cross, F. M. — "King Hezekiah's Seal Bears Phoenician Imagery." In *Biblical Archaeology Review*, 25(2):42–45. Washington, 1999.

Crowfoot, J. W. and G. M. Fitzgerald — "Excavations in the Tyropoeon Valley, Jerusalem 1927." In *Annual of the Palestine Exploration Fund.* London, 1929.

Dalman, G. — "Die Via Dolorosa in Jerusalem." In *Palästina jahrbuch*, 1906.

Fletcher, B. — *A History of Architecture on the Comparative Method.* 17th Md. London, 1963.

Geva, H. (ed.) — *Jewish Quarter Excavations in the Old City of Jerusalem.* Jerusalem, 2000.

Geva, H. — "The Tower of David: Phasael or Hippicus." In *Israel Exploration Journal*, vol. 31, 1981.

Geva, H. — "The Western Boundary of Jerusalem at the End of the Monarchy." In *Israel Exploration Journal*, vol. 29, 1979.

Goodwin, G. — *A History of Ottoman Architecture.* London, 1971.

Gray, J. — *A History of Jerusalem.* London, 1969.

Hamilton, R. W. — "Excavations Against the North Wall of Jerusalem, 1937–38." In *Quarterly of the Department of Antiquities in Palestine*, vol. 10. London, 1944.

Hennessy, J. B. — "Excavations at Damascus Gate, Jerusalem, 1964–1966." In *Levant*, vol. 2. London, 1970.

Hitti, Ph. K. — *Capital Cities of Arab Islam*. Minneapolis, 1973.

Jeremias, J. — *Jerusalem in the Time of Jesus*. London, 1969.

Johns, C. N. — "The Citadel, Jerusalem: A Summary of Work Since 1934." In *Quarterly of the Department of Antiquities in Palestine*, vol. 14. London, 1950.

Join-Lambert, M. — *Jérusalem: Israélite, Chrétienne, Musulmane*. Paris, 1956.

Kenyon, K. M. — *Digging up Jerusalem*. London, 1974.

Khusrau, N. — *Diary of a Journey Through Syria and Palestine, P.P.T.S.* London, 1893.

Le Strange, G. — *Palestine Under the Moslems*. Beirut, 1890.

Macalister, R. A. S. — *The Excavation of Gezer*. Vols 2–3. London, 1912.

Macalister, R. A. S. and J. G. Duncan — "Excavations on the Hill of Ophel, Jerusalem, 1923–1925." *Annual of the Palestine Exploration Fund*. London, 1926.

Margowsky, I. — "Bordi Kabrit et Environes (Chronique Archéologique)." In *Review Biblique*, vol. 78, 1971.

Marmadji, A. S. — *Textes Géographiques Arabes sur la Palestine*. Paris, 1951.

Mazar, A. — "Iron Age Burial Caves North of the Damascus Gate, Jerusalem." In *Israel Exploration Journal*, vol. 26, 1976.

Mazar, A. and B. Mazar — "Excavations in the South of the Temple Mount." In *QEDEM*, No. 29. Jerusalem, 1989.

Mazar, B. — "Jerusalem in the Biblical Period." In *Jerusalem Revealed*. Jerusalem, 1975.

Mitchell, H. G. — "The Modern Wall of Jerusalem." In *The Annual of the American Schools of Oriental Research in Jerusalem*, vol. 1. New Haven, 1920.

Muqaddasi — *Description of Syria including Palestine, P.P.T.S.* London, 1896.

Nebenzahl, K. — *Maps of the Bible Lands*. New York, 1986.

Pixner, B. — "An Essene Quarter on Mount Zion?" In *Studia Hierosolymitana*. Jerusalem, 1976.

Pixner, B. — "Noch Einmal das Prätorium." In *Zeitschrift des Deutschen Pälestina-Vereins*, vol. 95, 1979.

Poggibonsi, N. — *A Voyage Beyond the Seas (1346–1350)*. Jerusalem, 1945.

Pope Paul VI in the Holy Land. New York, 1964.

Prawer, J. — "Jerusalem in Crusader Days." In *Jerusalem Revealed*. Jerusalem, 1975.

Pritchard, J. B. (ed.) — *Ancient Near East in Pictures, Relating to the Old Testament*. Princeton, 1955.

Pritchard, J. B. (ed.) — *Ancient Near East in Texts, Relating to the Old Testament*. Princeton, 1955.

Pritchard, J. B. — *Gibeon, Where the Sun Stood Still*. Princeton, 1962.

Pritchard, J. B. — *The Water System of Gibeon*. Philadelphia, 1961.

Reich, R. and H. Geva — "Five Jewish Burial Caves on Mount Scopus." In *Jerusalem Revealed*. Jerusalem, 1975.

Richmond, E. T. — *The Sites of the Crucifixion and the Resurrection*. London, 1934.

Safdie, M. — *The Harvard Jerusalem Studio*. Massachusetts, 1986.

Safdie, M. — *Jerusalem, the Future of the Past*. Boston, 1989.

Schick, C. — *Der Tempel in Jerusalem*. Zurich, 1890.

Sharon, A. — *Planning Jerusalem, the Old City and Its Environs*. Jerusalem, 1973.

Shiloh, Y. — "Jerusalem, the City of David, 1981." In *Israel Exploration Journal*, vol. 32. Jerusalem, 1982.

Simons, J. — *Jerusalem in the Old Testament*. Leiden, 1952.

Storme, A. — *The Way of the Cross*. Jerusalem, 1976.

Stern, E. (ed.) — *The New Encyclopedia of Archaeological Excavations in the Holy Land*. Jerusalem, 1993.

Straton, A. — *Sinan*. New York, 1972.

Sukenik, E. L. and L. A. Mayer — *The Third Wall*. Jerusalem, 1930.

Tsafrir, Y. — "Muqaddasi's Gates of Jerusalem: A New Identification Based on Byzantine Sources." In *Israel Exploration Journal*, vol. 27. Jerusalem, 1977.

Tushingham, A. D. — *Excavations in Jerusalem 1961–1967*. 1. Excavations in the Armenian Garden on the Western Hill. Toronto, 1985.

Tzaferis, V. — "The Burial of Simon the Temple Builder." In *Jerusalem Revealed*. Jerusalem, 1975.

Ussishkin, D. — "The Original Length of the Siloam Tunnel." In *Levant*, vol. 8. London, 1976.

Vilnay, Z. — *The Holy Land in Old Prints and Maps*. Jerusalem, 1965.

Vincent, L. H. and F. M. Abel — *Jérusalem nouvelle*. 3 vols. Paris, 1914.

Vincent, L. H. and A. M. Stève — *Jérusalem de l'ancien Testament*. Vols. 1–4. Paris, 1954–1956.

Vogüé, M. de — *Le Temple de Jérusalem*. Paris, 1864.

Vriezen, K. J. H. — "Die Ausgrabungen unter der Erlöserkirche im Muristan Jerusalem (1970–1974)." *Abhandlungen des Deutschen Palästina-Vereins* 19, Wiesbaden.

Walker, P. — *Holy City, Holy Places: Christian Attitudes to Jerusalem and the Holy Land in the 4th Century*. Oxford Christian Studies. Oxford, 1990.

Warren, C. and C. R. Conder — *The Survey of Western Palestine—Jerusalem*. London, 1884.

Weill, R. — *La Cité de David*. 2 vols. Paris, 1920, 1947.

Wilkinson, J. — "Jerusalem as Jesus Knew It." In *Archaeology as Evidence*. London, 1978.

Wilkinson, J. — *Jerusalem Pilgrims Before the Crusades*. Jerusalem, 1977.

Wilson, C. — *Ordnance Survey of Jerusalem*. London, 1865.

Yadin, Y. — "The Gate of the Essenes and the Temple Scroll." In *Jerusalem Revealed*. Jerusalem, 1975.

INDEX

C

D

Dahariyya (loc.)   6–7

Dajani family   291

Damascus   4–5, 8, 56, 89, 174, 178, 213–214, 216, 218, 220, 226, 244, 262–263

Damascus Gate   13, 32, 69, 71–72, 118, 120–122, 137, 141, 145–147, 155, 159, 164, 198, 200, 203, 211–212, 225, 229, 232, 241, 246, 250–251, 256, 258, 267, 307, 315, 324, 326, 335, 339

Dan (loc.)   45, 56, 87

Dan (territory)   42

Daniel, prophet   76, 79

Danziger, Yitshak   333

Dar al-Salaam (Baghdad)   178

Darb al-Hajj   5
See also King's Highway

Darb al-Sultan   5
See also King's Highway

Darih, origin and meaning   238

Darius, king of Persia   88

Darom (loc.)   214

David, City of, see City of David

David, House of   23, 43, 60, 72-73, 84
genealogy chart   76

David, king   15, 23–25, 32–33, 40–49, 53, 62, 67, 72, 76, 79, 173, 363, 365
kingdom of   56

David, tomb of   314

David's Gate   201

David's Tower, see Citadel

David Street   256, 259, 305, 334–335

Dawadariyya, al- (Mamluk building)   233

Dayan, Moshe   345

Dead Sea   6–8, 11

Debir (loc.)   40

Decumanus (Roman street)   146
See also Cardo

Deir el-Adas (Monastery of the Lentils), see St. Eli, Church of

Deir Kremisan (monastery)   14

De Saulcy, Felicien   92, 325

Dibon (loc.)   56

Dickie, Archibald   325

Dome of the Rock   172–173, 175, 177, 180, 182, 197, 211–212, 219, 229, 233, 245–246, 251, 296, 310, 339, 349, 354, 363

Dominican Fathers   325

Dominus Flevit Church   310

Dor, Dora (loc.)   8, 56, 67, 78, 99

Doris (Herodian dynasty)   126

Dormition Church   273, 275, 339

Double Gate   193, 213, 339, 355

Druse   186

Drusilla (Herodian dynasty)   126

Drusus (Herodian dynasty)   126

Dumah (loc.)   5, 56

Dung Gate   86–87, 118, 162, 188, 229, 246, 253, 256, 258, 267, 300, 315–316, 319, 339

E

Early Arab period   168–169, 174–175, 340

Early Bronze Age, see Canaanite period

Eben-ezer (loc.)   46

Ecce Homo Arch   147, 155

Edelstein, Gershon   327, 331

Edrei (loc.)   214

Education, compulsory   132

Eglah (House of David)   76

Eglon (town)   38–40

Egypt   1–3, 6, 23, 28, 30–31, 35–36, 88, 91, 157, 182–183, 186, 194, 211, 213, 217, 219–222, 228, 235, 237, 243–245, 248, 265–266, 288, 292, 301, 306, 314, 345

Egyptian Expeditionary Forces   288

Eilat (loc.)   140–141, 216
See also Elath

217–219

French Hill, see Giv'at Shapira

Fulk of Anjou 202

Further Mosque, see Aqsa Mosque, al-

G

Gad, prophet 79

Galilee 4, 127, 129, 131, 133, 147, 163, 167, 265–266

Galilee, Sea of 6–7, 9

Gan Rehavia (neighborhood) 321

Garden of Eden 2

Garden Tomb 128

Gardner, Brian 289

Gate of Mercy 175, 225
  See also Golden Gate

Gate of the Chain 208, 213

Gate of the Jews 235

Gath (loc.) 38, 47, 56

Gath-hepher (loc.) 78

Gaza (loc.) 4–5, 7–8, 45, 56, 78, 82, 140, 182, 214, 262–263, 265

Gaza Strip 341

Ge'on Ya'akov Academy 187

Ge'ula (neighborhood) 9, 299, 307, 321

Ge'ulim (Bak'a) (neighborhood) 321, 361

Geba (loc.) 41

Gedor (loc.) 82

Geneva (loc.) 367

Genghis Khan 220–221

Genoa (loc.) 194

George, David Lloyd 288

Gerasa (loc.) 4, 146–147

German Center, see Teutonic Knights

German Colony 15, 72, 285–286, 307, 321, 361

Germany 220, 273, 275–276, 289–290

Germer-Durand, Joseph 325

Gerofina (loc.) 131

Geshem the Arab 83

Gethsemane 203, 225, 339

Gethsemane, Church of 201

Geva, Hillel 327

Gezer (loc.) 7, 20, 37–39, 42, 45, 56, 59, 82, 84–85, 87

Ghadariyya, al- (Mamluk building) 233

Ghor (district) 263

Gibbethon (loc.) 56

Gibeah of Benjamin (loc.) 25, 41, 44

Gibeah of Saul (loc.) 25, 44

Gibeath-kiriath-jearim (loc.) 47
  See also Kiriath-jearim

Gibeon (loc.) 20, 38–41, 46, 59–61, 82, 330

Gibeonites 39–40

Gihon Spring 14–15, 18, 20, 28, 41, 60, 62–64, 256, 284, 339

Gilead (region) 4

Gilo (neighborhood) 14, 72, 124, 319–320, 361

Giv'at Beit Hakerem (neighborhood) 320

Giv'at Hamivtar 307, 315

Giv'at Hananya (neighborhood) 321, 361

Giv'at Havradim (neighborhood) 320

Giv'at Mordechai (neighborhood) 320

Giv'at Oranim (neighborhood) 321

Giv'at Ram 139, 141, 312, 320, 330–331, 366

Giv'at Sha'ul (neighborhood) 311, 320, 361

Giv'at Shapira (neighborhood) 319, 321, 361

Godfrey of Bouillon 194–195, 197–199, 202

Golan Heights 4, 316

Golden Gate 169–170, 178, 201, 246, 339
  See also Gate of Mercy

Goldfuss, Chaim 328

Golgotha 13, 128, 149, 163, 197, 201

L

M

Q

Qa'itbay, sultan   236–237
  fountain of   233
Qalandiya (loc.)   14
Qalansuwa (loc.)   228
Qal'a, al-   233
  See also Citadel
Qal'at al-Shaqif (district)   263
Qalqashandi, al-, historian   191
Qaqun (loc., district)   228, 263
Qatana (loc.)   14
Qatna (loc.)   5
Qatuz, sultan   222
Qaysariyya, origin and meaning   238
Qilani, emir   234
Qilaniyya, al- (Mamluk building)   233–
  234, 237
Qubar, origin and meaning   238
Qubeiba, el- (loc.)   14
Quds, al- (Jerusalem)   24, 27

R

Rab', origin and meaning   238
Rabbanites   185
Rabbath (loc.)   38
Rabbath-bene-ammon (loc.)   4–5, 8, 56
  See also Amman
Rabin, Yitzhak   345–346
Raddai (House of David)   76
Rafah, Raphia (loc.)   7, 56
Rafidiyeh (loc.)   221
Rahab (House of David)   76
Ram, Er- (loc.)   14
Ramah (loc.)   41, 78
Ramallah (loc.)   6–7, 221, 319
Ramat Denya (neighborhood)   320
Ramat Rahel (loc.)   11, 14, 65–66, 121,
  124, 139, 299, 306, 308, 330–331
Ramat Shlomo (neighborhood)   361
Ramban, see Nahmanides

Ramban Synagogue   223, 226
Ramla (loc.)   182, 185, 215, 228, 262–
  263, 306
Ramot (neighborhood)   319, 361
Ramot Allon (neighborhood)   321
Ramot Eshkol (neighborhood)   319, 321
Ramoth-gilead (loc.)   4, 56
Ras el-Amud (loc.)   321
Rashid, Harun al-, caliph   180
Ravenna (loc.)   160
Raymond of St. Gilles   195, 197
Red Sea   1, 4–5
Redeemer, Church of the   273, 275
Rehavia (neighborhood)   11, 72, 299–
  300, 321, 361, 365
Rehob (loc.)   7
Rehoboam, king of Judah   53–54, 56,
  76, 79
Rehovot (loc.)   304, 312
Rephaim Valley   15–16
Restoration (Return to Zion)
  period   83–84, 340–341
Rhodes   89, 229
Ribat, origin and meaning   238
Ribat al-Mansuri   233
Ribat al-Mardini   233
Ribat Zammani   233
Ribat 'Ala al-Din   233
Ricart (Acra scholar)   92
Richard I the Lion-heart   215
Richard of Cornwall   217
Rimon, Yuval   332
Robert of Flanders   195
Robert of Normandy   195
Robinson, Edward   92, 280
Robinson's Arch   11, 31, 70, 72, 109–
  110, 168, 278, 339
Rockefeller Museum   297–298, 324
Rodin, Auguste   332
Rohan, Dennis   215
Roman Legion   136, 138, 142, 145, 258
Rome, Roman empire   78, 81, 88, 90–

Yolande (Crusader dynasty)   202
Yqr'm, king of Jerusalem   30–31
Yugoslavia   301

Z

Za'im, al- (neighborhood)   347
Zawiya, origin and meaning   238
Zealots   127, 132–133, 135–136
Zebidah (House of David)   76
Zechariah, prophet   50, 79
Zechariah, tomb of   101, 159
Zedekiah, king   43, 76, 79
Zemah (loc.)   7
Zephaniah, prophet   79
Zerubbabel ben (son of) Shealtiel   76,
    79, 81, 83, 84
Zibiah (House of David)   76

Zichron Moshe (neighborhood)   321
Zichron Rahamim (neighborhood)   321
Zichron Yosef (neighborhood)   321
Zinnor   62
    See also Water shaft
Zion   23
    See also City of David
Zion Cinema   336
Zion Gate   200–201, 211, 222–223, 225,
    229, 246, 252, 256, 267, 305, 307–308,
    339
Zionism, Zionist movement   288, 290,
    292–293, 301, 303, 314
Zionist Executive Committee   293, 304
Ziph (loc.)   57
Zoar (loc.)   5, 56
Zorah (loc.)   38